DEVELOPING WRITERS IN HIGHER EDUCATION

SWEETLAND DIGITAL RHETORIC COLLABORATIVE

Series Editors:
Anne Ruggles Gere, University of Michigan
Naomi Silver, University of Michigan

The Sweetland Digital Rhetoric Collaborative Book Series publishes texts that investigate the multiliteracies of digitally mediated spaces both within academia as well as other contexts.

Rhetorical Code Studies: Discovering Arguments in and around Code
Kevin Brock

Developing Writers in Higher Education: A Longitudinal Study
Anne Ruggles Gere, Editor

Sites of Translation: What Multilinguals Can Teach Us about Digital Writing and Rhetoric
Laura Gonzales

Rhizcomics: Rhetoric, Technology, and New Media Composition
Jason Helms

Making Space: Writing, Instruction, Infrastrucure, and Multiliteracies
James P. Purdy and Dànielle Nicole DeVoss, Editors

Digital Samaritans: Rhetorical Delivery and Engagement in the Digital Humanities
Jim Ridolfo

DIGITALCULTUREBOOKS, an imprint of the University of Michigan Press, is dedicated to publishing work in new media studies and the emerging field of digital humanities.

Developing Writers in Higher Education

A LONGITUDINAL STUDY

Edited by
Anne Ruggles Gere

University of Michigan Press
Ann Arbor

Published in the United States of America by the
University of Michigan Press
Manufactured in the United States of America
Printed on acid-free paper
First published January 2019

A CIP catalog record for this book is available from the British Library.

Library of Congress Cataloging-in-Publication data has been applied for.

ISBN 978-0-472-13124-2 (hardcover : alk. paper)
ISBN 978-0-472-03738-4 (pbk. : alk. paper)
ISBN 978-0-472-12481-7 (e-book)

https://doi.org/10.3998/mpub.10079890

This project was made possible in part through the University of Michigan's Humanities Collaboratory and its "Book Unbound" project grant.

For John W. Sweetland

ACKNOWLEDGMENTS

When I became director of the Gayle Morris Sweetland Center for Writing in 2008, I knew I wanted to undertake a longitudinal study of student writers, but I had no idea that it would take nearly a decade, call upon multiple resources, and involve dozens of collaborators. Grants from the University of Michigan's Center for Research on Learning and Teaching and Instructional Support Services supported the earliest stages of this study. Thanks to resources from the Dean's Scholarship provided by the School of Education, funds from the College of Literature, Science and the Arts, and, especially, the endowment of the Gayle Morris Sweetland Center for Writing, a succession of graduate student research assistants helped to move this project from concept to reality.

Tim Green and Laura Aull helped to launch the essay-based Directed Self-Placement that provided a common baseline for all students. Anne Porter led an investigation of writerly efficacy; Christie Toth drew on resources from the Institute for Social Research to draft and refine our survey; Sarah Swofford and Lizzie Hutton developed the coding system for interviews; Ben Keating found and used the aptly named Site Sucker app to preserve the contents of students' electronic portfolios; Anna Knutson wrangled coded interviews into searchable form; Ryan McCarty dove deep into students' electronic portfolios and archived writing to create "cases" for analysis; Emily Wilson organized and tabulated data for our digital resources; and Naitnaphit Limlamai coordinated our final push into publication.

A number of other graduate students augmented this small platoon of contributors. Michael Brown, Elizabeth Mann, and Alon Yakter made statistical sense of our survey data. Sheerah Cole, Merideth Garcia, Gail Gibson, Jonathon Harris, Michelle Kwok, Chris Parsons, Molly Parsons, Melody Pugh, Emily Rainey, Aubrey Schiavone, Nicole Wilson, and Crystal VanKooten conducted interviews. Ann Burke, Merideth Garcia, Gail Gibson, James Hammond, Jonathon Harris, Stephanie Moody, Amanda Presswood, Lavelle Ridley, Aubrey Schiavone, Bonnie Tucker, Nicole Wilson, and Crystal VanKooten helped code transcripts of interviews. Jathan Day, Michael Hoffman, Adrienne Raw, and Ruth Li assisted with the development of digital materials.

Throughout the coming and going of graduate students my most constant and valued collaborator was Naomi Silver, Associate Director of Sweetland. Thinking with her about virtually every aspect of this project, benefiting from her scrupulous attention to my prose, and learning from her deep knowledge of multimedia writing made this study both more effective and more fun. Naomi's leadership in developing the curriculum for Sweetland's Minor in Writing, her innovative approaches to teaching multimedia writing, and her enormous contributions to Sweetland's Digital Rhetoric Collaborative created the context that made this study possible. As I step away from directing Sweetland, one of the things I'll miss most is working daily with Naomi.

A grant from the University of Michigan's Humanities Collaboratory for the Book Unbound project gave digital life to this study. Originally this was to have been solely a print book project, but joining forces with colleagues Charles Watkinson, Director of the University of Michigan Press; Nicola Terrenato, a professor of classical archaeology; and Matthew Solomon, a professor of screen arts and cultures, led to a successful proposal that united our study of writing with one focused on the excavation of Gabii, a city that neighbored and rivaled Rome in the first millennium BC, and another on Orson Welles' planned but unmade film version of *Heart of Darkness*. Sharing ideas across disciplines as each of our projects prepared to mount scholarship and data on the Fulcrum platform emboldened many ideas, which took actual form thanks to the interventions of Kentaro Toyama, a professor in the school of information; Jeremy Morse and his colleagues in the publishing technologies group; Kevin Rennells, production editor; and Mary Francis, editorial director the Michigan publishing. These colleagues, along with very helpful anonymous reviewers and my stalwart writing group colleagues—Anne Curzan, Mary Schleppegrell, and Meg Sweeney—helped move this project to new levels of complexity and accessibility.

Of course none of this would have been possible without the generous cooperation of the students who participated in this study. Their willingness to complete lengthy surveys, participate in interviews, and regularly share their writing with us provided the materials on which this study is based. They opened windows into their learning and taught us a great deal about what writing development can mean. I cannot thank them all by name here, but their contributions are visible on every page of this book.

The authors of the chapters included in this collection shared my goal of making every contribution closely linked to all the others so that readers could experience it in more holistic terms. This meant close readings and discussions of one another's drafts, not just once, but multiple times. Across two summers and much of an academic year we met regularly, sometimes virtually and sometimes face to face, but always to share perceptions and make suggestions on one another's writing. I am deeply grateful to Emily, Justine, Ben, Lizzie, Gail, Ryan, Laura, Zak, Anna, Naomi, and Sarah for the many hours they invested in building bridges across chapters.

Through the long days and even longer nights of moving this book to completion, Budge Gere sustained me with home-cooked meals, regular swimming dates, and just the right combination of space and intimacy. Denali Gere entered the fourth grade during the earliest days of this project and graduated from high school as it wound down. She kept me grounded with continual reminders of life beyond work as well as comments about my "dorky medal" (received for a teaching award) and observations about my tendency to "just start another" as soon as I finish a project. My greatest blessing is the love and laughter they bring to my life.

I owe my deepest debt of gratitude to John Sweetland for his support and friendship. A very successful business person who understood the importance of writing, John endowed the Gayle Morris Sweetland Center for Writing and, thereby, provided the resources that made a longitudinal study of this scale possible. I count his regular visits to the Center, his active interest in every detail of our work, and his advocacy for all of our projects as precious gifts.

CONTENTS

Appendices

Digital resources for this book are available on our Fulcrum platform at https://doi.org/10.3998/mpub.10079890

INTRODUCTION

Anne Ruggles Gere

When graduating seniors fling their mortarboards into the air at college commencements, assumptions about these students and their capabilities also hover above them. One assumption is that these graduates are better writers than their first-year counterparts, that earning an undergraduate degree improves a student's writing. But this assumption prompts—or it should prompt—a number of questions: What does "better writers" mean? How do we know that the writing is better? Do all student writers become better in the same ways? What about the differences that students bring to college with them? What does writing development across the undergraduate experience look like? These questions and others like them show that we don't really know enough about the development of student writers.

Describing the ways students grow as writers poses challenges because "writing development" carries multiple meanings. Researchers have taken up a wide variety of definitions of writing development in the past fifty years, and they have employed various methods for investigating it. For example, one meaning focuses on surface features such as spelling, punctuation, and issues of usage, and some researchers discussed below have used error counts as a measure of writing development. In contrast, other researchers have posited disciplinary expertise as central to writing development and investigated how students take up (or don't) genres specific to a given field of study. A third way of defining writing development has emerged from longitudinal studies in which researchers have traced the varied and irregular paths students take as they move smoothly through one writing challenge and stumble on another. Methods and sites of investigation have, of course, varied with shifting definitions: error-seeking examination of student texts, comparison of student writing with that of disciplinary experts, and consideration of shifting syntactic and semantic patterns are among the ways studies of writing development have been approached.

For some researchers, the meaning of writing development is attached more to the writers themselves than to the texts they produce. Defining writing development in this way has meant considering what students do as writers—their responses to pedagogies of writing, the choices they make about forms and processes of composing, and the ways they employ various technologies, as well as the intersections between their academic and personal lives. It has also meant engaging students in discussions about their perceptions of writing in general, their own writing, and themselves as writers; about their hopes and goals; and about their emerging identities. Surveys, focus groups, and interviews as well as close reading of student texts have been employed to inform this view of writing development.

With both instructors and researchers in mind, this book avoids a single definition of writing development, because such a definition could lead instructors to expect students to follow a single path in their development as writers. It could also lead to a narrowing of definitions of and strategies for looking at writing development. Considering writing development from many angles led us to use surveys, statistical analysis, interviews, grounded theory coding, case studies, automated text analysis, and careful reading of a rich collection of student writing and digital productions collected across the undergraduate years. This introduction begins by asking what we can learn from existing research on the development of student writers, enumerating the various methods used and the meanings of writing development that have emerged, and suggesting some of the ways this study has complicated and expanded on these meanings. Then it turns to questions about the study reported here, the analysis of the materials collected, and the rationale for the book's organization.

Perspectives on Writing Development

This study aimed to avoid a single meaning of writing development, not only because existing research has articulated multiple meanings, but because of the inherent danger of seeing writing in monolithic terms. As King Beach notes, a singular perspective on development can become a yardstick for progress, and "at worst it will create a measuring stick for developmental progress derived from those who hold dominant and controlling interests in that society and will silence, coerce, and stigmatize others" (126). We did not want to hold ourselves or our student participants to a single standard that would not value the diversity of available methods and of students themselves. Rather, we began by assuming that writerly development can be seen in:

- Linguistic and rhetorical features of texts as well as in writers' perceptions
- Movement toward new capabilities as well as regression from previously learned ones
- Disciplinary and curricular experiences as well as student-created learning paths
- Individual students' social and psychological growth as well as the agency they claim for their own learning
- Both undergraduate extracurricular and academic contexts as well as the writing experiences that precede and follow after them

Inevitably, our view of writing development was shaped by previous studies, so it is worth recounting what we drew from our predecessors. A half-century ago, studies of writing development used cross-sectional approaches to determine the extent to which students increasingly excised errors—in punctuation and mechanics, spelling, paragraphs, material, words, structure, and sentences—as they moved through college. Albert Kitzhaber, for example, reported in his 1963 *Themes, Theories, and Therapies*—his cross-sectional analysis of freshman, sophomore, and senior writing at Dartmouth—that seniors made more errors than beginning first-years. Reflecting on this finding, Kitzhaber observed, "Backsliding after freshman English has been completed appears to be universal in American colleges and universities. . . . No one has so far discovered a way to keep students writing well in all their courses, nor does it seem at all likely that anyone will" (119). Dean Whitla's 1981 Harvard study of the "value added" by a college education framed writing development in terms similar to Kitzhaber's, coding student writing in a cross-sectional study for "spelling, grammar and organizational flaws" as well as "quality of the argument and counterarguments" (8). Whitla came to a somewhat more optimistic conclusion than Kitzhaber, noting that seniors in the humanities and social sciences wrote "with a finer pen" and "composed more forceful and logical essays, made fewer syntactical mistakes, and even spelled better than freshmen" (6). Although we recognize that "error," with all its contested meanings, plays a significant role in automated evaluations of student writing as well as in public conceptions of what constitutes "good writing," we resisted this conceptualization of writing development, because it is a measuring stick that could stigmatize many of our students and because it offers such a limited view of writing. However, as chapters by Laura Aull and Zak Lancaster show, framing attention to features of language in a larger context can reveal a great deal about students' writing development.

Whitla's observation that students in the humanities and social sciences wrote better than those in other areas gestured toward a relationship between discipline and writing development. Kitzhaber also pointed at this relationship in his survey report that 40 percent of faculty in the natural sciences said they required no extended prose, while faculty in the humanities and social sciences indicated that they required regular essays and papers. These early suggestions that writing development be considered in relation to disciplines connected, in our thinking, to Anne Beaufort's work on the role of subject matter knowledge and discourse communities in writing development, reminding us that linkages between disciplinary expertise and writing offer another perspective on how student writers grow. Yet as Ryan McCarty's chapter shows, students in our study resisted conflating disciplinary expertise and writing development as they pursued their own projects.

Richard Haswell's 1991 study included some attention to error but took a broader and more linguistically informed approach to language conventions. Haswell considered traditional features pertaining to error, including spelling and comma splices as well as more complex categories such as final free modifiers and clause length. His cross-sectional study looked at multiple features, such as students' increased fluency and flow, use of more technical (discipline-based) vocabulary, and better shaping of introductions and conclusions to describe writing development. In addition to offering a more complex and varied model of writing development, Haswell sounded a theme that echoed through much subsequent writing development literature, noting that "all along regressive sequences take place: final free modification grows along with comma splicing; bound modification increases along with embedding and reference errors; students quicken their pace and raise their rate of production mistakes; [they] attempt more midstream improvisation and write more awkwardly, focus more on ideas and less on specificity" (298). A number of scholars who investigated writing development in the years after Haswell's *Gaining Ground in College Writing* embraced this recognition of the unevenness of writing development, and it was prominent in our thinking about the great variety of paths our students took as they moved across writing contexts.

Although they define writing development somewhat differently, researchers such as Lucille McCarthy, Marilyn Sternglass, Anne Beaufort, Nancy Sommers, Laura Saltz, and Lee Ann Carroll echo Haswell's claim about "regressive sequences." Each resists describing students' writing development in linear terms, instead noting its unevenness, its irregular movements. McCarthy's longitudinal case study of one college writer, as he moves across multiple courses in three undergraduate years, leads her to conclude that writing development is so context-dependent that a student can move forward in one course or one discipline and not in another, which speaks to the issue of uneven development that was so prominent among students in our study. Sommers and Saltz explain that individual students in their longitudinal study did not develop in linear fashion, but progressed in irregular steps, backward and forward, a phenomenon common in our study as well. Sternglass's longitudinal case studies of four student writers portray development as a movement, however uneven, from "fact-gathering research to interpretation of material learned . . . from reliance on authoritative sources to analysis . . . [as students] adapt to the demands of specific tasks and specific instructors" (289). Carroll's qualitative portrayal of development, in her longitudinal study of twenty undergraduates, shows students who write not necessarily better but differently, "producing new, more complicated texts, addressing challenging topics with greater depth and complexity" (22). She also points to students' increased metacognitive capacities as a marker of development, describing them as those who can "assess their own proficiency and target areas where they are still struggling" (126).

Beaufort's longitudinal case study of one student points to the unevenness of development by creating a five-part model of cognitive processes that characterize writerly development in a given discipline. She finds that these processes, which include the use of rhetorical knowledge, writing processes, subject matter knowledge, genre knowledge, and discourse community knowledge, develop asymetrically, with genre and rhetorical knowledge showing the least growth in the student she studies. Studies such as these reinforce the argument for multiple perspectives on writing development by showing the mix of cognitive, social, and rhetorical capacities that student writers call on as they move through a variety of contexts. Such studies also demonstrate the value of employing multiple methods for deepening understandings of writerly development, a value we share and enact by taking many approaches to our data.

Two categories of subject matter knowledge and discourse community knowledge are integral to Beaufort's assertions about the relationship between writing development and disciplinary expertise. In Beaufort's telling, disciplinary knowledge cannot be separated from other dimensions of writing development, and she laments that "the influence of subject matter knowledge and critical thinking skills on written products" (143) is often neglected in research on writing studies. Although Beaufort's may be the most overt claim for this link between writing and disciplines, other researchers make related assertions. Carroll, for example, points to a relationship between writing development and discipline when she says that writing differently results from encountering new environments and taking on new roles, "not just getting better at the same task" (28). She amplifies this point by noting that development can be understood as students' "growing ability over four years to describe the methods and conventions of their disciplines" (126). It is not just that faculty in some disciplines provide more opportunities for writing development—although they do—but that the concept of writing development itself becomes imbricated in disciplinary knowledge or expertise. Yet, as Jonathan Monroe claims, even discipline-focused programs involve both "multidisciplinary decentering and discipline-specific explication" (5). The chapter by Lizzie Hutton and Gail Gibson reinforces this point by demonstrating how students also resist disciplinary genres in favor of their own constructions.

The model of writing development offered by Chris Thaiss and Terry Myers Zawacki's qualitative research—which included interviews, surveys, focus groups, assessment data, and student writing samples—is grounded in this linkage between writing development and disciplinary expertise. Their three-stage model begins with students intuiting disciplinary "rules" based on a few courses in the field. It continues in the second stage with additional course work where students encounter different "rules" and move away from a perception of consistency, attributing difference to instructor subjectivity rather than disciplinary conventions. In the third stage, which not all students reach, writers develop a nuanced understanding of the multiple ways of writing in a discipline and their place within it. Thaiss and Zawacki acknowledge that their model—of progression from authority-based knowledge, to a more relativistic stance, and finally to adapting previous practices to the diverse contexts of discipline-based writing—owes a debt to William Perry's model of ethical and intellectual development, a model that posits movement from dualism to relativism to commitment, but theirs is a discipline-focused adaptation. It is true, Thaiss and Zawacki note, that some students and faculty value writing "outside" disciplines, but the major thrust of their work, like the three stages they describe, indicates that writing development means growing capacity within a disciplinary framework. Although our study confirms that disciplines help shape writing development, it also shows how students complicate and subvert this connection, "reshaping the rhetorics of their disciplines," as Thaiss and Zawacki put it, "to meet their own individual needs and goals" (118). Furthermore, very few students in our study had just one major, so the idea of discipline-focused writing lay outside their experience.

Looking beyond texts and formal education, another set of meanings attached to writing development focuses on writers and their personal experiences. Elizabeth Chisseri-Strater opened this line of thought with her 1991 ethnographic study of two students, in which she found that students' development as writers can be impeded by the establishment of firm boundaries between their personal and academic lives. Herrington and Curtis's 2000 longitudinal study of four students via interviews, classroom observation, and writing samples portrayed writing as a self-constituting and relational activity in which social and psychological features of growth intersect with more academic ones. In this view of writing development, writers themselves cultivate a greater "sense of personal assurance and of purpose in communicating with readers" (357), and their writing becomes "more fully developed, more coherent, and more surely articulated" (357). For Herrington and Curtis, the self-development of students as individuals is inseparable from their development as writers. Sommers and Saltz take a related stance in their 2004 report on their qualitative study of first-year writers, claiming that "the story of freshman year is not one of dramatic changes on paper; it is the story of changes within the writers themselves" (144). They explain that "gaps between what a student knows about writing and what the student can actually do can be observed throughout all four years" as students encounter new genres, new disciplines, and new purposes for writing (144). Studies such as these call attention to a relationship between students' identity formation and their writerly development, and we found this a productive relationship in our study. Anna Knutson's chapter, for instance, shows how a student's constructs of effective writing alongside her perception of her ability to measure up to these constructs shaped her self-efficacy. Naomi Silver makes a similar point in chapter 8 as she notes how students conflate their writing development with personal growth or identity formation.

Another perspective on the relationship between students' personal and writerly development is offered by a 2015 large-scale statistical study by Paul Anderson, Robert Gonyea, Chris Anson, and Charles Paine. Using data produced by a collaboration between the Council of Writing Program Administrators and the National Study of Student Engagement (NSSE), these researchers found a high correlation between gains in students' personal and social development—as measured by the Personal and Social Development Scale of the NSSE—and three constructs of effective writing assignments. That is, students who had experienced writing instruction that used interactive writing processes, meaning-making writing tasks, and clear writing expectations indicated that college helped them develop a code of personal values, increase their understanding of themselves and others, participate in and contribute to their communities, and develop a deepened sense of spirituality. These results, obtained via regression analysis, offered an empirical, albeit correlational, basis for our further thinking about the interrelationships between students' personal development and their development as writers.

Jenn Fishman, Andrea Lunsford, Beth McGregor, and Mark Otuteye offer another way to approach the relationship between personal and writerly development. These authors consider two students who engage in writing performance or "live enactments of their own writing" through drama and spoken-word poetry

(226). Their extracurricular performances, which occur outside of classrooms, bring together body, rhetoric, and writing, and according to the students involved, such performances help to restore their flagging confidence in themselves as writers. Although students at Stanford express high confidence in their writing abilities when they arrive, that confidence diminishes during the first year. Experience with writing performances, however, contributes to a renewed sense of confidence, leading the authors to assert that "writing performances play a role in early college students' development as writers" (226). The authors argue that performance produces change because it fosters "social and self-reflection" (232). One dimension of performance via writing occurs, as the authors note, in digital spaces, as students compose at the intersection of "bodies, screens and documents" (246). Here, a heightened sense of audience awareness, the capacity for the visual as well as the verbal, and the flexibility of the medium create especially generative spaces for developing writers. In addition to enhanced confidence, the students described here increased their rhetorical awareness as writers, perhaps another dimension of the linkage between personal and writerly development. In a related article, Lunsford, Fishman, and Liew offer another perspective on personal and writerly development by showing how students develop an identification with writing and "come to see themselves as writers with something worthwhile to say" (486). Ben Keating's chapter explores and complicates this linkage as it delineates the role of peer feedback in writing development.

Recent studies suggest the special benefits that digital tools confer on developing writers. Crystal VanKooten, for example, found that video production in a first-year writing class gave students increased meta-awareness about composition, including the rhetorical dimensions of writing. She uses the term "rhetorical layering" to describe the "orienting, addressing multiple audiences and purposes and revising the parts and the whole" that student writers attribute to their experiences with video production (67, 2016a). Audience awareness is especially enhanced by the digital. As VanKooten explains, "This concept was the most prevalent across all students: all six talked about audiences for their work and made compositional choices that they linked to audience" (9, 2016b). Re-mediation, or transforming a written text into a different genre or medium, has likewise been shown to enhance the rhetorical awareness of student writers (Delagrange). Furthermore, as Naomi Silver's chapter in this collection shows, student development occurs in the digital realm, often in different directions and at different rates than in alphabetic forms, and the disjunctions between these two offer another perspective on the evolution of student writers.

The recent focus on transfer within composition studies reflects another dimension of writing development because of its attention to the ways students do (or do not) carry knowledge, strategies, and procedures from one context to another. Rebecca Nowacek's 2011 study of the rhetorical aspects of transfer serves as a reminder that writing development involves student agency. However, Elizabeth Wardle's 2012 description of "creative repurposing for expansive learning" makes it clear that transfer, like the writing development of which it is a part, does not always occur in the same way for all students, since the contexts in which they learn do not always support the problem-solving and meta-reflective dispositions that nourish transfer. Our study likewise found that curriculum, and the larger context in which it exists, play a significant role in writing development, as Anne Gere's chapter demonstrates. In turn, this reminded us anew that student writers follow a wide variety of (curricular) paths as they move through their undergraduate years.

Like transfer, threshold concepts recently emerged in composition studies, and the two share the assumption that students need to understand threshold concepts to engage in the metacognition necessary for transfer—and writing development. Developed by Myer and Land in 2003 as a framework for improving teaching and learning in economics by making the principal assumptions of the field visible, threshold concepts have been subsequently identified in many fields, including composition studies. Regardless of disciplinary markers, threshold concepts share common qualities: they are transformative in that they generate a shift in one's view of a subject; they are often irreversible because they cannot easily be forgotten; they are integrative and demonstrate how phenomena are related; they proceed iteratively and recursively; and they tend to involve forms of troublesome or counterintuitive knowledge.

These qualities of threshold concepts can be unpacked by considering them in relation to writing. For instance, when a student comes to understand that sentence-level features such as the use of what linguists call hedges, or words that qualify claims, can shape the strength of arguments in an entire essay, that student has a new—and transformed—view of writing. In conceptual terms, students will understand that specific words such as *perhaps*, *may*, and *possibly* can contribute to the effect of a piece of writing. At the same time, students' views of writing will be transformed ontologically because they will now see writing as an integration of sentence-level and whole-text features. Once students understand writing in these terms, it becomes difficult to think of sentence-level features as separate from the effect of the whole; the new way of seeing can become irreversible. This insight about the role of hedges can also enable students to see writing in more integrated terms, as they begin to recognize that features such as word choice and organizational structure relate to one another. Coming to such insights is not, however, a direct or smooth process; it proceeds incrementally, often with frequent returns to more familiar ways of thinking. Furthermore, students often resist new perspectives, preferring to avoid knowledge that troubles what they already know about writing and about themselves as writers, as Emily Wilson and Justine Post's chapter on student responses to feedback shows.

While this review doesn't do full justice to the array of meanings assigned to the term "writing development" or to concepts such as transfer and threshold, it does suggest larger bodies of research and theory that shaped our thinking in this study. We were prepared to consider a wide variety of texts produced by students, and also their reflections on their own writing, their observations about their various learning experiences and themselves as writers, and the effects of multimedia on writers and writing. We knew that we would need to employ a wide range of methods to analyze the enormous amount of data we would collect and to consider writing development from many angles, both quantitative and qualitative. And we understood that it would be impossible to describe the journeys of each of the students in our study, but we wanted to represent as many dimensions of their journeys as possible, acknowledging the progressions, regressions, and variations from verbal to digital.

The Context of This Study

Because curriculum numbers among the forces that contribute to writing development, we begin a discussion of context by filling in the details of curricular experiences shared by all students. Before they begin classes, every matriculating incoming student completes a directed self-placement essay to help them decide which writing course to take (see Gere et al. 2013 for details). The one-semester course that satisfies the first-year writing requirement is offered by seven departments, and very few students are exempted, so the several versions of the course, which follow common guidelines, provide comparable experiences for nearly all matriculating students. Peer review is a standard part of the curriculum, and students are required to participate in workshop sessions in which they give and receive responses to writing. The goal of the course is to help students develop the capacity to produce evidence-based arguments.

In addition, all students are required to complete a second course, the Upper-Level Writing Requirement (ULWR). While originally conceived as an opportunity for students to learn to write in their majors, this course has evolved into one where students pursue other areas of interest, follow a favorite professor, or develop additional skills (see Gere et al. 2015 for a detailed explanation). For some students, these two courses functioned as the only clear opportunities to develop as writers, while others ended up taking multiple ULWR courses. To provide additional opportunities to the former group of students and recognize the efforts of the latter group by offering credit toward a degree program, the Sweetland Center for Writing undertook the project of creating a minor in writing.

Launching this minor gave students from multiple disciplines an opportunity to extend their focus on writing, and it also set this study in motion. As we enrolled the first cohort of writing minors and recruited a number of them to participate in the study beginning in the fall of 2011, we also identified and recruited a group of nonminors who resembled them in terms of gender, academic achievement, and majors to see what we could learn about how the two groups developed as writers. After two years and four incoming cohorts (one each semester), 182 students had agreed to participate in our study, and by the end 169 remained, 60 minors (of whom 44 were women) and 109 nonminors (of whom 93 were women). Our 169 participants represented 47 different majors, an array spanning from American Culture and Anthropology to Sports Management, Statistics, and Women's Studies (see **appendix 1** for a full list of the 47 majors). Eleven of the study participants were peer tutors in the Sweetland Peer Writing Center. There were also eleven multilingual students and seven transfer students in the study. This participant group was obviously limited in some ways. Women, for example, were overrepresented. However, the gendered pattern parallels enrollments in the humanities more generally. Among current English majors at the University of Michigan, for example, 70 percent are women. Another limitation of the study is that all participants indicated an interest in writing—by enrolling in the writing minor, by agreeing to participate in surveys and interviews about writing, or by sharing selections of their writing each year—which may mark them as atypical.

The fifteen-credit Sweetland Minor in Writing Program required students to take both Gateway and Capstone courses within Sweetland, two ULWR courses (rather than just the one required of all students), and one more course focused on argumentative writing, creative nonfiction writing, professional writing, writing and other arts, or digital media writing. Fulfilling these requirements meant taking a writing-focused course nearly every semester, and encountering a broad range of genres, modes, and media.

Learning goals for the minor indicated that students would:

- Produce complex and well-supported arguments that matter in academic and nonacademic contexts.

- Explore different strategies for organizing, revising, and proofreading writing of varying lengths and genres.
- Identify and implement rhetorical choices that meet the demands of specific genres, audiences, and rhetorical situations.
- Compose in a variety of modes, including a range of new media such as blogs, interactive maps, online magazines, etc.
- Identify the expectations that characterize writing in the major, and use this knowledge to write effectively in a range of genres in that discipline.
- Learn the language to describe writing processes, rhetorical choices, genre expectations, and disciplinary discourse to discuss writing-in-progress and writing development over time.
- Collaborate with other writers to improve writing-in-progress.

The two courses required by the minor, the Gateway and Capstone (see **appendix 2**), addressed these goals explicitly and at the same time gave students a good deal of latitude in their ways of accomplishing them. One significant feature of the program was the creation of an eportfolio in both the Gateway and Capstone courses, creating a kind of reflective bookending of each student's writing experiences and growth. The major writing projects for the two courses also foregrounded student interests and commitments. Students were led, in the Gateway course, to reflect on the topic "Why I Write," and in the Capstone course to look back at their college experiences in a "Writer's Evolution" essay, accompanied by an annotated bibliography of their own writing. The Capstone course also required a special project of the student's choice, and many participants took this as an opportunity to explore diverse genres and areas of interest. Though both projects required a guiding idea and evidence, no format or genre was required, which allowed students to write poems, narratives, and manifestos as well as more conventional essays.

Reflection was cultivated throughout the minor, beginning with the application, which asked students to describe themselves as writers. The two eportfolios in which students wrote contextual reflections about each artifact, reflective introductions to the eportfolio as a whole, and reflections on their drafting processes furthered students' reflective capacities. It is also worth noting that courses and extracurricular writing experiences outside program requirements also fostered reflection, and many nonminors found the experience of selecting which pieces of writing to archive to be an experience of reflection.

Nonminors had no required writing courses beyond first-year composition and the ULWR course, both of which are required of all undergraduates. However, we found that many nonminors voluntarily took courses that required a great deal of writing—philosophy and English, for example—or decided to write a thesis, coauthor an academic article, or contribute to a campus publication. The university's Undergraduate Research Opportunity Program, which pairs undergraduates with faculty researchers, provided a gateway to writing for some students; an inspiring professor led others to focus on writing. For instance, Kris, a student profiled in Anne Gere's chapter, describes how an English professor helped her, a math major, realize she was a writer. Additionally, the experience of participating in the study probably contributed to nonminors' development as writers because they were required to archive selections of their writing each year and preface each selection with an explanation of the assignment. Simply looking at the growing archive of their work led some nonminors to think more deeply and systematically about their development as writers, as we discovered in student interviews.

Both nonminors and minors completed surveys (see **appendix 3**) during the sophomore year and again as they were graduating, and a subset of both groups took part in interviews (see **appendix 4**) as they entered the study and as they graduated. In addition to the information provided by surveys and interviews, we gathered institutionally provided demographic data for each participant and created an archive of their writing. For minors, this archive included the eportfolios, and for both groups it included a collection of writing produced across four years, beginning with the directed self-placement essay written by every matriculating student and extending to papers written at the end of senior year. This array of texts and other information enabled us to triangulate across multiple sources of evidence.

Overview of Analysis

This multiyear study involved 169 student writers, who produced 322 surveys, 131 interviews, 94 eportfolios, and 2,406 total pieces of writing. Given the large amount of data collected across five years, this was a highly collaborative project requiring many hands, and various configurations of us sat around the oak table in Anne Gere's office week after week and year after year to plan and analyze. As noted, we began by recruiting participants from Sweetland's new minor in writing in 2011, finding nonminor students with parallel institutional profiles to the minors who signed on, and developing survey questions and a protocol for entry and exit interviews. We designed the surveys to query a broad swath of students' prior writing experiences as well as their current experiences and perceptions of themselves as writers. We developed entry-survey questions that asked about high school and first-year composition writing practices and proficiencies and exit-survey questions that focused on upper-level writing courses and students' awareness of when they found themselves using strategies and skills they had learned in prior writing courses. Both surveys also incorporated the Experiences with Writing module from the National Survey of Student Engagement, as well as the full set of questions from the Daly-Miller Writing Apprehension Test. Our interview protocols, which appear in **appendix 4**, were designed to probe an equally robust range of writing practices and experiences. Recognizing that writing development begins long before college and extends well beyond it, we aimed to make our portraits of writers as full and extensive as possible.

During the first two years, we created naming conventions to identify each participant and links to all related quantitative and qualitative data. We built an online system for storing the ever-increasing collection of student texts, study responses, and institutional data, and endeavored to preserve everything included in the eportfolios using the Site Sucker application. All of this data was incorporated into the ever-growing project archive. As we began our analysis, the size and scope of the data required us to build a more manageable electronic archive of student interviews, survey responses, application materials, and writing samples. Ryan McCarty led the creation of the archive. Each student's data was stored in individual folders, facilitating some of the more in-depth case studies offered in this collection. The archiving of student writing presented an especially daunting task as we became aware early on that we would be interested in tagging each piece with a range of identifiers. Each piece was labeled with a textual identifier, followed by codes for whether the student was a minor or nonminor; whether the text was written for a STEM, social science, humanities, or extracurricular context; and the student's study number. We also designated each writing sample either "early" if it was written for a lower-division course or "late" if it was for an upper-division course. Although we did not explicitly ask them to do so, several students provided us with writing they did in high school. This material was labeled as "pre." In the case of students who provided us with multiple drafts of particular texts, folders were created to house each iteration, numbered from earlier to later (sometimes after a bit of careful reading to determine which draft probably preceded or followed another.

The process of constructing this archive and naming each of the texts constituted one of our first broad analytical encounters with the data as a whole. Naming the text involved actually opening each file and reading headings, titles, and early paragraphs, as well as occasionally making inferences about what general area the paper was written for if student headings did not clearly specify a course. Researchers kept early notes about participants who had given us an especially rich collection of writing in a particular academic division, or conversely, if students provided us with a range of writing from across disciplines. We also noted students who wrote on similar topics across their courses and those who provided texts that were particularly interesting in terms of genre or design.

Transcribing and coding interviews, analyzing interviews and responses to survey questions, and reading and rereading student writing filled the middle years of the study and continued through to the graduation of our final cohort in 2015.

Two central questions guided our study:

1. What can a longitudinal study of college student writers add to knowledge about writing development?
2. What comparisons can be drawn between nonminors and minors in writing?

We took multiple approaches in response to these questions. Our analysis of survey questions was largely statistical, comparing within-group responses from sophomore to senior year and comparing across groups to discern differences among and between minors and nonminors. We also compared groups across disciplinary areas; for instance, we considered STEM majors in relation to non-STEM majors. This form of analysis enabled us to discern trends within the entire group. For instance, after identifying survey items dealing with genre, we used factor analysis to determine correlations between students' experience with specific genres (such as five-paragraph theme, personal essay, evidence-based argument, etc.) and their understanding of rhetorical principles. Statistical differences between entry and exit surveys showed us that seniors were less likely to seek advice about beginning a writing project than they had been as sophomores, which we interpreted as indicating that as a total group these students had developed more confidence in their own capacities as writers.

We used open coding to analyze the interviews that had been recorded and transcribed, and after multiple conflations and combinations, established codes that identified concepts frequently visible in students' descriptions of their writing and of themselves as writers. We eventually settled on nineteen codes (see **appendix 5**), and the 11,156 excerpts identified by these codes provided the basis for further analysis as we attempted to understand relationships among students' various perceptions. Not surprisingly, we found significant co-occurrence among codes; for example, codes for "peer review" and "audience awareness" co-occurred as students found that the responses of their classmates made them much more sensitive to the needs of their various audiences. Similarly, "writerly self-conception," "kinds of writing," and "writing development" co-occurred as students looked back at the writing they had done in multiple contexts, considered how their writing had changed, and then assessed their strengths and weaknesses as writers. "Portfolio," "writerly self-conception," and "writing development" co-occurred as students' assessed how their two eportfolios had offered them insights into common themes and commitments that spanned their college writing. Such co-occurrences gave us deeper insight into the relationships students constructed for themselves as they developed understandings of key concepts in composition.

Analysis of student writing included both quantitative and qualitative approaches. Quantitative approaches included statistical analysis, primarily of student surveys, and automated text analysis, or corpus linguistic analysis to discern patterns in hundreds of texts written by all of the students in the study. For example, we compared students' use of boosters or intensifying words in their first and senior years to see trends in language use across the entire group. Chapters by Laura Aull and Zak Lancaster show how this kind of analysis, especially when combined with rhetorical analysis, can yield valuable insights into the macro-level effects of sentence-level choices student writers make. These chapters both complement and challenge early development studies focused on error because they invite a return to specific features of language and at the same time insist on embedding that attention in larger issues of discourse.

Coded interviews, students' written reflections, and papers collected in minors' eportfolios and in archives created by nonminors provided an environment where we could compare early and late selections, follow themes, and look closely at cases of individual students. We were able to read across interviews, selections of writing, and reflections to develop rich portraits of student writers. Reflections written by students also offered insights into the futures they imagined for themselves, suggesting how students constructed themselves professionally. In addition, we analyzed the digital features of eportfolios, including the navigation system, the use of multimedia including auditory and visual tools, and coherence of the various elements that comprised the whole. The collaborative nature of our research meant that more than one of us wrote about the same student, which resulted in even more fully elaborated and sometimes contradictory portrayals of an individual. **Appendix 6** lists the pseudonyms of all students included in this collection, along with an indication of the chapters in which they appear.

This multiplicity of approaches yielded an array of findings, each of which builds on earlier studies of writing development among college students. The chapters dealing with automated text analysis or corpus linguistics contribute to the language-focused aspects of writing development. The chapters centered on feedback, self-efficacy, and transitions add to the literature on the relationship between personal and writerly development. The chapters on genre augment studies of the connections between disciplinary expertise and writing development, and the chapters on digital texts speak to other studies of digital and multimedia writing. All of these findings elaborate on the principle that writing development never follows a constant or straight path; it is marked by starts and stops, by blind alleys and 180-degree turns, and by frustrations as well as unexpected discoveries.

Organizing Principles

Conducting all the studies associated with this project was challenging, but it was equally challenging to decide how to represent what we found. There is, as Anne Beaufort notes, "no grand theory of writers' developmental processes" (24) around which we could organize our work. There is not even an agreed-on set of terms to use. Beaufort's five-part model includes some dimensions that align with our study, but the strong emphasis on disciplinarity—evident in both subject matter and discourse community knowledge—does not resonate with our findings. To be sure, students in our study were aware of disciplinary discourses, but as we learned, they were as engaged in subverting them as in assimilating to them, and as we learned in an earlier study, even writing-in-the-disciplines courses are not always discipline-focused (see Gere et al. 2015). Both student agency and curricular design, then, led us away from the Beaufort model.

An alternative model of writing development entered writing studies with "The Value of Troublesome Knowledge: Threshold Concepts in Writing and History" (Adler-Kassner et al.) in 2012. In the ensuing years, threshold concepts have stimulated a good deal of conversation and debate. Indeed, their categories have shifted with time, as a comparison of the 2015 *Naming What We Know* (*NWWK*) with the 2016 *Critical Transitions: Writing and the Question of Transfer* (*CT*) demonstrates. While *NWWK* focuses on articulating core principles of the field, albeit with an emphasis on their contingent nature, *CT*'s threshold concepts serve as "a framework for designing for and understanding transfer of learning across contexts" (18). Both, however, describe threshold concepts as critical for those who want to help students learn to write more effectively. At the same time, theorists of threshold concepts acknowledge that concepts are continually shifting and emerging as we learn more about how students learn to write. This study demonstrates such claims by describing multiple aspects of students' writing development, and, thereby, building on and complicating threshold concepts.

The overarching concept prominent in both *NWWK* and *CT* is Writing Is an

Activity and a Subject of Study, which serves as a metaconcept for our study since both we and our student participants engage regularly in (the activity of) writing and at the same time deepen our understanding of the concepts that mark it as a bounded area of study. While we identified alignments between our findings and articulations of threshold concepts from both *NWWK* and *CT* as well as from Beaufort's model, our findings led us to create our own adaptations in response to what we learned from students. For example, the social aspects of students' approach to writing included an affective dimension, something not represented in existing threshold concepts but addressed in several chapters in this collection. While disciplinary subject matter knowledge and discourse communities did not loom as large in our study as they did in Beaufort's, they were a topic of discussion for many of our students. Other features that emerged from our data included the quality of high school preparation and the development of rhetorical stance. We also found that motivation and self-efficacy, capacities for generalizing and expressing certainty, and the reading-writing relationship registered as important for our students. All of these findings aligned with the claim that threshold concepts offer foundational assumptions about writing without linking these assumptions to specific goals or learning objectives. Even as we look to threshold concepts, we affirm the assertion that it is not possible or desirable to try to name and define all such concepts. This book takes up and extends the invitation to continue the effort of naming what we know—about developing writers.

Each section of this book casts a different light on how students and their writing follow various developmental paths. The first section, which considers both audience awareness and feedback from peers and instructors, centers on what Beaufort describes as rhetorical knowledge and the concept that writing is both social and rhetorical. The second section includes chapters on students' approaches to the conflation of disciplinary expertise and writing development and on the "types of writing" or genres described by students in our study. The third section contains chapters that focus on language, demonstrating how attention to sentence-level features illuminates entire texts. This entire collection embraces the idea that writers never reach a state of complete mastery; they always have more to learn. However, we focus on this concept specifically in section four. The final section looks at two sites of writerly development, the transition from high school to first-year writing and the transition from college to new writing environments. These descriptions suggest more bounded categories than we intend. Many of the chapters could easily be shifted to another section, and the sections themselves are as contingent as the models on which they draw. However, this organizational plan provides a framework on which to build further research. To that end we make our data available in the digitally expanded version of this book, which can be found on the Fulcrum platform at https://doi.org/10.3998/mpub.10079890. The basis for more generative conversation appears in the conclusion as it pulls together insights from the entire project to ask questions and offer suggestions to colleagues interested in fostering the development of student writers and to researchers who will sit around other tables in other rooms.

WORKS CITED

Adler-Kassner, Linda, John Majewski, and Damian Koshnick. "The Value of Troublesome Knowledge: Transfer and Threshold Concepts in Writing and History." *Composition Forum*, vol. 26, Fall 2012, http://compositionforum.com/issue/26

Adler-Kassner, Linda, and Elizabeth Wardle, editors. *Naming What We Know: Threshold Concepts of Writing Studies*. Utah State UP, 2015.

Anderson, Paul, Chris Anson, Robert M. Goyea, and Charles Paine. "The Contributions of Writing to Learning and Development: Results from a Large-Scale Multi-Institutional Study." *Research in the Teaching of English*, vol. 50, no. 2, 2015, pp. 199–235.

Anson, Chris, and Jessie L. Moore. *Critical Transitions: Writing and the Question of Transfer*. CSU Open Press, 2017, wac.colostate.edu/books/ansonmoore/. Accessed 6 June 2017.

Beach, King. "Consequential Transitions: A Developmental View of Knowledge Propagation through Social Organizations." *Between School and Work: New Perspectives on Transfer and Boundary-Crossing*, edited by Terttu Tuomi-Gröhn and Yrjo Engeström, Emerald Group Publishing, 2003, pp. 39–61.

Beaufort, Anne. *College Writing and Beyond: A New Framework for University Writing Instruction*. Utah State UP, 2007.

Carroll, Lee Ann. *Rehearsing New Roles: How College Students Develop as Writers*. SIU Press, 2002.

Chiseri-Strater, Elizabeth. *Academic Literacies: The Public and Private Discourse of University Students*. Boynton/Cook Heinemann, 1991.

Delagrange, Susan. "When Revision Is Redesign: Key Questions for Digital Scholarship." *Kairos: A Journal of Rhetoric, Technology, and Pedagogy*, vol. 14, no. 1, Fall 2009, http://kairos.technorhetoric.net/14.1/inventio/delagrange/index.html

Fishman, Jenn, Andrea Lunsford, Beth McGregor, and Mark Otuteye. "Performing Writing, Performing Literacy." *College Composition and Communication*, vol. 57, no. 2, 2005, pp. 224–52.

Gere, Anne Ruggles, Laura Aull, Moisés Perales-Escudero, Zak Lancaster, and Elizabeth Vander Lei. "Local Assessment: Using Genre Analysis to Validate Directed Self-Placement." *College Composition and Communication*, vol. 64, no. 4, 2013, pp. 605–33.

Gere, Anne Ruggles, Sarah C. Swofford, Naomi Silver, and Melody Pugh. "Interrogating Disciplines/Disciplinarity in WAC/WID: An Institutional Study." *College Composition and Communication*, vol. 67, no. 2, 2015, pp. 243–66.

Haswell, Richard H. *Gaining Ground in College Writing: Tales of Development and Interpretation*. Southern Methodist UP, 1991.

Herrington, Anne J., and Marcia Curtis. *Persons in Process: Four Stories of Writing and Personal Development in College*. National Council of Teachers of English, 2000.

Kitzhaber, Albert Raymond. *Themes, Theories, and Therapy: The Teaching of Writing in College*. McGraw-Hill, 1963.

Lunsford, Andrea A., Jenn Fishman, and Warren M. Liew. "College Writing, Identification, and the

Production of Intellectual Property: Voices from the Stanford Study of Writing." *College English*, vol. 75, no. 5, 2013, pp. 470–92.

McCarthy, Lucille Parkinson. "A Stranger in Strange Lands: A College Student Writing across the Curriculum." *Research in the Teaching of English*, vol. 21, no. 3, 1987, pp. 233–65.

Monroe, Jonathan, editor. *Local Knowledges, Local Practices: Writing in the Disciplines at Cornell*. U Pittsburgh P, 2007.

Myer, Jan H. F., and Ray Land. "Threshold Concepts and Troublesome Knowledge: Epistemological Considerations and a Conceptual Framework for Teaching and Learning." *Higher Education*, vol. 49, 2005, pp. 373–88.

Nowacek, Rebecca. *Agents of Integration: Understanding Transfer as a Rhetorical Act*. SIU Press, 2011.

Perry, William. *Forms of Intellectual and Ethical Development in the College Years: A Scheme*. Holt, Rinehart, and Winston, 1970.

Sommers, Nancy, and Laura Saltz. "The Novice as Expert: Writing the Freshman Year." *College Composition and Communication*, vol. 56, no. 1, 2004, pp. 124–49.

Sternglass, Marilyn S. *Time to Know Them: A Longitudinal Study of Writing and Learning at the College Level*. Lawrence Erlbaum, 1997.

Thaiss, Chris, and Terry Myers Zawacki. *Engaged Writers and Dynamic Disciplines: Research on the Academic Writing Life*. Boynton/Cook Heinemann, 2006.

VanKooten, Crystal. "'The Video Was What Did It for Me': Developing Meta-Awareness about Composition across Media." *College English*, vol. 79, no. 1, 2016a, pp. 57–80.

VanKooten, Crystal. "Identifying Components of Meta-Awareness about Composition: Toward a Theory and Methodology for Writing Studies." *Composition Forum*, vol. 33, Spring 2016b, compositionforum.com/issue/33/meta-awareness.php. Accessed 11 July 2017.

Wardle, Elizabeth. "Creative Repurposing for Expansive Learning: Considering 'Problem-Exploring' and 'Answer-Getting' Dispositions in Individuals and Fields." *Composition Forum*, 2012, http://compositionforum.com/issue 26

Whitla, Dean K. *Value Added and Other Related Matters*. US Department of Education, 1981.

SECTION ONE

Writing Is a Rhetorical and Social Activity

The rhetorical situation—the relationship of writer, subject, and audience—and its contextual variations embodies a foundational set of assumptions about writing. Without a solid understanding of the interactions of these three elements, undergraduates cannot address the writing challenges of higher education (and beyond). We open by focusing on the rhetorical dimensions of writing because understandings of the roles of writer, subject, and audience can grow as writers develop. Of the three, audience proved the most challenging for the students in our study. As they entered our study as lower-division undergraduates, our participants had a fairly clear understanding of their roles as writers, and they were well attuned to the need to focus on a specific topic or subject, but imagining or addressing an audience was more difficult for them. In interviews, a number of students said they would "just write" with no thought about the reader. The need to consider imagined or actual audiences, including what that audience knows and needs to know and their reasons for reading a given text, were largely beyond their ken.

Audience awareness took on major significance in our study because it was a site of growth and development for most students in our study. It wasn't just that students became more aware of their audiences as they moved through their undergraduate years; they also became concerned about the effect they wanted to have, the sort of relationship they wanted to create with audiences, connections they saw between audience and genre, and the ways they could use the affordances of digital writing to reach and influence audiences. Accordingly we assert that audience awareness—in its fullest sense—is an essential concept for epistemological participation in writing for students, instructors, and researchers.

A number of mentions provided the first indication of the importance of audience for our students. In entrance interviews, held after writing minors had taken the Gateway course and all participants had taken first-year writing, students were asked what constitutes good writing, and audience awareness was a frequent response, yielding over 600 coded entries. In part, students' talk about the importance of audience may have been a consequence of its relative novelty in their experiences as writers. Nicole's response in her entry interview typifies comments made about audience by many students:

> We had to talk a lot about audience at some point in the class. I think we had to write reflections saying who our audience was and like who our intended audience was. Having to pinpoint that was where it really like stuck in my mind because I'd never had to say like "Oh, I'm directing this at my classmates." I always thought it was a given, like, this is for my teacher, but it doesn't have to be that way.

Explicit attention to audience was a new experience for this writing minor, and the requirement to write a reflection apparently helped to complicate and solidify this rhetorical concept for her. The observation that "it doesn't have to be that way" suggests a new perspective on audience, a transformation, as the language of threshold concepts would explain it. Since high school writing instruction, particularly that shaped by standardized assessments, frequently asks students to write to no one in particular, it is not surprising that thinking about or beyond the instructor as audience was novel for many students. In both first-year writing and the minors' Gateway course, explicit curricular attention to audience in peer review and in required reflections helped move students toward a transformative rhetorical perspective.

The nature of that transformation varied, however. The default of the teacher audience remained strong for many students, and we found variations on "different professors want different things" in many interview transcripts, indicating that students, particularly nonminors, did not easily reach beyond the familiar teacher or professor audience. At the same time, however, many of our second-year students talked about the effects they wanted to have on audiences. Some emphasized clarity, so that readers wouldn't be confused about the point they were making. They talked about being "audience-friendly" and "reader-friendly" and went on to explain the ways they wanted to engage audiences, imagining themselves sitting next to someone and saying, as Kaitlin put it, "This is what I want you to get out of this piece." They also wanted to engage their readers; as Annie observed, "It's not boring—when people read through my paper they're not falling asleep." The desire to be engaging or entertaining as well as clear suggests that students wanted to do more than convey information to their audiences. They began to imagine readers who would have affective as well as intellectual responses to their writing.

Already as sophomores, students also probed the relationship between audience and genre. For example, Helen talked about writing literature reviews while working in a research lab during the summer and noted, "You learn from those types of people how they want their writing done, and it's not necessarily the same as a professor from the school." This nonminor makes it clear that the professor audience has different expectations than a supervisor outside the university, and those expectations extend to different types or genres of writing. Another student, Olivia, reinforced the point that moving from one audience to another could mean shifting to a different genre, explaining "The same core ideas can be transferred across to different projects and to different audiences and to different modes and different contacts too. . . . For example, if you want to write an article about shoes for the general public you're probably not going to overload them with your scholarly tones." Although neither student mentions genre, language such as "how they want their writing done," "modes," and "scholarly tones" shows that the concept of genre was guiding their thinking. Even without the metalanguage to describe an audience-genre relationship, students were able to talk about the complex ways that audience interacts with other dimensions of writing.

The prospect of online audiences for digital writing also heightened students' awareness of audience. Commenting functions on blogs, for instance, served as a clear reminder of their "unlimited audiences," a host of unknown but actual readers of their writing. As Isabella put it, "You turn in a paper and it's just gone and you don't think about the people reading it, but with the blog . . . people are reading this because they are commenting on it." Even students who didn't like the blog requirement in the minor in writing acknowledged that it was helpful because it enabled them to consider audience in their writing. Assignments that asked students to re-mediate or repurpose a piece of writing by using multimedia also increased audience awareness. For example, Kris, who wrote an academic argument debunking the idea that vaccinations lead to autism, described a conversation about repurposing that material for an online audience: "I'm thinking about making it into like a magazine article. What do you think about that? Everyone was like, 'Oh my gosh. That would be great, like you could do it as a parenting magazine.'" As this excerpt shows, the shift to a new medium led the writer to see a different audience—parents—for her academic work. The tools of digital writing made the rhetorical capacities of writing more visible to students, in terms of both how it could reach "unlimited audiences" and how it could be transformed to meet the needs of various audiences.

Two years later, as they were graduating, students still talked about audience awareness in their exit interviews in response to the question about what constitutes good writing. In over 800 coded responses (as compared with over 600 in the sophomore year), students referred to effects they sought, relationships they wanted to establish, linkages with genre, and the influences of digital media on their connections to audiences. The desire to have a particular effect on an audience remained strong; students such as Gabi, a nonminor, expressed a desire to write "things that people actually would want to read and care about reading," and to also get a point across, so that "whoever picks up and reads your essay, somebody who isn't necessarily familiar with the topic, can read it, and can understand it, and point out what the argument is and how you supported that argument." In specifying desired effects, students such as Natalie, a minor, described relationships with readers: "I love the feeling of . . . having someone else read my paper and they're like, 'Wow. I never thought of it like that before.'" They also called attention to the effect of audience response on themselves as writers, as Abby did: "It was nice to hear that other people really liked my piece and it had an impact upon them because it made me more confident with not only my writing abilities but what I have to say in general, people want to hear." The affective dimension evident in these comments shows how students' understanding of audience has become deeper and more complex. The delight in achieving a particular effect with an audience was echoed in students' comments about the pleasure of becoming more intimately connected to other readers and writers via peer review. These expressions of positive feelings associated with audience awareness suggest the need for further consideration of the ways we conceptualize writing development. The relationship between confidence and writing ability has received attention from researchers (Pajares and Johnson; Pajares), but very little notice has been given to the ways that the pleasures of writing might contribute to writing development. The comments of students in this study point to the need to learn more about the relationship between positive affect and writing development.

Graduating seniors also continued to talk about the relationship between audience and genre in describing their own ways of producing good writing, as Madeline did: "I could leave it in one form . . . or . . . turn it into another form so now it's maybe reaching double that amount of different people who the other form didn't reach." In using the term "form," Madeline makes a more explicit gesture toward genre than did her peers when they were sophomores. And like those peers, she points to a connection between audience and genre; with a different genre, she will be able to attract a different and larger audience.

These seniors reinforced the claim that multimodal writing heightened their awareness of and attention to audience, but they were more explicit about ways they used technology to shape readers' experiences; as Joy said: "[I was] trying to think about reader navigation while I designed [my electronic portfolio]." She continued, "I wanted it to be really clean . . . [for] you to stay in the site, not go outside of it and be able to move through it. Not quickly but have it be succinct enough you weren't overwhelmed by the amount of text." Courtney commented on the ways "design creates a different kind of experience for the reader," including issues of navigation, images, color, and overall "look." Statements such as these indicate an increased sophistication about how the affordances of digital writing can shape audience experiences, and students saw themselves as capable of using these tools to achieve desired effects on their audiences.

Students also described using multimedia writing to become readers of, and thereby audiences for, their own writing, and they cited blogs as doing this especially well. For example, Sadie kept a blog during her summer in Europe, and the blog became a space for "reflecting on the trip and what it taught me. The last few [posts] were definitely just like what I learned and what I wish I would have known and what I knew now. . . . When I go back and read it now, I'm impressed with what I was able to write." The pleasure this student expresses about rereading her writing echoes that expressed by students who took pleasure in audience responses from others. Taking on the role of audience not only gave this student a greater sense of audience awareness, it exposed her to the positive affect that the writer-audience relationship can evoke. Peer review inspired similar experiences and feelings. Carol explained, "I liked getting to know the other people through their writing because I felt I could really tell who they were by reading what they had written and where their heart's at. . . . You get a little sight into their soul when you read something somebody else has written. I really liked that." Susanne said, "It was just nice to be with a community of writers and just people who—and a lot of writing we were doing was really personal, so you got to make these personal connections." Not only was having the desired effect on one's audience a source of pleasure and of increased audience awareness for these students, but so was becoming an audience for one's peers.

Tracing students' expanding ideas about audience, reader relationships, genre, and medium suggests ways to broaden concepts that deal with rhetorical dimensions of writing. Audience awareness as represented by these students extends well beyond acknowledgment of readers to include perceptions and strategies that inform writing in specific ways. It is an awareness that positions the audience as a resource for insights about genre and digital tools as well as a motivating force for creating effects and building relationships. The growth of such expansive ideas about audience also speaks to writing development. Students did not move to complex views of audience uniformly or directly; they often stalled or moved sideways. Still, however, nearly all expressed different understandings of audience when they graduated than they had when they entered the study.

Despite the many common responses, there were important differences between graduating writing minors and nonminors. Writing minors evinced a wider range of perspectives on and approaches to audiences, while nonminors' view of audience remained more focused on the classroom, with more of them holding on to the concept of instructor as primary audience than they had initially expressed. For these nonminors, variation in instructors' expectations elicited frustration. Lauren recounted the experience of getting a low grade in her junior year because her instructor was "a new audience . . . completely and totally different than what [she] was used to writing for. You can be the best writer ever and get consistent A's on papers, but then you meet someone that doesn't understand how you write things, and he wants you to write it differently." The frustration born of seeing the audience as the instructor, and the grade as an indication of the quality of the writing, typifies the responses of many graduating nonminors. They expressed a firm understanding of the importance of audience in writing, but a majority focused on the context of the classroom, with grades and instructors' opinions assuming dominant importance. They could not see beyond the "local" to recognize that writers can push beyond one rhetorical context into myriad others. Minors, in contrast, more commonly engaged in what Elizabeth Wardle calls "creative repurposing," expanding from an initial concept of audience awareness into new variations by intermingling their ideas about audiences with thinking about engagement, pleasure, genre, and digital tools to develop new formulations.

These differences between minors and nonminors raise interesting issues about what it means to develop as a writer. Conceptualizing and expanding on audience awareness certainly marks an important element of development for all writers. Still, for some, that awareness remained relatively fixed across the undergraduate years, focused mainly on the instructor as audience, while others developed a broader concept of audience along with a capacity for creative repurposing. To some extent these differences can be attributed to the writing minor curriculum, which gave a good deal of explicit attention to the concept of audience awareness. However, another way to think about audience awareness in relation to writerly development is to consider how feedback might contribute to audience awareness: how might the social dimensions of feedback from instructors and from peers serve as mechanisms for developing audience awareness in its multiple forms?

The two chapters in this section look at feedback in terms of instructors' comments on and peer review of student writing, and show, albeit differently, how each contributes to audience awareness. Emily Wilson and Justine Post look at responses to instructor feedback in terms of critical engagement, which they define as seeing broad purposes for writing, imagining audiences beyond the instructor, reflecting on one's own writing, and evaluating feedback. Students who take up critical engagement develop an enhanced understanding of audience, because it becomes a more capacious category for them and because they come to understand the social nature of writing more fully. Students who face obstacles to critical engagement are frequently stymied by affective elements such as a poor relationship with an instructor, lack of confidence about high school preparation, or uncertainty generated by contrasting feedback. Such affective responses deprive students of the audience awareness made possible by critical engagement. Benjamin Keating's examination of students' varied experiences with peer review reveals a similar connection between affect and audience awareness, but in this case, affect centers on questions of authority. Keating posits collaborative and nonhierarchical authority as essential to effective peer review, a stance many minors and few nonminors embrace. Nonminors tended to express distrust of classroom-based peer review and doubt the abilities of their peers, thereby inhibiting their ability to develop the audience awareness that peer review can confer. A number of them do, however, see self-sponsored peer review in positive terms, because they have a different relationship to authority in groups they create for themselves. Minors, in contrast, tended to see authority in nonhierarchical terms and recognize their peers as authentic audiences. Together these two chapters demonstrate how the affect associated with feedback shapes audience awareness, a key element in writerly development.

WORKS CITED

Adler-Kassner, Linda, and Elizabeth Wardle, editors. *Naming What We Know: Threshold Concepts of Writing Studies*. Utah State UP, 2015.

Anson, Chris, and Jessie L. Moore. *Critical Transitions: Writing and the Question of Transfer*. CSU Open Press, 2017, wac.colostate.edu/books/ansonmoore/. Accessed 24 October 2017.

Pajares, Frank, and Margaret J. Johnson. "Confidence and Competence in Writing: The Role of Self-Efficacy, Outcome Expectancy, and Apprehension." *Research in the Teaching of English*, vol. 28, no. 3, 1994, pp. 313–31.

Pajares, Frank. "Self-Efficacy Beliefs, Motivation, and Achievement in Writing: A Review of the Literature." *Reading & Writing Quarterly*, vol. 19, 2003, pp. 11–22.

Wardle, Elizabeth. "Creative Repurposing for Expansive Learning: Considering 'Problem-Exploring' and 'Answer-Getting' Dispositions in Individuals and Fields." *Composition Forum*, vol. 26, 2012, compositionforum.com/issue/26/. Accessed 24 October 2017.

CHAPTER ONE

TOWARD CRITICAL ENGAGEMENT

AFFECT AND ACTION IN STUDENT INTERACTIONS WITH INSTRUCTOR FEEDBACK

Emily Wilson and Justine Post

In writing-intensive courses, instructors spend copious amounts of time providing students with written and oral comments on their writing. These extensive efforts have fueled a long line of research in writing studies devoted to instructor feedback. Across this body of scholarship, clear patterns have emerged that encourage instructors to make their feedback dialogic, reflecting an engaged conversation with students rooted in classroom contexts and instructor voices (Sommers; Connors and Lunsford); to place control over writing—as much as possible—in the hands of students (Sprinkle); and to prioritize students' purposes for writing, emphasizing the need for instructors to work both to understand those purposes and to help students realize them in their writing (Brannon and Knoblauch; Sommers). Although these best practices are widely agreed on by writing studies scholars and instructors alike, according to Brian Still and Amy Koerber, they have emerged from studies that "have framed the problem of instructor commenting from essentially the same perspective. . . . That is, they have sought to determine how instructors can comment on student writing in ways that they perceive as most beneficial to their students' long-term success as writers" (207). What is missing here, Still and Koerber argue, are "students' perspectives on commenting" (207).

This absence is as notable in the writing classroom as it is in the literature exploring instructor feedback. Instructors may not have the opportunity to learn how students feel about their feedback. In the absence of information about students' affective responses, instructors may focus on the actions that students take, noting whether they implement or ignore the instructor's suggested changes. In many cases, an instructor's only evidence about how a student is engaging with feedback is the final draft that shows how many of the instructor's comments the student decided to act on. In this way, understandings of students' engagement with feedback are often instructor-focused and narrowly defined, with little room for student perspectives to expand the notions of feedback that circulate in the writing classroom.

Even when researchers take students' perspectives into account, these perspectives often do not inform the notions of feedback that shape studies of student response.[1] Few studies have asked students what they identify as feedback in the writing classroom. Instead, researchers often ask students to complete surveys or questionnaires ranking or evaluating predetermined examples of instructor feedback, which may not even reflect the classroom context (Lynch and Klemans; Reed and Burton; Burkland and Grimm; Straub). In this study, we seek to build on existing narratives by representing students' dispositions toward and engagement with instructor feedback solely as *the students themselves* identified and described them in relation to their writing development. The students who participated in this study were never directly asked about the role that feedback played in their writing process. Instead, they were asked questions like "To what extent would you say you've grown as a writer?" and "How would you say that growth happened? What do you think influenced you?" as one interviewer asked a study participant.[2] Consequently, the depiction of feedback that emerges in this chapter is entirely student-generated, representing an important step toward filling this gap in the literature. From the perspectives of the students who participated in this study, it becomes clear that a student's decision to make a revision in response to the feedback he or she receives is only one small part of the full picture of that student's engagement with instructor feedback, particularly as it relates to his or her writing development.

For instance, if an instructor comments on a rough draft suggesting that a student delete a paragraph and in the final draft the paragraph is deleted, it is clear that the student has implemented the instructor's feedback. What is unclear, however, is whether the student actually agreed with the feedback. Did the student make the change willingly, thinking that it made the writing better? Or did the student resist the change, thinking that it made the writing worse, but make the change anyway due to the desire to earn a good grade? As they reflected on instructor feedback on their writing, students in this study expressed moments of *accepting*—where they articulated an openness toward feedback, a desire to receive feedback, or a willingness to change their writing in response to feedback. They also expressed moments of *resisting*—where they articulated closure toward some or all feedback, a desire not to receive feedback, or an unwillingness to change their writing in response to feedback. While moments of accepting and resisting were key to the students' experiences with feedback, these dispositions did not always align with the actions students reported taking when they revised their writing, suggesting a need to distinguish between affect and action when studying student response to feedback.[3]

Students' dispositions were the most salient feature of their engagement with instructor feedback, as minors and nonminors expressed moments of accepting and resisting across the data collected in this study. These moments emerged in students' entry and exit interviews and in the writing that minors included in their Gateway and Capstone eportfolios. However, these dispositions were not in and of themselves the most direct indicators of writing development. It might be tempting to assume that a student's acceptance of instructor feedback indicates writing development and resistance to feedback indicates a lack of development, particularly when those dispositions align with students' actions. In fact, instructors often draw such conclusions when they look with dismay at final drafts that seem to have disregarded most or all of the feedback that students received. From this perspective, the more accepting of feedback a student becomes, the more he or she appears to develop as a writer.

Implementing an instructor's feedback, however, did not always indicate that students were learning from the changes they made to their writing. One nonminor, Lauren, for instance, expressed considerable acceptance of instructor feedback. As she explained, "It really does help your writing to actually read what they have to say. . . . You have to know for the next time you write that you have to read that and see what they thought you did wrong." Feedback is important, according to Lauren, because instructors "are gonna be the people that are gonna be grading your paper, so like if you get feedback directly from them, you cannot go wrong, because you just follow what they say." In this moment, Lauren expresses not only openness toward instructor feedback, but a willingness to make changes in her writing in response to it. If an instructor suggested that a paragraph be deleted from one of her essays, Lauren would likely make this change willingly. The question that remains, however, is whether she would actually learn anything about her writing by doing so. By "just following what they say," Lauren simultaneously expresses an absence of critical engagement with the feedback she receives and a dependence on instructor feedback. If Lauren is not thinking about what she can accomplish in her writing by making this change, she is not developing an understanding of writing that could help her be more successful in the future. Because she equates success with directly following the feedback she receives on a draft, she is forced to rely on outside input instead of her own metacognitive awareness to revise her writing. Certainly this approach can lead students like Lauren to produce successful writing in academic settings, when feedback is readily available, but what impact does it have on writing development?

Lauren was not the only student who participated in this study to express this type of uncritical acceptance of instructor feedback. Nonminors and minors alike described using feedback to determine what their instructors wanted in their writing. One nonminor, Katie, explained that her understanding of writing was shaped by "going to the [instructor] in office hours and finding out what they're looking for in a paper, like what it means to them to be a strong writer." Sidney, a writing minor, similarly described going to her instructors' office hours and saying, "Okay. What do I have to do to get to that next level? What do I have to do to get that A?" In these moments, Katie and Sidney equate success in writing with directly implementing their instructors' feedback. Like Lauren, then, it seems unlikely that these students would engage critically with the feedback they receive, ultimately leaving them dependent on instructor feedback to produce successful writing.

These three examples offer only a snapshot of each student's engagement with instructor feedback, one that was taken from their entry interviews when they were presumably less developed writers. Even so, they demonstrate that a student's disposition—in terms of feeling accepting of or resisting toward feedback—is not a reliable indicator of writing development, just as a student's implementation of an instructor's suggestions does not indicate whether he or she has learned anything from that feedback. Instead, we argue that critical engagement with feedback plays a much more significant role in shaping students' development as writers. In this study, we define critical engagement with feedback in terms of one or more of the following actions:

1. Using feedback to develop awareness of purposes for writing beyond the assignment
2. Using feedback to develop awareness of broader audiences than the instructor
3. Using feedback as a springboard for reflecting on one's own writing
4. Analyzing or evaluating the feedback itself, rather than accepting it without question

In the remainder of this chapter, we share stories like Lauren's, Katie's, and Sidney's not only in snapshots but also over time, using evidence from students' survey responses, interviews, and the reflective writing included in the minors' eportfolios. We aim to show how students who participated in this study described their engagement with instructor feedback, both in terms of disposition and action, and how that engagement ultimately helped them develop as writers.

Feedback as a Key Factor in Writing Development

In this chapter, we add our voices to prior studies that have argued that feedback is a key factor in students' development as writers. In this study, instructor feedback was a frequent focus in both student interviews and the writing minors' eportfolios, suggesting that this pedagogical tool played an important role in students' experiences with writing. Of the 89 students who participated in at least one interview, 70 students—or 79 percent—discussed feedback. These figures are even higher for the students who participated in both entry and exit interviews, as 19 of the 24 minors and all 18 of the nonminors described experiences where they received feedback on their writing. The minors' eportfolios also frequently addressed instructor feedback (84 percent, 37 of the 44 eportfolios); students often noted direct ways that feedback had informed their writing process. Seven of the eportfolios, or 16 percent, included actual examples of instructor feedback, and three of these, or 7 percent, also included examples of peer feedback. One eportfolio even included examples of peer feedback the student had given to her classmates, highlighting both the value that minors ascribed to peer feedback—as Benjamin Keating argues in chapter 2—and the important role that feedback generally played for these students.

The value students placed on feedback was also reflected by the number of students who described efforts to actively solicit feedback from instructors. In their interviews, just over a third of the minors, 38 percent, described actively soliciting feedback on their writing, and the majority of nonminors—78 percent—also reported doing so. The discrepancy between these numbers might suggest that nonminors valued instructor feedback more than minors did, an interpretation that could be explained by the extent to which nonminors retained a focus on their instructors as their primary audience members, as Anne Gere observes in the introduction to this section. It would be reasonable, then, to conclude that the nonminors placed more emphasis on their instructors' feedback, as that feedback served as a direct indicator of their perceived audience's needs. Nonminors' emphasis on instructor feedback over peer feedback also appears to align with Keating's findings, which highlight nonminors' general opposition toward peer feedback in class. Nonminors tend to foreground instructor feedback much more than minors; however, the majority of minors incorporate references to and examples of their instructors' feedback in their eportfolios. This may indicate that these students either did not have to seek out instructor feedback as often as their nonminor counterparts (i.e., they regularly received instructor feedback in their writing minor courses without soliciting it) or that they did not find their efforts to seek out feedback interesting enough to bring up on their own during their interviews. In any case, that so many students discussed and wrote about feedback without prompting indicates that this pedagogical method is important not only to writing studies scholars and instructors, but also to students.

When students were prompted to report on their experiences with instructor feedback, these figures were even higher. Among the students who completed both entry and exit surveys,[4] 97 percent of minors and 95 percent of nonminors reported at the conclusion of the study that they discussed grades or assignments with their instructors at least some of the time, figures that represent increases of 10 percent and 2 percent, respectively, from what they reported in their entry surveys. In their exit surveys, every student reported receiving prompt written and oral feedback from faculty members at least some of the time, with 74 percent of minors and 68 percent of nonminors indicating they received this feedback often or very often. Students reported receiving a similar amount of instructor feedback during the drafting process. As figure 1.1 shows, in their exit surveys 71 percent of minors and 52 percent of nonminors reported receiving instructor feedback on some, most, or all of their assignments as they were developing their ideas. These figures demonstrate that the students who participated in this study were frequently exposed to instructor feedback on their writing.

Even more compelling is the number of students who directly attributed their writing development to engaging with the feedback they received from their instructors. In their Gateway and Capstone eportfolios, 13 of the 44 minors (30 percent) whose eportfolios are part of the study's data set (see endnote 4) described moments where their instructors' feedback directly contributed to their growth as writers. Jenna, for instance, wrote about the feedback she received from one instructor that pushed her to try a new revision strategy:

> I met with my [instructor], and she pushed me to reorganize my entire essay—completely switch up the structure. I had never done that. I felt like I was pouring my essay into a food processor and dumping the chopped up bits onto a new page, trying earnestly to make sense of it all. . . . Although I was initially resistant to rearranging my essay, pushing myself to try something completely different really strengthened my writing. It was the struggle that made me realize I could step out—or be forced out—of my comfort zone and be successful.

In this moment, Jenna suggests that her instructor's feedback encouraged her to try something she wouldn't have otherwise done, as she was "initially resistant" to the suggestion that she reorganize her essay. As she reflects on the effects of doing

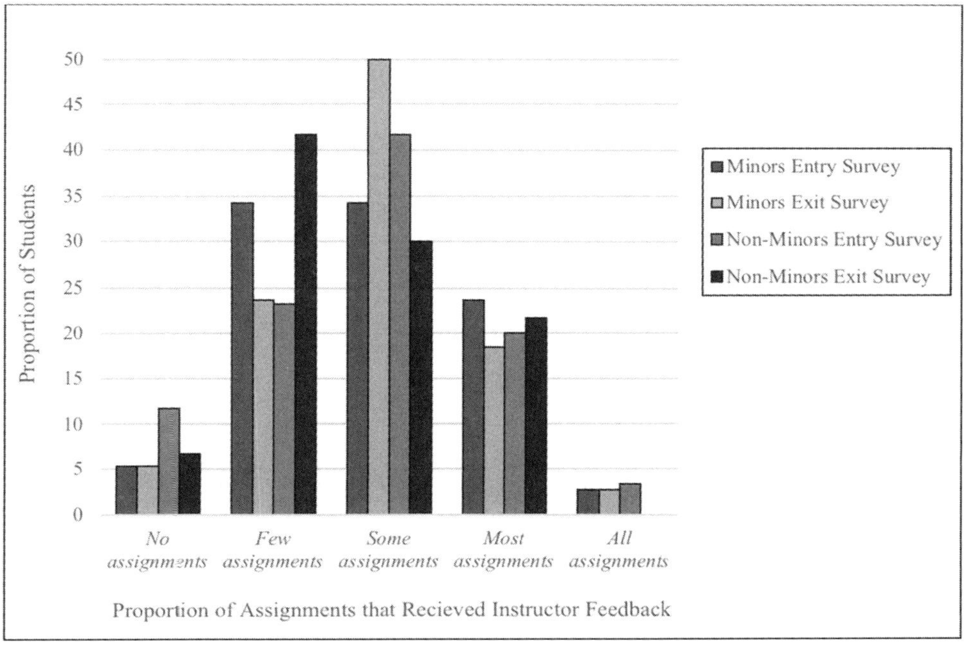

Fig. 1.1. Frequency of instructor feedback during drafting process, according to entry and exit surveys

so, however, she does not simply say that the draft she was working on improved, but that her writing as a whole became stronger. What Jenna learned about writing in this moment, then, was that she could try new approaches—even approaches that made her uncomfortable—and be successful. Consequently, this feedback was essential to her development as a writer, as she learned a lesson that could be extended to any future writing experience. In contrast to students who simply did what they were told in order to make a draft successful on an instructor's terms, Jenna was able to change her whole approach to writing, making it more likely that she would not only consider reorganizing her writing, but that she would continue trying new approaches in the future.

Similarly, one-third of the 42 students who participated in both entry and exit interviews also attributed their writing development to their experiences engaging with instructor feedback. For 4 of these students, comments from instructors on essays were particularly influential. When Natalie, a writing minor, was asked what had helped her develop as a writer, for instance, she explained, "I think the faculty at Michigan call you out on things, and they say, 'What are you trying to say?' or 'What does this mean? This doesn't mean anything to me. You have to make this mean something to me.'" As she concluded, "I think they push you to be more definitive in what you're writing. I think that was a big thing." For Natalie, critical comments from her instructors not only directly informed her development as a writer, but were actually the key factor she identified as shaping her writing.

A number of students, however, did not identify comments alone as contributing to their development as writers. Instead, ten students said that their writing development was informed more by their conversations about writing with one or more of their instructors. In her exit interview, for example, Ariana explained that her instructors' knowledge of her writing and writing assignments was an important reason that talking with them, as opposed to others, supported her writing development. "A key thing in my own development was talking with the [instructor]," she said, "'cause I think talking to someone who knows how you write, and knows what the assignment is, and knows the ideas you're grappling with is the most important thing to get to making something that you like." In this moment, Ariana prioritizes her own purposes for writing, suggesting that the conversations she had with her instructors were useful for her development because the instructors had enough context to help her achieve her goals, a conclusion that reinforces Anna Knutson's argument in chapter 7 that individualized feedback can support students' writing development. However, Ariana also indicated that she may not have perceived her development solely in terms of producing writing that *she* liked. As she went on to explain, "Talking to the [instructor] who has an awareness, a little bit, of who you are is more helpful than talking to someone else who's gonna critique it based on someone else's standards." Here, Ariana opens space for two distinct interpretations of the role that instructor feedback plays in her development. The first, in line with her comment above, suggests that instructor feedback is valuable because an instructor knows her writing goals and therefore can help her accomplish them. However, Ariana might also be suggesting that instructor feedback is valuable not because it contributes to her overall growth as a writer, but because it helps her to meet (or perhaps even exceed) her instructors' standards, which are ultimately used to evaluate her writing. In either case, what is clear in this moment is that Ariana privileges her instructors' feedback over all other types of feedback she might receive, suggesting that it has a powerful impact on her development as a writer, regardless of whether she understands her development in terms of achieving her own goals or her instructor's. Other students described the relationship between instructor feedback and their writing development with much more emphasis on fulfilling their instructors' expectations. For example, Sidney—the student who reported visiting her instructors' office hours solely to figure out how to earn an A on her assignments—recalled:

> My issue was making sure I was getting all of my arguments across. I think it had more to do with the classes and the content and learning what was most important to make my argument. I think office hours was the biggest help for that. I don't think I ever sat down in a class and learned. I think through trial and error and through seeing what teachers wanted included, talking to them one-on-one like this. I think that is probably where I learned to get better at that and what I needed to do.

For Sidney, getting better at writing entailed getting better at giving teachers what they wanted, something that she reported learning to do by using her instructors' feedback. Sidney was not alone in the emphasis that she placed on meeting her instructors' standards. In their exit surveys, every minor and 95 percent of nonminors reported working harder than they thought they could at least some of the time in order to meet an instructor's standards or expectations. The emphasis that students placed on fulfilling instructors' expectations increased over time; in their exit surveys 84 percent of minors and 73 percent of nonminors reported striving to do so often or very often, an increase of 11 percent and 3 percent, respectively. For these students in particular, instructor feedback would likely influence their development as writers, because it directly communicates instructors' standards and expectations. For those unwilling to move beyond this focus, however, that development may be limited.

Across the examples considered here, it is apparent that the largest impact on students' writing development is not simply whether they choose to use instructor feedback, but how they engage with that feedback. Consequently, in the next section, we more carefully explore moments of accepting and moments of resisting as students described their engagement with instructor feedback, always with an eye toward the criticality they expressed in the process and the ways that criticality (or lack thereof) contributed to—or hindered—their development as writers.

Accepting, Resisting, and Critically Engaging with Feedback: What Matters for Development?

Across the entire set of interviews, entry and exit, minor and nonminor, and even within the same interview, students articulated varying moments of acceptance of and resistance toward instructor feedback. In this section, we examine two students who primarily discussed moments of resisting (Adrienne and Tim) and three students who mainly articulated moments of accepting (Dariella, Sidney, and Joy). For each student, we dig a little deeper than their expressed dispositions to understand the nuances of how they critically engaged with their instructors' feedback and what that engagement meant for their development as writers. Some students expressed resistance toward instructor feedback without critically engaging with that feedback. In her entry interview, Adrienne, a writing minor, expressed perhaps the strongest moments of resisting across all the interviews when she described written comments she received from an instructor on a paper about *Jane Eyre*. She stated:

> I was just like done. I felt like I had written a good paper, but I didn't get the grade I wanted on it and I didn't feel like it was appreciated. It was just like, *am I going to take class after class where I have to write what the teacher thinks and write what the teacher's opinions are*? I feel like English gets a really bad rap for doing this and sometimes I think it's deserved, in my biased opinion.

While this moment does not fully represent Adrienne as a writer, this is a case in which resistance, in the form of sheer frustration, caused her to "quit thinking about English as a major." She did not analyze or evaluate the instructor feedback she received, nor did she use it to reflect on her writing. Instead, she concluded that the only option was to tell instructors what they want to hear, and as a result, she disengaged from her course work. Consequently, Adrienne's uncritical resistance in this moment is a move that likely constrained her development as a writer.

Although Adrienne was willing to meet instructors' expectations for her writing, she went on to observe that fulfilling their seemingly subjective requirements had sapped her confidence as a writer. In response to the question of how she views herself as a writer now that she has taken some challenging courses, Adrienne stated, "I would say I'm much more concerned with fulfilling the requirement of my [instructor] and making sure that my paper is clear and concise. . . . For me, I'm just less confident because I've realized that there's not an ideal paper, like it doesn't exist. Even if I wrote it, an [instructor] wouldn't think it was the ideal paper." Instructors would be likely to read her implementation of their directions as evidence of development, but they might be surprised to learn that uncritically fulfilling requirements had resulted in Adrienne feeling diminished confidence. She attributed her lack of confidence to the belief that good writing was utterly arbitrary, a matter of opinion that differed from one instructor to the next. Focused on giving instructors what they wanted to read, Adrienne had begun to feel that she herself did not know what good writing was—or even if it existed.

In her exit interview, Adrienne's relationship to instructor feedback had changed significantly. In response to one instructor's feedback, she explained: "I wanted more, 'How is it working as a whole? What is your feeling as a whole? . . . I feel like I didn't get enough feedback. At the same I—the feedback I got wasn't what I wanted." Her disposition seems like a moment of resistance in that she did not like the feedback she received. However, she actually desired and was open to receiving feedback in general; in fact, she wanted more feedback than she received. Rather than implementing feedback unquestioningly, Adrienne analyzed her instructor's comments and made choices about what kinds of feedback she found most helpful. In this moment, she was resistant to the feedback she received from one instructor, while being open toward receiving other kinds of feedback. Her analysis of her instructor's feedback is an indicator of critical engagement.

Later in the exit interview, Adrienne expressed even more of an accepting disposition toward the feedback she received in a different class in which her instructor radically redirected her writing to meet the expectations for a specific genre. "My Gateway course was with my faculty advisor, and she gave me more of the kind of feedback I wanted," she said. "It was more looking at the overarching thing. She was really great at keeping in mind form." In this moment, Adrienne was specifically accepting of what she perceived as tough-yet-generative feedback she received from her advisor:

> In my developmental essay, she made me—I said I wanted to do a CNN news report. Instead, I wrote a very lovely creative non-fiction piece. . . . She was just like, "No, this is not what you—" [*laughter*] "This is not what you did." I wrote something that would be a news article. It was killing my darlings, but it was learning form and purpose.

Across both exit-interview examples, Adrienne was open toward instructor feedback, but she strongly distinguished what she perceived as more and less helpful questions and comments, indicating that she only found certain kinds of feedback conducive to her development. She wanted instructors to direct her attention to global concerns and build her knowledge of discipline-specific genres, so that she could acquire knowledge of such things as "form and purpose," even if it meant "killing her darlings." While instructors might view Adrienne's resistance toward certain kinds of feedback as stubbornness, the fact that she analyzed and evaluated the feedback she received, rather than implementing it unquestioningly, demonstrates a critical engagement with feedback, and therefore, an important step in Adrienne's development as a writer.

There were times when students expressed the same disposition in both entry and exit interviews, but subtle changes occurred beneath the surface in those moments of accepting or resisting. For example, a writing minor, Tim, expressed moments of resisting instructor feedback in both his entry and his exit interviews.

In his entry interview, Tim stated that he felt receiving instructor feedback was not helpful: "Yes, you can go to your [instructor] or whatever, but I feel like they're not as open to helping you or whatever. . . . It's more just like, 'Well, what do you think?' It's like, 'That doesn't help me, 'cause I'm asking what you think." Like Adrienne in the exit interview, Tim expressed acceptance toward certain kinds of feedback—he believed that learning the instructor's thoughts was helpful—and resistance toward questions that prompted his own thinking, which he perceived as unhelpful. Unlike Adrienne's, Tim's resistance to the specific feedback these instructors gave him was rooted in a desire to produce the kind of writing his instructors wanted. His frustration is understandable; Tim was closer to the beginning of his undergraduate experience and was trying to navigate various expectations for coursework. From his perspective, being asked what he thought was a waste of time, because he wanted to give his instructors the writing they wanted so that they would give him the grade he wanted. However, his development as a writer would be limited if he were told exactly what to do and then followed directions without some kind of critical engagement with feedback, including a broader consideration of the purposes and audiences for his writing.

Although Tim expressed moments of resisting his instructors' feedback, there is evidence that he implemented that feedback, albeit without much indication of substantive critical engagement. In the reflective introduction to one of the essays he included in his Gateway eportfolio, Tim stated, "Once I had had some time away from my 'Why I Write' paper, I took my instructor's suggestions and ran with them." In an introduction to another assignment, where Tim was tasked with repurposing an essay he had previously written, he noted, "Once my original [first-year writing] paper had been repurposed into a personal letter, I then looked to remediate it into a new media presentation using PowerPoint. After some discussion with my [instructor], however, I was later encouraged to create a video instead." These excerpts do not indicate that Tim evaluated or analyzed his instructors' feedback, used it as a springboard for reflecting on his writing, or decided how to synthesize it with his own ideas. While directly following instructors' suggestions and being able to meet their standards is a kind of development, it does not encourage broad rhetorical awareness or cultivate a sense of agency within the student writer.

In his exit interview, Tim talked differently about how he interacted with instructors' expectations in his writing process. He reflected on moments when his instructors required him to write multiple drafts:

> [One instructor] made me do multiple drafts, which I don't do. . . . I write and I edit as I go, so if I can't think of something I'll go back to what I've written and just tweak it or

> make it sound better, but it takes a long time for me to do that. I don't write like—[the other instructor] was all about the shitty first draft, like you write a bunch of crap and then you take those ideas and you write it again. In my mind that's a waste of time—to waste your time writing crap—and then you take your crap and turn it into gold. It doesn't make sense to—for my style. It works for some people.

Even though Tim followed his instructors' directions, this quote represents some distance from his assertion that he did not want to be asked what he thought. His resistance in this quote did not stem from wanting to be told what to do with his writing, but from *not* wanting to be told what to do with his writing process. Like Adrienne, he believed he knew what worked best for him as a writer, and he expressed opinions about the writing process that were informed by experience. He articulated an understanding of why his instructors set those requirements: he knew that multiple drafts worked for some people. Although Tim indicates in both the entry and exit interviews that he implemented his instructors' directions, there is more nuance in his exit interview statements regarding his resistance toward the specific instances of feedback he received.

Critically engaging with feedback is something that many students in this study learned to do during their undergraduate years, including those who expressed primarily accepting dispositions toward feedback. For example, Dariella, a nonminor, enthusiastically accepted feedback during her time at Michigan, but moved from a generally uncritical acceptance of feedback toward a more critical engagement. In her entry interview, she demonstrated the same unquestioning acceptance that other students evinced in many of the entry interviews, explaining that her instructor "told me what she thought could be improved, and then I just followed those instructions." Like Tim, Lauren, Katie, and Sidney, Dariella described employing a strategy that is useful in the short term to help her achieve success in her classes, but might not be as successful over time in promoting agentive, rhetorically sophisticated development.

Dariella's strongly accepting disposition toward feedback was evident in her exit interview, in which she stated that her writing style had been influenced by "catering to different instructors and really learning what they liked from you." However, later moments suggest that she was doing more with writing assignments than merely catering to her instructors' whims. When Dariella was asked what advice she would give to students about writing, she advised that they begin with overarching goals for their writing:

> I always start off with—I guess it depends on the kind of paper I'm writing but you should—they should really think about the overall goal of what they're writing when

> they start. Because I think that gives you a clear sense of where you're headed and how you're going to get there. . . . [Instructors] give out the goal of the paper—you know what you want to get out of a research paper I guess. Who your target audience is and the best way to write to them.

Even though she was still attuned to instructors' expectations, Dariella saw a broader purpose in writing than just the assignment and a broader audience than just the instructor, both attributes of critical engagement. She advised students to prioritize the instructor's goal for the paper, but also to consider their own desires for their writing and their knowledge of their target audience. While there was less clear criticality in Dariella's comments than in other students' comments in this section, the subtle back-and-forth she expressed between instructors' purposes and students' purposes suggests that she has developed as a writer, in terms not only of rhetorical awareness, but of how she would likely approach the writing process and consequently engage with instructor feedback.

For some students, the shift toward critical engagement was primarily about the development of independence, as they used instructor feedback to learn strategies for evaluating their own writing. Sidney, the writing minor for whom going to office hours was initially all about "seeing what teachers wanted included," remained open to receiving feedback during her time at the university, but developed her ability to assess and question her own writing rather than relying so heavily on her instructors to tell her what to do. In the evolution essay of her Capstone eportfolio, Sidney directly attributed her growth as a writer to her engagement with instructor feedback. She wrote:

> When I came here freshman year, I would frequently receive feedback in my classes that my papers needed to be more specific. . . . Many times my [instructors] would circle a sentence and mark in the margin, "this could be its own paragraph," or "develop this idea, what do you mean?" I was taking complex arguments or ideas and not giving them the amount of space they deserved to be explained fully. . . . It took practice and a lot of red writing in the margins, but I started to get a hang of this specificity in my academic writing. *What is my argument here? Does this sentence support that argument? Is this idea fully developed for my reader? This sentence seems too off topic? Cut it.* I started to have these conversations with myself as I prepared drafts and eventually I started to produce highly persuasive academic papers.

In this moment, Sidney still expressed a highly accepting disposition toward instructor feedback and a desire to implement instructors' suggestions for her writing. But as she reflected on her development, she demonstrated that she was less dependent on feedback, less focused on figuring out what instructors wanted to see in a paper, and more focused on learning strategies that she could apply independently and transfer to new situations. She gained perspective on her writing and developed a critical awareness that enabled her to see strengths and weaknesses in her writing. In this way, Sidney directly attributed the development of self-assessment skills that could be applied across writing assignments to her engagement with instructor feedback.

For other students, accepting feedback while critically engaging with it involved using feedback as a springboard for reflection. Discussing her experience in the Capstone course, writing minor Joy described engaging in dialogic feedback with her instructor as something that helped push her writing in new directions:

> Every day, [my instructor] would have a different topic that we would talk about. He would just ask questions. I can't really remember particular examples. It's just the questions he asked and follow-up questions that really make you think twice about things in general. If you thought you wanted to write something going in this direction, he might ask you questions. Then you're, like, "Oh, wait. Actually, I could see it going in this direction." It kind of just opened up the realm to experiment more than I typically would. It was just nice with having more options to experiment with writing through those conversations.

Joy suggests that her instructor's probing questions and discussion topics encouraged innovation and experimentation in her writing. Their conversations invited her not only to reflect productively on her writing, but to consider alternate choices and to experiment more with her writing than she typically would have on her own. Joy's description of her instructor's questions that caused her to "think twice about things in general" suggests that she was learning broader principles about writing that could be transferred across contexts. Feedback was not only about improving single drafts but about creating a wider space for learning about writing. Joy's experience illustrates the critical attribute of using instructor feedback as a springboard for reflecting on her writing, and suggests that her instructor's feedback was a catalyst for Joy's development as a writer.

However, in her eportfolio, Joy described engaging with feedback that did not allow her the kind of innovation she wanted in her writing. The evolution essay she wrote for her minor-in-writing Capstone discussed receiving feedback on a policy brief, in which "my [instructor] noted that I 'missed the mark' in terms of specificity and evidence because there was too much abstraction and too many assumptions being made without enough data to support the claims." This feedback caused her to take a step back and reflect on her writing, which is a sign of critical engagement. She expressed resistance, however, to the way she was being told to write, observing that, "Though writing this policy brief provided an insightful exercise into data collection and analytical writing, I was unable to effectively mold my affinity for informality and creativity into this piece." There is a question of whether Joy is more resistant to the feedback itself or to the expectations of the disciplinary genre. However, she acknowledged elsewhere in the evolution essay that following the forms required by genre was important, but that it need not stifle expressiveness completely. She argued that "students will inevitably still need to write in those traditional academic structures, but allowing them to put a creative spin on their assignments can help students find value and satisfaction even in those rigid academic styles." Joy believed that individual expression was possible, but that instructors needed to allow students some freedom for creativity within the genre. She believed that the result would be that students would find more "value and satisfaction" in their writing assignments. Her thoughtful analysis of different types of feedback and her cogent argument for instructors' encouraging students' creativity within more rigid disciplinary genres suggest robust development as a writer.

As each of these examples demonstrates, critical engagement with instructor feedback is something that students expressed more frequently at the conclusion of the study than they did at its start. Minors and nonminors alike increased in mentions of critical engagement with instructor feedback from their entry to exit interviews, as figure 1.2 illustrates. In addition, students enrolled in the writing minor were considerably more likely to critically engage with instructor feedback than those who were not. None of the 18 nonminors who participated in entry and exit interviews described critically engaging with instructor feedback at the start of the study, but 8 described doing so by the study's conclusion.

The writing minors, in contrast, identified moments of critical engagement with instructor feedback in both their entry and exit interviews. In their entry interviews, 4 of the 24 minors described moments where they critically engaged with instructor feedback. By their exit interviews, that number had increased to 15. Given that 6 minors did not discuss instructor feedback in their interviews at all, 83 percent of the minors who talked about feedback in their exit interviews (15 of 18) described critically engaging with that feedback. This suggests that students' participation in the writing minor likely contributed to their efforts to critically engage with instructor feedback, something we argue also promoted their writing development.

In each of the previous examples, minors and nonminors alike describe mo-

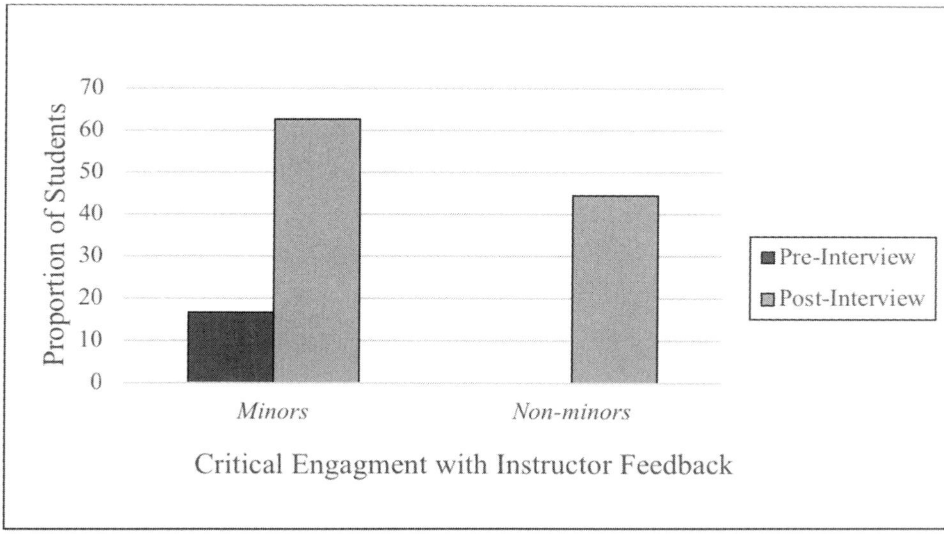

Fig. 1.2. Proportion of students expressing critical engagement with instructor feedback

ments where they critically engaged with their instructors' feedback and moments where they were unable to do so. For the students who participated in this study, obstacles emerged that at times hindered their ability to critically engage with instructor feedback and consequently to develop as writers. In the final section, then, we turn to explore the obstacles that students encountered and to shed light on how—at least in some cases—students learned to overcome these obstacles to further their development as writers.

From Obstacles to Engagement: Toward a Critical Engagement with Instructor Feedback

As students described their experiences engaging with instructor feedback, they at times identified obstacles that hindered their ability to do so. These obstacles, and students' efforts to overcome them, played a direct role in their development as writers, as students described the varying ways they learned to more critically engage with instructor feedback over time. Roughly a quarter of the students who participated in both entry and exit interviews reported encountering these obstacles. These reports, however, were considerably more common among nonminors, with 8 of the 18 nonminors (44 percent) and only 2 of the 23 minors (8 percent) describing obstacles they encountered. For the students who did encounter obstacles, the difficulties they identified primarily emerged from contrasts between the feedback they received across contexts. These contrasts emerged in students' perceptions of the types of feedback they received, the quantity of feedback they received, and even their relationships with instructors as they shifted from high school to college or from one college-level class to another.

Several students expressed the view that differences between the feedback they received in high school and college made college-level feedback difficult to engage with. As Sarah Swofford argues in chapter 9, writing development begins long before students arrive in first-year writing classes, and the experiences with feedback that the students in our study brought with them to college writing profoundly shaped how they interacted with instructor feedback. Five students, for instance, described moments where the feedback they received in college sharply contrasted with the feedback they received in high school. For Adrienne, the writing minor who chose not to pursue an English major because of her experiences with feedback, this contrast was particularly frustrating and led her to become more resistant early on, not only to engaging with her instructors' feedback, but to engaging in the writing process at all. As she explained in her entry interview:

> I have written good papers and not gotten good grades on them, well, a good grade for me, which means an A. I feel like that's kind of shaken my confidence, but it also made me realize how subjective writing is and how unlike maybe at the high school level, [instructors] aren't filling out a checklist and even if they are, that checklist, their interpretation of what makes something clear, what makes an idea important, is different. . . . I feel like having to write for [instructors], for academic settings, has made me less empowered as a writer and less—I don't know—less passionate about it because it's not really for me.

In this moment, Adrienne identified a number of obstacles that seemed to prevent her from critically engaging with her instructors' feedback. First, she described the feedback that she received in college as subjective, an observation that she drew from contrasting college-level feedback with the presumably objective checklists her high school teachers previously offered, and from the fact that she was no longer earning A's on her writing. In suggesting that instructors have varying notions of what makes writing effective, Adrienne also indicated that instructor feedback differs widely across contexts, an understanding that certainly would decrease the incentive for her to critically engage with that feedback. This contrast from high school to college not only changed Adrienne's understanding of writing, it changed the way she felt about herself as a writer, leaving her with less confidence and less motivation to work on her writing. Adrienne indicated that these factors directly informed her approach to writing, leading her to focus on her instructors' shifting expectations instead of her own goals as a writer, and making it less likely that she would critically engage with her instructors' feedback.

For other students, shifts in both the type and quantity of feedback received from high school to college informed their ability to critically engage with instructor feedback. As Rebecca, a nonminor, explained in her exit interview, "It's super overwhelming when you get all red, and you're, 'Well, I thought it was good. I didn't have any spelling errors.' That's all my high school teachers looked for." In this moment, Rebecca indicated that the feedback she received in her college-level writing classes differed both in focus—addressing more than spelling errors—and in quantity from what she had received from instructors in high school. Because her notion of good writing had been shaped by her high school instructors' feedback, which led her to equate good spelling with good writing, responding to the shifts in the feedback she received on entering college was likely even more challenging. Rebecca had to not only learn to process more feedback than she was accustomed to, she had to reconsider her understanding of good writing. While these differences made it more difficult for Rebecca to engage with her instructors' feedback, for some students, the same contrasts had the opposite effect.

Some students suggested that it was actually a lack of feedback—not an abundance of feedback—that made it difficult to engage in the writing process. In these cases, students indicated that feedback itself—or a lack thereof—could be an obstacle to their engagement. Like Rebecca, Dana recalled getting very little feedback on her writing in high school. For this writing minor, however, the absence of feedback left her with a sense of insecurity about her writing. "I guess coming from high school," she said in her entry interview, "I had no confidence with writing at all. I thought I was a terrible writer. I hated it. Yeah, I guess I just had no good experience with it, and all the feedback I would get would just be a grade. It wouldn't be like, I guess, ways to improve. I was very, I guess, insecure about writing." In this moment, Dana links her sense of self-efficacy to the feedback she received on her writing, suggesting that grades alone were not enough to help her understand whether and how she was making effective choices in her writing. In terms of the link between self-efficacy and feedback, Dana's story bears a resemblance to Natalie's, as described by Swofford (chapter 9). For both Dana and Natalie, feedback played a key role in their development as writers. Natalie needed positive feedback to develop her self-efficacy, and Dana indicated that she could not gain a sense of her own development without additional input from her instructors.

In some cases, then, contrasts in the feedback students received in different contexts were not obstacles, but actually increased their engagement in the writing process. Dana and one other writing minor, for instance, suggested that the increased quantities of feedback they received in their college writing courses, in contrast to high school, motivated them to become more invested in the writing process. As Dana recalled, "Then I took the intro, [first-year] writing class. I just had an amazing teacher, a great experience. I guess each assignment, I got the feedback and it gave me more confidence. By the end, I was like, 'I guess I'm a good writer!'" This experience, Dana recalled, "made me want to do the minor or take more classes with writing." In contrast to Rebecca, receiving more feedback on her writing was not an obstacle, but actually increased Dana's self-efficacy and her motivation for writing. The differences in these students' experiences could be connected to the types of feedback they received; Dana recalled receiving positive feedback that helped her develop confidence in her writing abilities and Rebecca described receiving an overwhelming amount of red ink focused on issues in her writing. Alternatively, they could reflect differences in the students' dispositions, with one perhaps being more accepting of and one more resistant to instructor feedback. In either case, these examples demonstrate that the obstacles that hinder students' abilities to critically engage with instructor feedback vary from student to student. Though contrasts across contexts were not always obstacles, for a number of students, such contrasts made it difficult to critically engage with feedback or even in the writing process itself, often in ways that impaired their development as writers.

One final obstacle that emerged as significant for several students was their relationships with their college-level instructors. As Janie, a nonminor, explained, "If I'm very comfortable with the [instructor], I feel more at ease writing a paper. But, if I feel like the [instructor's] really strict, it's a lot more stressful to get a paper because you're trying so hard to target it." In this moment, Janie indicates that her perception of her instructor would likely influence the degree to which she could engage with that instructor's feedback. Though she is not talking about her specific uses of instructor feedback here, her emphasis on targeting what her "strict" instructors want suggests that she would be much more likely to implement their feedback without critical engagement. With her "comfortable" instructors, then, the student's more-relaxed writing process suggests that she would place less emphasis on giving those instructors what they want, opening space for her to analyze and evaluate their feedback in relation to her other goals.

The instructor-student relationship was as important to students enrolled in the writing minor as it was to nonminors. As she reflected on her experiences in the minor, Madeline expressed a desire for more of a mentoring relationship with her advisor in the program. "Had I had a good relationship," she explained, "maybe I would have gone in and asked for advice for different pieces I was writing on, especially during the Capstone project. If I'd had a mentor who I could have bounced ideas off of, I think I would have valued that." Because she did not have this relationship with her advisor, however, and because she felt constrained by the grading system in her Capstone course, Madeline did not feel she had the freedom to critically engage with the feedback she received on her Capstone project. "I want to be able to write in kind of—especially with the Capstone project—kind of do what I want to do without this pressure of knowing that there's someone grading me," she said. "I think that actually contributed to why I didn't like the Capstone as much. I felt like I didn't get as much out of the project because I was forced to somewhat conform myself into what [my instructor] wanted me to do." In these moments, Madeline clearly linked her relationship with instructors to her ability to solicit and critically engage with feedback, suggesting that she was only able to use feedback as a springboard for reflection when she had a strong relationship with that instructor. Without that relationship, her writing process was constrained, leaving her unable to even evaluate or analyze what her instructors suggested and forcing her to conform to their expectations. In this way, Madeline—like Adrienne—privileged instructor feedback over her own writing goals to ensure that she achieved the grades she desired on her writing. This difference would certainly have hindered Madeline's writing development, because in this experience, she concluded, she was not able to learn as much from writing her Capstone project.

Though the instructor-student relationship was equally important to students whether or not they were enrolled in the writing minor, survey responses showed differences in students' perceptions of the quality of relationships they had with their instructors. For instance, when students were asked to rate their relationships with faculty members in terms of their availability, helpfulness, and sympathy for students, 26 percent of minors reported the highest possible score (seven on a scale of one to seven), whereas only 13 percent of nonminors reported the same on their exit surveys. A considerably higher proportion of the writing minors rated their relationships with faculty members within the top two scores, with 63 percent of minors and only 42 percent of nonminors reporting a six or seven on their exit surveys. In addition, whereas minors reported a small increase in the quality of relationships they had with faculty members from the entry to the exit survey, with average scores of 5.1 and 5.7 respectively, nonminors actually reported a slight decrease in the quality of these relationships, shifting from an average of 5.2 to 5.1. These contrasting shifts occurred despite the fact that both minors and nonminors reported increases in the frequency with which they emailed their instructors and discussed ideas with them outside of class from their entry to exit surveys.

This difference could explain, at least in part, why nonminors were more likely to identify obstacles that hindered their ability to critically engage with instructor feedback. If these students have lower perceptions of their relationships with faculty members, they may feel more pressure to conform to what they believe those faculty members want them to do in their writing. Other factors also influence the differences that have emerged across these students. Students who are willing to minor in writing may have a stronger desire to develop their writing, making it more likely that they would want to critically engage with feedback and push through the obstacles that they encounter in the process. Furthermore, it seems quite likely that participating in the writing minor helped these students learn to engage with feedback in more critical—and consequently more productive—ways.

Certainly, the obstacles that students encountered did not prevent them from critically engaging with instructor feedback altogether, as students such as Adrienne still described moments where they were able to do so. These obstacles did, however, make engaging with feedback more difficult. An essential aspect of students' development as writers, then, is learning how to seek out and critically engage with their instructors' feedback. Although only 3 of the 70 students in our data set who discussed feedback in at least one interview actually described how they learned to solicit or engage with instructor feedback, it seems likely that this dearth reflects the fact that students were never directly asked about instructor feedback in interviews more than it reflects the number of students who actually had to work through this process.

This possibility is reinforced by the number of students who indicated via surveys that they never learned how to solicit feedback on their writing during their time in college. When asked how prepared they felt to decide where to go for help with new writing tasks, for instance, 15 percent of nonminors reported in their exit surveys that they were not at all prepared or not very prepared, suggesting that the vast majority of students felt prepared to seek out instructor feedback. Even more interesting, however, is the fact that this number represents an increase of 5 percent over what the same students reported on their entry surveys, meaning that over time, nonminors actually felt less prepared to find help with their writing. Furthermore, when asked to select all aspects of academic writing that cause students difficulty, 10 percent of nonminors identified "knowing where to get feedback" as an issue in their exit surveys, which represents an increase of 5 percent over what the same students reported in their entry surveys. Even when students were assigned academic writing by an instructor, then, nonminors reported increasing difficulty knowing where and how to get feedback on their writing over time.

In their exit surveys, every minor reported being somewhat prepared or very prepared to find help with their writing, with the majority of minors—71 percent—reporting they felt very prepared, an increase of 16 percent from their entry surveys. This suggests that participation in the writing minor helped students learn where and how to receive help with their writing. Similarly, fewer minors reported experiencing difficulty knowing where to get feedback; on the entry survey the figure was 13 percent, and on the exit survey 3 percent, a decrease of 10 percent. These shifts in the responses of writing minors indicate that nonminors would have benefited from additional support regarding where and how to seek help with their writing, something the minors, in contrast, clearly learned.

When students did get help with their writing, they still had to learn how to engage with the feedback they received, a process in which students found varying degrees of success. For Lauren, the nonminor who at the start of this study was inclined to wholeheartedly accept her instructors' feedback, learning to engage with instructor feedback—even in uncritical ways—was not intuitive, but represented an initial step in her development as a writer. Prior to coming to college, she explained, she had gained a sense that her writing was as good as it would ever be:

> I've always been really, really good with writing. When I had mastered—so you know, AP English scale is graded one to nine—when I'd hit my nine, I was like, "Obviously, I'm at the top." Like, "I already have what I need to pass this test. I don't really need to improve here." I think that attitude carried over because towards the end of my AP English it was like, I was getting nines on everything. How else could I improve it if I was at the top? I think that carried over into college.

In this moment, Lauren indicates that the grades she earned on her writing had a direct impact on her efforts to improve her writing, because she concluded from her high scores that there was no need for her to think critically about her writing or her approach to the writing process. This belief ultimately informed her approach to the instructor feedback that she received on her writing, which, as she reported, she did not even begin reading until she reached college:

> I can't take feedback very well. When I first was in an English class like that, I used to—whenever I got my paper back—I never used to read what they wrote. And here, when I started going to college, it was like I was consistently getting the same grade on every paper, and so it was—obviously, I needed to change. I actually started to read the feedback and try to incorporate it.

In this moment, Lauren suggests that her decision to begin engaging with instructor feedback emerged from a desire to earn higher grades. In contrast to Adrienne, who expressed a resisting disposition in response to feedback that was accompanied by lower grades than she expected, Lauren's desire to perform better actually led her to develop a more accepting disposition, as she expresses an openness toward instructor feedback and a willingness to change her writing in response.[5] Lauren's high grades and Adrienne's low grades were initially obstacles to critically engaging with instructor feedback. In addition, Lauren indicated that she began to see feedback as a key factor that could promote her development, as she identified her efforts to read and incorporate this feedback as the strategy she used to change her writing.

This shift toward a more accepting disposition was a crucial step in Lauren's development as a writer. However, she still experienced difficulty being open to the feedback she received. In reflecting on how she learned to open up to feedback, Lauren recalled, "I had [instructors] that liked mandatory meeting with them to talk about the papers. It really opened me up to more feedback." She went on to share how she found a required full-class peer workshop to be similarly beneficial:

> You have to bring in ten pages and then everyone just reads it and you have to sit through an hour and a half of them telling you what's wrong with your paper. That really helped me ease into accepting criticism. It wasn't necessarily a reflection on my person. It was just like, "This is how we wanna help you make your product better, by pointing out to you what you could improve."

In these instances, Lauren described moments where she was required to receive extensive feedback in person and suggested that the act of receiving feedback itself—from both her instructors and her peers—is what helped her to become more open. In part, this shift likely resulted from Lauren's growing awareness that she had not mastered writing to the extent she initially believed. Receiving feedback that identified areas for growth—which in each of these cases she had no choice but to hear, in contrast to the written feedback she had never previously read—almost certainly contributed to the student's new level of awareness about her writing. Lauren also suggests that she found the face-to-face feedback she received during peer workshops to be particularly beneficial, because it helped her realize that the criticism she received was not directed toward herself as a person, but toward her writing, with the ultimate goal of making her writing more effective. These experiences with feedback helped Lauren develop a new understanding not only of her writing, but of the role that feedback could play in her writing development, ultimately leading her to become more accepting of this pedagogical tool.

In learning to become more accepting of feedback, then, Lauren made an important step in her writing development. This step on its own, however, is only a starting point. She did not describe critically engaging with instructor feedback in either her entry or exit interview. When asked at the conclusion of the study what advice she would offer other students, she explained:

> I would say be prepared to forget everything you think you know about writing. . . . I just think that each stage of writing you've ever done in your life is different. From the beginning when we were first learning to write, it was all about the five paragraph, beginning, middle, end. Then when I got to high school, my AP English teacher was like, "Throw all that out. We're not gonna do that." Then when I got here, it was like, "Throw all of that stuff out. We're not gonna do that." 'Cause each institution has a different way of doing things. I'm assuming even when I go to my career, they're probably gonna be like, "Throw it all out. This is how we want you to write."

Even at the conclusion of her college career, then, Lauren expressed an understanding that particular writing skills and strategies do not always transfer across contexts. This understanding would likely hinder Lauren's ability to critically engage with instructor feedback, because that feedback would only hold value in the specific context in which she was writing. However, Lauren also indicated that she was in the process of developing a more nuanced understanding of writing, as she suggested that the contrasts she identified are not due solely to the subjective nature of writing, but instead extend from institutional differences. Consequently, it is possible that Lauren would critically engage with instructor feedback to the extent that it enabled her to transfer her learning across experiences within the same context. "If somebody would've told me to realize that you have to adapt your writing to the audience that you're writing for," Lauren said, "it probably would've saved me a lot of hassle with rewriting and not understanding why it was not working." In this moment, then, Lauren shows promise that she is moving toward a more critical engagement with feedback and with her writing, as her perception is clearly beginning to shift from the notion that writing should directly follow what an instructor wants to the notion that writing is a complex task that involves adapting to the needs of various audiences.

Instructor Feedback as a Tool for Promoting Writing Development

These students' stories create a picture of feedback that is as varied as the students who participated in this study. For some, feedback was an empowering tool that inspired them to think about writing—both the product and the process—in new ways and that helped them make informed choices about their writing. For others, receiving differing feedback across instructors became an obstacle that caused them to view writing as subjective and arbitrary, making it more difficult for them to engage in the writing process. These dispositions not only informed how students engaged with instructor feedback, they influenced their attitudes toward writing and conceptions of audience.

Ultimately, the findings presented in this chapter suggest that moments of accepting and resisting are easy to spot, but that they are not what matters most in terms of development. Nor is implementation of instructor feedback, in and of itself, the most reliable indicator of student growth in writing. Instead, students' movement toward more critical engagement with instructor feedback matters more than changes in affect or in action. Students who described moments of critical engagement with instructor feedback—using that feedback to develop a broader understanding of their audience or purpose, evaluating or analyzing that feedback, or using it as a springboard for reflecting on their writing—also indicated development in terms of rhetorical sophistication and agency. Students who did not critically engage with feedback, however, at times suggested they learned nothing from this pedagogical tool. Consequently, more than anything else, this chapter suggests that one powerful way to promote students' development as writers is to teach them to seek out and critically engage with instructor feedback.

NOTES

1. In this body of literature, *response* is used broadly to address the following: (1) students' perceptions of feedback, often in terms of what they find useful or not useful; (2) students' behaviors, in terms of their decisions to take up or not take up particular comments or in terms of their affective responses; and (3) students' writing performance, in terms of the quality of their subsequent writing.

2. Questions such as these were asked of all students who participated in this study. On the interview protocol, interviewers were instructed to ask students, "How would you describe yourself as a writer when you began here at the University of Michigan?" and then to probe students' answers to this question by asking, "To what extent would you say you have grown as a writer? To what would you attribute this growth?"

3. Throughout this chapter, we use the term *dispositions* specifically to refer to the feelings of acceptance or resistance that students expressed as they described their experiences with instructor feedback. We refer to these dispositions as moments of accepting and moments of resisting in order to emphasize the temporal nature of these affective responses; many students described both accepting and resisting feelings toward the feedback they received, at times even in response to a single instructor comment. This use of the term is related to but also distinct from other uses of the term in writing studies (for example, it is distinct from Driscoll and Wells's discussion of dispositions in terms of personal characteristics).

4. To facilitate the comparison of survey results from the start and end of the study, all of the

statistics reported here were taken from the subset of students who fully completed both their entry and exit surveys. This data set included 38 minors and 60 nonminors.

5. This contrast reflects divergences in the findings of studies that have specifically explored the relationship between grades and students' motivation for engaging in the writing process, with some scholars arguing that grades are an important motivator for encouraging students to work on their writing (Reed and Burton) and others claiming just the opposite (Burkland and Grimm). Consequently, though grades clearly mediate students' engagement with instructor feedback, the role they play seems to vary from student to student in complex ways.

WORKS CITED

Brannon, Lil, and C. H. Knoblach. "On Students' Rights to Their Own Texts: A Model of Teacher Response." *College Composition and Communication*, vol. 33, no. 2, May 1982, pp. 157–66.

Burkland, Jill, and Nancy Grimm. "Motivating Through Responding." *Journal of Teaching of Writing*, vol. 5, no. 2, Fall 1986, pp. 237–47.

Connors, Robert J., and Andrea A. Lunsford. "Teachers' Rhetorical Comments on Student Papers." *College Composition and Communication*, vol. 44, no. 2, May 1993, pp. 200–223.

Lynch, Catherine, and Patricia Klemans. "Evaluating Our Evaluations." *College English*, vol. 40, no. 2, Oct. 1978, pp. 166–80.

Reed, W. Michael, and John K. Burton. "Effective and Ineffective Evaluation of Essays: Perceptions of College Freshmen." *Journal of Teaching Writing*, vol. 4, no. 2, 1985, pp. 270–83.

Sommers, Nancy. "Responding to Student Writing." *College Composition and Communication*, vol. 33, no. 2, May 1982, pp. 148–56.

Sommers, Nancy. *Responding to Student Writers*. Bedford/St. Martin's, 2013.

Sprinkle, Russell S. "Written Commentary: A Systematic, Theory-Based Approach to Response." *Teaching English in the Two-Year College*, vol. 31, no. 3, March 2004, pp. 273–86.

Still, Brian, and Amy Koerber. "Listening to Students: A Usability Evaluation of Instructor Commentary." *Journal of Business and Technical Communication*, vol. 24, no. 2, 2010, pp. 206–33.

Straub, Richard. "Students' Reactions to Teacher Comments: An Exploratory Study." *Research in the Teaching of English*, vol. 31, no. 1, Feb. 1997, pp. 91–119.

CHAPTER TWO

"A GOOD DEVELOPMENT THING"

A LONGITUDINAL ANALYSIS OF PEER REVIEW AND AUTHORITY IN UNDERGRADUATE WRITING

Benjamin Keating

Peer review, a collaborative learning tool that emerged in the 1980s as a response to the failure of traditional writing pedagogy to meet the demands of students previously excluded from higher education (Bruffee; Trimbur), is intended to help students cultivate a sense of authority over the texts they produce and to support them as they position themselves as new members of scholarly or professional communities. Research from the 1980s and 1990s suggests that peer review[1] can help students develop as writers by destabilizing traditional hierarchies between instructors and students that had previously limited student authority (Berkenkotter; Gere and Abbott; Nystrand; Stanley). However, research has also shown that peer review could in fact reproduce the inequitable effects it intended to mitigate, not only between instructors and students, but between students, especially around gender (Spear; Stygall), race (Fox; Villanueva), language difference (Allaei and Connor; Silva and Matsuda), and ideological difference (Horner; Myers; Trimbur). Therefore, more research is needed to understand whether peer review works as intended (Kerschbaum; Leverenz; Moss et al.; Ruecker; Stygall; Trimbur). Does peer review actually enhance writing development by empowering students, destabilizing instructor authority, and encouraging students to see themselves as participants in an authentic community of writers and critics?

If peer review is designed to do these things—in short, to instill a sense of authority in students—it is important to expand our knowledge of how students experience and perceive it in their development as writers, especially since the bulk of research on peer review took place in the 1980s and 1990s and therefore cannot account for current student demographics or current institutional contexts. Further, no recent scholarship takes a longitudinal view of peer review as a potential factor in writing development or considers it in terms of student perceptions. In this chapter, I use quantitative and qualitative data to trace conceptions of peer review over time and between the writing minor and nonminor groups, examining or analyzing what role authority—the extent to which students felt that their peers were authorized, by each other and by their instructors, to give feedback—plays in student perceptions of and experience with peer review. Further, what are the connections between audience awareness, authenticity, and authority? While my findings indicate that peer review *can be* a key aspect in writing development, stark differences emerged between minors and nonminors regarding their beliefs about and experience with peer review; as I show below, for the minor group, peer review was foundational to writing development, while for the nonminors, it played a less central and more complex role. I argue that these beliefs and experiences were shaped by notions of authority and authenticity in the classroom, so that the value of peer review in writing development was determined largely by how students viewed the authority of their peers relative to the authority of their instructors.

Most students perceived peer review as a useful developmental tool. As Natalie, a writing minor, put it in her entry interview, "Something about that class, it was like a workshop 24/7, which was a good development thing. I know it helped all of us." Peer review, then, had durable consequences for students as they embraced a view of writing as a social process consistent with the threshold concepts in Linda Adler-Kassner and Elizabeth Wardle's *Naming What We Know*. By the latter stages of their college careers, both the minors and nonminors realized the value of peer review in the writing process, but they came to and practiced this realization in very different ways. A vital distinction arises here between two categories of peer review that emerged from my analysis: (1) "school-sponsored," as I will call it, in which peer review was required by an institutional authority figure, and (2) "self-sponsored," in which students sought to give or receive feedback outside of class from friends and family.[2] Almost without exception, the minors located school-sponsored peer review as indispensable to their growth as writers and students. Almost without exception, however, nonminors were ambivalent about or disappointed in school-sponsored peer review. Instead, they turned to self-sponsored peer review, reporting generally that it was an important, though not vital, part of their writing development.

To illustrate these differences, I begin by analyzing what seemed like an apparent point of convergence between the minors and nonminors: the experience of frustration with peer review. While all of the participants acknowledged that school-sponsored peer review could be frustrating, minors and nonminors explained their frustration in notably different ways. When the nonminors expressed frustration with school-sponsored peer review, they had an ambivalent and sometimes overtly negative view of it. On the other hand, the frustration of the minors was rooted in the recognition of how potentially useful peer review could be. As Celeste put it in her entry interview, "For me, [peer review] was a frustrating process because I feel like it didn't have to be a frustrating process." Other minors displayed a similarly confident attitude toward peer review, talking, for example, about gleaning valuable editing experience even when the reviews they received were not useful to them. As I detail below, despite their frustrating experiences, minors spoke enthusiastically about school-sponsored peer review as central to their writing development over time.

The nonminors, on the other hand, found school-sponsored peer review frustrating because they saw it as a "subjective" and fraught process of sorting through conflicting or unreliable feedback. As one nonminor, Stephanie, said in her entry interview, "I don't know. I've grown to love and hate [workshops] simultaneously," since, as she explained, although some feedback helped her see her own assumptions more clearly, she found the process of resolving conflicting feedback overwhelming. In her exit interview, another nonminor, Charlotte, made a similar point about her ambivalence: "I'm kinda torn about workshops. I like them and I don't because I think that you get a lot of feedback at once and sometimes that's too much." These two students demonstrate a theme in the data: the nonminors remained ambivalent toward peer review over time.

A longitudinal comparison of nonminor entry and exit interviews supports this assertion. For example, in her entry interview, Dariella said, "It's always kind of really dependent on the situation because when we do peer review, sometimes, most of the time, I don't find it that useful." In the exit interview, when asked about more recent peer review work, she said, "In terms of peer review, that's a process that you have to go through in every single class at U of M. It is useful sometimes." Here, "sometimes" is the key term. Dariella's mixed experience was typical, though some students were much more negative about their experience. While nonminors recognized the potential of self-sponsored peer review to help them improve their writing, they did not perceive school-sponsored peer review as central to their development as writers over time. This difference between the minors' and nonminors' view of peer review's potential to be frustrating demonstrates the divergent perceptions of its role in writing development.

Below, I present a brief theoretical framework before turning to a comparative analysis of the interview data, looking first at the nonminors and then the minors. Between these qualitative analyses, I present two "survey data interludes"[3] in which I use longitudinal and comparative statistical analysis to supplement my claims about the role of peer review in writing development. This quantitative analysis, the methods of which I detail below, is based on the survey responses of both minors and nonminors.

Authority and Authenticity in Peer Review

When, in college classrooms, instructors assign peer review activities to decenter their own authority and model a more social theory of writing, students often resist. This resistance is based in the notion that authority resides not in students, as novices, but in instructors, as experts, invoking the problematic cliché of the "blind leading the blind." This view of authority depends on hierarchical and individualistic notions of not only the student-instructor relationship, but the process of writing itself—for example, an individual student writes for an individual instructor, who is authorized to assess that writing (Bruffee). Peer review, in nearly any form, begins to disrupt this dynamic. Yet instructors who seek to decentralize authority in these ways may find that students will de-authorize their peers, as some students did in this study.

This basic problem is related to larger questions around authority that have long concerned scholars in writing studies, where work on classroom discourse invites wider debates about authorship, capitalism, and intellectual property (Ede and Lunsford; Grobman; Mortensen and Kirsch; Penrose and Geisler; Spigelman, *Across Property Lines*; Trimbur). *Authority* is a vexed and vexing term, as Andrea Lunsford points out. On one hand, it suggests domination, institutional or individual, while on the other, it suggests the possibility of collaboration and knowledge-making, so that to *authorize* students is to *empower* them as writers in relation to both their peers and their instructors. The purpose of peer review, after all, is not to reproduce hierarchical power dynamics. Rather, one of its defining goals is to support discursive transgression; as Kenneth Bruffee writes, "By helping one another feel more comfortable crossing [discursive] boundaries, [students] initiate one another into the larger discourse communities they are joining" (47). Thus, collaborative learning strategies such as peer review empower students to "initiate" each other instead of relying on an instructor for this initiation. Following Peter Mortenson and Gesa Kirsch, Lunsford argues that to move beyond conceptions of authority as based in power, control, and individualism, instructors should attempt to model—through collaborative learning techniques such as peer review—a conception of authority based in knowledge, creation, and collaboration.

However, when the question of authority occurs in close proximity to writing, as in the context of peer review, the relation between authority and authorship becomes more immediate and more problematic. If, as Candace Spigelman argues, "Classroom writing groups are, in fact, a way to help students gain textual authority by identifying themselves and each other as writers" ("Habits of Mind" 253), then the move to claim authority depends on students' willingness or ability to identify each other as authors. Indeed, not all students in this study identified themselves or their peers as such. This suggests that authority in peer review is *relational* in the way it is claimed among students themselves. As Stuart Greene notes, authority is "always provisional" and it is "a relational term that calls attention to the fact that writers are always situated within a broad sociocultural landscape" (213). In the landscape of this study, I show how hierarchical and individualistic notions of authority competed with collaborative and communal notions of it. Since the contexts of school-based peer review—and perhaps self-sponsored peer review as well—were different for the minors and nonminors, students' experiences with and perceptions of themselves and their peers as authors also differed.

I refer to *authority* in broad terms as the capacity to be seen as a competent source of knowledge and power in the writing classroom. To claim authority is to use this knowledge and power to persuade in peer review. Following the concern that Spigelman brings up about "textual authority," I take up *authenticity* as the capacity to be seen as a "real" writing peer, as a "real" audience for writing, in short, as an author. The following questions loomed large in the data, as students explored their experience with peer review and its relation to their writing development: What counts as an *authentic* audience in the writing classroom? Who can be seen as an *authentic* peer? Who has *authority* in the context of peer review, and what kind of authority is it? These questions inform this chapter's mixed-methods[4] comparison of student perceptions of peer review, weaving together an analysis based on data from entry and exit interviews and surveys to show how the minors and nonminors differed in their perceptions of and experiences with self- and school-sponsored modes of peer review. In order to address these questions, I turn first to the nonminors.

"Not My Favorite Process": Nonminors on Peer Review

For many nonminors, school-sponsored peer review remained focused on surface-level concerns. When asked in her entry interview about what she would advise instructors to keep in mind in their writing pedagogy, Katie responded, "Get rid of the peer reviews—because I hate those. I'd rather them take a class day to just sit in their office and we can go in there individually and talk with the teachers, than have our peers look at it." Katie's comment also previews a point I will focus on below: the ways many nonminors saw their instructor as the only person authorized to give them feedback. In the exit interview, despite reporting extensive practice with it, Katie seemed even more dismissive of school-sponsored peer review, this time citing students' similar levels of grammar competency as the reason it was not useful:

> I think it's a complete waste of time. No one wants to do anything other than correct grammar mistakes and we argued. At UM everyone has pretty decent grammar so it's a complete waste of time. No one wants to talk about how to make your idea better. . . . Teachers like it for some reason but we all end up talking about other things.

This student pointed out two challenges. The first was incoherent pedagogy. If instructors do not articulate the value of peer review—*why* instructors "like it"—students will not see its value. Moreover, if peer review is focused on grammatical correctness rather than "how to make your idea better," it becomes a "waste of time" when there are few mistakes to correct, that is, when there is parity in grammatical skill, and no hierarchy to justify the claiming of authority. With no way to measure authority, the peer review devolved into counterproductive "arguing." This view of peer review as a "waste of time" was representative of students in the nonminor group, though they offered different reasons for this view.

Other nonminors did not see their peers as "decent" in grammar. Instead, these students dismissed peer review because of a deficit-oriented assessment of their peers' writing. The usefulness of peer review was then rooted in a calculus that equated authority in peer review with the perception of "strong writing," so "good" writers could give "good" reviews and "bad" writers would give "bad" reviews, with "good" and "bad" describing grammatical correctness. For example, when asked in her exit interview about a recent encounter with peer review, Janie linked her perception of the low quality of her peer's writing with the low value of class-sponsored peer review:

> I hate [peer review]. Like I said earlier, I had [to review] a 15-page paper where every sentence started with "However." That was probably one of the most miserable experiences in my life. I had over a—you know the review function on Word? Where you can count it? . . . I had over 100 comments and at that point I gave up on saying, "This is not how you use 'however.'" It also makes you look extremely dumb to contradict yourself every sentence.

Several other students positioned their peers as unauthorized and deficient in relation to themselves. Indeed, Janie claimed authority in relation to her peer as she took on a teacherly stance to correct her peers' writing. Janie saw class-sponsored peer review as an occasion to exert a traditional kind of hierarchical authority on her peers, whose writing she saw as needing correction. Where Janie thought she was authorized in this relational way, another student, Angela, argued in her entry interview that peer review was not useful because of what she saw as a collective de-authorization of herself and her peers:

> [Peer review] is not my favorite process because it's like we're all students. . . . We're all at the same; I don't feel like anyone is so superior that they would be really giving me any great ideas nor do I think I'm so superior that I should be giving anyone great ideas. I guess it's fine. I would never seek it out. I've never asked any friends to read my stuff.

But this view shifted in Angela's exit interview, when her view of peer review became more deficit-oriented, much like Janie's. Instead of a collective lack of authority, the problem became one of deficient instruction, or low writing standards, with the result that her friends were "not good writers." At this point, Angela felt authorized to provide feedback to help her friends improve their "bad" writing:

> To be honest, working with other writers—I mean, some of my friends have asked me to help them with their papers and help them with their essays, and they're not good [*laughter*] . . . They're not good writers, particularly their organization is really bad, which I feel like is a fundamental skill that you should've learned in high school. I don't know how they got past high school without this. They're really smart people . . . I'm like, "How did you get to this point?" . . . God, I sound condescending. I'm sorry. I don't mean to sound condescending. They're really great people.

Like Janie, Angela claimed to be authorized to give self-sponsored peer review to her friends, while her friends seem unauthorized to give feedback to her. Importantly, while Angela dismissed both school- and self-sponsored peer review in her entry interview, she at least acknowledged her involvement in self-sponsored peer review in her exit interview. When the interviewer asked if Angela's practice with self-sponsored peer review had been useful for her own writing, she said she was "probably more conscious about my own writing" and that it "probably helped me a little bit." While neither mode of peer review was central to Angela's writing development, it had the potential to play a larger role, as it had already been somewhat helpful.

Even students who spoke negatively about peer review in any mode allowed that it, as an idea—or ideal—could be valuable. For example, Janie, who spoke in very negative terms about peer review in both her entry and exit interviews, asserted "I was never taught how to peer review, so the way I peer review is a lot of editing for grammar" ("Entry"). Because grammatical correction remained the default mode for students in our study faced with their peers' work, it is all the more vital for peer review to be taught as a recursive and reflexive skill. Without this training, the powerful urge to hunt for grammatical errors may continue to undermine peer review's developmental possibilities. It is also important to note that Janie recognized that there are other, more useful ways to respond to writing, ways that remain out of reach. A clear finding, then, is that when students report that the purpose of peer review is unclear to them, they are likely to fall back on dominant ideologies regarding not only grammatical correctness, but, as I argue, regarding a transactional view of writing expertise that privileges instructor authority over student authority, undermining the stated goals of peer review.

The nonminors' beliefs about peer review tended to be embedded in a deficit-oriented view of both writing and peer review, reflecting larger ideologies about authority as a hierarchical construct (Lunsford, "Refiguring Cassroom Authority") in which better writers can claim more authority, mimicking the traditional teacher-student power dynamic that allows them to correct their peers' writing. The nonminors also tapped into crisis rhetoric about literacy and education, which positions most student writers as deficient (Rose). Given the durability of these ideologies, it is unsurprising that students embraced, and then enacted, these assumptions about peer review. For many nonminors, the experience with school-sponsored, and in Janie and Angela's cases, self-sponsored peer review became evidence for the truth of these ideologies. Here, peer review acted as a constraint on student power by de-authorizing rather than authorizing students in relation to their peers and their instructors, or distributing authority in uneven ways.

If anything, as I will show below, the instructor took on an even more central role when students experienced school-sponsored peer review in ways that drove them to resist the notion of their peers as authorized. When they pushed back, they recentered and reified the authority of the instructor, correcting and assessing rather than connecting and critiquing. Indeed, for many students, being an authoritative peer reviewer meant enacting an authority based in power and control, rather than what Andrea Lunsford calls a "refigured authority" in which writers claim the right to develop their work in conversation with each other and out of mutual interest and respect.

How the students viewed their peers in relation to their instructors determined whether they embraced both self- and school-sponsored peer review, and whether they embraced one over the other. The nonminors often spoke with distrust about their classmates' authority as reviewers. "I think peer reviews are pointless. . . . I would've rather given a draft to my [instructor] because she's the one who's gonna be grading it," said Lauren in her exit interview, continuing, "The suggestions that she gives me, I know are actually helpful."[5] Here, Lauren granted no authority to her peers and total authority to her instructor, a representative of institutional authority, who Lauren viewed as the *real* audience for her paper. Because she did not see her peers as the real—or authentic—audience for her paper, it follows that they should have no authority over it. Moreover, Lauren refused to participate in peer review, saying in her exit interview, "a lot of times, like when I was doing my peer reviews, I was just making stuff up so I could say something and get the grade for it." In resisting peer review, Lauren de-authorized herself as well as her peers as reviewers, since students put little trust in their peers' reviews if they themselves are "making stuff up" for a grade. For Lauren, school-sponsored peer review, as compulsory and graded, was a distracting and perhaps counterproductive step in the writing process, which elicited a fake engagement based in grades rather than collaboration. As Emily Wilson and Justine Post point out in chapter 1, in the specific context of an advanced screen-writing course, Lauren did develop her capacity to accept feedback from her peers. Nevertheless, Lauren maintained a stance of noncritical engagement with instructor feedback, alongside a general rejection of peer feedback. This instructor-centric view of school-sponsored authority and grading was representative of the nonminor group as a whole.

A central finding of this analysis is that since the feedback they received in school-sponsored peer review was unauthorized and unreliable, students turned to self-sponsored peer review. Their embrace of this mode of peer review was a marker of their writing development, since it acknowledged that writing is ultimately social: writers need feedback to produce valued text. For example, although Charlotte, a nonminor, remained wary of school-sponsored peer review, she developed an appreciation of self-sponsored peer review. In her entry interview, she asserted, "I haven't found that workshopping in college is as helpful just because, especially now, it's really hard to depend on people to workshop your papers and do it in a good and well-reviewed manner." As I have shown, many nonminors talked at length about their peers as unauthorized and untrustworthy reviewers, but they also talked about self-sponsored peer review as a key aspect of their writing process. Charlotte's narrative from her exit interview is representative of this phenomenon:

> Well, I do use peer editing as a huge thing. . . . I don't really enjoy using peer editing in class . . . I like using people who I know I can trust as far as peer editing, which usually happens to be my mom a lot, or my friends that work at the *Daily* or past teachers.

As Charlotte outlined the benefits of peer review, calling it a "huge thing," she pivoted to the problem of authority and trust, addressing it through self-sponsored peer review. For Charlotte, peer review was an important part of the writing process, one that spanned the continuum of revision—from larger questions about audience, evidence, and structure to sentence-level concerns about grammar.

But it was process external to the classroom. In short, self-sponsored peer review allowed students to get feedback from an authentic audience, that is, an audience motivated to give trustworthy feedback that was not required by an instructor. In this sense, self-sponsored peer review was a social activity in which students authorized their friends and family rather than their peers. Importantly, the limitations of school-sponsored peer review that nonminors such as Charlotte saw were very real. When students were not invested, when they resisted the kinds of collaborative authority that school-sponsored peer review required by "making stuff up" for a grade, nonminors were making a savvy choice about how to best gather feedback on their writing. Yet as they disengaged from school-sponsored peer review, they reinforced the ideologies of traditional schooling, in which students transact knowledge with instructors but not with their peers, and authority remains a matter of power, control, and hierarchy.

Survey Data Interlude One: Sponsorship, Practice, and Transfer

This finding from the interview data—that nonminors valued self-sponsored over school-sponsored modes of peer review—was supported by an analysis of the survey data. Before I present statistical data and findings, a note on methods. The following analysis is based on *t*-tests of difference in means, a method used to determine whether differences in the average scores of two representative populations are real or rather the result of chance. The level of confidence in a *t*-test is estimated using a *p*-value, a number between 0 and 1 that reflects the odds of wrongly inferring a real difference between the groups. A lower *p*-value thus implies stronger confidence that the groups are truly different. The closer a *p*-score is to zero, the more statistically significant the difference is said to be; the closer to 1, the less significant.

In this analysis, the chosen threshold for statistical significance is a *p*-value of 0.05 or below. Therefore, the term *significant* means that there is a 95 percent certainty that a difference between the groups is not the product of chance. Thus, a *p*-score above 0.05 is deemed not significant, while a *p*-score of 0.00004 is very significant, indicating a nearly 100 percent chance that the difference is not random. Below, we performed *t*-tests on the means of specific survey questions to make an inference about the differences between the minors and the nonminors and differences over time. For each survey question *t*-test, I supply the *p*-score so that readers can gauge the level of statistical confidence in the group differences.

Two questions in the entry and exit surveys were focused on self-sponsored versus school-sponsored modes of peer review. The first question (Q.A.), which concerned the self-sponsored mode, asked students to report the number of assignments for which *they sought* feedback on their writing. Q.A. was as follows:

> *During the current school year, for how many of your writing assignments have you received feedback from a classmate, friend, or family member about a draft before turning in your final assignment?*

The second question (Q.B.) asked students to report the number of assignments for which their *instructors required* in-class peer review. Q.B. was as follows:

> *During the current school year, for how many of your writing assignments has your instructor asked you to give feedback to a classmate about a draft or outline the classmate had written?*

For both survey questions, students could then choose from the following answers: no assignments (1), few assignments (2), some assignments (3), most assignments (4), all assignments (5). A number of statistical inferences become possible by comparing how minors and nonminors answered these questions. It is also possible to compare the questions themselves within each population.

First, a comparison between the nonminors answers for Q.A. (self-sponsored peer review) and Q.B. (school-sponsored peer review) showed statistically significant differences in both entry and exit surveys for the nonminors, who reported seeking their own feedback more often than they reported being directed to seek feedback by their instructors. A *t*-test of the entry surveys yielded a *p*-value of 0.001, a highly significant difference.[6] A *t*-test of the exit survey yielded another significant difference, with a *p*-value of 0.025, well within the 95 percent confidence interval.[7] This suggests that more nonminors got feedback autonomously from their friends and family than from their classmates, a finding that supports the qualitative analysis above, in which nonminors demonstrated a distrust of school-sponsored peer review that made them more likely to seek and view favorably self-sponsored modes of peer review.

However, this is not to suggest that the nonminors did *more* self-sponsored peer review than the minors. A comparison between the groups' responses to Q.A. and Q.B. shows that the minors reported doing *more of both* modes of peer review for their writing assignments than the nonminors did during both years they were surveyed. A t-test comparison between the minors and nonminors' responses to Q.A. showed a statistically significant difference suggesting that the minors received more self-sponsored feedback than the nonminors in both years they were surveyed, with a p-value of 0.031 comparing entry surveys and a p-value of 0.039 comparing exit surveys. On average, the minors reported self-sponsored feedback for "most assignments," while the nonminors reported self-sponsored feedback for "some assignments."[8]

Using the same method, an analysis of Q.B. showed that minors reported a highly statistically significant difference compared to the nonminors, in both the entry and exit surveys, in school-sponsored peer review, the number of times instructors required them to give (and probably seek) feedback. Comparing entry surveys, there was a p-value of 0.003; comparing exit surveys, there was a p-value of 0.000.[9] The minors were asked to give feedback on between "some" and "most" assignments, whereas the nonminors' fell between "few" and "some assignments." These significant differences between the groups in terms of how much self- and school-sponsored feedback they received demonstrates that minors had much more experience with peer review than nonminors.

The exit surveys show that in addition to *practicing* peer review more often than the nonminors, the minors reported *learning* more about peer review in general than the nonminors reported learning. The exit survey contained the following question:

> *Q.C. How much did you learn about giving and receiving feedback on writing-in-progress in your courses at the University?*

Students could then choose from the following answers: very much (1), some (2), not much (3), and nothing (4). Comparing exit surveys yielded a p-value of 0.021, with minors reporting a mean closer to "very much," while nonminors had a mean closer to "some."[10] This statistically significant difference was probably related to another: in the entry survey, the minors, more than nonminors, reported that they were able to transfer peer review skills they had learned in first-year writing to other courses. This assertion is based on a t-test of Q.D.:

> *How frequently do you use what you learned in your First-Year Writing Requirement course about giving and receiving feedback on writing-in-progress when writing for other courses?*

To respond to this question, students could choose very often (1), sometimes (2), not very often (3), never (4), or I didn't learn about this in my first-year writing course (5). Analysis of this question about transfer yielded a *p*-value of 0.049, just within the 95 percent confidence threshold to be called significant. The mean of the minors fell between "very often" and "sometimes," whereas the mean for nonminors was very close to "sometimes."[11] Interestingly, this *p*-value suggests a less certain difference between the groups, which suggests, alongside the interview data, that both groups appreciated their experience with peer review in their first-year writing courses, particularly the nonminors, who reported good experiences with first-year writing peer review in their interviews.

To conclude this interlude, the survey data illuminate why and how the minors practiced *more* peer review, *learned more* about it, and *used what they learned about it* more often (after their first year) than the nonminors. Taken together, these differences confirm that minors found more benefit in school-sponsored peer review than the nonminors, though the minors seemed to value self-sponsored peer review as well. Paired with the data from the interviews, the data from the surveys also suggest a link between the frequency at which instructors ask students to perform semiautonomous peer review and students' propensity to act autonomously. That is, the more students practiced peer review in class, the more likely they were to do it outside of class. Further, as is clear from differences in the interview data between the groups in terms of their perceptions of peer review, with practice seems to come a positive view of peer review. Below, I turn to the interview data to show how minors came to value school-sponsored peer review in such stark contrast to the nonminors, and how that valuing of peer review becomes a marker of writing development.

"Holistic Instead of Nitpicky": Minors on Peer Review

While the nonminors positioned school-sponsored peer review as both focused primarily on surface-level correction and generally unauthorized—compared to instructor feedback and self-sponsored feedback—the minors as a whole described a developmental arc that began with surface-level revision and moved to an in-depth revision process that positioned peers as an authorized and authentic audience. As Kaitlin, a minor, put it in her exit interview, peer review became "more holistic instead of nitpicky." This arc is clear in a comparison between Sidney's entry and exit interviews. In her entry interview, Sidney's description of peer review is generally representative of the minors' entry interviews: "I really enjoy peer editing and breaking down in small groups to workshop things. I think that that's very powerful. . . . I find that very, very helpful." The focus is on the transactional function of peer review as a revision tool—that is, what peer review can *give* writers to help them improve their writing, often in terms of sentence-level corrections.

This statement stands in contrast to the function of peer review described in Sidney's exit interview, which is more relational. In the exit interview, Sidney asserted that the minor curriculum allowed students "to write about really real things," that is, to choose their own topics for their own reasons. Students wrote about *authentic* subjects, perhaps in ways that encouraged them to enact an authentic writing persona, to claim authorship, and to position their peers as fellow authors whose feedback was important. Sidney chose to write about depression, and described the peer review sessions as "constructive," continuing, "they weren't everyone [just] saying, 'Oh, great job.' You got honest feedback, but it was a safe space where people were also telling you what they liked, and you felt okay bringing big ideas to the table." Wilson and Post (chapter 1) trace a similar arc in Sidney's relationship with instructor feedback, showing how she moved from a transactional and noncritical acceptance of instructor feedback to a more collaborative and dialogic process. In her exit interview, as Wilson and Post argue, she started "to have these conversations with [herself]" about how to revise her writing, which suggests she had used the feedback processes from both instructors and students to develop her ability to revise her writing (p. 42).

Yet Sidney's description of peer review captures another phenomenon of the minors' relationship with peer review, one that extends beyond questions of writing improvement, assessment, or trust in their peers or instructors. For many students, peer review reached into liminal spaces in which students developed their awareness and respect for the experiences of others. The minors saw class-sponsored peer review as a dialogic process, energized by encounters with different points of view, different media, and different disciplines. As Natalie reported in her exit interview:

> My project ended up being way in a completely different mode and displayed way differently because a girl that was like—she plays the bass, she's in the music school—she's like, "Oh, I've done this before and you should try this." . . . It was very kind of push and shove kind of revision . . . I think my writing and me intellectually as a whole I think was pushed forward because of the people and the different array of measures and backgrounds I guess. That was really cool.

What "pushes" Natalie forward is not just the diversity of skill and the dynamics of peer review within the class, but dialogic contact with a diversity of experience. As in the excerpts above, Natalie positioned herself as a writer with an authentic audience, whose feedback pushes beyond the surface level. Natalie's development, as a writer *and* as a thinker, was driven by the contact that school-sponsored peer review afforded her. Other students spoke in similar ways about peer review: less as a means to an end—as a tool given to them by their instructors for the purpose of improving their grades—and more as a chance to incorporate new ideas from and connect with their readers. Sarah Swofford's analysis of Natalie's development (chapter 9) also highlights her relational and flexible disposition around writing. Indeed, her ability to connect with other writers in self- or class-sponsored peer review, Swofford argues, helped smooth her somewhat turbulent transition from secondary writing to postsecondary writing.

The minors not only positioned peer review as a key—and generally consistent—aspect of their writing development, they did so by highlighting the value of peer feedback in relation to instructor feedback, crediting both as useful in different ways. For example, in response to the question in his exit interview, "What have your experiences been of working with other writers throughout the minor?" Zach answered,

> You get a lot from your instructor 'cause obviously they're professional teachers in writing and stuff, but there's nothing quite like the feedback that people who are in the same situation as you have. [Peer review] was insanely valuable for learning how to frame it in ways that we as students wanted to frame it.

Zach positioned peer review as a unique kind of feedback that supplemented and decentered instructor feedback. Peer feedback, then, was useful in ways that instructor feedback was not, despite the fact that the instructor was a "professional teacher," and thus authorized by the institution to give official feedback. Zach also described his peers as an authentic audience and peer review as a way to connect with that audience. Another student, Joy, positioned peer review in a similar way in her exit interview: "Honestly, my project wouldn't have been as successful without the feedback, not only from [the instructor], but the other girls in the class. Because they were in my target market for the magazine that I was writing, so it was really nice to get firsthand feedback about what a reader would think about it. That's been very valuable." Like Zach, Joy positioned her peers' feedback as in some ways more authorized than her instructor's feedback.

Both of these students framed peer review as an activity that destabilized the traditional binary between instructor and student authority: here, students as peer reviewers had a degree of power in their position as both target audience, or authentic audience, and community member. They suggest that peer review, as practiced in the minor, allowed feedback to emerge from a community of writers rather than from a single authority figure. However, this is not to suggest that instructor feedback was less developmentally important to students such as Joy. As Wilson and Post argue (chapter 1), when students engaged critically with instructor feedback, which often meant a "dialogic" engagement with their instructors, students had much to gain. In Joy's case, argue Wilson and Post, her instructor's practice of posing challenging questions acted as a "springboard" for Joy's self-awareness and as a "catalyst for Joy's development as a writer" (p. 43). Indeed, when instructors cultivate the kind of writing environment where peer feedback is valued, instructors might find themselves free to give a different kind of feedback—for example, to ask more challenging questions.

Most of the students in the minor group viewed their classmates and their instructors as valuable collaborators, even though they did not see themselves as engaged in collaborative writing per se. This suggests that these students did not see themselves as solitary writers pursuing solitary projects. Rather, they connected their production to the group it was composed in and for. Since their writing was no longer an individual transaction with their instructor, their peers became an authentic audience, not one placed awkwardly between themselves and the assessment of their instructors. Because they saw their peers as an authentic audience, students valued the feedback they received.

In other words, a connection emerged between authenticity and authority, so that an authentic audience of peers held a *nonhierarchical authority*, one founded on collaboration rather than competition, transaction, or control. This view of writing echoes what expert writers hope for when they imagine receiving feedback from their audience of peers: when an audience is not only a willing consumer of text but also an active responder, authority and audience are mutually constructed. These students' relational view of writing and authority positioned them less as *students* and more as *authors*.

This analysis also suggests that the ability to appraise and critically revise one's own writing, a crucial step of writing development, is intimately related to peer review. Many students made the connection between peer review and self-reflection explicit, like Shannon, in her exit interview:

> The one skill that I've actually picked up in the Gateway course was self-reflective comments. . . . That's just really, really helped me to define where I'm struggling in my papers. Then, also if I have a peer or an instructor look at my paper, I know exactly what areas I want them to address, so that's been really helpful.

The term the student uses, "self-reflective comments," is an embodiment of this movement from internalization and reflexivity to revision. When students were able to independently see their uncertainties and "define" their struggles, a recursive process occurred in which they exercised autonomy in subsequent review sessions with both peers and instructors.[12] The movement from external experience to internal, independent development seems connected to students' skills in self-reflection. This movement from peer review to internalization, and from internalization to reflection, is clear in Shannon's talk about "struggling." Indeed, this struggle is indicative of the process of writing development.

The minors' experience with school-sponsored peer review suggests a robust level of writing development. Indeed, they practice Andrea Lunsford's conception of writing as

> [b]oth relational and responsive, always in some way part of an ongoing conversation with others. This characteristic of writing is captured in what is referred to as the classic *rhetorical triangle*, which has at each of its points a key element in the creation and interpretation of meaning: writer (speaker, rhetor), audience (receiver, listener, reader), and text (message), all dynamically related in a particular context. ("Writing Addresses, Invokes, and/or Creates Audiences" 20)

Students in the minor were writing in these "relational and responsive" ways, with peer review as a key site for this work that allowed students to realize—make real—each side of the triangle. As Sidney's example shows, where peer review started as a function of how to improve writing, it evolved into a vehicle for social relation in which students, as rhetors, wrote "real" rather than "mutt" genres, to invoke Elizabeth Wardle's label for written genres that only approximate the genres at work in communities of practice. As Sidney suggested, the minors were able "to write about really real things," which made the feedback more valuable. Jonah, another minor, put it this way in his exit interview,

> It was nice to be surrounded by people who I was more comfortable in discussing my works with them and it didn't feel like an exercise. It actually felt helpful and like I could get useful feedback. I think having us all together like that made the feedback feel more confident.

For Jonah, being "together" with his peers made the feedback more trustworthy. Therefore, when school-sponsored peer review was more than an "exercise"—when the rhetorical triangle was real, or authentic—peer review took on a new, more complex meaning, one that expert writers immediately recognize in their own writing practice. Without the presence of a trusted community, peer review loses much of its power.

Survey Data Interlude Two: Affect

Turning again to the survey data, quantitative evidence supported the notion that, for the students in our study, peer review was a relational activity that depended in part on the affective dimension that Anne Gere references in the introduction to this section. The data showed that although discussing their writing may not be a very enjoyable experience for most students, there were significant differences between our two study groups regarding this question.

First, in the entry survey, and again in the exit survey, the minors reported that they found discussing their writing with others more enjoyable than the nonminors did. In Q.E., students rated their agreement with the following statement: "Discussing my writing with others is enjoyable." Students could then choose from the following answers: strongly agree (1), agree (2), uncertain (3), disagree (4), or strongly disagree (5). A comparison of the responses in the entry survey yielded a p-value of 0.010, with the minors and nonminors both falling between "uncertain" and "disagree." The nonminors, though, were much closer to "disagree." The same trend continued in the exit survey, where the p-value was 0.003, and the difference between the group was even larger.[13] This statistical inference is consistent with the interview data so far presented in the chapter, where the minors spoke with such enthusiasm about peer review. Yet it is also notable that despite this enthusiasm, the minors still viewed discussing their writing with others in ambivalent and uncertain terms. The data certainly do not suggest that most students find discussing their writing to be an "enjoyable" activity.

Despite this, the nonminors experienced a greater difference between their entry and exit surveys: their enjoyment of talking about writing grew significantly over time, with the mean for the entry exam at 2.97 and the mean for the exit 2.64 (n = 45), a difference that yields a 0.030 p-value. This was not the case for the minors, who, although they found discussing writing more enjoyable than the nonminors, did not experience a significant difference over time: enjoyment grew from entry to exit, but not in a statistically significant way, from an entry mean of 2.3 to an exit mean of 2.19 (n = 26), a difference that yields a p-value of 0.052, just over the 95 percent confidence threshold required for *significance*.

Thus, while the minors showed more enjoyment in general, the nonminors' ability to enjoy talking about writing grew more than the minors'. This finding might connect to the positive ways in which nonminors spoke about the feedback from their friends and family. As they advanced in their disciplinary discourses, they might have experienced more fulfilling experiences with self-sponsored peer review. Again, it is not that the nonminors did not experience peer review as a developmental tool; rather, they did so outside the confines of the classroom.

For the study group as a whole, including all minors and nonminors who completed both an entry and exit survey, students indicated that discussing their writing with others had become more enjoyable as they progressed through their course work. The difference was statistically significant over time, with a p-value of 0.030 ($n = 71$). This finding further supports Gere's observation in her section introduction about the link between affect and writing development: that both groups of students found talking about their writing more enjoyable indicates that there is much to learn about the potential connections between affect, feedback, and writing development.

Conclusion

In their exit interviews and surveys, the minors displayed what I have argued is a sophisticated understanding of the relationship between writing and peer review. With their extensive experience in peer review, a mainstay of the minor curriculum, these students showed a marked change in their view of peer review over time, not only in moving away from a focus on surface-level editing, but in their fundamental stance toward the writing and revision process. For minors, peer review took place primarily in a classroom setting where students were able to choose their own writing projects and claim authority over them. Overwhelmingly, they perceived peer review as a highly useful and enjoyable experience.

Peer review emerged as a vehicle for recursive movement from group capacity to individual capacity: from peer review to self-review, and back again, so that reflexivity (awareness of self in relation to others) was a key element in writing development. Further, minors saw peer review as a dialogic process, during which they were energized by encounters with different points of view, different media, and different disciplinary perspectives. Peer review was seen less as an assessment tool given to them by their instructors to improve their grades and more as a chance to address an authentic audience whose feedback mattered. Indeed, there are parallels in how students such as Sidney developed their stance regarding instructor *and* student feedback. As they developed their self-awareness as writers, they also embraced a more dialogic and critical notion of feedback.

The nonminors had a very different way of conceptualizing the value of peer review over time. They did not experience a coherent peer review curriculum, and, by and large, they reported more negative experiences with school-sponsored modes of peer review. Because of these negative experiences, the data suggest that many nonminors relied primarily on self-sponsored peer review. This reliance grew out of a sense of distrust of school-sponsored peer review. For some nonminors, this distrust and disappointment was intertwined with deficit-oriented views of their peers' writing that, for example, equated a perception of mastery over Standard Edited American English with writing competence, and in some cases, a perception of a hierarchical authority in relation to their peers. Fluency and authority were conflated in ways that led to a continuing focus on surface-level concerns. In other words, when students saw themselves as authorized because of their "skill" in grammar, their writing development slowed.

The nonminors' preference for self-sponsored peer review points to an opportunity to learn more about what self-sponsored peer review looks like. How might self-sponsored peer review offer the kinds of affective and dialogic rewards the minors spoke of? How do students reconcile self-sponsored feedback with school-sponsored feedback, including that of the instructor? How might students see self-sponsored feedback in relation to questions about authority? In other words, what kinds of authority are enacted in self-sponsored modes of peer review? Do they adhere to traditional notions of authority, or do they progress toward a collaborative and plural notion of both authority and authorship?

The question of self-sponsorship leads to another about equity. Not all students have friends or family willing or able to respond usefully to college-level academic writing. For example, transfer students, a growing demographic of students in higher education, often need to build a network of peers to use self-sponsored peer review; further, since transfer students may come from less privileged backgrounds or may be first-generation college students, their family connections might prove less useful for self-sponsored peer review than the connections of students whose parents hold advanced degrees (Gere et al.). For historically underrepresented or marginalized students, school-sponsored peer review may be the best option, in which case there is an urgent need for instructors to do a better job demonstrating its value and training students to use it effectively.

For both groups, the ways that students engaged with peer review often involved a litany of vexing questions about their peers' authority. Students were essentially forced to engage critically with the feedback their peers offered. Often, at least in their first years, this critical engagement tended to dismiss rather than accept peer feedback; at the same time, as Wilson and Post demonstrate (chapter 1), inexperienced students often showed a propensity to accept instructor feedback uncritically. As they developed their capacity as writers, however, many students learned to engage critically with their instructors' feedback, an engagement that Wilson and Post argue is a marker of writing development. This beginning asymmetry in students' reactions to feedback is telling—in basic terms, the propensity to reject peer feedback while accepting instructor feedback can evolve, certainly in the case of the minors, to a practice of engaging critically with both peer and instructor feedback. For the nonminors, this engagement with peer feedback might occur in self-sponsored rather than class-sponsored modes of peer review, which points to the need to open lines of investigation into self-sponsored peer review.

Further, the asymmetrical reception of feedback also seems to be linked to the competing notions of authority that students and instructors both grapple with. If a hierarchical notion of authority remains dominant, shaping student-student as well as student-instructor relationships to feedback, asymmetrical receptions of feedback remain the default. If a collaborative notion of authority gains traction, students empower themselves, their peers, and their instructors as critics and writers. Of course, a problem arises when instructors assign peer review, hoping to cultivate a collaborative and formative kind of feedback in the classroom, but then maintain the singular and summative authority to shape their students' careers by stamping their papers with A's, B's, or C's. If students are to engage critically—rather than dismiss—their peers' feedback, instructors may need to reframe what Lunsford calls the "troubled authority" of classroom discourse—a hierarchical authority that maintains its power in part by authorizing students to de-authorize their instructors.

That is, despite the institutional authority that instructors may wield to require students to participate in school-sponsored peer review, that authority is actually quite tenuous; instructors cannot force students to carefully consider peer feedback. As the nonminors showed us, undermining school-sponsored peer review is not difficult. It is simply the choice to not listen, to do it only for the grade, or to dismiss it out of hand compared to instructor feedback. The extent to which peer review was a factor in writing development, then, might be correlated to the extent to which instructors have been able to frame peer review as a nonhierarchical, dialogic, collaborative form of authority-making, where peers are authentic audiences.

Reframing peer review is clearly possible, as the minors show us, yet as scholars who value peer review in our classrooms in part because we value it in our scholarly careers, we are at constant risk of under-theorizing it in our research. Charlotte Brammer and Mary Rees suggest that peer review, in both its professional and pedagogical applications, is "practically instinctive" (71) for many instructors. This renders it less visible as a research topic, since what is "instinctive" is generally harder to position as an object of study. Making the case *to students* about peer review as a worthwhile tool will mean continuing to research the enactment of collaborative kinds of authority in classroom discourse.

NOTES

1. In this chapter, I refer to student-to-student feedback processes simply as *peer review*, since it is the more general and widespread term. See Armstrong and Paulson for a discussion of terminology for peer review.

2. I use these terms based on Anne Ruggles Gere's distinction between autonomous and semi-autonomous writing groups, where the former is compulsory, convened by an authority figure. The latter is voluntary, with no immediate connection to the authority of an institution.

3. I have chosen not to integrate this quantitative analysis into the qualitative analysis so that readers can concentrate on one methodological argument at a time.

4. With few exceptions, the qualitative and quantitative data are complementary, but they are not perfectly parallel. That is, since the interviews were semistructured, not every survey question has an equivalent interview question. However, as we detail in the introduction, students filled out an extensive set of entry and exit surveys that contained multiple questions specifically about peer review. The interview protocol also contained questions about collaborative learning and peer review.

5. Instructor feedback is seen as more valuable when grades are of paramount concern.

6. Entry: 3.01 on Q.A.; 2.53 on Q.B.; p-value: 0.0009; $n = 67$.

7. Exit: 2.72 Q.A.; 2.36 on Q.B.; p-value: 0.025; $n = 61$.

8. Freshmen year: minors: 3.51; nonminors: 3.01; p-value: 0.031; $n = 104$. Senior year: minors: 3.18; nonminors: 2.72; p-value: 0.038; $n = 98$.

9. Entry: minors: 3.21; nonminors: 2.53: p-value: 0.003; $n = 104$. Exit: minors: 3.16; nonminors: 2.36; p-value: 0.00004; $n = 98$.

10. Exit: minors: 1.35; nonminors: 1.64; p-value: 0.021; $n = 101$.

11. Entry: minors: 1.63; nonminors: 1.96; p-value: 0.049; $n = 104$.

12. Hyland and Hyland make a similar point: "Students can make their own revisions without feedback and improve their writing significantly. It is therefore important not to overlook the writers themselves as critical readers and reviewers of their own texts. . . . In fact, most writing teachers would acknowledge that the ultimate aim of any form of feedback should be to move students to a more independent role where they can critically evaluate their own writing and intervene to change their own processes and products where necessary. . . . To do this, students need to develop metacognitive skills" (86).

13. Entry: minors: 2.29; nonminors: 2.8; p-value: 0.010; $n = 104$. Exit: minors: 2.10; nonminors: 2.78; p-value: 0.003; $n = 97$.

WORKS CITED

Adler-Kassner, Linda, and Elizabeth Wardle. *Naming What We Know: Threshold Concepts of Writing Studies*. UP of Colorado, 2015.

Allaei, Sara Kurtz, and Ulla Maija Connor. "Exploring the Dynamics of Cross-Cultural Collaboration in Writing Classrooms." *Writing Instructor*, vol. 10, no. 1, 1990, pp. 19–28.

Armstrong, Sonya L., and Eric J. Paulson. "Whither 'Peer Review'? Terminology Matters for the Writing Classroom." *Teaching English in the Two-Year College*, vol. 35, no. 4, 2008, pp. 398–407.

Berkenkotter, Carol. "The Power and the Perils of Peer Review." *Rhetoric Review*, vol. 13, no. 2, 1995, pp. 245–48.

Brammer, Charlotte, and Mary Rees. "Peer Review from the Students' Perspective: Invaluable or Invalid?" *Composition Studies*, vol. 35, no. 2, 2007, pp. 71–85.

Bruffee, Kenneth A. "Collaborative Learning and the 'Conversation of Mankind.'" *College English*, vol. 46, no. 7, 1984, pp. 635–52.

Ede, Lisa S., and Andrea A. Lunsford. "Collaboration and Concepts of Authorship." *Publications of the Modern Language Association of America*, vol. 116, no. 2, 2001, pp. 354–69.

Fox, Tom. "Basic Writing as Cultural Conflict." *Journal of Education*, vol. 172, no. 1, 1990, pp. 65–83.

Gere, Anne Ruggles. *Writing Groups: History, Theory, and Implications*. SIU Press, 1987.

Gere, Anne Ruggles, and Robert D. Abbott. "Talking about Writing: The Language of Writing Groups." *Research in the Teaching of English*, 1985, pp. 362–85.

Gere, Anne Ruggles, Lizzie Hutton, Benjamin Keating, Anna V. Knutson, Naomi Silver, and Christie Toth. "Mutual Adjustments: Learning from and Responding to Transfer Student Writers." *College English*, vol. 79, no. 4, 2017.

Greene, Stuart. "Making Sense of My Own Ideas: The Problems of Authorship in a Beginning Writing Classroom." *Written Communication*, vol. 12, no. 2, 1995, pp. 186–218, http://doi.org/10.1177/0741088395012002002

Grobman, Laurie. "The Student Scholar: (Re)Negotiating Authorship and Authority." *College Composition and Communication*, vol. 61, no. 1, 2009, pp. 175–96.

Horner, Bruce. "Students, Authorship, and the Work of Composition." *College English*, vol. 59, no. 5, 1997, pp. 505–29.

Hyland, Ken, and Fiona Hyland. "Feedback on Second Language Students' Writing." *Language Teaching*, vol. 39, no. 2, 2006, pp. 83–101.

Kerschbaum, Stephanie L. *Toward a New Rhetoric of Difference*. Conference on College Composition and Communication, National Council of Teachers of English, 2014.

Leverenz, Carrie Shively. "Peer Response in the Multicultural Composition Classroom: Dissensus—a Dream (Deferred)." *Journal of Advanced Composition*, 1994, pp. 167–86.

Lunsford, Andrea A. "Refiguring Cassroom Authority." *The Ethics of Writing Instruction: Issues in Theory and Practice*, edited by Michael A. Pemberton, Ablex Publishing Corp., 2000, pp. 65–78.

Lunsford, Andrea A. "Writing Addresses, Invokes, and/or Creates Audiences." *Naming What We Know: Threshold Concepts of Writing Studies*, edited by Linda Adler-Kassner and Elizabeth Wardle, UP of Colorado, 2015, pp. 20–21.

Mortensen, Peter, and Gesa E. Kirsch. "On Authority in the Study of Writing." *College Composition and Communication*, vol. 44, no. 4, 1993, pp. 556–72.

Moss, Beverly J., Nels P. Highberg, and Melissa Nicolas. *Writing Groups Inside and Outside the Classroom*. Routledge, 2004.

Myers, Greg. "Reality, Consensus, and Reform in the Rhetoric of Composition Teaching." *College English*, vol. 48, no. 2, 1986, pp. 154–74.

Nystrand, Martin. "Learning to Write by Talking about Writing: A Summary of Research on Intensive Peer Review in Expository Writing Instruction at the University of Wisconsin–Madison." University of Wisconsin–Madison, 1984.

Penrose, Ann M., and Cheryl Geisler. "Reading and Writing without Authority." *College Composition and Communication*, vol. 45, no. 4, 1994, pp. 505–20, https://doi.org/10.2307/358762

Rose, Mike. *An Open Language: Selected Writing on Literacy, Learning, and Opportunity*. Bedford/St. Martin's, 2006.

Ruecker, Todd. "Analyzing and Addressing the Effects of Native Speakerism on Linguistically Diverse Peer Review." *Peer Pressure, Peer Power: Theory and Practice in Peer Review and Response for the Writing Classroom*, edited by Steven J. Corbett et al., Fountainhead Press, 2014, pp. 91–105.

Silva, Tony, and Paul Kei Matsuda. *Landmark Essays on ESL Writing*. Routledge, 2013.

Spear, Karen I. *Sharing Writing: Peer Response Groups in English Classes*. Boynton/Cook Publishers, 1988.

Spigelman, Candace. *Across Property Lines: Textual Ownership in Writing Groups*. Southern Illinois UP, 2000. Studies in Writing & Rhetoric series.

Spigelman, Candace. "Habits of Mind: Historical Configurations of Textual Ownership in Peer Writing Groups." *College Composition and Communication*, vol. 49, no. 2, 1998, pp. 234–55.

Stanley, Jane. "Coaching Student Writers to Be Effective Peer Evaluators." *Journal of Second Language Writing*, vol. 1, no. 3, 1992, pp. 217–33.

Stygall, Gail. "Women and Language in the Collaborative Writing Classroom." *Feminism and Composition Studies: In Other Words*, edited by Susan C. Jaratt and Lynn Worsham, MLA, 1998, pp. 252–75.

Trimbur, John. "Consensus and Difference in Collaborative Learning." *College English*, vol. 51, no. 6, 1989, pp. 602–16.

Villanueva, Victor. "On Writing Groups, Class, and Culture: Studying Oral and Literate Language Features in Writing." *Writing With: New Directions in Collaborative Teaching, Learning, and Research*, edited by Sally B. Reagan et al., SUNY Press, 1994, pp. 123–41.

Wardle, Elizabeth. "'Mutt Genres' and the Goal of FYC: Can We Help Students Write the Genres of the University?" *College Composition and Communication*, vol. 60, no. 4, 2009, pp. 765–89, http://www.jstor.org/stable/40593429

SECTION TWO

Genre Awareness Contributes to Student Writing Development

The field of writing studies has given considerable attention to genre in the past few decades. Spurred by Carolyn Miller's theorization of genre as a communicative act rather than merely a formalist term, scholars including Charles Bazerman, Anis Bawarshi, Amy Devitt, and David Russell, among many others, have contributed to the ongoing discussions of genre as social action. Scholars such as these have described genres as habitual responses to specific rhetorical contexts. The subfield of rhetorical genre studies emerged as these discussions continued, delineating the ways that social, cultural, institutional, and disciplinary forces shape writing into recognizable forms that are stabilized by repetitive social actions. With the recognition of genre as social action has come attention to the ways genres are both shapers of and shaped by those who use them. A genre tells us what members of its discourse community expect us to know and do, whether filling out a form or giving an academic paper, and we in turn can conform to or push against the genre, adding categories to the form or challenging academic expectations. Although the implications of this mutual process of shaping have been explored in multiple contexts, relatively little attention has been given to the specific ways students participate in this process.

Disciplinary forces have been given special attention in discussions of genre as social action, usually by crediting the discourse community of a discipline with shaping its genres. Bazerman, for example, explains how scientific practices interacted with writing in creating the article form common in scientific journals. In his telling, the recurring pattern of introduction, methods, results, and discussion in scientific research shaped the format for scientific articles. Ken Hyland and Carmen Sancho Guinda point to citation practices—the use of parentheses, footnotes, or attribution—as another indication of the shaping force of disciplines on genres, arguing that each practice reflects disciplinary values. At the same time, scholars such as Chris Thaiss and Terry Zawacki have emphasized that disciplinary knowledge-making is an ongoing process that responds to changing norms and technologies.

The concept of genre has also figured prominently in discussions of transfer, particularly the extent to which writing knowledge gained in a first-year composition class transfers to successful writing in other academic contexts. Amy Devitt, among others, suggests that such courses can foster genre awareness or a critical consciousness of the ideological effects of genre forms. Elizabeth Wardle, for example, employs the term "mutt genres" to argue for the futility of assuming that first-year writing courses can teach genres or even awareness of them and should instead focus student learning on writing about writing or general principles of writing. These discussions of transfer have decreased the emphasis on addressing disciplinary genres in first-year composition, or even attempting to address them.

With regard to writing development, however, most scholars hold that expertise in disciplinary genres is essential. Anne Beaufort, for instance, claims, "What writing expertise is ultimately concerned with is becoming engaged in a particular community of writers who dialogue across texts, argue, and build on each other's work" (18). The conceptual model she offers embeds writing expertise in discourse community knowledge and includes subject matter knowledge among its features. Beaufort is not alone in describing a tight linkage between writing development and disciplinary expertise. Indeed, as Ryan McCarty notes in his chapter below, "The centrality of this conflation of [writing] development and [disciplinary] expertise can be found in some of the most important work of the discipline" (p. 114).

Scholars such as Mary Soliday, Chris Thaiss and Terri Zawacki, and Nancy Sommers and Laura Saltz all argue for the importance of guiding students toward disciplinary expertise, toward understanding the content, methods, and epistemologies of a given area of inquiry to develop them into effective writers. The students in our study complicate these assumptions with both their actions and assumptions.

While students in our study did not entirely dismiss the importance of taking up the discourses of specific disciplines as part of their writerly development, they complicated this equation in two significant ways: they challenged the boundaries of disciplines, and they created their own categories for describing genres. Students challenged disciplinary boundaries as they created their own programs of study, combining majors and minors, selecting specific courses, and participating in extracurricular activities. These challenges led to others as students drew on multiple fields and activities to develop ways of writing that they saw as important to their academic success as well as to their future selves. In creating their own categories for genres, they focused on the purposes the given piece of writing was designed to fill, and they also noted how it did or did not allow them to grow on their own terms.

Many students in our study did not see any one discipline as an area for exclusive focus. They declared various combinations of double majors or majors and minors, often to achieve goals they defined for themselves, and they did not necessarily seek to apprentice themselves to any one discipline. All of the writing minors, of course, majored in a field other than writing, and a significant majority of all participants (142 of the original 183 who signed up for the study) had either a double major or a major and one or more minors. Of the 64 minors who remained in the study, 26 had either one major and two minors or double or triple majors and one minor. Among the 104 nonminors, all but 36 had some combination of double or triple majors or a single major with one or more minors. One reason many students put together combinations of majors and minors was because they saw the mixed perspective as more valuable, and they testified to that value in interviews where they recounted the various sources—majors, minors, specific courses, instructors, and multiple extracurricular experiences—that supported their growth as writers.

Even students who had a single major were likely to see other fields as central in their writerly development. Kris, for example, a student who appears in both Ryan McCarty's and Anne Gere's chapters, combined philosophy courses with her biology major because she found that philosophy gave her a way to think about and assess the science she was studying: "The philosophy course provided more of a contrast, I think more of a development, because it was a different form of writing. It also helped me reflect upon the way we write in science" (p. 122). Kris also participated in collaborations with physicists, and learned, among other things, how the standards for "proof" varied across the two fields: "From the physics standpoint, they're like, 'We've got this number here. The number is solved. The equation is set. We're good.' At least, that's how we perceive their side. We're like, 'But the number is not of biological relevance unless we put it in this framework.'" As McCarty puts it, "For Kris, then, development as a writer certainly involves the goal of developing expertise in one disciplinary discourse. But her understanding of that development is distinctly *not* isolated to her discipline. Instead, she sees her disciplinary expertise developing in dialogue with her other writing experiences" (p. 122).

Jonah, another student McCarty discusses, also looked beyond his major to foster his writerly development, but rather than another academic discipline, he looked to multiple locations, including the extracurricular world of online gaming, to develop fluency and dexterity as a writer. Although he became competent in writing about science, he did not see that as his main goal. He wanted, instead, to develop a repertoire of writerly capacities so that he could, as he now does in his role as a professional writer, respond effectively in a variety of rhetorical contexts. As McCarty says, "For Jonah, like many students, the ability to write with dexterity across a range of situations is more valuable than disciplinary expertise" (p. 128).

Other students put two majors or a major and minor together for specific purposes. Stephanie, a student who appears in Anne Gere's chapter, majored in both math and English, and explained that the combination of the two made her a better student in both. The precision of math enhanced her focus and organizational skills in English, and the interpretive aspects of reading literature led her to seek more complex explanations in math. With these and other configurations of majors, minors, and courses, many students in this study demonstrated the benefits of moving beyond discipline-based expertise and constructed their own versions of writerly development.

Given the very close connection between disciplines and genres, it is not surprising that students' challenge to disciplinary boundaries extended to academic genres. Since genres constitute the means by which members of discourse communities—disciplines in the academy—demonstrate their affiliation, students who challenge disciplinary structures also challenge genres. If students don't want to become part of the discourse community of a discipline, they can respond by resisting its genres, as David Russell and Arturo Yañez found. In their case, students in an introductory history class did not aspire to become historians and resented the instructor's expectation that they adopt the genres of that disciplinary discourse community: "These are his writing tasks and he wants me to write in his way" (NP). Russell and Yañez conclude that genres can be sites of contestation because "the expectations created by the genre may not allow one to do the kind of work—or learning—that one wants or needs to" (NP).

The contestation Russell and Yañez describe is somewhat different from what we found in our study. Student participants had chosen majors, an indication that they wanted to become part of that discourse community, and many of them became competent writers in the appropriate disciplinary genres, but they sought access to a broader repertoire. The success they achieved is evident in data from a survey of all participants. Responding to a survey question asking about their ability to write in different forms, all students showed a statistically significant (p-value 0.007) increase between the entry and exit survey. Both minors and nonminors felt they had learned to write in many different rhetorical contexts—in many different genres—as a result of their college writing experiences. Responses to a related question about their ability to "approach new kinds of writing" also showed statistically significant growth (p-value 0.033). The entire group of study participants indicated an increased confidence in their ability to take on new kinds of writing as they left the university; they apparently felt the repertoire of writing strategies they had developed as undergraduates would serve them well in new writing contexts.

In their search for a more extensive array of genres of writing, students did not use traditional terminology to describe the writing of various discourse communities, but even without benefit of a social activity theory of genre, they effectively conveyed their understanding of the forces shaping genres. In their chapter, Hutton and Gibson draw on students' own talk to explain how students tended to categorize their writing into two main and apparently mutually exclusive categories. Students used "academic" to describe writing that communicates thought through reproducible forms, and "creative" to describe a context-transcending writing that focused more on invention. As Hutton and Gibson explain, students understood these two macro genres to "enable different *types* of transfer—one reliant on recurrent written forms, the other on a durable writerly self" (p. 92). Unlike the macro genres described by Michael Carter, which focused on the knowledges and activities characteristic of writing within clusters of disciplines, or the more traditional genres associated with specific disciplines, the genres identified by students were defined by what they aimed to accomplish. Like the students interviewed by Heather Lindenman, who described genre in terms of what they saw as its central activity, such as "writing for a grade," "writing for money," or "reactionary writing" (NP), the students in this study framed types of writing in terms of goals. The overall categories spoke to the extent to which the task fostered writerly development; what they called "academic" did not and "creative" did.

Hutton and Gibson recount that only a few students appeared to embrace the possibility of a third approach to writing as a hybrid of these two conceptions. These were students who could, as Hutton and Gibson put it, "negotiate between views of writing and their writerly growth as entailing both generative activity and adherence to communicative norms, instead of viewing these approaches as requiring an either-or-choice" (p. 105). In describing their experience of writing, these students looked to "kinds of writing" neither as repetitive practice of narrowly framed forms nor as less structured generative strategies. Rather, they framed writing in more flexible terms, as a set of understandings and abilities that could be easily transferred across various contexts and forms. In some sense these students were able to look beyond the details of one piece of writing toward a more holistic and positive view of themselves as writers and of the ways writing figured in their lives. As Hutton and Gibson note, the largest number of students who fell into this category were writing minors, and one explanation the authors offer is the minor's curricular emphasis on a wide range of genres, on reconceptualization of writing, and on considerable reflection, as described in **appendix 2**. As Hutton and Gibson are careful to note, however, some nonminors also arrived at the more integrated stance, which suggests the value of looking carefully at other factors.

One factor that merits more attention is the nature of the assignments to which students write. The urgency of attending to the quality of assignments is underscored by students such as Katie, who appears in McCarty's chapter and who says, "I guess maybe that's what developed me into the writer I am today, the different assignments and the different maybe audiences that I'm supposed to be writing to, the different purposes of the assignments" (p. 117). Recent attention from scholars such as Dan Melzer and the collaboration of Paul Anderson, Robert Gonyea, Chris Anson, and Charles Paine suggests that faculty in all disciplines can improve the quality of assignments. Assignments offer one way for instructors to foster student awareness of genres and their roles in disciplinary discourses—and for students to identify the activity systems in which discipline-defined genres function, even if they choose to move beyond them. The two chapters in this section not only interrogate the conflation of writing development and disciplinary expertise, they include hints about ways that assignments can foster the development of student writers.

WORKS CITED

Anderson, Paul, Robert M. Gonyea, Chris M. Anson, and Charles Paine. "The Contributions of Writing to Learning and Development: Results from a Large-Scale Multi-Institutional Study." *Research in the Teaching of English*, vol. 50, no. 2, 2015, 199–237.

Bawarshi, Anis. *Genre and the Invention of the Writer*. Utah State UP, 2003.

Bazerman, Charles, and David Russell. *Writing Selves/Writing Societies: Research from Activity Perspectives on Writing*. The WAC Clearinghouse and Mind, Culture and Activity. Available at http://wac.colostate.edu/books/selves_societies/

Beaufort, Anne. *College Writing and Beyond: A New Framework for University Writing Instruction*. Utah State UP, 2007.

Carter, Michael. "Ways of Knowing, Doing, and Writing in the Disciplines." *College Composition and Communication*, vol. 58, no. 3, 2007, 385–418.

Devitt, Amy. *Writing Genres*. SIU Press, 2004.

Hyland, Ken, and Carmen Sancho Guinda, editors. *Stance and Voice in Written Academic Genres*. Palgrave Macmillan, 2012.

Lindenman, Heather. "Inventing Metagenres: How Four College Seniors Connect Writing Across Domains." *Composition Forum*, 31, 2015. Available at https://files.eric.ed.gov/fulltext/EJ1061560.pdf

Melzer, Dan. *Assignments Across the Curriculum: A National Study of College Writing*. Utah State UP, 2014.

Miller, Carolyn. "Genre as Social Action." *Quarterly Journal of Speech*, vol. 70, 1984, 151–67.

Russell, David, and Arturo Yanez. "'Big Picture People Rarely Become Historians': Genre Systems and the Contradictions of General Education." Bazerman and Russell. *Writing Selves/Writing Societies*. Available at http:/wac.colostateedu/books/selves_societies

Soliday, Mary. *Everyday Genres: Writing Assignments Across the Disciplines*. SIU Press, 2011.

Sommers, Nancy, and Laura Saltz. "The Novice as Expert: Writing the Freshman Year." *College Composition and Communication*, vol. 56, no. 1, 2006, 124–49.

Swales, John. *Genre Analysis: English in Academic and Research Settings*. Cambridge University Press, 1990.

Thaiss, Chris, and Terry Zawacki. *Engaged Writers, Dynamic Disciplines*. Heinemann, Boynton/Cook, 2006.

Wardle, Elizabeth. "'Mutt Genres' and the Goal of FYC: Can We Help Students Write the Genres of the University?" *College Composition and Communication*, vol. 60, no. 4, 2009, pp. 765–89.

CHAPTER THREE

"KINDS OF WRITING"

STUDENT CONCEPTIONS OF ACADEMIC AND CREATIVE FORMS OF WRITING DEVELOPMENT

Lizzie Hutton and Gail Gibson

Asked about her writing development, Joy tells a narrative that illustrates the circuitous and networked nature of her learning. She draws on extracurricular and professional experiences as much as academic ones; she shows writing facility and interests that range across fields, goals, and identities. She speaks of entering the university to study engineering, then switching to communications. She describes writing both for the school newspaper—the "serious side of writing"—and for an online campus magazine, focused more on what she calls "girly things, fashion." She takes a summer internship in "corporate America," a marketing and communications position where she writes for the company's internal newsletter and social media platforms. In her spare time, she also works on a "young adult teen type novel about romance," which by her senior year she speaks of hoping to self-publish. In both her entry and exit interviews for our study, Joy talks fluently of argumentative credibility, of connecting with her audience, of differences and similarities across genres. Yet when she is asked in the exit interview about the effect a particular political science class had on her as a writer, Joy's usual enthusiasm and rhetorical broadmindedness take a sharp turn:

> Honestly, that was a terrible experience. The one assignment that I'll tell you about was the policy brief. It was a very structured assignment, where we had to just analyze a piece of legislation in a state, and just go through the process of what we would do differently, recommendations and things like that. The biggest problem I had with that [was] the professor did not let us explore this from a creative angle at all. I remember one girl . . . in the same class with me. She started her brief off with a little background

> story. . . . They did not like that at all. They suppressed any form of creativity. That just made me unhappy with the class. It had to be very structured. It was just not so good.

We begin with this example not to defend Joy's perspective on her instructor's insistence on rhetorical conventions, but because of how vividly Joy's comment illustrates larger patterns that emerged across our study: when asked to discuss their own development as writers, students commonly turned to talk about specific "kinds of writing" that divided writing—as activity *and* as product—into the categories of "academic" and "creative." While on their surface, these classifications may seem unsurprising, we show that, examined more closely, these terms function as a kind of shorthand for much larger questions and struggles, and thus offer an instructive window onto students' emerging beliefs about writing development and their identities as writers. In this chapter, we explore how these categories point to different constructs of development—growth in an "academic" domain or in a "creative" domain—and how these categories thus structure two distinctive ways for students to explore rhetorical awareness, to think about transfer and genre, and to conceptualize a writerly self in both school contexts and other spaces.

As we argue, the students who align their writing development with the "academic" tend to see writing as constituting the *communication* of thought; they thus define writing development as the provable, product-based, context-sensitive mastery of specific and often static disciplinary forms, as illustrated by their ability to reproduce these forms (similar to what Ryan McCarty discusses in chapter 4 of this volume). Meanwhile, students who talked about their growth as writers as more closely tied to the "creative" tend to understand writing instead as constituting the *generation* of thought; these students thus define writing development through their increased ability to produce new, relatively original, and often personally relevant ideas and texts.

Moreover, students' talk also implies that students see these two concepts of writing and writing development as weighted with different educational value. For some students, the academic is the premiere construct of writing forwarded by their college course work, which school has allowed them to develop *into*. In this framework, communication through reproducible and often discipline-specific forms is the main mark of the kind of development their college career has encouraged. For others, however, the academic represents the construct that the more "creative" work of their college education in writing has allowed them, fruitfully, to develop *out of*. By this process, students' "creative" growth beyond the academic stands as the main mark of this alternate strand of development, even as such development continues to take place in a college context. That said, students' talk also reveals a number of these two constructs' shortcomings and blind spots, perhaps most significantly in the strict binary through which a number of students discuss these two views of writing and the apparently mutually exclusive kinds of writing development they appear to entail. For most students interviewed, the academic and the creative seemed to represent approaches to writing and constructs of development that were not only separable but irreconcilable. Only among a small number of students did a third construct emerge, which we will explore in the final section of this chapter: an integrative vision of how these paradigms of writing and of writing development might work more in tandem, signaling the self-conscious negotiations these students saw themselves as staging between the generative forces of invention and the pressures of communicative norms.

Of course, such patterns in student talk might be interpreted in some alternate ways. One might understand "creative" and "academic" most transparently as only representing large-scale genre divisions: between the scholarly and school-based genres of traditional disciplinary fields, on the one hand, and varieties of fiction, poetry, and creative nonfiction on the other. Indeed, these are the very genre-based categories maintained by our own university's English department, which—like many English departments across the United States—presumes a clear and bright line between its first-year writing program, which centers on "academic" writing and inquiry, and its creative-writing program, which centers on literary and essayistic productions. However, given the capacious way our study participants were sorting their writing into these categories—and connecting these categories to their development as writers—this analysis does not quite satisfy; students did not use these terms only to signify specific fields or contexts and the genres these contexts typically espouse. Nor do students' use of "academic" and "creative" seem to indicate what Michael Carter has identified as "meta-genres," which he aligns with larger metadisciplinary "ways of doing" (385) (such as "performance" or "empirical inquiry," e.g., 394). Though many students' use of "creative" and "academic" descriptors includes gestures toward genres, and especially toward those textual features and forms that, by Amy Devitt's description, "trace" the existence of genre (575), such taxonomies of genres and metagenres do not fully capture the way these categories of "academic" and "creative" seem to function for our study participants.

Another explanation of these creative and academic paradigms might draw on Linda Bergmann and Janet Zepernick's 2007 study of students' perceptions of first-year writing. Unlike the genre-based distinctions outlined above, these researchers found students distinguishing *all* English course work, including for first-year writing, as "creative" (130), and found students placing this kind of writing work in sharp contrast to "the important work of professional socialization that occurs in their 'content-area' courses" (138) (and which our participants might classify as "academic"). Even more striking, Bergmann and Zepernick found that these distinctions indicated students' perceptions of these writing types' different levels of transferability—with "creative" and process-focused constructs of writing and instruction transferring little across fields, and the more academic, discipline-specific kinds carrying over productively into new contexts. Yet this framework does not fully explain the patterns we found in our study participants' talk, either. To be sure, Bergmann and Zepernick found students relying on dichotomous language notably similar to what we observed, yet our participants did not align these terms so categorically with negative or positive instances of transfer. Further, many students, like Joy, did not see the "creative" as confined only to English or first-year writing (or, indeed, to its particular "genres"); instead, many presented the "creative" as a larger, context-transcending construct of writing itself that was applicable across a variety of fields—as with Joy's suggestion that her political science instructor should have allowed a fellow student's "creative" tweaking of certain disciplinary norms. Indeed, when Joy promotes the "creative," she also acknowledges the importance of what she calls "train[ing]" in academic forms: as she says, "I'm not saying [instructors] should dismiss the structured writing because students do need to learn that." Unlike Bergmann and Zepernick's findings, we argue that for many of our study participants, even though they do not always have clear and concise language at hand to discuss these patterns and distinctions, these different constructs of writing and development enable different *types* of transfer—one reliant on recurrent written forms, the other on a durable writerly self.

In many ways, Jean Anyon's foundational 1981 study of students' perceptions of knowledge and its sources provides perhaps the best precedent for our findings. Anyon's investigation of students from three very different US school systems leads her to distinguish two main paradigms within which these students operate: "reproductive" constructs of knowledge (31), which reinforce existing practices and norms, and more "transformative" constructs of knowledge, which, as she writes, instead cultivate the "creative" and learners' abilities to "think for themselves" (36). We do not here pursue the crucial issue of social class that Anyon also analyzes through this framework; but her larger categories are still germane. Like the constructs that Anyon identifies in her students' talk, the constructs we identify are often implicit or still emerging. Indeed, we read our participants' talk about "creative" and "academic" kinds of writing and development as placeholders for larger concepts for which these students have little vocabulary—and little opportunity—to otherwise explain and explore. Even so, the concepts we find these students grappling toward show a significant similarity to the two school-based frameworks of knowledge production that Anyon also identifies, and our study showcases the more specific implications these frameworks have for students' varied understanding of writing and of their own writing development, across their college experience.

As such, the classifications of writing development we explore in this chapter emerged not from our own predetermined categories, but from students' own talk when they were asked about kinds of writing and their development as writers while in college. In this, we follow recent research that has begun to explore issues of transfer, genre, and development from students' points of view (e.g., Fraizer; Reiff and Bawarshi; Lindeman). Further, and although we open here with the specific instance of Joy, our discussion draws from broader patterns observed across our study participants' varied taxonomies of their own writing and the kinds of writing development they espouse. Through their talk about kinds of writing, and about "creative" and "academic" kinds more specifically, we strove to capture the larger tendencies implicit in students' suggested or stated constructs of writing and writing development.

Finally, a note on our methodological approach to these study participants. The patterns we describe in this chapter—which we found through an analysis of all entry and exit interviews with students who completed the interview portion of our study—do not split tidily between students enrolled in the Sweetland Minor in Writing Program and those who were nonminors. In the interest of drawing larger conclusions about the relations between constructs of writing and constructs of development common across both populations, we deliberately resisted analyzing our data by those divisions. That is not to say, however, that we found no signs that different curricula had affected these trends. A greater number of students in the first, "academic" category—who saw writing and writing development as entailing mainly learned competence in the genre-specific communication of thought—tended to be nonminors, whose writing-intensive course work involved mainly writing-in-the-disciplines courses. A greater number of the students in the second, "creative" category—who saw writing development as entailing competence in the generation of thought, and who emphasized the development of a highly personal writerly identity—tended (including Joy) to be writing minors, whose course work also included writing classes detached from a specific disciplinary affiliation beyond writing studies itself.

Moreover, the students falling into our third category—who were beginning to describe their development as the integration of both these domains of writing—also tended to be writing minors, and they often praised the space that the minor courses provided for processing these different constructs. Nonetheless, these population patterns were not hard and fast. The fact that these patterns do not entirely align with minor/nonminor distinctions, combined with the fact that minors were themselves split between championing a more exclusively "creative" construct and a more integrative construct, suggests that these tendencies are not merely a by-product of the disciplinary training that the writing minor provides; instead, these may be larger cultural patterns of thought that writing instructors of all kinds could more effectively acknowledge and harness.

"You Have to Write Like That": The "Academic" Construct of Writing Development

For many of our study participants, the most common way to classify and discuss their development as writers was to talk about writing within specific courses or disciplines and writing that closely followed distinct school-based structures. Across interviews for this study, students commonly spoke about their comfort with writing a "research paper," for instance, or with experiences writing lab reports for science courses. Consider, for instance, Courtney's assessment of her own writing growth to begin to examine this view of writing development, one in which students describe writing not as an opportunity to generate new ideas, but as the necessity to replicate existing ideas and information—what we describe here as writing that functions for the *genre-specific communication of thought.*

During her exit interview, conducted as she approached graduation, Courtney discusses her experiences with writing as almost exclusively following highly prescriptive and standardized approaches to "academic" forms of writing. In contrast to Joy, Courtney framed writing development as adherence to perceived rules and formats, and she significantly set issues of exploration, or the "creative," in stark opposition to this work:

> Every class I've essentially taken, I've never been asked to do creative writing, necessarily. Every paper I've always had to write for any class has always been for a specific purpose. Like, "Argue this." Very structured-type things. . . . I'm like, "I have probably written 100 papers since I've come here." They're all so similar, that it's like, once you get the hang of it, they—it's so easy.

In Courtney's reflection on her growth as a writer during college, this kind of "structured-type" writing serves as evidence for her writing development, and she attributes that development to repeated practice, or the idea that "once you get the hang of it . . . it's so easy." In this view, writing development is closely linked to knowledge of, and historical experience with, various types of school-based assignments and their attendant audience expectations.

Indeed, this can describe one distinct strand of writing development as entailing students' mastery—often through the kind of repeated practice that Courtney recounts—of what Linda Adler-Kassner and Elizabeth Wardle have referred to as the "recognizable forms" of school-based writing (35–47). This understanding of writing and writing development can contribute to a clear sense of self-efficacy in student writers as they begin to see themselves taking on writerly identities tied to their fields of academic and professional interest and begin to show ownership over the kinds of writing most often practiced and valued in those fields. Importantly, this view of writing development also points to distinct kinds of rhetorical knowledge, as students come to recognize specific audiences and purposes for the writing that they commonly describe as academic. For many students, this implies a kind of transfer tightly tied to the knowledge of conventions—as when Courtney expresses self-assurance in her ability to successfully reprise structured academic forms, which she sees as easy to duplicate.

Yet as students themselves identify in some instances, this form of writing development also can be weighted by certain constraints. For students who viewed writing development primarily as the successful reproduction of specific academic forms of writing, a clear binary existed between writing that allowed for expression of new ideas and the generation of new knowledge, on the one hand, and on the other, writing that we came to identify as existing primarily to record or communicate highly localized and genre-specific thoughts or information. Indeed, these students often saw themselves as highly capable students and thinkers, but they generally did not see their skill as writers as traveling across strictly drawn boundaries.

Rather, students who tracked their growth as writers primarily around "academic" kinds of writing reflected surprisingly narrow beliefs about the possibilities and power of writing. They commonly saw themselves as "writers" only in the sense that they were able to successfully write for school assignments, and they commonly located evidence of success in writing externally—in an instructor, a grade, or in comparison to other students' work. These restrictions also reflected the scant freedom, and scant sense of coherent writerly identity, that these students felt, as discussed by Dana in an exit interview conversation near graduation:

> I would say that as a writer my main focus has been academically. I'm not a free writer. I don't know. I'm still in the period of deciding if I call myself a writer or not. Most of my experience with writing has been purely academic, but for internships or stuff like

> that I have done some other types of writing. I guess I would just call myself a student writer, if that makes sense.

Dana explicitly connects her growth to academic forms of writing and aligns it with her tendency to bar other forms of writerly identity. She not only rejects the idea of herself as a "free" writer, she even hesitates to call herself a writer more generally. Indeed, Dana shows little understanding of the ways that her strengths as a "student writer" may have transferred to professional spaces ("for internships") or to other extracurricular contexts.

Talk such as Dana's suggests that students who approach writing primarily as the communication of thought also commonly show intense concern with form and structure, and such students saw little possibility that these forms or structures might be applicable to other purposes or contexts—not just outside of school, but even in other academic contexts. Chassi, for example, states with confidence in her exit interview that "sociology requires you to analyze. I don't really see much of that in psychology." In this way, some students suggest that the apparently autonomous nature of these disciplinary categories implies a rigid exclusivity, in which any specific "kind of writing" appears applicable *only* to a specific academic field; and in which their writerly growth, in turn, is restricted to that same space. Ashley, for instance, in her exit interview, describes the writing requirements for a movement science class as helping her perfect the kinds of writing required distinctly for that discipline and its typical requirements, but as good for little else, especially any affective or personal sense of accomplishment:

> I didn't enjoy that class very much actually. It's just a little dry because it was the same thing over and over again. The style is just very—it's so straightforward and so—you have to do it the same way every time. I just got a little bored with it. I can see the value in it because if you ever wanna do research or write scientific papers, you have to write like that.

For Ashley, development as a writer has involved mastery largely through reproduction, and she ties this reproductive quality implicitly to academic writing, in which forms are seen as static, predetermined, and uncontested ("you have to write like that"), rather than being shaped by potentially shifting exigencies or values.

Also suggestive of the link (or absence of a link) students seemed to feel between genres and transfer is the trend among students to fail to see that the writing they do in courses even counts as "writing." When asked in her entry interview about the "opportunity to do writing in your field," Eva responds,

> I've done—okay, so for Econ this semester, I've done some article responses, so those are small pieces of writing that refer back to what we've learned, so I wouldn't call them really writing not much, just getting the concepts across that we learned more.

For this student, the textual productions required in her course work stand less as a constructive activity she would call "writing" than as the transparent communication of discipline-specific knowledge ("just getting across the concepts"). This suggests that, in this student's mind, these assignments do not draw on one or another set of generalizable conventions but represent the pure transmission of information. Moreover, some students aligning themselves with this construct of development voiced explicit discomfort about writing assignments that strayed beyond the familiar boundaries of the academic. Asked in her exit interview about how confident she felt as a writer as she neared graduation, Teresa holds tightly to beliefs about herself as a writer within the framework of her academic concentration:

> My major is business, so I think in professional writing or academic writing, I'm a little more confident because it's not so much about my opinion as just, "Oh, this is the argument that I'm trying to prove." Here is my hypothesis, my thesis. These are my supporting evidence. Maybe have a counterargument and the wrap-up.

For this student, a sense of writing development and sense of self-efficacy seems achieved less through the expression of her own perspective or "opinion" and more through the mastery of argumentative forms and conventions.

Further, we found that this adherence to disciplinary boundaries and belief in writing development as the communication of genre-specific thoughts was often linked to related moments of uncertainty for student writers, especially when they anticipate how the writing will be evaluated by an external reader. The belief that writing should be crafted for a singular reader—the professor, for instance, or the employer—arose commonly among students who understood their writing development through this academic construct. These students could be seen using largely reproductive strategies to meet the perceived demands of those external audiences, a move that further restricts the purpose of writing only to the communication of information. Consider, for instance, Jake, who—identifying in his entry interview "writing that I do work on and spend time with" as "just mainly an academic thing"—spoke about some of his early experiences writing within his major area as well as upcoming deadlines to produce professional letters. Jake says that, "I feel confident that I can write effectively for the things I'm interested in. Within the classes, it depends, just 'cause the thing that frustrates me the most about writing in college: it's different professors want different things. Sometimes it's hard to anticipate that."

Jake's response is compelling both for the rhetorical understanding he demonstrates—here, awareness of audience—and for how it still stops short of recognizing the rhetorical principle of invention. Students who describe growth in writing as primarily growth in academic writing give nods to notions of purpose (responding to the prompt), of arrangement (addressing specific page requirements, for instance, or following standard formats), and of audience (most commonly, the instructor who has assigned the writing). Yet there is less explicit acknowledgement that writing, as an activity or product, might also persuade readers to adopt new perspectives, speak to multiple audiences, or help to shape the writer's own ideas.

When students measure their writing development by its success in meeting a purely academic end—that is, to pass a specific course or achieve a specific grade—they also view their own identities as writers as restricted to the defined spaces of school. Just as Dana calls herself a "student writer," other study participants also do not see space for themselves as professional writers, or more broadly as writers conveying ideas to a wider audience or in order to develop new knowledge. To be a strong academic writer, as expressed across many student interviews, is to master distinct formulas and the expectations of external reviewers. Consequently, writing development as framed by the academic also meant, for many students, that they needed to expressly set aside the creative—that is, the kinds of writing that they described as "free" or "personal." Indeed, many students frame their growth as writers in college and in college courses as expressly apart from creative forms of writing. Dariella, describing in her exit interview her experiences in an anthropology-biology course, talked about the class as requiring "just a giant research paper"—and she linked the formulaic nature of the assignments and expectations as explicitly disallowing the "creative," even as she acknowledged that the topic was left up to students to choose:

> I didn't [laughter] have to be super creative with how I wrote things. It was just divided into sections. It was, "Tell us about your species." "Tell us the feeding habits of your species." Like, "What are their mating habits?" . . . [T]he most creative liberty I had with it was like, "Talk about something that's interesting about your species that you chose."

Like Teresa saying "here is my hypothesis" and "these are my supporting evidence," this graduating senior tidily categorizes her past writing experience as the fulfillment of highly specific writing conventions. But significantly, this also proves to be a practice that to her was not particularly memorable or meaningful, at either a disciplinary or personal level. As we explore next, some students see more opportunity for personal exploration and meaningful development of ideas as involving a paradigm quite different from the academic. Building from a more "creative" construct of writing development, students suggest that they have found newly authentic ways to express themselves and to claim clearer authority over their own writing and ideas. Nonetheless, as we explore, this second construct of writing development carries its own constraints.

"The Chance to Make Up Your Own Everything": The "Creative" Construct of Writing Development

For many students, the alternate construct of writing development that they align with the "creative" entails seeing themselves as writers newly capable of producing original ideas that transcend what they frequently see as the rigidly disciplinary categories they understood an "academic" framework to require. Writing in and for this "creative" framework is therefore a distinctively epistemic construct, where writing serves as a thought-generating activity in its own right. As Olivia describes it in her exit interview, the "creative" means that you can "kind of give yourself permission to be kind of a crappy writer at times and follow these really interesting ideas." Such creative work is thus valuable not for its written products—laughing, she describes her creative work as the "kind that you try to bury under a stack of paper"—but because it allows for a process that is "more liberated and free" than other notions she holds of "how I should be writing academically." As this comment exemplifies, students sharing Olivia's view often position the "creative" as a liberating alternative to both the genre-bound "academic" domain and the specific kind of development this construct appeared to promote.

Unlike the writers of the previous section, who understand writing as the appropriate response to highly local and explicit readerly demands, a creative construct of writing and development implies a new attitude toward the sources of authority and the writer's construction of knowledge. In her exit interview during her senior year, Lauren describes creative exploration as writing that "causes you to get outside of the rigorous academic sometimes dry writing and get into something way more creative where you actually have to give a voice to someone that you have never met, someone that actually doesn't exist." For Lauren, this marks a dramatic break from past habits: "It's definitely a new way of thinking." The imaginative demands of such work result for many students in a newly constructivist view of evidence and a novel turn to internal rather than purely external criteria for a sense of validity. In the domain of the creative, writing is seen to be generative in and of itself, and as such, a healthy relief from more typically "academic" approaches: "It kinda is like a break," Lauren says. Indeed, the emphasis on invention seems, for Lauren, to create a propagative momentum of its own: as she argues, work within this domain feels like "I stepped out, got a creative breath of fresh air, which allowed me to continue writing."

Moreover, these students who talk about writing development as the ability to invent and explore also report more "personal" investment in their writing and the development of more durable identities as writers. For many, this is both freeing and enables transfer across new contexts; however, as we will also explore below, this construct appears for many students to also preclude more nuanced understandings of genre, especially through students' overemphasis on voice and independence from structure, and underemphasis on the shaping power of rhetorical exigency. In both freeing and limiting ways, then, the "creative" seems to suggest a form of development that students link most tightly to their writerly selves, and to writerly products and processes seen exclusively—and sometimes narrowly—through the lens of individual convictions. When Raquel, for example, describes herself in her exit interview writing "more personal reflection, personal narrative, creative non-fiction, and re-purposing essays," she offers as her sole example "an argumentative essay without any research, like you weren't allowed to do anything *so you had to just really develop your own ideas*" (emphasis added). For Raquel, this work is developmental not for enabling a new level of expertise in some preexistent knowledge domain, but for enabling more personal connections to the making of knowledge, and an attendant theory of invention:

> Obviously having evidence helps, but just helping develop your own tone and your style like that was really beneficial in just opening my eyes. Like if I view this topic and this is my opinion, I need to be able to explain why I view that before I even start backing it up, like how does that apply to my life, how do I relate to it.

As Raquel seems to understand it, this "creative" approach encourages her to explore how the writer and her topic interrelate, especially by emphasizing the writer's own experiences and beliefs. As such, the writing and developmental construct underlying this approach involves more than just communication through rhetorically effective (in this case, evidence-based) forms, but the realization and cultivation of one's own more personal perspective.

In this way, this construct of development also seems to encourage a more cohesive concept of the writerly self than their more "academic" experiences, with their apparent over-focus on formulaic concepts of genre. For these students—as echoed by many writers from the previous section—the academic construct of writing requires obedience to the outside prescriptions that Olivia describes as the internalized "mental picture of how I should be writing academically." In contrast to that construct, Olivia and Raquel suggest that certain more writer-centered concerns—personal relevance, associative processes, comfort with speculation—are an alternate means of achieving writerly development. Many students even saw their newly "creative" construct as a progressive development away from academic writing: developing away from the construct that Leo, for instance, implies in his exit interview is a kind of academic rule-following, and developing into a newly generative independence.

Indeed, Leo argues that before turning to the "creative," he was overly reliant on external criteria and formulas, to the detriment—as he sees it—of his own writerly self-conception: "I realized that I was taking inspiration from other writers and using their styles. Ultimately, I didn't know who I was as a writer." Subsequently, as he then explains, "I did a lot of creative non-fiction because I was thinking that that would help me figure out who I was as a writer." In short, the generative construct of writing that students align with the creative seems to enable a turn away from identifying only as what Dana called a "student writer" and toward a new ability to connect their writing to a highly individualized but newly coherent sense of writerly self.

Yet while a secure and durable sense of writerly identity can be a boon to writerly self-efficacy, many students' comments also illustrate how this epistemic construct of writing is often imagined to exist entirely independently of outside influence. In this way, it is a construct that verges close to an outright rejection of a social-rhetorical view of writing and the writer. For, in addition to positioning a new relationship to evidence and the writerly self, the "creative" also seems to posit a new skepticism about the "recognizable forms" that also shape written knowledge. For many students, writing activity that operates within this "creative" sphere rejects the academic sphere's apparent propensity for reproducing norms that already exist, so that, as Lauren puts it, "I'm not just strictly getting drawn out with the same academic jargon over and over and over again." Ashley, for example, who describes her senior year creative writing class as encouraging her to "explore a little bit more," presents this exploratory function as unbound by the kinds of generic knowledge her other academic experiences promoted. As she explains in an exit interview, "before this semester, I . . . wrote to a form, and, again, very straight forward"; however, "now I'm delving into more of a creative field, and I don't need a form as much as I did anymore."

In this way, the rigid mutual exclusion by which many students seem to understand these two writing constructs suggests that for many, these two strands of development impinge little on one another. Dan offers a powerful example in his entry interview of a student unaware of the extent to which his "creative" construct of writing and development may be affected by audience demands or by the reproduction of forms that he disavows because they entail overly "academic" modes of writing. Indeed, Dan understands his generative construct of writing and voice to require abandoning the "academic" formalism that many students see previous school experiences as having overemphasized. As Dan describes his first-year writing course, he draws hard distinctions between that formalism, on the one hand, and his teacher's apparent focus on fostering a more personal voice and more personal sources of authority, on the other:

> Well, I had a teacher my freshman year . . . and he's in the creative writing department. . . . He kicked my butt on one of my first papers, and I was like, "Oh, crap. This is gonna be a bad year already." . . . I did really poorly on that, and I talked with him, and I said, "Well, what have I gotta do?" He said, "I feel like you're trying to write this, and you are reinforced to write this. Just write it for me as you would say it." That was what helped make the differences, that I stopped realizing that I need to write something formal, and I can just write what I would say, or whatever I wanted, and it would be easier like that.

Dan understands his teacher as promoting an expressivist writing construct wherein "I can just write what I would say, or whatever I wanted" to achieve a new writerly fluency. And this approach, by Dan's telling, helps him foster a newly authentic and self-assured sense of himself as a writer. Further, Dan implies that this has a significant impact on his development and on his transfer of writing knowledge across contexts. For, as Dan argues, internalizing his teacher's advice means that

> [t]hen papers were easier to write. I could get them done quicker or I would be less stressed because I knew that I wasn't being forced, and that [the] professor wasn't looking for some strict style, he was just looking for you to make your point.

In Dan's understanding, his development involved moving beyond concerns with what he calls "strict style" and has meant instead embracing an idea-driven (or "point-driven") model of writing—similar to Raquel's claim that the "creative" forced her to attend less to outside evidence and more to the internal coherence of her own claims and beliefs. This construct of writing development thus has a crucial practical function for Dan, establishing a strong sense of self-efficacy that seems to encourage learning transfer across genres and fields. For just as Lauren explained that the creative provided a "breath of fresh air, allowed me to continue writing," Dan seems to understand this new focus on the discovery and expression of "what I would say" to promote the continuing cultivation of an authentic and confident writerly self. And this is a construct, Dan suggests, that affects all the work he produces for "professors," indicating that he views the construct as useful across school circumstances, even those that don't operate within the generically "creative" domain he affiliated with this particular teacher.[1]

Even so, and to return to Dan's original description of the influence of this teacher, Dan seems to understand such expressivism, and its implied construct of writing and development, in absolutist terms: as freeing him of any of the conventions he was previously taught, especially the prescriptive formalism his teacher seems to presume was encouraged by his past and even present schooling ("He said, 'I feel like you're trying to write this, and you are reinforced to write this. Just write it for me as you would say it'"). Indeed, Dan does not seem aware of the extent to which "writ[ing] what I would say, or whatever I wanted" still remains, in this course-specific case, just as shaped by audience expectation as was his more "formal" prior work. After all, and by his own description, Dan's first-year writing stays focused toward the particular demands of a teacher. Nor is this somewhat narrow view of audience complicated by this teacher; instead, at least by Dan's telling, this view is explicitly confirmed, as when he reports that his teacher has told him to "just *write it for me* as you would say it." Indeed, this small narrative reveals the unresolved tensions inside many students' understanding of this "creative" construct of writing in which Dan continues to define his writerly purpose by one reader's preferences, even while he imagines that its "creative" nature engenders total freedom from such fetters. As such, it remains significant that Dan continues to present this construct as entirely separable from the academic formalism of his previous educational experiences: it does not provide fresh nuance to his understanding of rhetorical exigency, but instead encourages an apparently outright rejection of his previously "forced" and "stressful" attention to readers' formal expectations.

Indeed, one wonders what Dan might do with a curriculum such as that in Ashley's movement science class ("you have to [write it] the same way over and over")—and whether his freedom from "forced" and "stressful" writing constructs would survive when confronted with more stringently convention-bound course work or future professional demands. One possibility is that students like Dan are self-selecting courses that allow these "creative" constructs of writing and development to flourish unchallenged. The exit interview comments of another study participant, Tim, suggest that, for other students, this notion of highly personal and autonomous invention might actually prove inapplicable to all other college course work. What Tim understands as the creative domain's "chance to make up your own everything" represents an option, in his description, that "I never really applied . . . to anything else." For Tim, then, this "aspect of making everything"—which he here aligns with a fiction-writing course—did not transfer. While he nods vaguely to the notion that such writing "made it more well-rounded, I guess," he also argues that the kind of writing it promoted did not travel to other contexts. Instead, "it was kind of just a unique experience in itself."

What remains consistent among Dan and Tim, and among the students such as Ashley who are more inclined to identify purely with an academic construct of development, is that the academic and the creative constructs of writing and writerly development appear for them entirely incompatible. For Tim and Ashley, they do not travel or transfer usefully across contexts; for Dan, transfer only occurs when one (the "creative") completely subsumes the other. Again, this incompatibility may be attributed to students' understanding of the differences between genres and disciplines themselves, as when Shannon explains that "I guess I can mold my style to any different venue or audience and purpose for what I'm writing," and that, if she is writing a "creative, non-fiction piece, I can put my voice into more and have my personality show through"; in contrast, "If it's a research academic paper, I know to be more formal in tone and to cite studies." At one level, comments like this merely illustrate a commonsensical kind of genre-sensitive rhetorical savvy—writing knowledge that is a mark of development in and of itself. But it remains significant that these constructs continue to be understood by many students in such tidily binary terms, requiring the student to simply swap out an "academic" emphasis on "form" and outside evidence for a "creative" emphasis on "voice" and "personality." By hewing to such a neat equation, students such as Shannon also leave unexplored the formal, audience-sensitive elements that help shape invention and creative expression, and the sense of personal investment and genuine inquiry that gives disciplinary work its argumentative traction.

To be sure, the experiences and ideas these students relate show the real constraints that many students understand genre-based academic work to impose on their writerly selves. Moreover, their comments reflect the hunger many students seem to feel for the alternate construct of writing and the writer that this creative domain can promote: a constructive, epistemic view of knowledge, and the self-discovery project implicit in the activity of putting personally significant words on a page. Nonetheless, interview data also show how difficult it appears to be for many students to reconcile these two constructs of the creative and the academic, or to see them as dialogically related. Whether discussing transfer, or genre, or voice, students show a stubborn propensity to entirely replace the features implicit in one for the features implicit in the other, instead of understanding these constructs of writing and strands of development as possibly intertwined and even mutually constitutive. In the next section, we consider the experiences of students who are beginning to put these two domains of writing development into conversation—and into action.

Integrating the Academic and the Creative: A Third Construct of Writing Development

Across the study, many students could be seen classifying themselves, more or less neatly, within the two domains—the academic or the creative—that we have operationalized in this chapter to frame constructs of writing development. Yet the study data also point to a third, more integrative construct of writing development, one that appears to allow students to move beyond some of the constraints that either of the two spheres we have discussed here presents. Within this third construct, we saw students who were able to recognize and draw from both creative and academic forms and experiences in the ways they conceptualized writing assignments and themselves as writers.

Indeed, this finding adds a new dimension to Rebecca Nowacek's concept of "agents of integration." Nowacek's work sees students as integrating knowledge of different genres to enable transfer across writing contexts and to develop new abilities and writing identities. Here, we find students doing integrative work at an even more conceptual level: integrating different constructs of writing and development themselves, the one defined by its knowledge of disciplinary norms, the other defined by a more self-reliant form of invention. In this third, blended construct of writing development, students negotiate between views of writing and their writerly growth as entailing both generative activity and adherence to communicative norms, instead of viewing these approaches as requiring an either-or choice. We thus conclude with a discussion of students who appeared to operate in what we call an *academic-creative hybrid*. These students appear to understand writing and their development in more capacious ways than their peers—even, as we note, when they struggle to describe and discuss this work with the same ease that others display through their neat taxonomies of the academic and the creative.

We see three distinct strengths of this more integrative approach for student writers. First, students discuss writing tasks and opportunities in ways that display greater confidence and agentive power than students who framed writing development within the domain of either the academic *or* the creative. Next, these students display greater flexibility within given contexts and, as important, they appear able to more easily navigate the transfer of writing skills across different spaces and among different forms. Finally, these students are able to reflect on writing as both a topic and a tool and can discuss development in terms of both their conceptions of themselves as writers and the varied roles that writing might play in their lives.

As discussed at the outset of this chapter, students who fit in this more expansive category of writing development also tend to be those who minor in writing. This pattern probably reflects the influence of the these students' course work, including projects (described in **appendix 2**) that explicitly require students to think across disciplinary boundaries regarding how they conceive of and present writing, and to be open to broad reconceptualizations of their own writing and their approach to writing. Students in the writing minor, for instance, are asked in one assignment to repurpose a piece of writing into a different form or medium; they also are asked to transfer written work into digital formats through online portfolios and Capstone projects. This course work also includes frequent self-reflection assignments, encouraging students to gain more meta-awareness of their own writing processes, the forms in which they write, and their sense of writerly self-efficacy. Still, it is relevant to note that this construct of development was something also forwarded by some students who were not writing minors. Indeed, a number of exceptions existed in which students from a range of disciplines could be seen working to find ways to bridge their understanding—and their use—of academic and creative forms in their writing practice.

Students operating within this hybrid construct of writing development were more likely to indicate that they see various "kinds of writing" not as repetitive practice in one or another narrowly conceived skill set or form, but as an open-ended exploration of rhetorical features and generative strategies. These students discussed writing as an opportunity for growth that transcended the narrow confines of course requirements, or even the larger academic setting, and they thus framed their own development neither as bound by specific disciplinary conventions nor as tied to absolute creative freedom. This more expansive view of how we grow as writers indicates that these students imagine their own development as a kind of movement across and beyond the categories that other students' taxonomies of "kinds of writing" might suggest are sealed off.

The way these students talk about writing is especially instructive regarding the forms of respectful and relative independence they see themselves as having achieved as writers. They can acknowledge the powers of local audience awareness or a situation's "recognizable forms" while also showing a new willingness to navigate among, rather than entirely capitulate to, these forces or reject them altogether. Moreover, and as a mark of development, students suggest that this new construct supports their growth into newly "confident" and agentic writers, able to respond to discrete assignments yet also able to restructure some formats or preconceived notions of what successful writing looks like in a range of contexts and categories. Near graduation, in her exit interview, Stephanie discusses writing development in terms of her ability to form arguments that deviate, at points, from expected responses, and she explains this as resulting in a newfound confidence:

> I think just, yeah, being able to shape my ideas independently—that's really how they affected me. As far as, as I practiced and as I became more confident as a writer, I was also becoming more independent, especially in the ideas, where I'm not afraid to take a different stance than a professor, and say, "Hey, maybe you are wrong in this." I'm not gonna change your opinion, but, hey, let's pretend that you would for a second. That independence has really helped.

Stephanie's willingness to imagine that she might "change" her professor's opinion is a sign of her faith in writing as a means of generating new ideas that have possibly transformative consequences in the world. Yet she does not understand this generative power as existing in a vacuum; such "independence" is shaped, instead, by a deep familiarity with her professor's own "stance," and an understanding of how she might position herself accordingly. For her, then, this "independence" is not absolute, but contingent; it functions as a belief that she can intervene in known opinions and may be able to reshape existing ideas. Likewise, Grace, in her entry interview, draws together expertise in math with exploration in English to rethink the ways that writing is shaped but not rigidly bound by the "recognizable forms" through which it communicates, as Anna Knutson (chapter 9) also explores. Grace's cheerful analysis admits the complications of this understanding and of carrying it out in practice, as can be seen in her detailed parsing of the terms "system," "formula," and "organization"—the two former terms functioning as markers of the conceptual rules in the discipline of math, and the latter describing the notion of a structure that is legible yet unfettered by strict formulas and that she aligns with the "art" of writing:

> With math you're just like, "Well, I have to put this variable on this side of the equation first," and then there's a system. When you're writing there is no system. As a writer, my writing had always been really formulaic . . . [But] writing is a kind of art and shouldn't

> be so formulaic. It's something that has to be creative—but also can't be all over the place. It has to be organized, and then I'm always trying to figure out how to match the creativity with the organization. It takes me forever to write!

In their comments, each of these students demonstrates an approach to writing that reflects confidence not only in their own skills and preparation as writers, but in their ability to rethink what others might see as constraining forms of writing in order to explore new ideas or generate new knowledge. These students recognize the value of form and organization in this exploration, but they draw from a mix of disciplinary experiences and broader ways of conceiving writing. And when Grace closes with the quip that "It takes me forever to write," we also see students' recognition that this hybrid approach to writing development is not easier or faster; nonetheless, they show themselves to be remarkably invested in the work of writing and in the power it holds for them.

Students whose talk about writing development puts the domains of the academic and the creative in conversation also show greater flexibility in their ability to transfer skills and approaches to writing across courses and disciplines, and between academic and nonacademic contexts. Stephanie, for instance, pointed in an exit interview to an insurance course as allowing her to recognize the broad potential reach of writing:

> I think that the class really—it taught me that there is more to math than just math. That really is where it bridged my math and my English majors. . . . Saying that the skills that I was learning in the English classes weren't going to be tossed on the wayside in the math world. That knowing how to analyze and explain situations through writing is definitely necessary, especially in the insurance business.

As they make sense of new kinds of writing and in various school, personal, and professional settings, students who view the academic and the creative in tandem also display awareness of the ways that that their development as writers reaches across boundaries that may seem more restrictive to other emerging writers. In many ways, this is achieved through developing a more durable sense of writerly self whose skills and sense of self-efficacy remain relatively consistent across contexts. Ayanna explained in her exit interview her gradual move away from thinking about writing in exclusively school-based terms in this way:

> Most of the writing I did when I started at Michigan was very much for school, and it was very much driven by the classes I took and the topics I encountered that way. Now,

> I think, coming out of Michigan I've developed writing more as a personal hobby as well, alongside the class stuff, and I think I've broadened my view of writing a bit more. I think before, writing for me was mostly, like, five-paragraph essays and a lotta papers, and now there's much more of a reflective component about it. It's less about writing about other people, which I still do, but finding myself within the writing, too, I think, I've realized more now than I did before.

This expanded construct of writing development reflects connection to personal purpose and exploration. For Ayanna, thinking of "writing as writing" allows a construct of writing development that makes space for reflection and allows a personal sense of purpose to interact with rhetorical demands.[2] Naomi Silver's chapter in this volume further explores Ayanna's emerging sense of writerly identity and its connections to the explicit work of reflecting on writing that Ayanna engages through the eportfolio process.

In these reflective comments, students who can discuss their own writing as drawing from both academic and creative constructs point, finally, to an understanding of a wider role for writing in their lives and to stronger self-conceptualizations as writers. More broadly, their comments highlight the ways that the exploration and integration of different constructs of writing allow students to use writing for broader purposes and to see themselves more fully as writers. Another study participant, Mike, echoes this idea in his exit interview, discussing the importance of helping students to recognize that "what they're doing everyday, whether they realize it or not, is valuable writing—so how we talk with our friend and text, and how we write little notes or how we organize our thoughts." As students bridge writing experiences that they sense are more academic or more creative, their development can be defined by their new ability to operate across contexts in more flexible and confident ways. This same pattern extends as well to how students integrate disciplinary with extracurricular knowledge in their upper-level college writing, as explored in more detail in McCarty's chapter in this volume.

Finally, Mike's comment—however unwittingly—also points to the complexity of this hybrid approach to considering student writing development. When Mike suggests that students are gaining rhetorical flexibility "whether they realize it or not," he indicates how enormously difficult it can be for students to envision themselves in this integrated space, one in which they cannot rely on reductive notions of themselves as strong "academic" writers or free and expansive "creative" writers. For instance, even as Jonah discussed "overlaps" between various kinds of writing in his entry interview—and hinted at his own growth within that blended space—he also voiced his own uncertainty:

> There's more than overlap between different English types of writing than there is between science writing. The lab report versus, I don't know what exactly it was, but it was like a report on a society. There's a lot of difference between those, 'cause one you're citing sources, you're still trying to make an argument, but it's a concise argument. The lab report is just a write-up of facts, whereas English writing kind of spans. I mean, I'm getting more confident at it, but I'm not 100 percent there.

While not "100 percent there," Jonah is working hard to articulate the ways that clearly distinct kinds of writing—"English types" and "science writing"—are both characterized as types of "report," in both of which "you're still trying to make an argument." The difference is one he seems to intuitively sense, and we can see him beginning to discern the push-and-pull between discipline-specific writing approaches and the fact that these approaches may be drawn from more generalizable rhetorical moves and goals. Ultimately, this gray space—and the more complex negotiation it requires of students (and of their instructors across disciplines)—may point toward richer and more lasting growth in college student writing.

And it is perhaps most important to remember how difficult it seems to be for many of our articulate and enthusiastic participants to recognize and embrace this gray space as a productive integration of these academic and creative constructs. One of our core arguments is that many of these students' taxonomies are not attributable to the writing minor curriculum alone, although that curriculum may well have helped to crystallize certain patterns of thought. Instead, we would suggest that these categorizing tendencies emerge from a larger lack of available constructs with which students can conceptualize in a genuinely dialogic way both the generative and the reproductive kinds of activity entailed in writing. The student who opened our chapter, Joy, also provides an apt coda for this argument; like many of her peers, she seems to be groping toward a new construct of writing that could help her transcend the polarizing categories through which she currently understands her own work and development. For her, in fact, like many of the students quoted here, these overarching domains of the "academic" and the "creative" appear to emerge from a base-level frustration with how academic writing, consciously or not, is most broadly presented in school contexts—as a inflexible construct determined exclusively by static formulas and an overly local sense of audience (the instructor). For these students, this construct fails to engage notions of invention or the writerly self, and thus creates a vacuum that only a radically defined "creative" domain, focused instead on epistemic activity alone, can fill. Or so Joy forcefully argues when asked what researchers into undergraduate writing development ought to consider when designing curricula:

> I guess they could learn that there is a student dissatisfaction with the very structured academic writing. I remember in the class [in the minor] . . . I brought up the point that, for example, in my poli sci class, the teacher really suppressed creativity. Everyone seemed to agree with that. . . . It's just, I guess they could learn that students need freedom to develop as a writer. It's great to train them in professional writing. I'm not saying they should dismiss the structured writing because students need to learn that. . . . It just seems like there's not many opportunities for creative thinking throughout the Michigan curriculum in general.

Significantly, Joy's statement, by its end, moves from the realm of writing to the realm of thought, and to the need to teach a kind of "creative thinking" that many students believe an over-focus on "academic writing" has somehow edged out. That said, and as these students' talk also illustrates, an overly extreme shift to the "creative" construct of writing and development risks, in its turn, students' discounting the rich rhetorical knowledge that an "academic" focus on genre and audience has also provided. The challenge for writing studies, as we see it, is therefore to provide students with more integrative language and constructs for students' own sense of their writing and their development as writers, in which the generation *and* the communication of thought through writing can be experienced and understood to always be working in tandem.

NOTES

1. Anne Ruggles Gere's discussion, in chapter 10, of Dan's postgraduate musings on the significance of peer feedback—and his regret about having disregarded peer feedback for much of his college career—suggests that Dan's postgraduate experiences as a workplace writer have given him new insight into the social nature of writing. In his new professional context, Dan's sense of the creative may likewise have developed from the individualism implied here to a more situation-sensitive acknowledgment of the shaping powers of genre and form.

2. Ayanna's ability to think through "writing as writing"—and her attempts to disentangle "*writing* writing" from multimodal communications, as glossed in Silver's chapter (chap. 8, this vol.)—can be attributed to the self-reflective realm the writing minor provides. In many ways, this realm is similar to the "'third space' environment" that Fraizer recommends for developing college-level writers: "where writers can reflect across disciplinary boundaries and generalize about what they're learning outside of the activity system of their work in progress" (52).

WORKS CITED

Adler-Kassner, Linda, and Elizabeth Wardle. *Naming What We Know: Threshold Concepts of Writing Studies*. Boulder: University Press of Colorado, 2015.

Anyon, Jean. "Social Class and School Knowledge." *Curriculum Inquiry*, vol. 11, no. 1, 1981, pp. 3–42.

Bergmann, Linda, and Janet Zepernick. "Disciplinarity and Transference: Students' Perceptions of Learning to Write." *WPA: Writing Program Administration*, vol. 31, no. 1–2, 2007, pp. 124–49.

Carter, Michael. "Ways of Knowing, Doing, and Writing in the Disciplines." *College Composition and Communication*, vol. 58, no. 3, 2007, pp. 385–418.

Devitt, Amy J. "Generalizing about Genre: New Conceptions of an Old Concept." *College Composition and Communication*, vol. 44, no. 4, 1993, pp. 573–86.

Fraizer, Dan. "First Steps Beyond First Year: Coaching Transfer After FYC." *WPA: Writing Program Administration*, vol. 33, no. 3, 2010, pp. 34–57.

Lindenman, Heather. "Inventing Metagenres: How Four College Seniors Connect Writing across Domains." *Composition Forum*, vol. 31, 2015.

Nowacek, Rebecca. *Agents of Integration: Understanding Transfer as a Rhetorical Act*. Southern Illinois University Press, 2011.

Reiff, Mary Jo, and Anis Bawarshi. "Tracing Discursive Resources: How Students Use Prior Genre Knowledge to Negotiate New Writing Contexts in First-Year Composition." *Written Communication*, vol. 28, no. 3, 2011, pp. 31.

CHAPTER FOUR

COMPLICATING THE RELATIONSHIP BETWEEN DISCIPLINARY EXPERTISE AND WRITING DEVELOPMENT

Ryan McCarty

ARIANA: *I think that the fact that I took—I've taken courses all over the place. I've taken econ. I've taken sciences. I've taken poli sci. I've taken English. I've taken Hebrew classes. All these different disciplines. Learning how to read and write within those disciplines, I think that I learned that good writing changes depending on the situation and the academic discipline.*

INTERVIEWER: *Do you consider yourself better at one kind of writing than another, depending on the class?*

ARIANA: *No. I think that I don't know if I necessarily adapt to these different writing styles because it's not like I'm a professional in one of these fields. I don't really think that I'm better at one just because I don't think I know enough about one to really write in that style.*

One of the difficulties with discussions of writing development is that development is often conflated (or at least talked about in tandem) with theories of disciplinary expertise, a tendency that might not align well with the views of a student like Ariana, who sensed that she was developing writing abilities that differed across settings, but without actually developing—or even necessarily seeking—expertise in any particular disciplinary context. Instead, she reflects that her development as a writer hinged on her ability to learn to distinguish between the ways that writing and its varied forms are enacted in different contexts for different purposes. It is this broad array of writing experiences, not an in-depth focus on one site of writing, that characterizes her sense of what it means to learn and write in college. So it seems that at least in the case of Ariana—a successful student by most institutional standards, graduating with a 3.74 undergraduate GPA and acceptance into the University of Michigan medical school—there is very little evidence that she would agree with conventional wisdom about writing development that tends to focus on students' abilities to move from novice to expert status in one distinct academic context.

However, the centrality of this conflation of development and expertise can be found in some of the most important work of the discipline. Mary Soliday discusses the ways that professors in the disciplines share their genre expertise, illustrating how this helps students develop discipline-specific features in their writing. In their reading of the findings of the National Research Council–sponsored *How People Learn*, Kathleen Yancey, Liane Robertson, and Kara Taczak argue that, while gaining expertise might be an ephemeral pursuit, writing development consists mainly of developing the often highly specialized expert practices common to a particular context (38–42). Similarly, Anne Beaufort notes that what someone looking to gain "writing expertise is ultimately concerned with is becoming engaged in a particular community of writers who dialogue across texts, argue, and build on each other's work" (18). In the tradition of studies in discourse communities and communities of practice, such conceptions of writing development position students in the complex role of negotiator among texts, mentors, and individual situations, all with the goal of learning to approximate a particular form of communicating. Nancy Sommers and Laura Saltz emphasize the importance of novice status in writing development, but note that this must eventually give way to a single disciplinary expertise, lest students become "globetrotters, moving from course to course, constantly breaking new ground in new subjects every time they write, never cultivating the disciplinary expertise in content and method that is necessary to question sources, develop ideas, and comfortably offer interpretations" (146). Chris Thaiss and Terry Myer Zawacki's three stages of writing development position student development as a progression toward understanding the methods, genres, epistemologies, and contents of a particular discipline. Writing development, it appears, is a question of picking a particular academic or professional language and style, then striving to gain fluency in it.

As we moved further into our longitudinal study, though, it became clear that this kind of target-language assumption, in which students see their writing development as a striving to develop unmarked fluency in one disciplinary academic language, was simply not what we were hearing from some participants or seeing in their writing. Students might agree with Beaufort that part of developing writing fluency means they "must also develop knowledge of genres whose boundaries and features the discourse community defines and stabilizes" (20). Zach, a pre-med student majoring in ecology and evolutionary biology and minoring in writing, emphasizes this kind of development in a reflection on his development as a writer, completed as part of the writing minor Capstone course: "I am now a perfectly well-adapted scientific writer, streamlined to convey concepts and findings in a concise and objective manner. . . . It has historically been a necessity to write this way in science in an effort to convince skeptical readers that your findings are based on truth rather than opinion." His sense of scientific writing is a common one, privileging concision and markers of objectivity and nodding toward the functional reasons that STEM writers have adopted those practices.

As his reflection continues, though, it becomes less clear that Zach is content to allow these genres and discourses to remain stabilized in the ways that Beaufort and others frame them vis-à-vis disciplinary expertise: "However, I believe that even more societal value can be drawn from scientific truths by conveying them in a way that draws on the passion of the audience, not just the rationality. As I have learned though, such an endeavor must be undertaken carefully and subtly so as not to distract from the empirical evidence." While he maintains the exigencies attached to presenting empirical evidence in scientific writing, Zach also insists that "good writing" consists of more than what he has learned about writing in the sciences. For this reason, he sought out different writing experiences by minoring in writing. The program's acceptance of genres that Zach did not often encounter in his STEM courses allowed him to develop other abilities to address a wider range of audiences and purposes.

As Zach's case illustrates, students often viewed their development as writers in ways that went far beyond the boundaries of expertise in particular settings, though it is important to reiterate that this is not necessarily because students cannot or are not willing to produce writing that conforms to the expectations of those settings when the situation requires it. Still, they frequently express the desire to infuse their writing with features of writing from other contexts—sometimes to satisfy the desire for narrower conceptions of personal voice, as Zak Lancaster describes in chapter 6 in this collection—but often to address what they perceive to be the needs of their audiences, as Zach's comments do. That is, for some students, writing development seems to entail both learning the practices expected for a particular situation and incorporating—or at least thinking about—other practices that might be useful for readers to either understand or appreciate the text. Accordingly, then, many students echo Beaufort's sense that real gains in writing expertise only happen "in the context of situational problem-solving" or through real-world "apprenticeship situations" (22). However, many students see this kind of disciplinary expertise as just one distinct knowledge that they integrate with other writing experiences in other contexts to form a larger sense of what it means to be a good writer.

Often, the recognition that they can leverage disciplinary expertise in other contexts is central to students' own narratives of their writing development. In case after case, we found students such as Leo, a minor who felt that his writing development was facilitated not only by a focus on disciplinary expertise, but also by reflecting on writing across his college experiences, as he notes in his exit interview: "I've become very self-aware of how I'm writing, and what I'm writing. I think that that has been a culmination of every class I've taken; little fragments of writing." Like Ariana, Leo views his writing experiences not as discrete and bounded by established disciplines, but as contributing to a sense of writing development that prioritizes dexterity and cross-connection. It is this view of writing development that I explore here: one that highlights students' tendencies to see their writing development as a process of learning many genres and practices from a range of disciplines, professions, and extracurricular contexts, often holding these practices up for comparison, with the goal of leveraging all of those knowledges against each other to be more effective across all of the contexts in which they write. However, students' constant references to the contexts in which they learned to write in certain ways keep their pursuit of "good writing" grounded in the particularities of actual writing situations. They want to be better writers, but do not fall into the trap of believing in what Brian Street terms the "autonomous model of literacy," in which skills and practices can be learned apart from contexts of actual use (19). Instead, it is through their reflections on times when they leveraged their range of writing experiences from across contexts that many students come to develop a richer sense of the nuances of writing in particular disciplines, professions, and extracurricular activities.

Students gained striking insights about specific writing contexts by holding them up for comparison with writing in other contexts. An excellent example is Katie, a nonminor communications and international studies double major. In her exit interview, she described herself as initially struggling to understand how to navigate between the writing she had learned in a public relations summer internship and academic writing in her majors:

> I guess when I first came back I thought, "Okay, great. I know how I'm supposed to write for PR. That's communication. It's what I want to do so I'm going to try and apply that here." I started writing and then I hadn't turned it in yet, luckily, but then I realized, "Oh, wait, that's a different setting. I have to go back to how I was writing before the summer" and I did much better on those assignments after that.

Her realization that there were distinct rhetorical differences when addressing audiences in public relations and communications deepened her sense of exigency beyond "good communication." Instead, she began to recognize that influences from these different contexts positioned her as a more nuanced communicator, free to draw on diverse understandings of writing. While other students might attribute this difference to a simple academic/professional dichotomy, delegitimizing the work of college writing in the face of a concise and to-the-point writing style, Katie instead focused on how information is presented differently for different audiences and purposes. For instance, she distinguishes between differing genres' presentations of information, pointing out that

> [a] press release is written like a newspaper article. You have to lead with the most important thing, and then you give the background information later on. Whereas, in college I'd been writing, have the background information at the top and then get more and more specific or get to your point at the bottom.

For Katie, then, the process of developing as a writer involves first seeing writing in public relations as more or less equivalent to writing in communications, but later recognizing more nuanced requirements for each different setting. Ultimately, she claimed that it was this collection of writing experiences that developed her sense of self as a writer: "I guess maybe that's what's developed me into the writer I am today, the different assignments and the different maybe audiences that I'm supposed to be writing to, the different purposes of the assignments." The emphasis on a broad collection of writing experiences is noteworthy, illustrating that, for Katie, the writer she has become is one who can effectively distinguish between exigencies of particular contexts, drawing on the appropriate resources in her writing repertoire.

Again, we see that the students described in this chapter are not discounting the importance of learning the languages and styles of their respective disciplines—on the contrary, we saw time and again through analyses of interviews and writing that the students in this study make significant moves toward adapting the linguistic features of their new disciplines. Similarly, I will make the case that some students exhibit exemplary disciplinary writing abilities and problem-solving approaches. If, as Jenny Rice puts it, "expertise is less an individual quality than it is a description of the *activity of posing problems* (and consequently of solving them)," then these students frequently can be seen as developing experts, shifting their approaches to writing to suit the purposes at hand (122; emphasis original). However, their understanding of how and why they develop writing for particular purposes is centered not on a single way of posing and solving problems, but on the incorporation of knowledges and writing conventions from across many contexts. These students speak of themselves and their writerly exigencies as spanning many intellectual, personal, and future-professional spheres, and while they often acknowledge the need to conform to particular expectations at times, they see their most substantial moments of writing development in cases when they draw from across a wide repertoire of writing resources.

To further complicate the relationship between disciplinary expertise and writing development, this chapter presents two cases that illustrate the rich range of resources that students learn to draw on when writing. These two cases were selected for the contrast they provide, with one student directing her attention toward developing disciplinary expertise—though not always in the ways we might expect—and the other looking for ways to leverage disciplinary writing knowledge in other contexts. They are also interesting because they offer such very different approaches to writing in the STEM fields. Both students recognize the need to understand the highly specialized nature of writing in the sciences, but they also both find it necessary to take classes in other departments to further their own writing development. Finally, these cases offer an opportunity to contrast students who minored in writing with those who did not. In many of the chapters in this collection, we see evidence that writing minors develop more nuanced abilities to talk about writing, to reflect on their processes, and to shift their knowledge about writing to new situations. However, this minor/nonminor distinction is not airtight, as Lizzie Hutton and Gail Gibson suggest in their discussion of students who favor a more integrative view of "kinds of writing" (chapter 3). While it is true that many of the students who did not minor in writing appear to lack the ability to use the language of writing that writing researchers find most familiar, these two cases suggest that writing development happens in many ways, sometimes conforming to the expectations of teachers and researchers of writing, and sometimes in ways that are so discreet and nuanced, we might hardly notice them if students did not point them out.

To draw out these distinctions, I discuss how these two students are developing markers of disciplinary language in their writing and how they are thinking about blending those norms with features of other writing, often in ways that are difficult for readers to notice. Still, these students' stories of their writing development illustrate ways that even the most seemingly straightforward disciplinary writing might be a product of what Thaiss and Zawacki describe as the third stage of writing development, where "the student uses the variety of courses in a major: varying methods, materials, approaches, interests, vocabularies, etc., toward building a complex but organic sense of the structure of the discipline," and also of dialogue with the methods, materials, approaches, etc., encountered in courses far from the students' majors (139). Like the student comments included earlier in this chapter, these cases illustrate how students think about disciplinary expertise as one factor in their overall writing development. While developing such expertise is sometimes an explicit goal of these students' wide-ranging explorations of writing within various genres during their college years, at other times that expertise is developed as a tool to be leveraged with expertise developed in other contexts.

Kris: Developing Expertise through Dialogues

At first glance, Kris might seem like the most straightforward example of the overlap between disciplinary expertise and writing development. Unlike most students in this study, she did not carry a minor or double major, instead choosing to focus solely on the discipline of microbiology. Eventually, her collected writing developed into one of the most thorough approximations of disciplinary discourse that we found in the study, making it seem as if she developed as a writer in the most discipline-focused sense. Indeed, as represented in Anne Gere's chapter on students' writing experiences after completing college, Kris's success as a graduate student in microbiology at UM further solidifies her status as a burgeoning disciplinary expert. However, her interviews suggest a much more nuanced story, as she describes a process of negotiation that might otherwise go unnoticed when looking at her writing samples. These negotiations span considerations of developing individual style within the discipline as well as how to dialogue with other disciplines when thinking about her research. In this way, Kris's case illustrates how even students who seem to be striving for expertise in a single disciplinary discourse do so by drawing from much further afield than we might assume.

Though Kris became a highly successful disciplinary writer, her relationship with writing started as a struggle. After coming to the UM and receiving a recommendation to enroll in the Transition to College Writing course available for students who need support before enrolling in first-year writing, she eventually found a deep commitment to writing, sparked by her work in a microbiology lab where she conducted and wrote up research that earned her honors and led to her acceptance in a graduate program. Over the course of her undergraduate career, she read voraciously from the major publications of the field, learning to write in many of the major and supporting genres of her discipline with high levels of success (see Gere's conclusion for more on Kris's development as a reader in the discipline). Kris's honors thesis, titled "Identification of 5-methylcytidine and N6-methyladenosine DNA Modifications in the *Bacillus subtilis* Genome" is an unmistakably disciplinary piece of writing, exhibiting high levels of lexical, syntactic, and rhetorical conventions, as this excerpt illustrates:

> While *ccrM* expression is itself tightly controlled by CtrA, the master cell cycle regulator, it regulates many cell cycle genes via **methylation status of various promoters**, including *ctrA* and **genes encoding cell division proteins, polarity determining proteins, proteins involved in cell shape, division, and DNA replication** [21]. *C. crescentus* CcrM homologs have been identified in at least 20 other α-proteobacteria [38] and are essential in *A. tumefaciens* [39], *S. meliloti* [40], and *B. abortus* [41]. (emphasis mine)

This excerpt, taken from the literature review in her introduction, illustrates command of a specialized lexis, as well as a tendency toward discipline-appropriate use of nominalizations, such as "*ccrM* expression" and noun clusters, which are bolded above. Such condensation of participants and processes into dense noun groups is prevalent across scientific writing, allowing writers to make processes themselves the subject of discussion, and compacting those processes into single lexical items or noun groups (Halliday, Kirkwood, and Martin; Fang and Schleppegrell).

Kris's writing displays successful development of such disciplinary features, and her interviews also show signs that she is developing some metalinguistic awareness of these practices as well. This awareness is notable in her exit interview description of her realization that the content of her writing was meaningfully linked to the language of the discipline:

> At first when I was starting to read papers, I thought scientists used unnecessarily large words to describe things. Then what I found as I started writing was that we have a specific vocabulary, just like any field does, and it's just way easier to communicate in that way. You can use one word to describe what would have to be used as a whole sentence.

Though she does not use linguistic terms such as *nominalization* or *noun clustering*, her conscious recognition of the language patterns is more important than the terms themselves. Kris's reference to individual words that can replace whole sentences is probably pointing at least partly to the kinds of specialized language that encodes processes as nouns in cases such as "expression" and "replication," which would require a great deal more writing to unravel, as Michael Halliday, Alexander Kirkwood, and James Martin point out in their studies of scientific discourse. Kris's recognition that the dense forms of scientific writing exist for practical purposes leads her to see such writing as more than a rigid pattern to be emulated. Instead, her development of metalinguistic awareness with respect to her disciplinary writing allows her to begin to take on such discourse features as her own, as Thaiss and Zawacki's third-stage students learn to do while working their ways into disciplinary expertise. See Lancaster, chapter 6 of this volume, for an in-depth discussion of the ways that students conceptualize the relationship of *voice* to disciplinarity and overall writing development.

As Kris takes on the identity of a member of her disciplinary community, she often attributes this development to her deep participation in labs, research projects, and journal clubs. Her reflections on scientific writing and her writing itself seem to suggest that Kris is developing her writing by becoming an expert in her discipline—she is learning to write like a microbiologist by being a microbiologist, and her growing understanding of the ways that such writing functions allows her to stake out a place for herself. Most importantly for her, she is conscious of the need to develop an individual style without straying from the conventions of the discipline. She describes her experiences learning this skill during her exit interview: "you're not told how to do it, so you don't automatically pick up on somebody else's style, and make that your own. You still have to form it in such a way that it's your own style, but that you can communicate it in a more effective way with the person that's reading it." This talk about her development of style is individualized insofar as Kris seems to be referencing an approach to writing that is distinct to each writer, but she avoids the pitfalls of seeing style as "my voice" in the way that Lancaster describes them. Instead, she conveys a sense of developing awareness of how others in the field might write, balancing that against her own approach, all while considering the rhetorical necessities of her audience. Expertise, then, is a matter of not just mimicking a given set of conventions, but of understanding how to find a place for herself within the space of that particular disciplinary style.

But Kris also develops an awareness of her approach to writing outside of her own discipline, through interdisciplinary interactions in the lab, where she is able to weigh the cardinal understandings and approaches to writing about microbiology against those of collaborators from physics. She describes in her exit interview the process of collaborative research and writing as an interaction between two distinct ways of knowing and writing:

> As biologists, we think that the biology perspective is very important. We know what's important for other biologists to read, and what they think. From the physics standpoint, they're like, "We've got this number here. The number is solved. The equation is set. We're good." At least, that's how we perceive their side. We're like, "But the number is not of biological relevance unless we put it in this framework." You see that back and forth.

The distinction between how biologists and physicists think about matters of proof when writing is quite rhetorically savvy in its discussion of shifting exigencies in writing, provides yet another striking example of Kris's development of metalinguistic awareness, with an emphasis on not only the content emphasized by each discipline, but also on the ways those disciplines write about such content. Importantly, though, Kris reflects that it was through this interdisciplinary interaction that she developed this awareness; her development of disciplinary expertise was a result of negotiating differences with other disciplines and ways of communicating.

Similarly, she reflected that one of the most significant steps in her writing development came from the writing she did in a course well outside her major. In a philosophy course on medical ethics, Kris wrote an argument for mandated vaccinations, drawing on the argumentative structures of that course and discipline to talk about a topic related to her own disciplinary work. Shifting to argumentative methods from outside of her usual STEM contexts forced her to reexamine the kinds of thinking and writing she did as a microbiologist. Emphasizing the usefulness of this experience in her exit interview, she equates writing about science in a philosophy course with writing to a nonspecialist audience for a grant proposal. Both help her to see the form and content of her STEM writing with new nuance:

> The philosophy course provided more of a contrast, I think more of a development, because it was a different form of writing. It also helped me reflect upon the way we write in science. Between the two, it showed me how I can communicate effectively when we do talk about—okay, so you're talking to more of a lay audience as opposed to the scientific community in communicating your research. Let's look at different ways to read and write.

Kris credits the contrast provided by cross-disciplinary and nonspecialist writing with helping her to understand her disciplinary work. In the philosophy course, it is the adoption of new forms of writing that makes her more aware of the forms she would regularly use, while the assumed readers of the grant proposal—who are often nonspecialists and not familiar with the technical jargon of the discipline—require her to think more about the link between ideas, language, and audience.

For Kris, then, development as a writer certainly involves the goal of developing expertise in one disciplinary discourse. But her understanding of that development is distinctly *not* isolated to her discipline. Instead, she sees her disciplinary expertise developing in dialogue with her other writing experiences. Her own expert voice developed through comparison with other members of the discipline and other ways of writing across the curriculum. She reflects on this in the last moments of her exit interview, when asked to give her advice to novice writers early in their college careers: "I would encourage them to read broadly, to write broadly, to try different techniques, and, most importantly, to not be afraid of failure." The note about not being afraid of failure provides an important reminder that Kris initially struggled with writing, and her process of drawing from a wide range of influences as she developed as a writer grew out of these struggles. Thus, she suggests a notion of development that recognizes that even when students produce the most seemingly monologic disciplinary texts, it is important to note the extent to which they are influenced by engagement with a wider range of texts and practices.

Jonah: Developing a Hybrid Approach to Writing

If Kris reminds us that it is important to look far outside the student's home discipline for influences contributing to writing development, Jonah's case is important insofar as it shows how a writer can develop by drawing on disciplinary expertise in nonacademic writing. The goal is not just to develop as a disciplinary expert, but to be able to leverage that expertise in new situations. So, as he tells it, Jonah's is the story of a student consciously broadening his repertoire with the goal of hybridizing the texts he writes as well as his own writerly self-conception as he pushes against notions of what it might mean to be a "science" or "English" writer.

When he first enrolled in the study, Jonah was a pre-med student, majoring in evolutionary anthropology. He applied to the minor-in-writing program because he felt that he would benefit in his future career as a doctor if he could "learn more ways in which to perfect various forms of writing," as he put it in his application essay. However, he was already eagerly taking classes in the English department, and during his entry interview he spent more time talking about the work he was doing in those courses than in his STEM concentration. Midway through his junior year, Jonah switched his major, eventually earning a less-common BS in English, with minors in biochemistry and writing. After finishing his undergraduate work, he was hired to write for *Blizzard Watch*, a website devoted to the online gaming communities associated with Blizzard Entertainment, the production company responsible for creating and maintaining such massive online game franchises as *Diablo*, *Overwatch*, and *World of Warcraft*, which Jonah wrote about extensively for his minor in writing courses. These fairly in-depth writing experiences across contexts left Jonah with a range of writing resources to draw on. Indeed, in the reflections written while minoring in writing and in his interviews, he describes his writing development as an ongoing recognition of the ways that diverse kinds of writing can be leveraged for seemingly unrelated situations. That is, he recognizes that writing differs across the contexts he has encountered, but argues that his development as a writer comes not from simply acquiring fluency in particular discourses, but by learning how to write more effectively by drawing on and adapting resources from across his repertoire.

This process of drawing from a range of resources began, perhaps predictably, as Jonah started to develop an awareness that writing functioned differently depending on the situation. Because he wrote in a wide range of contexts, from English courses to labs to online gaming spaces, and because of his tendency—in his estimation—to write more like an English major than his peers in the pre-med track, Jonah developed a strong sense early on that writing in different contexts was to be kept separate. Early comments on his development of writing in STEM courses as well as analysis of writing from those contexts illustrate attempts to adopt a very standard disciplinary style. For instance, in his entry interview, his discussions of writing feedback in STEM courses generally focus on learning to edit out elements that are considered unnecessary:

> I guess a lot of the times I have to go back and look at old stuff that I've written, and when the instructors, "You don't need to say this," I go, "Okay, don't say that." I guess I just have to constantly remind myself, just say what you wanna say and be done and move on. It's more of as I'm writing, a constant reminder to myself, "Hey, you stated the fact, you don't need to say anything else."

Jonah's early sense of writing in the sciences is normative, emphasizing the separation of this discourse from others by deleting unnecessary explanations beyond simple reporting of "facts." Though he would eventually develop a more nuanced approach to thinking about the relationship between "facts" and "explanation," when he first enrolled in the study, Jonah identified a clipped and concise style as one of the most important factors when writing in the sciences.

Indeed, analysis of his writing confirms Jonah's sense that he was developing discipline-specific concision. STEM writing from earlier in his undergraduate years, like this biochemistry lab report, illustrates a more straightforward disciplinary style:

> <u>TLC spotting of the crude solid and the starting material (PABA)</u> was done, as well as a co-spot of both. **Results** showed an R_F value of .35 for the crude product, and R_F value of .16 for the PABA, and two separate spots with R_F values of .35 and .16 for the co-spot. **The separate RF values** indicate that the product is different from the starting material, and the <u>complete separation of spots in the co-spot</u> indicates that the product is pure. When performing melting point analysis, our crude product melted at 88.6° C. This

> melting point matches the known data for Benzocaine, which has a melting point range of 88–90° C. (bold and underlining added)

There is much to be said about the ways that Jonah achieves a "forward, to the point, no fluff" style of writing here, as well as the level of metalinguistic awareness that he has developed to conceptualize such writing. The passive voice and agency shift from researchers to abstractions, as bolded above, is a general rhetorical move in the sciences (Gross, Harmon, and Reidy), and is one of the most familiar linguistic differences noted by students beginning to develop lab and research writing. The nominalizations and noun clusters that characterized Kris's writing are also present, as underlined. While Jonah regularly employs these practices in his writing, he does not mention them explicitly when describing his writing in STEM courses. Still, Jonah's approximation of both of these linguistic features illustrates a development of language considered appropriate for this disciplinary context and is evidence of his steps toward disciplinary expertise in lab and research writing.

Similarly, in a chemistry paper written the same year, Jonah successfully approximates the linguistic tendencies common to writing in the sciences in ways that might be considered clear and straightforward, while also showing a developing ability to use familiar academic narrative structure to describe previous research:

> [1] Primary attempts to create luminescence in plants were accomplished using firefly luciferase by Ow et al. in 1986. **[2]** By adding luminescence to the plants, researchers were able to use the luciferase as both a genetic marker and a genetic tag that could be used to identify other target proteins within the cells of the plant. **[3]** However, use of the firefly luciferase as opposed to the other forms of luciferase led to a dependence on externally applied luciferins to induce the luminescence. **[4]** In addition, this method of luminescence did not protect against the transgenic contamination of other plants. (underlining and numbering added)

Jonah's continued use of dense noun groups, as underlined, illustrates a growing comfort with this feature of writing, particularly in the third sentence, which posits one large nominal group leading to another equally dense nominal group. There are signs of larger genre-based development as well. This paragraph follows a familiar pattern for creating a research space (Swales) within previous findings, as Jonah (1) topically introduces previous research, (2) describes how such research has approached the topic, then (3) problematizes and (4) further problematizes that approach. After following these steps, Jonah is situated to continue his discussion of developments in genetic modification research in this area.

Thus, it would appear that Jonah was on his way to developing his writing in terms of disciplinary expertise, not only recognizing the need for clarity and concision, but also beginning to deploy grammatical resources particular to the register of the discipline. However, as he continued his college studies, Jonah became less content with maintaining this strict division learned in his disciplinary courses, instead developing a sense of himself as a writer drawing on a wide range of styles to best suit the needs of his audiences. This shift is most visible in the layout of the eportfolio Jonah designed for the Capstone course in the minor. Jonah chose to use a large caffeine molecule to serve as his central image, with each of the molecule's constituent atoms linking to a different text from his undergraduate career. As Naomi Silver notes in chapter 8 in this collection, such multimodal design elements are an especially effective way for students to "make even more literally visible the innovative negotiations and play" they engage in as hybrid writers (p. 244). For Jonah, these negotiations are a matter of combining experiences and abilities from across a range of contexts, including both academic sites that favor text-heavy expression and gamer communities based around graphics and video.

He explains this choice, noting in his exit interview that an important "part of the sciences is the microscopic scale and how things come together. What I wanted this to show was different pieces of my writing coming together to show who I am as a writer. Like the different parts of this molecule they all come together" to create a larger whole. Importantly, Jonah does not propose an autonomous view of writing and literacy in which a skill such as writing is learned free of contexts and then applied to situations as the need arises. Instead, Jonah views his own writing development in terms of experience with many different forms of writing, each contributing to his greater dexterity as a writer. As he reflects on his growth as a writer in his eportfolio, making "characteristics" of different writing work together effectively was one of the difficulties that he grappled with most during the minor Capstone course:

> All of these characteristics have improved over my years of being a student writer—the *World of Warcraft* piece I wrote certainly utilized some of these aspects and was arguably better for it! In their own right, they certainly have value and can contribute to the betterment of a piece. But making them all work together, and then some, is more difficult.

Jonah's desire to integrate influences from across his academic experiences is most visible in his final project for the Capstone course: a large multimedia text introducing newcomers to aspects of gameplay and culture in *World of Warcraft*, a massive online game in which players develop their own characters, hone specialties, create alliances with other players, communicate and plan via text and voice-based features, and keep track of updates to the sprawling landscape of the game. In twenty-one pages of introductions, descriptions of basic controls, explanations of norms and practices in the online community, and presentations of testimonials from other players, Jonah draws on narrative elements he associates with writing from his English and writing minor courses, as well as conventions he learned as a member of the *World of Warcraft* gaming community. But in his exit interview he also notes places where he drew on writing knowledge developed in STEM courses, identifying one page that included an infographic with particularly in-depth figures and his own discussion of the kinds of things players could learn from reading such texts, describing "a lot of the time where I would take that scientific approach where I would try to say as much as I can about numbers and facts. Without going too far above people's heads, but also without dumbing it down too much." Though simplistically stated and somewhat deficit-oriented in its view of how scientists write for nonspecialists, Jonah's sense that he is better able to write this page because of his experiences writing in STEM courses is noteworthy insofar as it seems to support the integrative-view-of-writing theme of his eportfolio.

However, it is difficult to find significant examples of the grammatical patterns identified in his other STEM writing:

> The picture to the left is an example of how **one might visually represent** a boss encounter. While <u>such a visual representation</u> might be limited in its capacity to demonstrate the entirety of an encounter, it is still useful for boiling an encounter down to its bare essentials and making for a quick overview. For this particular fight, the image conveys what each role must do through the use of role icons; demonstrates key traps in the fight raiders must watch out for through the use of still images; and makes note of the special phase of the encounter by off-setting the description to the bottom. In short, the salient details are all present for raiders who need a quick rundown/refresher of the fight.

Significant use of nominalizations and dense noun clusters is limited, with only one example in which the process of representing something (bolded above) is nominalized as the subject in the beginning of the next sentence (underlined). This pairing is a frequently used pattern in scientific and "school-based" texts (Fang and Schleppegrell; Schleppegrell). Such limited carry-over of these features of writing could call into question the validity of Jonah's claim that he is writing in this text like he does when he is writing like a scientist, since the two styles differ in such a notable way, grammatically speaking. However, this analysis might further indicate that Jonah had developed these features in his disciplinary writing but was still in the process of consciously developing the metalanguage to recognize or describe them; if this is the case, it might be unsurprising that there is only limited transfer of these features from STEM writing to Jonah's *World of Warcraft* text, given the importance of meta-awareness to transfer, as Anna Knutson discusses in chapter 7 in this volume.

One feature that Jonah does carry over more significantly from his STEM writing is a tendency to shift active agency to abstractions, particularly numbers and figures. His organic chemistry lab writing contained several "results" and "values" that were acting as main participants in sentences, while his *World of Warcraft* piece discusses a "visual representation" that has limited "capacity to demonstrate," and an "image" is tasked with conveying, demonstrating, and even making note of special phases. There are, of course, differences in the ways he is presenting these active numbers and figures, but what is important to consider is how Jonah sees writing as directly linked to his science writing.

So, unlike Kris, Jonah does not see the goals of his writing development in terms of building expertise in a single disciplinary discourse. Instead, he privileges the development of a broad repertoire of writing approaches, which he can draw on for particular rhetorical and communicative effects. When he needs to convincingly phrase a description of laboratory research, he can employ the appropriate language features, but when he needs to explain a technical concept, he can draw on the structured logic of scientific writing to make his explanation clear and concise. Importantly, he has become a professional writer through his pursuit of this wide range of approaches to writing. Having cultivated the ability to write "scientifically" in his explanations of online gaming, Jonah used the space of the minor in writing to further develop an individualized approach that moves fluidly between resources from across his writing experiences. Graduating from college, he felt less like an expert in a single disciplinary discourse than Kris, but that was not his goal. For Jonah, like many students, the ability to write with dexterity across a range of situations is more valuable than disciplinary expertise.

Conclusion

Though they do so in different ways, these cases suggest that students' theorizations of their own writing development do not always limit this development to expertise in a single disciplinary discourse. Instead, they locate their writing development at the intersections of many sites of learning and writing, as they negotiate between the ways of writing they might encounter in their majors and those they might bring from other courses and extracurricular contexts. While not all students were as successful at identifying and putting into practice these diverse elements from across their writing experiences (see Knutson, chapter 7 of this volume, for a discussion of the ways that Grace spends a good deal of time struggling to develop the rhetorical agility that might facilitate such moves), an unexpected number did see their writing development in more expansive terms. Here at Michigan, this trend should perhaps not be altogether surprising, as it builds on previous research that revealed students' complicated relationships to disciplinarity and upper-level writing course selection (Gere et al.). Initially aimed at assessing the efficacy of upper-level courses for apprenticing students into practices common to their majors, Gere et al. revealed that "students instead take up the requirement [to take upper-level writing courses] in a more selective way: as an entry into networks of strategies, audiences, and relationships that will help prepare them for their post-undergraduate academic and professional lives" (258). Often, students take these writing courses in departments far from their majors, explicitly to develop their writing in ways that their disciplines do not encourage. For many of these students, such diverse course selection is the best or only way that they feel they can develop as well-rounded writers, prepared for the range of tasks they expect to encounter in the future.

However, it is worth noting that this isn't a disposition that is unique to students in privileged positions at this particular institution. In their longitudinal study of students who began their college paths struggling in basic writing courses, Anne Herrington and Marcia Curtis describe a similar tendency, with students working to make links across a range of academic and private interests. While they provide a rich discussion of the relationship between the student's private communities and the discourse community of the student's chosen area of study, they caution that their "framing of discourse community . . . focusing as it does on each student's formal or informal 'major,' does not account for the important function that specific classes, including ones outside of that cluster, played in helping these individuals make the link between private and social and between personal and academic" (375).

Like the students in this study, Herrington and Curtis's participants understood their development as multifaceted, drawing on a range of personal interests, general education courses, courses in their majors, work experiences, and extracurricular pursuits. The shortcomings of their study are replicated in this one, insofar as this chapter is certain to only scratch the surface of the broad range of influences on these students' writing development. Deepening our understanding of this kind of development should certainly highlight what Doug Brent simply calls "a rhetorical education," which "could be defined narrowly as the sum of courses or programs designed explicitly to teach rhetorical knowledge and skill," including first-year writing, disciplinary writing courses, and traditional advanced composition and rhetoric courses, but might also "be defined in the broadest possible terms as the sum of all experiences in a person's life, both inside and outside formal educational settings, that help him or her develop rhetorical knowledge and skills" (559). Such a definition of writing development is related to disciplinary expertise, to be sure, but also asks what else contributed to that disciplinary understanding, what students plan to do with it, and how it relates to their developing sense of themselves as educated communicators across a range of contexts.

WORKS CITED

Beaufort, Anne. *College Writing and Beyond: A New Framework for University Writing Instruction.* Colorado UP, 2008.

Brent, Doug. "Crossing Boundaries: Co-op Students Relearning to Write." *College Composition and Communication*, vol. 63, no. 4, 2012, pp. 558–92.

Fang, Zhihui, and Mary J. Schleppegrell. "Disciplinary Literacies across Content Areas: Supporting Secondary Reading through Functional Language Analysis." *Journal of Adolescent & Adult Literacy*, vol. 53, no. 7, 2010, pp. 587–97.

Gere, Anne Ruggles, et al. "Interrogating Disciplines/Disciplinarity in WAC/WID: An Institutional Study." *College Composition and Communication*, vol. 67, no. 2, 2015, pp. 243–66.

Gross, Alan G., Joseph E. Harmon, and Michael S. Reidy. *Communicating Science: The Scientific Article from the 17th Century to the Present.* Oxford UP, 2002.

Halliday, Michael, Alexander Kirkwood, and James R. Martin. *Writing Science: Literacy and Discursive Power.* Taylor & Francis, 2003.

Herrington, Anne J., and Marcia Curtis. *Persons in Process: Four Stories of Writing and Personal Development in College.* National Council of Teachers of English, 2000.

Rice, Jenny. "Para-Expertise, Tacit Knowledge, and Writing Problems." *College English*, vol. 78, no. 2, 2015, pp. 117–38.

Schleppegrell, Mary J. "Linguistic Features of the Language of Schooling." *Linguistics and Education*, vol. 12, no. 4, 2001, pp. 431–59.

Soliday, Mary. *Everyday Genres: Writing Assignments across the Disciplines.* SIU Press, 2011.

Sommers, Nancy, and Laura Saltz. "The Novice as Expert: Writing the Freshman Year." *College Composition and Communication*, vol. 56, no. 1, 2004, pp. 124–49.

Street, Brian V. *Literacy in Theory and Practice.* Cambridge UP, 1984.

Swales, John. *Genre Analysis: English in Academic and Research Settings.* Cambridge UP, 1990.

Thaiss, Chris, and Terry Myers Zawacki. *Engaged Writers and Dynamic Disciplines.* Boynton/Cook, 2006.

Yancey, Kathleen, Liane Robertson, and Kara Taczak. *Writing across Contexts: Transfer, Composition, and Sites of Writing.* Utah State UP, 2014.

SECTION THREE

Writing (and Writing Instruction) Benefits from Attention to Language-Level Features

Language-level features generally receive little attention in current discussions of students' writerly development, and they are not listed among threshold concepts. This is not altogether surprising given the complicated relationship between writing studies and linguistics. Yet it is worth pausing to consider why a language-level approach to writing is not seen as foundational. After all, as Charles Cooper claimed about strategies such as sentence-combining and the generative rhetoric of the sentence, "No other single teaching approach has ever consistently been shown to have a beneficial effect on syntactic maturity and writing quality" (72). George Hillocks, after an extensive review of research on language-level pedagogies, affirmed and amplified Cooper's claim. Study after study showed that students' writing improved when they received language-level instruction. During the period between the mid-1960s and the early 1980s, teaching approaches that drew on linguistics enjoyed wide approval. Articles on language-level approaches appeared regularly in journals, and several conferences on sentence-combining were held at Miami University.

A quick look at the history of writing studies provides one explanation of why such successful instructional practices would have been banished from the field. In the mid-1960s, as the field of writing studies or composition and rhetoric took shape, the generative rhetoric of the sentence as articulated by Francis Christensen received a great deal of attention for its capacity to help students create periodic sentences. This was followed by sentence-combining, which Kellogg Hunt and John Mellon showed to be highly effective in enabling students to produce more complex syntax. The work of linguist Noam Chomsky provided a theoretical basis for sentence combining, lending it further stature, and many in the field received training in or claimed affinity with linguistics. Tagmemics, introduced by Richard Young, Alton Becker, and Kenneth Pike, added a rhetorical dimension to a language-level approach, but it proved difficult to teach. As language-level writing instruction was taking shape, the field of writing studies began moving in another direction. Proponents of a process-based approach to writing, such as Janet Emig, Donald Murray, and James Moffett, criticized language-level approaches for removing context from writing. Their desire to push language-level approaches aside was made easier by the turn of linguistics toward ideal rather than actual users of language. To the extent that linguistics or language study received attention from scholars in writing studies after the early 1980s, it took the form of a sociolinguistic focus on issues surrounding African American vernacular as articulated by Geneva Smitherman, or discussions of writing instruction for students who use English as an additional language by scholars such as Ilona Leki, Alister Cumming, and Tony Silva.

Robert Connors offers another explanation for the decline of language-level writing instruction. He argues that critics framed language-level approaches as formalist, behaviorist, and empirical, setting them in opposition to more holistic, student-centered, and process-focused strategies. Connors goes on to claim that the reason colleagues in writing studies became so actively antiformalist, antibehaviorist, and antiempirical was because they found their "departmental home in the same place its primary course identity—first-year composition—resided[; . . .] the graduate students after 1975 who would make up the core of composition studies were, for better or worse, English graduate students, and they would go on to become English professors" (121). The current number of writing departments now separate from English departments raises questions about Connors' claim, but English departments still house many scholars of writing studies. Given that current language-level approaches to writing instruction call on computer-aided approaches, and given English departments' increased interest in the digital humanities, there may be reason to think that attitudes and perspectives in today's English departments have shifted.

In any event, it is time to bring language-level approaches back into the field of writing studies, and the two chapters in this section demonstrate what our field can learn from doing so. During the time that we in writing studies have been looking elsewhere, linguistics has developed theories and practices that can inform our approaches to writing. Among other things, helping students develop an understanding of how certain features of language can shape the larger effect of a given piece of writing gives them a metacognitive perspective that may be easily transferred to other rhetorical contexts. Language-level attention to writing can help address common writing problems such as overgeneralization, use of ineffective words, and the struggle to assume an authoritative stance. Moreover, language-level approaches can be effectively combined with the more familiar rhetorical genre studies (Miller; Russell; Devitt).

Linguistics has also developed new methods of analysis using computer technologies that reveal patterns of language use that are impossible for an individual reader to discern. Like Franco Moretti's distant reading, computer-aided analysis or corpus linguistics makes different, large-scale, aspects of writing visible. Corpus linguistics begins by creating a collection or corpus of texts in a principled way, such as copies of student essays from the same course or institution, and then, often, comparing this corpus with another, perhaps student essays written by a different group of students or an established reference corps such as the Contemporary Corpus of American English or the Michigan Corpus of Upper-Level Student Papers. In a comparative study, a tool or concordance such as AntConc (Anthony) or WordSmith Tools (Scott) identifies keywords or words that are distinctively salient in each corpus, and statistical analysis determines if the differences between the two sets of keywords occurred by chance or were significant in the statistical sense. In some cases, a corpus is divided into subcorpora to examine differences such as gender or major in a large body of writing. A concordance can also generate lists of collocations or groups of words that occur together in a given corpus. Reflecting important patterns and distinctions across texts, both keywords and collocations can show textual choices that have a considerable effect on entire pieces of writing.

In recent years, corpus analysis has been used to study first-year student writing (Aull; Aull and Lancaster) and writing constructs valued in US composition instruction (Dryer). Corpus studies show that teachers and students often respond to patterns that are tacit and invisible, and they can reveal unconfirmed intuitions about writing. For example, Zak Lancaster's recent corpus study tests the intuition-driven writing templates in the widely used textbook *They Say, I Say*. He finds that the templates do not reflect discourse practices of published academic writing; for instance, the templates encourage students to directly entertain objections, using phrases such as *many will probably disagree*, while academic articles and essays instead favor indirect phrases such *as it could be argued that* (251).

Both of the authors in this section analyzed corpora or collections of texts written or spoken by students in our study using a concordancer. Each of the authors addressed a different research question, but they both used similar methods in that they created corpora, used a concordance to identify words or phrases that were distinctive in two or more corpora, and compared the results with another corpora. Applying this method of analysis to various collections of student writing, sorted by categories such as gender, minor or nonminor, major, or student level in college can show how language-level choices contribute to much larger effects.

Laura Aull's chapter takes on the problem of overgeneralization, as it frequently appears in the writing of relatively inexperienced students, signaled by words such as *every*, *always*, and *people*, among others. These uses are analyzed alongside assertions of certainty. By considering the appearance of such language in writing sorted by genre, discipline, and student level, she provides insights into the writing development of seven students in our study based on analysis of the entire collection of their writing across their undergraduate years. She begins with the Directed Self-Placement (DSP) essays written by each student as part of their matriculation into the university, and she concludes with papers written in the senior year. As she looks at each category of student writing, she compares it with a similar corpus. For example, in analyzing the DSP essays, she compared her sample with a larger corpus of DSP essays collected between 2009 and 2013. In analyzing more advanced student writing she uses the Michigan Corpus of Upper-Level Student Papers for comparison. For the most advanced student writing the Contemporary Corpus of American English, which includes published academic writing, served as the reference corpus. While not exactly parallel to the student writing under consideration, these three corpora provide a means of comparing students' use of language that marks generality and certainty across three levels of writing.

In addition to words that mark generality, Aull's study focuses on qualified generalizations such as *almost all*, *virtually every*, and *some people*, along with lists of hedges, words such as *perhaps*, *approximately*, and *plausible* that qualify claims, and boosters, words such as *conclusively*, *extremely*, and *doubtless* that amplify claims to show how students' use of such language shifts across their undergraduate writing careers. Not surprisingly, generality markers along with boosters appeared most frequently in the writing of first-year students, and advanced student writing showed more hedges and qualified generalizations. These variations suggest that the epistemic stance created by the languages of generality and certainty serves as an indication of broad patterns of writerly development.

To show further nuances in the ways students use markers of generality and certainty and to deepen her analysis, Aull considers subcorpora of particular genres; discipline-specific texts; three divisional groups of humanities, social sciences, and natural sciences; and student and professional writers. This analysis, in addition to that focused on the full corpus, makes visible the differences between the writing students do when they arrive at the university and when they leave. Aull's analysis implies, among other things, that genre and discipline can have a shaping effect on language-level choices made by student writers, and these choices, in turn, contribute to rhetorical constructs such as audience and purpose.

Zak Lancaster also employed automated text analysis, but instead of focusing on student writing he examined what students say in interviews about the metalinguistic constructs of *style* and *voice*. Specifically, he analyzed responses to questions raised in 131 interviews about students' views of "good" writing as well as their writerly identities and goals. Using the concordancing software AntConc, he identified 454 instances of students using *style* and *voice* in responding to interview questions. After differentiating what he calls the individualist (expression of the writer's unique inner self) and social (culturally embedded language performance, sometimes called *stance*) views of voice, he reviews scholarship on the various ways these constructs have been described, asserting that most scholars who take one view or the other would probably agree that "voice is best understood in dialogic terms, through specific discoursal interactions" (p. 167). Lancaster does not review all the scholarship on style, but he notes a similar division between viewing style as prose unique to an individual author and style as more socially constructed. Most importantly, he observes that writers draw on linguistic resources to construct community-valued voices (p. 167), thereby making clear the need to learn more about what resources student writers draw on and how they deploy them.

Combining two groups—minors and nonminors—Lancaster reports that *style* appears more commonly than *voice* in the responses of the entire group, and he suggests that its frequent appearance may result from the multiple meanings students attach to it. These meanings include style as individual language use, as register, as genre, and as usage conventions. Significantly, minors and nonminors apply specific meanings at different frequencies, with nonminors increasingly referring to individual style, perhaps using it as a substitute for voice, and minors describing style as register. Lancaster observes that the minors' description of style as register is "more congruent with current theoretical conceptualizations" (p. 171). This observation suggests that the curriculum experienced by minors may have enhanced their ability to think about style in more complex terms, especially since minors referred to voice more than twice as much as nonminors during their entry interviews. Without the minor curriculum, this group might have continued to focus on *voice* in relatively simplistic terms.

With regard to *voice* Lancaster found that individualist terms tended to surface in discussions of specific forms such as assignments, while students used social terms in more general discussions of writing goals. Both minors and nonminors described voice less frequently in individualist terms as they moved toward graduation and increasingly framed it in social terms. Still, though, minors referred frequently to *voice* in their entrance and exit interviews, and it was usually represented in individualist terms, while their references to style usually emphasized social terms. From a developmental perspective, one of the most interesting findings with regard to students' use of both *voice* and *style* is the extent to which students move between individualist and social meanings for both, sometimes in the same sentence. This fluidity suggests that even graduating seniors are still developing concepts of writing and of themselves as writers.

Lancaster's analysis of two individual selections of writing offers an intriguing discussion of the resources and strategies these students call on to create a writerly self-image. Through careful reading and identification of both linguistic and rhetorical features, Lancaster shows how these student writers establish roles for themselves and their readers at the same time that they enact some of the meanings of *style* and *voice* that they articulated and/or contradicted in their entrance and exit interviews. Through this analysis, Lancaster further demonstrates the enormous complexity that surrounds students' negotiations with taking a stance in writing.

Together these two chapters demonstrate how much we can learn about writerly development by looking through a language-level lens at both the writing students produced and what they say about writing and themselves as writers. By looking at the large patterns made visible with automated text analysis, we can begin to understand how developing writers actually progress from one type of writing to another because language-level changes contribute so much to the overall effect of a piece of writing. Features such as boosters and hedges may seem relatively incidental, but as Aull shows, they help shape the stance of the writer regarding the extent to which the writing does or does not conform to the discourses of the academy and/or confer authority on the writer. If a goal of college writing is to guide student writers to take up academic discourses, the tools of corpus linguistics can indicate the developmental levels achieved by a group of students, particularly with regard to a threshold concept such as *writing is a social and rhetorical activity*. Students' use of hedges and boosters can, among other things, provide an indication of students' rhetorical sensibilities as well as the extent to which they seek to engage the reader in dialogic terms.

Similarly, linguistic analysis of the language students use to talk about their own writing, especially if done in concert with analysis of samples of their writing, can provide insights into their understandings of writing. As Lancaster showed, the terms students use and the meanings they apply often vary from those used by professionals in writing studies, but nonetheless they offer a window into the thinking that contributes to writing choices. Of course, this does not mean that there is always symmetry between what students say about writing and what they actually write, as Lancaster's analysis of Joe shows. Even though Joe talks about voice in individualistic terms, he uses patterns of language and rhetorical moves that invite interaction with the reader.

Contradictions such as these point to another aspect of language-level analysis. Even though large-scale patterns and smaller-scale examination of linguistic features can provide some insights into students' writerly development, it is never steady or uniform development. As the variations between minors and non-minors, different genders, and lower and upper division students, to say nothing of the variations within groups, show language-level development is irregular and dynamic; we cannot point to stages or levels of linguistic development in student writers. But we can point to the value of giving students opportunities to develop metalinguistic awareness. Such awareness can lead to productive discussions about writing that capitalize on students' uneven and shifting writerly development.

WORKS CITED

Adler-Kassner, Linda, and Elizabeth Wardle, editors. *Naming What We Know: Threshold Concepts of Writing Studies*. Utah State UP, 2015.

Anson, Chris, and Jessie L. Moore. *Critical Transitions: Writing and the Question of Transfer*. CSU Open Press, 2017. Available at wac.colostate.edu/books/ansonmoore/

Anthony, Laurence. AntConc (version 3.4.3) (computer software). Waseda University, 2014.

Aull, Laura L. *First Year University Writing: A Corpus-Based Study with Implications for Pedagogy*. Springer, 2015.

Aull, Laura L., and Zak Lancaster. "Linguistic Markers of Stance in Early and Advanced Academic Writing: A Corpus-Based Comparison." *Written Communication*, vol. 31, no. 2, 2014, pp. 151–83.

Chomsky, Noam. *Aspects of the Theory of Syntax*. MIT Press, 1969.

Christensen, Francis. "A Generative Rhetoric of the Sentence." *College Composition and Communication*, vol. 14, no. 3. 1963, pp. 155–61.

Connors Robert J. "The Erasure of the Sentence." *College Composition and Communication*, vol. 52, no. 1, 2000, pp. 96–128.

Cooper, Charles R. "Research Roundup: Oral and Written Composition." *English Journal*, vol. 64, 1975, pp. 72–74.

Devitt, Amy. *Writing Genres*. SIU Press, 2004.

Dryer, Dylan B. "Scaling Writing Ability: A Corpus-Driven Inquiry." *Written Communication*, vol. 30, no. 1, 2013, pp. 3–35.

Emig, Janet. *The Composing Process of Twelfth Graders*. National Council of Teachers of English, 1971.

Hillocks, George, Jr. *Research on Written Composition: New Directions for Teaching*. National Council of Teachers of English, 1986.

Hunt, Kellogg. "Teaching Syntactic Maturity." *Applications of Linguistics*, edited by G. E. Perren and J. L. M. Trimm. Cambridge University Press, 1971.

Leki, Ilona, Alister Cumming, and Tony Silva. *A Synthesis of Research on Second Language Learning in English*. Taylor and Francis, 2008.

Mellon, John. *Sentence-Combining: A Method of Enhancing the Development of Syntactic Fluency in English Composition*. National Council of Teachers of English, 1969.

Miller Carolyn. "Genre as Social Action." *Quarterly Journal of Speech*, vol. 70, no. 2, 1984, pp. 151–67.

Moffett, James. *Teaching the Universe of Discourse*. Houghton Mifflin, 1968.

Moretti, Franco. *Distant Reading*. Verso, 2013.

Murray, Donald. "Teaching Writing as Process Not Product." *The Leaflet*, Fall 1972; rpt. in *The Essential Don Murray: Lessons from America's Greatest Writing Teacher*, edited by Thomas Newkirk and Lisa C Miller. Boynton/Cook, 2009.

Russell, David. "Activity Theory and Its Implications for Writing Instruction." *Reconceiving Writing, Rethinking Writing Instruction*, edited by Joseph Petraglia. Taylor and Francis, 1995, pp. 51–78.

Scott, M. *Wordsmith Tools* (version 6.0) (computer software). Oxford University Press, 2014.

Smitherman, Geneva. *Talking and Testifying: The Language of Black America.* Wayne State UP, 1986.

Young, Richard, Alton L. Becker, and Kenneth L. Pike. *Rhetoric: Discovery and Change.* Harcourt, 1970.

CHAPTER FIVE

GENERALITY AND CERTAINTY IN UNDERGRADUATE WRITING OVER TIME

A CORPUS STUDY OF EPISTEMIC STANCE ACROSS LEVELS, DISCIPLINES, AND GENRES

Laura L. Aull

Consider the following sentences written by incoming college students:

Since the beginning of time, people have feared new technologies.
Our culture today stresses perfection and nobody wants to be less than perfect.
Pressure always brings out the worst in people.
Every mature, established person has control over what they say and do.

Sentences such as these provoke the common lament that students overgeneralize, making claims they cannot support, or worse, intimating a presumptuous, homogeneous view of the world. The sentences apply observations and predictions across time, contexts, and people— suggesting not only that *pressure brings out the worst in people*, for example, but that it *always* does.

Of particular concern are students transitioning into higher education. Instructional materials from across the United States warn new college writers against generalizations as a fallacy. In just two examples, Bowdoin College and the University of North Carolina (UNC) cite generalizations as among the most common characteristics of ineffective introductions: Bowdoin warns students against "absurdly general phrases" such as "humans have always . . ."; UNC encourages students to avoid openings addressing "human beings" writ large.[1] These recommendations indicate that such generality is viewed as imprecise, unnecessary, or not credible to instructors. Instead, as noted in the Writing Program Administrators Outcomes

Statement, students must learn to craft credible, "appropriately qualified" claims.[2] Due to the importance of college writing in educational access and attainment, these expectations are crucial for traditional and nontraditional students alike (Berlin; Penrose). They especially matter in a time of divisive and uncivil media discourse in light of the ethical implications of generalizing, since responding effectively to diverse perspectives requires global citizens who can distinguish when views apply across people and contexts and when they do not.

Curiously, generalizations are addressed in instructional materials far more often than in research. The research we do have suggests that many students either perceive they *should* generalize or struggle to avoid generalizing relative to more experienced writers. For instance, Ellen Barton's discourse analysis of professional versus undergraduate essays shows that the greatest distinction between the two is generalizations. All of the student essays in the study contain generalizations, not only in introductions but also, in "striking contrast" to the professional essays, in idea development within body paragraphs (763).

Corpus analysis of writing by students transitioning into university likewise shows that incoming students are significantly more likely than advanced student and professional writers to suggest that claims are *always* or *never* the case (Aull; Aull and Lancaster; Hyland "Undergraduate Understandings"). A corpus analysis of a more expanded list of "generality markers"—*always*, *never*, indefinite pronouns (e.g., *everyone*), and generic nouns (e.g., *people*)—further shows that incoming college students generalize more than advanced students and published writers. Additionally the study shows that both genre and developmental level may explain these patterns, because generalization decreases by level but remains higher in essays than academic articles (Aull, Bandarage, and Miller). Moreover, research suggests that assignment design may influence student generalizing. For example, analysis of incoming college student writing shows a significant correlation between open-ended writing prompts and certain broad, generalized claims, suggesting that standardized writing exams may solicit generalized responses by intimating that students can reasonably argue about large-scale phenomena (e.g., tradition vs. technology) and heterogeneous groups (e.g., teenagers) without representing diverse views (Aull).[3] Finally, generalizations seem related to student success: in a corpus analysis of advanced placement (AP) writing by secondary students attempting to gain college course credit, low-scoring AP essays are characterized by "emphatic generality," in contrast to the "elaborated specificity" of higher-scoring essays (Brown and Aull).[4]

Aside from these studies, we still know little about generalizations in student academic writing, aside from the sense that students seem to generalize and should not. My anecdotal experience is that some instructors assume generalizing is a result of developmental immaturity and academic level, but this may overlook important caveats, including that in certain genres, an urgent and widely applicable claim may appear convincing and confident. Such a caveat highlights a broader issue: we know little about the relationship between generalizing and various aspects of student writing, including developmental level, genre, and discipline.

This study adds to our understanding of students' writing development by distinguishing and analyzing two aspects of stance, certainty and generality, and by exploring the impact of genre, discipline, and student level on use of related stance features.[5] A key reason for distinguishing generality and certainty is that generalization markers such as those in the sentences above—references such as *nobody*, *people*, and *our culture today*—seem to address not whether something is true, but the extent to which it applies across people and circumstances. More specifically, certainty, or the extent of the commitment or truth value expressed about a statement, is often expressed in hedges and boosters (e.g., that something *may* happen); and generality, or the extent to which an argument can be generalized, is often expressed in indefinite pronouns (e.g., that *everyone* agrees) and extreme intensifiers (e.g., that something *always* happens). This examination of certainty and generalization illustrates the larger point that language-level research provides an additional means for identifying writerly development.

Although certainty is addressed regularly in research on academic stance, generalization markers remain underanalyzed. They merit more attention not only because student writers often use them, but because they are generally associated with vagueness or nonacademic, conversational discourse (e.g., Biber et al.; Hinkel; Labov) and therefore may thwart student success. In other words, while generality and certainty are overlapping, distinguishing them seems important in studies of student writing, since achieving a credible, academic stance relates to both a credible level of certainty and a credible level of generality. Students must learn how much caution or certainty to express about a claim, thereby showing diplomacy toward other views and appropriate care with risky claims (Hyland, "Stance and Engagement"), and they must learn to express an appropriate level of generality to avoid extending a claim beyond a reasonable level of applicability.

This study explores the use of certainty and generality markers over time in the writing of seven undergraduate students studying humanities, social science, natural science, and business, to investigate how they craft a written stance before and after undergraduate writing instruction, and across different genres and disciplines. This includes examining the extent to which these undergraduate writers use certainty and generality features, in contrast to more advanced students and published academics. The following questions guided the analysis:

1. To what extent do markers of generality and markers of certainty show distinct trends in selected student undergraduate writing?
2. To what extent do stance features of generality and certainty change over time in selected examples of student writing?
3. To what extent do stance features of generality and certainty appear to be influenced by genre, discipline, and student level?

Analysis Methods and Corpora

I have argued that context-attentive corpus analysis in composition can blend both more traditional attention to context and individual texts with patterned meaning exposed by corpus analysis (Aull).[6] Along these lines, this study includes a small-scale corpus linguistic analysis of recurring discourse features alongside attention to the discipline, genre, and academic level of the writers and the texts. Though this study focuses on a small number of students, it examines stance patterns in writing by the same students across three kinds of writing tasks: placement essays at the start of university courses, reflective and personal writing in non-discipline-specific courses, and discipline-specific writing in major-level courses. In so doing, the study explores discourse patterns associated with student levels, genres, and disciplines, and examines connections between those patterns and related writing expectations.

The writing analyzed in this study was completed by seven University of Michigan (UM) students as they moved through the Sweetland Minor in Writing, which is described in the Introduction and detailed more fully in **appendix 2.** The students were selected with four main criteria in mind: (1) students who had written Directed Self-Placement (DSP) essays as part of their initial UM writing course placement (Gere et al.), (2) students who had written general, non-discipline-specific writing (such as in general writing courses prior to major-level courses), (3) students who had written major-level, discipline-specific writing, and (4) students from a mix of disciplinary majors. This precluded, for instance, students who were writing minors and had submitted a DSP essay but had not yet taken major-level courses, as well as writing-minor students who had taken major-level courses but had not submitted a DSP essay. With these criteria, I aimed to examine a range of writing tasks commonly confronted by US students across their undergraduate writing development, from placement essays completed prior to college-level writing instruction, to non-discipline-specific undergraduate writing generally completed in the first two years of college, to discipline-specific writing generally completed in the final two years of undergraduate study.[7] Ultimately, these criteria narrowed the study to seven students majoring in distinct and common undergraduate disciplines, enabling a context-informed corpus-based analysis of stance features in seven DSP essays and forty-four undergraduate texts.

Distinctions among the forty-four undergraduate texts further enabled analysis of stance patterns according to genre, the broadly recognizable prototypes (or "family resemblances") in the social actions of texts (Grabe; Miller). Reading through the undergraduate writing, I identified three genre-based categories beyond the two initial categories of non-discipline-specific and discipline-specific writing: (1) discipline-specific writing in the student's major discipline, such as reports or argumentative essays focused on discipline-specific questions; (2) non-discipline-specific, formal academic writing focused on an observed issue or problem and written for a general audience; and (3) personalized and reflective writing about student writing and other personal experiences.

The first genre category includes essays, reports, and research papers that focus on a discipline-specific issue, for instance, a research-based essay on anxiety disorders in psychology or a lab report on an aldol condensation experiment in chemistry. The second genre category includes students' general academic essay writing, for example, an essay on how the media blame the victim in sexual assault cases, written for a general audience outside the discipline. The third genre category includes reflective, personalized writing. These categories capture valuable distinctions, because discipline-specific discourse can be distinct from non-discipline-specific discourse even on similar topics (Myers). Furthermore, corpus research on undergraduate writing tends to examine discipline-specific texts rather than general essays or reflective writing, probably because open-access corpora include the former (e.g., see Hardy and Römer; Nesi and Gardner). In this way, this study offers a unique look at a range of undergraduate writing assignments confronted by students. The undergraduate (non-DSP) writing genres in the study are noted by discipline and discipline group in table 5.1 below.

Interestingly, most of the texts fall into two mutually exclusive categories: discipline-specific genres and general essay genres. Both seem relevant to analyze in a study of undergraduate writing. Specifically, because "undergraduates are now expected to write 'in the discipline' or 'across the curriculum,'" and as a result will "need to write in a way that conforms to the practices of a discipline they may not (yet) be familiar with" (Hardy and Römer 184), it is worthwhile to identify what discursive distinctions emerge across the students' discipline-specific writing and in contrast with more general academic writing. Furthermore, even though general, argumentative essays have been critiqued as school genres (Russell; Wardle), they are the single most common genre in undergraduate courses and merit study in relation to student writing development. Such study could be coupled with investigations of student perceptions of genre, such as Lizzie Hutton and Gail Gibson's in chapter 3.

Though the above two categories were the most common, the third undergraduate writing category also emerged in the non-discipline-specific texts: personalized and reflective texts that appeared generally short and less formal stylistically—for example, a student's open letter to her boyfriend's parents about cross-cultural

Table 5.1. Description of Student Writing-Minor Texts and Categories

Discipline Group	Discipline	Genres
Humanities	Language and Literature	Discipline-specific: literary analysis (2), research paper
		Non-discipline-specific: personal essay, reflective essay
	Communication	Discipline-specific: advertising comparison, critical analysis, project proposal
		Non-discipline-specific: personal essay, blogging promotional piece
Social Sciences	Political Science	Discipline-specific: brief, research paper
		Non-discipline-specific: creative writing/letter, general writing argumentative essay, personal essay
		Reflective/why write essay
	Psychology	Discipline-specific: argumentative essay (3), case study, conversational paper, final research paper
		Non-discipline-specific: cultural studies essay, definition essay, open letter to discriminatory parents
Natural Sciences	Biology	Non-discipline-specific: argumentative essay, personal/creative writing, reflective writing essay, writing tutor reflection
		Discipline-specific: scientific report, summary
	Chemistry	Discipline-specific: scientific report (5)
		Non-discipline-specific: media commentary essay, personal essay
Business	Marketing	Discipline-specific: editorial, critical analysis
		Non-discipline-specific: argumentative essay, summary cultural essay, summary essay

dating, or reflective pieces on "why I write." Therefore, to see what additional features emerged across these texts, I created a "personalized" category to capture all texts in which there is an explicit, first-person narrator offering an experiential point of view, often in reflective commentary on the students' writing. Together with the DSP essays as their own category, these four genre categories captured all of the academic writing submitted by the University of Michigan minor students in the study; the details of each are noted in table 5.2. In addition to the levels and genres noted in table 5.2, the minor discipline-specific texts are further divided by the discipline groups noted in table 5.3.

As noted in the section three introduction, I use three corpora as reference corpora for three levels of writing, that is, as representative of more examples of writing at the same level.[8] A larger corpus of DSP writing by all incoming UM first-year students between 2009 and 2013 serves as a reference corpus for incoming college writing at UM; all of these first-year students responded to a similar reading, writing, and reflecting task prior to college writing instruction (see Aull; Gere et al.). The Michigan Corpus of Upper-Level Student Papers (MICUSP) serves as a reference corpus for advanced student writing. MICUSP is the largest open-access corpus of student writing to date, consisting of over eight hundred A-graded pieces of writing across sixteen disciplines and seven genres (e.g., essays, reports) by students in their final level of undergraduate through the third level of graduate

Table 5.2. UM Writing Minor Corpora Texts and Token Numbers by Genre

Corpora by Level and Genre	Minor Students' DSP Essays	Minor Undergraduate Writing Texts[a]		
		Minor Discipline-Specific Texts	Minor General Essay Texts	Minor Personalized Texts
Text Number	7	21	14	9
Word Tokens	6,294	37,154	32,486	8,819

[a]Overall, the minor undergraduate writing corpus includes 44 texts and 78,459 word tokens.

Table 5.3. UM Writing Minor Subcorpora Texts and Token Numbers by Discipline Groups

Minor Discipline-Specific Texts by Discipline Group	Minor Humanities	Minor Social Science	Minor Natural Science	Minor Business
Text Number	7	5	7	2
Word Tokens	8,331	13,558	12,065	3,220

school (Römer and O'Donnell). Finally, the academic corpus of the Contemporary Corpus of American English (COCAA) serves as a reference corpus for published academic writing. COCAA contains published articles as well as essays across disciplines; it therefore approximates published academic writing in a range of genres rather than just formal academic research articles. These reference corpora, noted in table 5.4, are not assumed to be exactly parallel to the writing minor, but they provide approximate comparison points for how the stance features analyzed tend to be used across three general levels of academic writing. They capture hundreds or thousands of texts from the same student levels, and hundreds of thousands of texts of professional academic writing.[9]

Markers of Generality and Certainty

As noted in the introduction, exploring generality and certainty means targeting the words that mark these concepts. Certainty markers include hedges and boosters. Hedges, which indicate qualified or cautious certainty, are such words as *perhaps*, *might*, and *possibly*; boosters, by contrast, indicate full certainty about a proposition and include words such as *clearly*, *definitely*, and *without a doubt*. For instance, the following MICUSP example from a graduate-level psychology text includes the hedge *unlikely*, which qualifies a statement about a study participant's autonomy: "Since Adam is suffering from FAS which will affect his life in every domain in significant ways, it will be *unlikely* that he will be able to achieve or will be expected by others to achieve autonomy as much as other children." In

Table 5.4. Reference Corpora Text and Word Token Numbers

Reference Corpora	UM DSP (2009–13)	MICUSP	COCAA
Text Number	17,029	743	~4 million words per year[a]
Word Tokens	16,836,976	1,917,748	85,092,288

[a]Within COCAA, the nine disciplinary subcorpora were used to compare features across the following: history, education, geography/sociology, law/political science, humanities, philosophy/religion, science/technology, medicine, and miscellaneous. The academic disciplines and discipline groups were selected to cover the range of the Library of Congress classification system (Davies), and the sizes of each subcorpus at the time of the study, 2015, follows: COCAA (all) (90,168,162 tokens), history (12,245,202 tokens), education (9,443,293 tokens), geography/sociology (16,180,080 tokens), law/political science (8,600,386 tokens), humanities (11,926,481 tokens), philosophy/religion (6,740,288), science/technology (14,075,316), medicine (6,700,484), and miscellaneous (4,256,632). Davies states that the balance between the size of discipline and discipline groups remains stable from year to year.

one more example, the following statement from a UM incoming student DSP essay includes the booster *dramatically* and the hedge *relatively*, which show more and less certainty, respectively: “Developing and implementing a more discriminatory process for recruiting teachers will *dramatically* increase the educational standards of this country in a *relatively* inexpensive way.” In these examples, the hedges and boosters modulate epistemic commitment, or give the writers’ “assessments of possibilities and probabilities” (Vande Kopple 97). Thus, certainty indicates the extent to which something might be true and is marked by hedges and boosters.

Though it overlaps with certainty, generality can be seen as a distinct and underexamined aspect of stance (Aull, Bandarage, and Miller). Generality refers to the scope of an argument, or the extent to which something can be applied across people and contexts. In this study, markers of generality include unqualified uses of indefinite pronouns and several generic nouns that appear in over 96 percent of student writing across the corpora. These pronouns and nouns are noted in linguistic research as markers of generalized and indefinite references. Specifically, studies of “universal and negative pronouns” *none*, *all*, *each*, and *no** and *every** pronominals (*nothing*, *no one*, *nobody*, *everything*, *everyone*, and *everybody*) are described as “marked exaggeratives” (Biber; Hinkle; Quirk et al.). Similar studies use the term “vague indefinite pronouns” to refer to *any** and *some** pronominals (e.g., *anything*, *someone*), which are cast as hedges because the reference remains unspecified (Hinkel; Quirk et al.). Generic nouns include *people*, *world*, *society*, *human(s)*, and *human being(s)*, as well as certain uses of *today* (e.g., *students today*). In addition, qualified uses of generalizations—those markers of generality modified by *not* or a hedge, such as *almost anyone* or *not all people*—are treated as a separate category, since these phrases emphasize applicability but do not imply that a claim is fully generalizable. Aull et al. show that not only uses of generalizations but also qualified generalizations distinguished incoming college writing from expert academic writing; expert academic writers use not only fewer generalizations but more qualified generalizations than students. This pattern suggests that generality is not unwelcome in academic writing, but that qualified generalizations may be one way that academic writers show emphasis while avoiding claims that imply there are no exceptions.

A full list of the generality and certainty markers analyzed in this study is included in the online appendix 8 (https://doi.org/10.3998/mpub.10079890.cmp.6), and analysis of these features in the reference corpora provides empirical support for focusing on these features.[10] In other words, analysis of the certainty and generality markers in first-year UM student DSP writing, upper-level student writing in MICUSP, and expert academic writing in COCAA suggests the importance of focusing on these features and differentiating certainty and generality.

Hedges, boosters, generality markers, and qualified generalizations appear in notably different frequencies across these three reference corpora. With one exception, all four sets of features were significantly different across all three levels ($p < .001$)—so significant, that is, that the likelihood that the distinction occurred by chance is less than 1 in 1,000. Furthermore, the trajectories across the three levels were compelling. Uses of generality markers and qualified generalizations were both significantly different across all three levels ($p < .001$), and they showed an opposite trend: the generality markers were highest in the incoming first-year writing and lowest in the published academic writing in COCAA, with the advanced student use falling in between. By contrast, qualified generalizations were lowest in the incoming first-year writing and highest in the published academic writing, with the advanced student use falling in between. Hedge use was highest in the advanced student writing, next highest in the published academic writing, and lowest in the incoming first-year writing. This difference in hedge use may draw attention to genre distinctions between the advanced student writing in MICUSP and the published academic writing in COCAA; MICUSP contains only discipline-specific writing, which tends to include more hedges than writing for a general academic audience (Hyland *Disciplinary Discourses*; Hyland *Metadiscourse*). This variation may likewise help explain the only distinction that was not significant, booster use between the incoming first-year writing and the published academic writing in COCAA. The published academic writing aimed at a general academic audience may permit more boosters. At the same time, it includes more hedge use, so even while booster use is not significantly different, the published academic writing contains more of a balance between certainty and qualification than the incoming first-year writing (Aull).

Analysis of Findings

Textual Examples

The minor writing in this study bears out these patterns. Their DSP essays, written prior to their UM matriculation, contain frequent generality markers. Furthermore, the scope of the generalizations appears especially wide, for example, across very large groups. As they begin to write for undergraduate courses, the minor writers show adjustments in their levels of both generality and certainty. The following examples in various minor texts help illustrate stance feature use across student level, genre, and discipline.

Minor DSP text examples:

Generality:

1. *The children of today* are the leaders of tomorrow, so if we do not put great significance on the way in which teachers are chosen, children will be deprived of an effective education and won't be able to handle *society's* money. (DSP essay of Shannon, communications major)

Qualified Generality

2. Each quality may *not always* be exhibited, but we have the flexibility that computer programs do not to take into account. (DSP essay of Amanda, English major)

The first excerpt includes generalization markers *(children of) today* and *society's*. It seems to use the generalization about children to project urgency about a shared ideal (Aull, Bandarage, and Miller). This excerpt also extends the generalization to definitive, causal projections about what will happen if teacher selection is not prioritized. By contrast, the second excerpt includes a qualified use of generality by using the phrase *not always*. The next two example passages include *may* and other examples of certainty markers.

Certainty:

3. This method would *undeniably* improve America's educational system by replacing the bottom six to ten percent of public-school teachers that currently hinder it. (DSP essay of Owen, political science major)
4. For example, how a celebrity interacts with people *may* be *very* different from how a mechanic *may* interact. (DSP essay of Ayanna, business major)

Here excerpt three includes the booster *undeniably*, which draws attention to the writer's full certainty about the claim about how to improve the hiring of teachers. The fourth example includes the following certainty markers: the hedge *may* and the booster *very* as well as the generalization marker *people*. In this example, the booster *very* highlights the level of difference the writer describes, while the hedge *may* avoids suggesting that the writer can definitively prove that celebrities and mechanics behave differently. The use of the generality marker *people*, though, makes the claim less precise than most academic arguments. The same DSP essay goes on to suggest that "As humans, we are versatile in our responses and behavior. It is impossible to find one single pattern." These generality markers indicate very broad predictions, so that while generality markers are also used in more advanced academic writing, the scope of these incoming first-year student predictions is much wider than claims made by more experienced writers. In their argumentative essay writing prior to undergraduate instruction, then, the students often construct a stance characterized by generalized predictions and observations.

Minor essay genre text examples:

Generality:

5. The media leads *general society* to believe that the "sexual situation" [e.g., late at night] that results is the victim's fault, and therefore not rape. There is a common misconception in our *society* that victims should choose their actions more wisely if they don't want to be involved in that situation. (Argumentative essay by Amanda, English major)
6. Choices are a part of *everyone's* lifestyle everyday [sic]. We live with them, treasure them and can be disappointed by them at any time. Choices can have both good and bad consequences. (Argumentative essay by Ayanna, business major)
7. By maintaining normality in *society*, order is also sustained. With the same idea, *no one* would want "crazy" people walking around on the streets. (Argumentative essay by Justin, psychology major)

Qualified Generality

8. Anyway, the very words that humans created can be insufficient to describe this meaning. *Not everything* can be described with words. (Reflective essay by Ayanna, business major)

Excerpt five includes the generalization marker *society* twice. The first use is modified by *general*, but both uses as well as other uses of *society* throughout the full essay seem to refer to the same entity—readers of and commenters on social media and online news outlets—though neither *society* nor *media* is explicitly specified along these lines. Example six opens with a generalization about *everyone*, which is followed by the use of *we* and the projection of shared experiences. All of the statements are broad insofar as they do not address the topic of "choices" in terms of kinds of decisions. The seventh example includes the generalization markers *society* and *no one* in what appears to be an effort to imply that "normal" and "crazy" are socially constructed and maintained; in this case, *no one* seems to refer to a typical person, without exception, who is influenced by said social norms. Excerpt eight shows the use of a qualified generalization that explicitly counters a potential generalization.

Certainty

9. When weapons of *any* kind are made permissible in public schools, equal access to learning cannot be attained. Students will be confronting daily with the knowledge that their pupils carry swords, which will *undoubtedly* interfere with their learning. (Argumentative essay by Owen, political science major)
10. Ethnographic fieldwork is dependent on the development of intimate relationships with members of the society being studied. The ability to initiate, foster, and maintain these relationships is *greatly* influenced by the background of the ethnographer. (Argumentative essay by Susanne, biology major)

Passage nine includes the generalization *of any kind*, which intimates that the writer sees no exception to the claim that weapons should be kept out of public schools. The passage also includes the booster *undoubtedly*, which explicitly conveys full certainty about the claims—imagine, for example, the same claim without the booster. Excerpt ten includes a claim intensified by the booster *greatly*, though like many boosters in advanced academic writing, the booster intensifies a rather specific claim—this one about the influence of ethnographer background on ethnographic fieldwork.

Minor discipline-specific text examples:

Generality:

11. As marketers, we recognize that we not only serve our organizations but also act as stewards of *society* in creating, facilitating and executing the *transactions* that are part of the greater economy. (Marketing brief by Ayanna, business major)
12. In order to strengthen our data we should have each run the five reactions ourselves. Each individual has a different way of performing the experiment regardless of how uniform we try to design the experiment. One individual may scrape out the round-bottom flask until *every* visible speck of the precipitate is out, and another may not. (Lab report by Abby, chemistry major)

Qualified Generality

13. His references *almost always* have other underlying messages that a typical scholar of today must search for more deeply, but at the time were usually well known within the intellectual sphere. Images involving religion or classical mythology do not necessarily agree in today's world, but they worked well for Milton to address multiple perspectives that his audience could comprehend no matter what they believed in. (Research paper by Amanda, literature major)

The generalization marker *society* in excerpt eleven refers to marketers as stewards of the social lives of people writ large, while excerpt twelve includes the generality marker *every* to emphasize the necessity for thorough work in lab preparation, helping to convey the students' understanding of how they can improve. This lab report example also includes the hedges *may* and *may not* to further emphasize the variability of experiment execution. The thirteenth excerpt from a discipline-specific literature research paper includes a qualified generalization, *almost always*, to make a claim about references in Milton's literature; this matches the use of qualified generality to make a "near-generalization" (Aull, Bandarage, and Miller 38). The passage also contains several other stance markers, including the generalization markers *of today* and *today's world*, as well as the hedges *usually* and *not necessarily*.

Certainty:

14. The next peak occurs at 6.7 and corresponds to the multiplet that has an area of three so it *must* correspond to Group C and E. (Scientific report by Abby, chemistry major)
15. This factor [chronic and excessive worry or anxiety] *certainly* applies to Austin who explains that he can spend at least 3 hours and sometimes the entire day in "worry land," a term that he coined himself to explain the time when he thinks about little events that occur in everyday life and worries about what will happen in the future. (Case study by Justin, psychology major)

The passage in excerpt fourteen indicates certainty in a statement that demonstrates knowledge: *must* intensifies a discipline-specific statement about correspondence between the noted peak and the groups in the study. Likewise, the fifteenth excerpt demonstrates knowledge, suggesting that a factor of a psychological disorder not only applies, but applies without doubt, to a patient discussed in a psychology case study.

As do corpus patterns across the texts displayed in the next section, these example uses appear to confirm that the minor students make some changes in their written stance as they develop as writers and encounter more genres and discipline-specific courses. The changes suggest that in minor course work, and perhaps as well in extracurricular settings discussed by Ryan McCarty in chapter 4, the students are implicitly or explicitly encouraged to find ways to craft credible claims, by avoiding certain generalizations and showing certainty vis-à-vis supported claims that demonstrate their knowledge.

Corpus Patterns

Corpus analysis of stance markers across the corpora point to several distinctions based on writing level, genre, and discipline. In terms of all stance features in the minor writing—generality markers, qualified generalizations, hedges, and boosters—the greatest distinctions emerge between the DSP essays and all of the undergraduate writing (minor essays and minor discipline-specific writing).[11]

Differences based on student level

In the comparison of the minor DSP writing versus all minor undergraduate writing—both essays and discipline-specific texts—there are several significant differences. Somewhat significant distinctions include that qualified generalizations increase to a moderately significant degree ($p < .05$), and boosters lessen significantly ($p < .01$). The only highly significant differences ($p < .001$) occur in generality marker use, across all three levels: use of generality markers is highest in the minor DSP and lowest in the minor discipline-specific texts, while the minor essay texts fall in between. Interestingly, there are no other significant differences between the minor essays and the minor discipline-specific writing; in other words, in terms of qualified generalizations, hedges, and boosters, there are no significant differences across the writing completed by minors after at least some UM writing instruction. These patterns therefore imply evidence of writing development as soon as minor students begin practicing undergraduate writing, in that after their DSP essays, the students modify their use of all certainty and generality stance markers across the genres they write. Furthermore, given that students qualify more, and intensify and generalize less, the specific modifications they make point to a coherent theme in writing development, toward more circumspect writing.

Differences based on genre

Other findings suggest additional genre-based trends. In terms of qualified generalizations and hedges, there are no significant differences between minor DSP essay writing and minor essay writing, suggesting that students, regardless of level, qualify generality and certainty less often in essay writing and more often in nonessay, discipline-specific writing. The essay genre, then, appears to influence qualification (or downplaying) of both certainty and generality, even as such downplaying increases by level. Along with level-specific minor writing patterns, these findings furthermore suggest that generality marker use appears to be influenced by both genre and student level. In other words, even as students generalize less and qualify more once they begin undergraduate course work, they still generalize more and qualify less in essay writing. (See tables A and B at https://doi.org/10.3998/mpub.10079890.cmp.6 for more detailed findings.)

Comparative use of stance features is also interesting across the three genre-specific categories within the minor in undergraduate writing: minor discipline-specific writing, minor general, essay writing, and minor personalized/reflective essay writing. All three of these corpora consist of writing by the minor students after some college instruction (thus, the DSP texts are excluded). These corpus patterns show that discipline-specific writing and the personalized writing are most distinct from one another, a finding similar to that of Lizzie Hutton and Gail Gibson in chapter 3. More specifically, though, they are most distinctive in terms of generalization marker use as well as booster use ($p < .001$). They are not significantly distinct in terms of use of hedges. Furthermore, the general essay genre and personalized writing appear only significantly distinctive from one another in terms of boosters, which are used most in the personalized writing. Here too, these patterns suggest cases in which genre, rather than level, especially influences the minor students' written stance.[12] They also show that these writers use generality and certainty markers distinctly, or in distinct frequencies from one another, which supports the idea that it can be analytically useful to differentiate them in research on stance. For instance, minor students use generality markers significantly more in their personalized writing than in their essay writing, but there is no significant difference in their use of hedges between the two. The minor students may therefore be developing genre-specific stance features even as they are also making broader adjustments: overall, the students seem to develop their use of features related to a more circumspect stance—one with less generality and more qualification—but students furthermore use the most circumspect features in their nonessay writing. (See table C at https://doi.org/10.3998/mpub.10079890.cmp.6 for more detailed findings.)

Differences based on discipline group

Consider next the minor students' stance feature use across the minor discipline-specific writing, according to three common discipline groups: humanities, social sciences, and natural sciences. In these comparative corpus analyses, there are a few highly significant differences. One is that generalization marker use is significantly higher in minor humanities writing than in minor natural sciences writing ($p < .001$), and it is also significantly higher in minor social science compared to the minor natural science writing ($p < .001$). At the same time, minor social science writing contains significantly more qualified generalizations than the natural science writing ($p < .001$). A final highly significant distinction is that boosters are more frequent in minor humanities writing than in natural science writing ($p < .001$); they are also moderately significantly higher in minor social science than in minor natural science writing ($p < .01$).

Interestingly, the minor humanities writing includes the most generality markers as well as the most certainty markers, in both hedges and boosters. The certainty marker patterns match those found in Hyland ("Stance and Engagement"), in which academic research articles in the humanities contain the greatest relative frequencies of hedges and boosters, followed by social science and finally by natural science writing, which contains the fewest. Hyland attributes these patterns to the importance of showcasing writers' interpretive reasoning in the humanities, in contrast with the more empirical evidence used as the basis for claims made in social science and especially natural science writing. It is important to note that this is a matter of relative frequency of stance markers across disciplinary groups, rather than use and nonuse. That is, all disciplinary groups use features to adjust stance; for instance, as evidenced in the textual examples in the last section, a booster in a natural science lab report can emphasize the writer's knowledge and the reliability of the results. But boosters and hedges appear to be a more frequent part of a credible academic stance in the humanities than in the natural sciences, with social sciences often falling somewhere in between, in both the writing in Hyland's ("Stance and Engagement") research article analysis and in the minor writing. These patterns therefore indicate that the minor students may be approximating discipline-specific writing expectations consistent with published research articles, perhaps reflected in the discipline-specific texts they read for class and guided by instructor feedback that mirrors discipline-specific norms. These discursive distinctions point to discipline as another dimension of the students' writing development. (See table D at https://doi.org/10.3998/mpub.10079890.cmp.6 for more detailed findings.)

Differences based on student and professional level

Finally, to explore how stance feature use in minor-discipline-specific writing compares to that in more advanced academic writing, we can turn to the two advanced reference corpora: MICUSP, the reference corpus for slightly more advanced student writing, and COCAA, the reference corpus for published academic writing.

In terms of generality, the minor discipline-specific writing appears similar to both corpora: there are no significant differences in the frequencies between minor discipline-specific writing and either advanced student or published academic writing in generalization marker use. There are also no significant differences between minor-discipline-specific writing and advanced student writing in terms of qualified generalizations.

In terms of certainty, the minor student writers use significantly fewer hedges and significantly more boosters than the advanced student writers in MICUSP ($p < .001$). They likewise use fewer hedges ($p < .05$) and significantly more boosters ($p < .001$) than the published academic writers in COCAA. This pattern in minor student writing—of both more often intensified, and less often qualified, epistemic commitment—suggests that even though they begin to qualify their claims more as they move from secondary to undergraduate writing, students may still not be modulating stance to convey as much caution as more advanced writers, a point discussed further below.[13]

Conclusion

The focal corpora in this study are too small to draw broad conclusions, and more research is merited to explore stance features across level, disciplines, and genres. Still, notable discourse patterns emerge that point to student development, including: (1) an apparent developmental trajectory in use of stance features such as hedges and boosters, in which hedges increase and boosters decrease over time in academic writing (cf. Aull and Lancaster); (2) hedge and booster patterns in discipline-specific minor writing that appear to approximate professional academic expectations (cf. Hyland "Stance and Engagement"); and (3) the curbing of generalizations as a potential way that minor students begin to negotiate academic writing expectations.

One take-away from these findings is that generality and certainty markers are distinct in terms of student use, indicating that it is analytically and pedagogically useful to differentiate these aspects of stance. Both appear to be influenced to some extent by developmental level, genre, and discipline, but to different degrees. Specifically, the minor writers use certainty features significantly differently in their writing before UM instruction than they do after any UM writing instruction. In addition, relative to generality marker use, the certainty marker use in minor writing approximates that of more advanced writing across the genres they write: after some undergraduate instruction, these writers begin to use more qualification, and less definitive certainty, regardless of genre or field, and they also adjust in field-specific ways. For instance, minor humanities writing includes the most markers of generality and also the most markers of certainty, in both hedges and boosters, indicating that the minor students may be approximating discipline-specific writing expectations consistent with published research articles. The minor discipline-specific texts are furthermore similar to advanced discipline-specific texts in terms of generality markers.

These trends indicate that as students read and write more academic texts, some of their stance marker use shifts, and they do adjust levels of certainty and generality, at least to some extent, across rhetorical situations. Because these students receive instruction and engage in reflective writing practices as part of their writing minor, the patterns may indicate that students have benefited from these explicit practices. Specifically, students in writing minor courses may have received clear course-, genre-, and field-specific expectations, and been asked to reflect on these expectations. Other students may likewise benefit from clear expectations related to the generality and certainty of claims appropriate to a given task, including clear guidance about whether a writing goal is to approximate professional academic writers or not. Several other studies in this collection, including those by Ryan McCarty and Zak Lancaster, show what we can learn about student writing development from language-level analysis, and in turn, how insights from such analysis can support the development of student writers.

More specifically, insofar as the minor students qualify more and boost less after some UM undergraduate writing instruction, the students seem to have developed a greater understanding of how to qualify certainty and generality as part of negotiating the expectation that academic writing will show diplomacy and caution (cf. Hyland, "Stance and Engagement") and will be careful and open-minded toward competing positions (cf. Thaiss and Zawacki 5–7). At the same time, several studies in this collection indicate that many instructors do not aim for students to approximate the norms of professional academic writing in their discipline-specific course assignments. It may therefore be true that circumspect claims are welcome in undergraduate writing for a range of audiences and purposes. It may also be necessary and valuable for instructors to clarify whether they hope students will follow the norms of discipline-specific academic publishing or have alternate goals, such as making their ideas legible for a more general, popular audience. Specifically, as I hope this study shows, discourse-level choices can help illuminate macro-level constructs such as audience and purpose by connecting them to how they are realized and discoverable in language-level choices. Attention to discourse patterns in students' own and others' writing can help highlight distinctions in expectations related to stance, as well as specific choices students have for fulfilling them.

In a similar vein, the findings illustrate that students are learning multiple expectations related to expressing stance in different genres and disciplines. They therefore point to broader considerations for assessment, corpus research, and teaching. In terms of assessment, the findings suggest that we have more to learn about the intersection between stance patterns and genres regularly assigned in writing courses and standardized assessments. A specific finding is that stance features differ significantly between undergraduate essay genres and undergraduate discipline-specific writing. Research already suggests a mismatch between standardized secondary writing prompts and college-level writing assessments (Gere et al.), and this analysis further suggests that students must negotiate clear differences in stance expectations between early college and discipline-specific writing. Along these lines, we could see essay patterns such as generalizations as support for shifting "from nearly exclusive use of the essay" in early college writing to genres such as proposals that are more often expected in upper-level courses and workplaces (Burstein, Elliot, and Molloy 134), based on the idea that the generic conventions of the essay do not necessarily support the kinds of social and rhetorical actions students will encounter later. But if students can make discursive adaptations across genres, an apt question is instead, or additionally, how to help facilitate such adaptation. This brings us to considerations for research and teaching, which in turn can help inform writing assignment design.

An important research implication is that we need more studies of how language-level choices are shaped by genre and discipline, as well as other influences discussed in other chapters. Accordingly, we need more corpora that are organized and balanced vis-à-vis these facets of student writing development. Such corpora, with equal representation (to the extent possible) of different genres, fields, levels, etc., make it possible to expose distinctions that resonate with the interpersonal and genre-based expectations of different rhetorical tasks.

A final implication, and one I pose as a call for greater understanding, relates to how we conceptualize and examine what constitutes a credible and also civil claim. This study suggests that these minor students move away from emphatic and generalized claims and toward more circumspect ones as they practice and study writing. The findings in turn highlight several significant possibilities, as well as a responsibility to learn more. They point to discourse as a direct contributor to how writers position their own views. Incoming first-year writing tends to position the writer's claim as the only one; as the students write in undergraduate courses, they begin to position their claims as *one* credible option, especially in the nonpersonalized writing. These are shifts that highlight patterned discourse as evidence of distinctions across levels, genres, and disciplines. By that measure, they show that patterned discourse can help expose challenges and expectations that students face in crafting judicious claims: discourse can be part of students' analysis of genres and disciplines and can be an important part of recognizing writing that is inhospitable to nuance and multiple perspectives. The practiced ability to recognize such distinctions can help fuel awareness of the power of discourse and its socio-rhetorical effects. These choices include identifying when it may be fair to generalize and emphasize, and when it is most fair to be circumspect about the claims we make.

The lexical lists used in the analysis and the findings from the corpus analysis are available on our Fulcrum platform at https://doi.org/10.3998.mpub.10079890

NOTES

1. See, for instance, online writing guidance for incoming US college students, which regularly warns students against the "fallacy of hasty generalizations"; we see this, for example, from the University of North Carolina, University of Richmond, Purdue University, and Utah State University. Also see Clauss and Pinto (2011). See https://www.bowdoin.edu/writing-guides/three%20parts.htm; http://writingcenter.unc.edu/handouts/introductions/. Interestingly, the Bowdoin materials also suggest that students should "Make sure you convey that the topic is of vital concern," just after the recommendation that they should avoid general statements. It is worth considering whether students might perceive these two recommendations as being at odds.

2. The WPA Outcomes Statement identifies "appropriately qualified" generalizations as "foundational" for first-year college writers. For the WPA Outcomes Statement, see http://wpacouncil.org/positions/outcomes.html

3. Aull showed significant differences in claims made in the three task-based categories of student Directed Self-Placement (DSP) essays; corpus 3 included features closest to expert academic writing and corpus 2 included features the least like those of expert academic writing. An example of an open-ended prompt is "why do students cheat?" versus a source-text-based prompt such as "argue for or against Gladwell's proposal."

Corpus 1: Task invites personal evidence + source-text evidence; source-text-based writing prompt

Corpus 2: Task invites personal + source-text evidence; open-ended writing prompt

Corpus 3: Task invites source-text evidence only; source-text-based writing prompt

4. Comparisons between native and nonnative English-speaking students are outside of the scope of this study, but research also shows that relative to their native peers, English language learners intensify and use more generalized references (Hinkle; Hyland "Undergraduate Understandings"; Hyland and Milton).

5. Research on stance in academic writing tends to refer to two kinds of stance, "epistemic stance," which modulates truth value, and "attitudinal stance," which modulates affect. Epistemic stance markers, conventionally boosters and hedges that show more or less certainty, show writers' "assessments

of possibilities and probabilities" (Vande Kopple 97). Attitude markers show affective rather than epistemic stance, displaying the "degree of desirability" toward propositional information (Vande Kopple 100), such as by showing surprise, frustration, or importance (Hyland *Metadiscourse* 180). Recent work has argued that epistemic stance is communicated not only through adjusting certainty but by modulating generality (Aull, Bandarage, and Miller), as discussed more below. For concision, I refer throughout this chapter to the "stance markers" in the study, though they are more specifically epistemic stance markers.

6. It is likewise worth noting that corpus tools do not generate word and phrase frequencies alone; they generate word patterns, in lines of text and common word clusters, which are all linked to each full individual text in the corpus. See Römer and Wulff.

7. These criteria also precluded discipline-specific texts written by minor students outside of their major (e.g., a paper written by a chemistry major student for an upper-level anthropology class), because it was neither general writing nor writing in the discipline in which the student was receiving major-level training.

8. The UM DSP corpus is a rather specialized reference corpus, in that compared to the minor DSP, it is representative of a wider range of writing on the same particular task, level, and context. *Reference corpus* is defined generally as a corpus that is representative of a certain language (Cheng; Kübler and Zinsmeister), or as "usually a larger corpus of a more general type" (Römer and Wulff 105), and so in this case (relative to the minor DSP writing), the DSP corpus provides an appropriate reference. However, while the MICUSP and DSP corpora are useful in this case, studies such as this highlight the need for more reference corpora for student writing.

9. MICUSP is available at http://micusp.elicorpora.info/ and is comprised of writing by nonnative and native English-speaking students in their final year of undergraduate through their third year of graduate school. Because some texts appeared unusable when converted to .txt form for concordance analysis, the study includes 743 texts.

10. To attend to uses in individual texts as well as various corpus comparisons, each marker of generality, certainty, and attitude was analyzed in the selected minor student writing as well as in WordSmith Tools 6 concordance and collocation patterns across the corpora (Scott). All figures are normalized by 1,000 to provide comparative frequencies, and statistical significance was based on log likelihood (LL) values (e.g., see Gries).

11. As measured by log likelihood values; see table B at https://doi.org/10.3998/mpub.10079890.cmp.6 for values.

12. In this collection, Lizzie Hutton and Gail Gibson also suggest that genre distinctions are influenced by cultural patterns.

13. Though it does not concern minor writing, it is also interesting that MICUSP shows more hedges than COCAA ($p < .05$) and also significantly more boosters ($p < .001$). This suggests that these highly discipline-specific texts written by advanced student writers show more qualification than published academic essays and articles, which may be based on genre, in that general academic essays are a less formal academic genre and therefore contain less qualification.

WORKS CITED

Aull, Laura Louise. *First-Year University Writing: A Corpus-Based Study with Implications for Pedagogy*. Springer, 2015.

Aull, Laura Louise, Dineth Bandarage, and Meredith Richardson Miller. "Generality in Student and Expert Epistemic Stance: A Corpus Analysis of First-Year, Upper-Level, and Published Academic Writing." *Journal of English for Academic Purposes*, vol. 26, 2017, pp. 29–41.

Aull, Laura Louise, and Zak Lancaster. "Linguistic Markers of Stance in Early and Advanced Academic Writing: A Corpus-Based Comparison." *Written Communication*, vol. 1, no. 33, 2014.

Barlow, M. "Software for Corpus Access and Analysis." *How to Use Corpora in Language Teaching*, edited by J. M. Sinclair. Amsterdam: John Benjamins, 2004, pp. 205–21.

Barton, Ellen L. "Evidentials, Argumentation, and Epistemological Stance." *College English*, vol. 55, no. 7, 1993, pp. 745–69.

Berlin, James. *Writing Instruction in Nineteenth-Century American Colleges*. SIU Press, 1984.

Biber, Douglas, et al. *Longman Grammar of Spoken and Written English*, vol. 2, MIT Press, 1999.

Brown, David West, and Laura Louise Aull. "Elaborated Specificity vs. Emphatic Generality: A Corpus-Based Comparison of Higher and Lower Scoring Advanced Placement Exams in English." *Research in the Teaching of English*, vol. 51, no. 4, 2017, pp. 394–417.

Burstein, Jill, Norbert Elliot, and Hillary Molloy. "Informing Automated Writing Evaluation Using the Lens of Genre: Two Studies." *CALICO Journal*, vol. 33, no. 1, 2016, pp. 117–32.

Cheng, Winnie. *Exploring Corpus Linguistics: Language in Action*. Routledge, 2011.

Clauss, Patrick, and Pinto, Laura. "Is Data the Plural of Anecdote? Inductive Arguments in Composition." OSSA Conference Archive, 49, 2011. https://scholar.uwindsor.ca/ossaarchive/OSSA9/papersandcommentaries/49

Cortes, Viviana. "Lexical Bundles in Freshman Composition." *Using Corpora to Explore Linguistic Variation*, edited by R. Reppen, S. M. Fitzmaurice, and D. Biber. Amsterdam: John Benjamins, 2002.

Dryer, Dylan B. "Scaling Writing Ability: A Corpus-Driven Inquiry." *Written Communication*, vol. 30, no. 1, 2013, pp. 3–35.

Gere, Anne Ruggles, Laura Aull, Moisés Damián Perales Escudero, Zak Lancaster, and Elizabeth Vander Lei. "Local Assessment: Using Genre Analysis to Validate Directed Self-Placement." *College Composition and Communication*, vol. 4, no. 64, 2013, pp. 605–33.

Grabe, William. "Narrative and Expository Macro-Genres." *Genre in the Classroom: Multiple Perspectives*, 2002, pp. 249–67.

Gries, Stefan. "Useful Statistics for Corpus Linguistics." *A Mosaic of Corpus Linguistics: Selected Approaches* 66 (2010): 269–91.

Hardy, Jack A., and Ute Römer. "Revealing Disciplinary Variation in Student Writing: A Multi-Dimensional Analysis of the Michigan Corpus of Upper-Level Student Papers (MICUSP)." *Corpora*, vol. 8, no. 2, 2013, pp. 183–207.

Hinkel, Eli. "Hedging, Inflating, and Persuading in L2 Academic Writing." *Applied Language Learning*, vol. 15, no. 1/2, 2006, pp. 29–42.

Hyland, Ken. *Disciplinary Discourses: Social Interactions in Academic Writing*. Michigan classics ed. University of Michigan Press, 2004.

Hyland, Ken. *Metadiscourse: Exploring Interaction in Writing*. Continuum Discourse Series, Continuum, 2005.

Hyland, Ken. "Stance and Engagement: A Model of Interaction in Academic Discourse." *Discourse Studies*, vol. 7, no. 2, 2005, pp. 173–92.

Hyland, Ken. "Undergraduate Understandings: Stance and Voice in Final Year Reports." *Stance and Voice in Written Academic Genres*, edited by Ken Hyland and C. S. Guinda, Palgrave Macmillan, 2012, pp. 134–50.

Hyland, Ken, and John Milton. "Qualification and Certainty in L1 and L2 Students' Writing." *Journal of Second Language Writing* 6.2 (1997): 183–205.

Kübler, Sandra, and Heike Zinsmeister. *Corpus Linguistics and Linguistically Annotated Corpora*. Bloomsbury Publishing, 2015.

Labov, William. *The Several Logics of Quantification*. Annual Meeting of the Berkeley Linguistics Society, 1985.

Lancaster, Zak. "Do Academics Really Write This Way? A Corpus Investigation of Moves and Templates in '*They Say/I Say*.'" *College Composition and Communication*, vol. 67, no. 3, 2016, pp. 437–64.

Lancaster, Zak. "Stance and Reader Positioning in Upper-Level Student Writing in Political Theory and Economics." PhD diss., University of Michigan, 2012.

Miller, Carolyn. "Genre as Social Action." *Quarterly Journal of Speech*, vol. 70, no. 2, 1984, pp. 151–67.

Myers, Greg. "Lexical Cohesion and Specialized Knowledge in Science and Popular Science Texts." *Discourse Processes*, vol. 14, no. 1, 1991, pp. 1–26.

Nesi, Hilary, and Sheena Gardner. *Genres across the Disciplines: Student Writing in Higher Education*. Cambridge University Press, 2012.

Penrose, Ann M. "Academic Literacy Perceptions and Performance: Comparing First-Generation and Continuing-Generation College Students." *Research in the Teaching of English*, 2002, pp. 437–61.

Puma, Vincent D. "Relationships between Writer-Audience Proximity, Register, and Quality in the Essays of First-Year College Students." 1986.

Quirk, Randolph, et al. *A Comprehensive Grammar of the English Language*. Longman, 1985.

Römer, Ute, and Matthew Brook O'Donnell. "From Student Hard Drive to Web Corpus (Part 1): The Design, Compilation and Genre Classification of the Michigan Corpus of Upper-Level Student Papers (MICUSP)." *Corpora*, vol. 6, no. 2, 2011, pp. 159–77.

Römer, Ute, and Stefanie Wulff. "Applying Corpus Methods to Written Academic Texts: Explorations of MICUSP." *Journal of Writing Research*, vol. 2, no. 2, 2010, pp. 99–127.

Russell, David. "Activity Theory and Its Implications for Writing Instruction." *Reconceiving Writing, Rethinking Writing Instruction*, edited by Joseph Petraglia, Routledge, 1995, pp. 51–78.

Scott, M. *Wordsmith Tools*. (vers. 6.0) (computer software). Oxford University Press, 2014.

Thaiss, Chris, and Terry Myers Zawacki. "Engaged Writers Dynamic Disciplines." *Engaged Writers Dynamic Disciplines: Research and the Academic Writing Life*. Boynton/Cook Heinemann, 2006.

Vande Kopple, William J. "Metadiscourse, Discourse, and Issues in Composition and Rhetoric." *Discourse Studies in Composition*. Hampton Press, 2002, pp. 91–113.

Wardle, Elizabeth. "'Mutt Genres' and the Goal of FYE: Can We Help Students Write the Genres of the University?" *College Composition and Communication*, vol. 60, no. 4, 2009, pp. 765–89.

CHAPTER SIX

TRACKING STUDENTS' DEVELOPING CONCEPTIONS OF *VOICE* AND *STYLE* IN WRITING

Zak Lancaster

Participants in the Writing Development Study (WDS) were asked complex questions during interviews about their writing experiences and beliefs, including their views of "good" writing and of their identities and goals as writers. Understandably, many stumbled through their explanations, often drawing on slippery terms such as "style" and "voice" in the process. Consider Tim's responses to the question, "How would you describe yourself as a writer?" These were recorded approximately two years apart, the first around the end of his sophomore year and the second during his senior year.

- Obviously, in college, you get exposed to a lot of different styles; English creatives [*sic*], professional, and stuff like that, so you have to adopt [. . .] like different voices as you write. In general, the kind of writing that I tend to do is very informal in style, and just kind of personable, as opposed to a very academic style, or big words and stuff like that.
- Writing has always been a strength of mine through all of school; middle school, high school, stuff like that. I kind of have a creative, like, informal voice, but my writing has always been very solid. That's always been my strength.

Such interview comments illustrate the complex ways many WDS participants used the terms *style* and *voice* to articulate their conceptions of writing. For Tim, the terms appear to be at once interchangeable and polysemous. In one breath, he refers to his exposure to "a lot of different styles" and the need to "adopt different voices" in writing, suggesting that styles and voices are multiple and vary by context. In the very next breath, he refers to the kind of writing he "tend[s] to do" as "very informal [and personable] in style," in contrast to a "very academic style," which is a view of style akin to what linguists call *register*. Two years later, Tim refers to his individual *voice* (the voice "I kind of have") as "informal" and "creative." For Tim, then, it seems that *voice/style* is both something one personally "has"—and can learn to express in writing—and something one can choose to "adopt" depending on the rhetorical context.

Tim's complex uses of *style* and *voice* recall long-standing debates in writing studies, especially those centered on voice (see overviews by Matsuda; Tardy). As I discuss in greater detail below, Tim's reference to "different voices" suggests a social-constructionist view, which sees voices as multiple and as constructed within social contexts. In contrast, his reference to voice in individualized terms (e.g., "I kind of have a creative . . . voice") is more in line with an expressivist view, or what I will call here an individualist view, which sees voice as an expression of one's authentic self. Similar distinctions have been made with regard to *style* (see, e.g., Johnson and Pace; Olinger). As shorthand, we may refer to these two conceptions as *individualist* and *social*. What is especially noteworthy about Tim's responses is that they suggest he sees voice and style in both their individual and social dimensions. Does this mean he is confused? Or does it mean the individualist/social dichotomy is limited? Or might it point to the unevenness and messiness of writers' developing conceptions about writing?

Inspired by these questions, this chapter examines interview data in the WDS study to explore both quantitatively and qualitatively how the participants' beliefs about writing are illuminated through their uses of two constructs, *style* and *voice*. It examines every instance of students' explicit use of these terms in all 131 WDS interviews. In so doing, it pays special attention to the potential impact of the writing minor curriculum on students' articulations by comparing the minors' and nonminors' implicit definitions of *voice* and *style* at two stages in their development, just as they were setting out on their major and minor concentrations (around their second year) and then as they were preparing to graduate.

In pursuing this investigation, this chapter raises questions about trajectories of development in students' underlying views of *style* and *voice*, and about the kinds of assignments and activities that may aid in that development. In this way, it approaches writing development in terms of language-level discussions about writing—that is, the language we use to talk about writing and the concepts that underlie that talk. A great deal of scholarship in both writing studies and linguistics has begun to explore writers' explicit knowledge about writing, from discussions of threshold concepts, to pedagogical approaches to enhancing students' explicit awareness of language use, to frameworks for studying meta-awareness and metacognition. Following in this tradition, this chapter explores the extent to which students' views of *style* and *voice* align with current conceptualizations of these constructs in writing studies, as seen in research by Paul Kei Matsuda, Christine Tardy, Andrea Olinger, Ken Hyland, and others. If writing is understood "as a social and rhetorical activity" and one that "enacts and creates identities and ideologies" (Adler-Kassner and Wardle), then we might expect that students, especially those who have chosen an interdisciplinary writing minor, would come to see *voices* and *styles* in increasingly social and rhetorical terms. What this chapter shows, however, is that just as students' performances of writing do not develop neatly and linearly over time, neither do their metalinguistic capacities to discuss their writing. Metalinguistic development, like writing development generally, is uneven and sporadic, happening in fits and starts. But, as this chapter also shows, it is a dimension of writing development that may be especially responsive to opportunities to engage in explicit dialogue about writing.

Voice and *Style*: Individual and Social Conceptions

To probe students' conceptions of *style* and *voice*, it is necessary to understand how these constructs have been conceptualized in writing studies. Regarding *voice*, the individualist-social division is a reductive but useful starting point for gauging the range of perspectives. The *individualist* view regards voice as the writer's expression of her unique inner self, whether understood as her personal opinions, passions, and commitments, as her distinct ways of using language, or both. This conception is suggested in advice to express, find, or own your voice, and it is the view that seems to be most frequently articulated in US-based composition textbooks, as shown by Vai Ramanathan and Robert Kaplan, and by high school English teachers still today, as Jill Jeffery shows. The individualist view has also been juxtaposed with "academic writing" generally, which is often perceived as dull, lifeless, and voiceless. With enough skill and willpower, according to this view, the writer may be able to *infuse* voice into her otherwise dry and stuffy research article. Understood this way, voice is a quality of language use that can be "allowed" or "injected" into academic discourse. As Christine Tardy notes, this individualist view is frequently wrapped up with notions of strength, commitment, ownership, and authenticity.

Writing scholars have challenged the individualist perspective of voice on a number of fronts. In addition to overlooking the ways writers vary their authorial self-representations depending on audience and genre (see, e.g., Ivanič), it reflects cultural assumptions about writing and selfhood that not all students share.

In particular, many students who are raised outside dominant US cultures or who write in English as an additional language may find advice that they should project a strong, individualized voice to be inaccessible or objectionable (Ramanathan and Kaplan). This is partly because such advice elevates the "I" above the "we" (see, e.g., Shen), which is an understanding of the self that can confuse and marginalize students who come from cultures with different understandings of the self and who have less extensive experience with genres of writing that foreground an individual voice.

Partly as a response to such critiques, *social* views argue that voices are rooted (and shaped and reinforced) in specific social contexts, including academic discourse communities. From this view, the voice projected in a text is "a language performance—always social, mediated by experience, and culturally embedded" (Sperling and Appleman 71). Charles Bazerman suggests such a view when he points out that college writers are expected to "learn to speak with voices recognizable as legitimate, warrantable and powerful within the disciplines" (25). This sense of voice is closely associated with communities and genres. A scientist reading a fellow scientist's research article, a genre often thought to be voice*less*, would recognize and identify with a certain kind of *scientific voice* projected by the text, one that carries authority within the specialist community.

From a social view of voice, then, it is not simply that a writer can or cannot (or should or should not) express her voice in writing; it is rather that all writing, because it is embedded within communities of readers and writers, responds to and reflects a socially based voice for those readers, whether or not the writer consciously aims for a certain kind of voice. In this sense, voice has been seen as an *inevitable* quality of discourse, coconstructed between writer and reader in specific discursive interactions. Matsuda's definition captures these points. *Voice*, he argues, is "the amalgamative effect of the use of discursive and non-discursive features that language users choose, deliberately or otherwise, from socially available yet ever-changing repertoires" (40). And that amalgamative rhetorical effect, interpreted as "voice," is "successful" if it is recognized and valued by members of the community where the writing is taking place.

Despite these sharp differences in conceptions, the individualist/social dichotomy does not hold firm for very long if pressed. Peter Elbow, for instance, who has frequently been identified with individualist views of voice, has acknowledged that voice is not limited to the individual or to only certain kinds of prose. "The voice" in a piece of writing, he suggests, "can be blah, impersonal, bureaucratic, or even computer-speak, but there's always a voice" ("Voice in Writing Again" 178). He has also argued that students need to develop a variety of voices in their writing because, as he explains, "selves tend to evolve, change, take on new voices and assimilate them" ("What Do We Mean" 5).

Conversely, scholars more closely associated with social views have acknowledged the importance of writers' individual perspectives. In his recent work ("Undergraduate Understandings"), Ken Hyland has teased apart "stance" from "voice," arguing that the former is writer-oriented and the latter reader-oriented. In this framework, it is *stance* that individual writers express when they mark their presence as authors and signal their attitudes, judgments, and feelings. It is, in contrast, the community-oriented *voice* they are creating that allows for their stances to be heard in the first place. If writers want their stances to be heard, that is, they must create a "voice" for their texts that resounds with "the authorized ways of speaking as a community member" (134). Of course, this is a very different perspective on *voice* from the individualist one. But it is still the case for Hyland that academic writers express their individual views, attitudes, and feelings. Philosophers or historians may do this more prominently than engineers or physicists, but all academic writers do it to one degree or another.

Even closer to the individualist notion is Roz Ivanič's concept of the writer's "autobiographical self." In her theorization of identity in writing, Ivanič distinguishes between, on the one hand, the writer's sense of her own roots, including her personal history, values, and motivations (i.e., who she "really" is), and, on the other, how the writer uses language to project an authorial presence in the text. Ivanič terms the first dimension *autobiographical self* and the second *discoursal self*. These two dimensions do not always align, of course, and Ivanič is especially interested in exposing how writers may resist or accommodate to certain discoursal selves.

A point on which Hyland, Ivanič, and Elbow (among others) would probably agree is that voice is best understood in dialogic terms, as negotiated through specific discoursal interactions. Stretches of discourse can also be viewed for the ways they weave multiple voices together: the writer's, other scholars', putative readers', and the social voices that are *implied* by the writer's choice of genre. Seeing voice from this perspective suggests Mikhail Bakhtin's notion of *heteroglossia*, or multivoicedness. Linguists working in the tradition of systemic functional linguistics, furthermore, have drawn on Bakhtin's work to model how developing writers learn to use resources in the language to move from a position of monogloss, or singlevoicedness, in their course-work writing, to a more heteroglossic position marked by dialogic diversity (see, e.g., Coffin; Hood). Such research emphasizes the linguistic resources that writers draw on to construct community-valued voices. Other traditions have focused more on the role of readers and how they interpret and evaluate voices based on linguistic cues (see, e.g., Matsuda and Tardy).

The scholarship on *style* is far too enormous and diverse to do it justice here. I would remark, however, that the perspectives on voice just sketched out are applicable to *style* as well. For instance, literary conceptualizations of style have focused on prose qualities that are unique to an individual author—qualities recognizable as his or her personal stamp or linguistic signature. On the other hand, discussions of linguistic resources used to construct an "academic style" overlap significantly with social views of voice. Mary Hiatt acknowledged this split in 1978:

> Some stylisticians hold that style is totally a matter of one individual's writing . . . others take an opposing view and maintain that it is possible to describe the characteristics of a group of writers or of writers in a certain era. Stylisticians further differ on whether style is the sum total of the characteristics of the writing or whether it describes in what way the writing departs from the norm. . . . The state of the theory itself is therefore conflicting and confusing. (222)

As suggested here, "style" may be thought of as an extraordinary use of language, that which "departs from the norm." But it may also be thought of as synonymous with what linguists call *register*, defined by Douglas Biber and Susan Conrad as "a variety [of language use] associated with a particular situation of use" (6). If style is seen as purposeful, situated language variety, we can talk about "styles of writing" such as journalistic, legal, and academic styles—a very different concept from "my style" or "her style."[1]

Individual and social views of language use do not have to be mutually exclusive, especially as dialogic views offer a bridge between the two. So, how did the study participants use the terms *style* and *voice*? What shifts, if any, are evident in their uses of these constructs between entry and exit interviews? And finally, what might these shifts suggest about learners' metalinguistic development?

The Study: Exploring Students' Conceptions of Style and Voice

To explore these questions, I examined every instance of *style* and *voice* in the 131 interviews conducted as part of this study. While there are many related terms worthy of investigation, including *tone*, ethos, *persona*, *identity*, *language*, and *grammar*, my aim was to better understand students' conceptions of *style* and *voice* in particular. As scholars such as Roz Ivanič, Rebecca Nowacek, and Mary Soliday have argued, attending closely to students' talk about writing—including the specific terms they use—can help to illuminate their attitudes and beliefs about writing, which often run below their fully conscious awareness.

To aid my analysis, I converted all the interview transcripts to plain text files and examined them through AntConc (Anthony). Unlike Aull's analysis in this volume, mine did not require sophisticated corpus searches. I used the software mainly to retrieve all uses of the two terms, which I then examined and sorted into categories. In addition to ensuring that I did not overlook any instances, the software enabled me to perform basic analyses of collocations. These included the pronouns *my* and *your*, as in *my/your voice* and *my/your (own) style*, and verbs such as *have*, *find*, and *own*, which indicate something about how students understand the two constructs. Through these basic tools, I was able to retrieve quantitative information that informed my approach to the qualitative analysis.

In total, the corpus search retrieved 454 related uses of *style(s)* and *voice(s)*.[2] I pasted these into an Excel spreadsheet, and for each instance I included the surrounding co-text—typically several turns in the interview—to interpret how participants were using the terms; in some cases, I referred to larger sections of the transcript. I also compared individual students' uses of *style* and *voice* within single interviews and, where applicable, across entry and exit interviews.

Participants' Conceptions of *Style* and *Voice*: A Quantitative Overview

At the most general level, the corpus results show that the term *style* was used more frequently than *voice*. Approximately 70 percent of the participants used *style* in at least one of their interviews, while just 50 percent used *voice*. This difference points to the greater variety of meanings that participants used the term *style* to articulate, as I explore below.

Table 6.1 shows the percentages of interviews where the respective terms were used. For example, the top row shows that, among the 34 entry interviews conducted with the writing minors, 21 minors (61.8 percent) used the term *voice* while 23 (67.7 percent) used the term *style*. Table 6.1 also shows differences between the minors and nonminors. Primarily, the term *voice* was used by more minors than nonminors, in both entry and exit interviews, while the term *style* was used by more nonminors than minors. The difference in references to *voice* was especially large in the entry interviews, where 61.8 percent of the minors use the term compared to just 26.5 percent of the nonminors. This percentage did increase for the nonminors by their exit interviews, when nearly half (48.3 percent) referred to *voice*.

Table 6.1. Explicit Mentions of Voice and Style

Status	Interviewees (*n*)	Students Referring to *Voice*		Students Referring to *Style*	
		n	%	*n*	%
Minors (Entry)	34	21	61.8	23	67.7
Nonminors (Entry)	34	9	26.5	25	73.5
Minors (Exit)	34	23	67.6	23	67.6
Nonminors (Exit)	29	14	48.3	21	72.4
TOTAL	131	67	51.1	92	70.2

Students' Uses of Style

To explain the greater use of *style*, my analysis uncovered four recurring references. As illustrated in table 6.2, these are: *style as individual language use*, *style as register*, *style as genre*, and *style as usage conventions*. **Style as individual language use** is akin to the notion of *individual voice*, in that it concerns the writer's expressions of her distinct ways of using language. Under this category, I placed all references to *my (writing) style* and *your/their style*, as well as explicit mentions of *unique*, *individual*, and *my personal style*. **Style as register** refers to variation in language use by situational context. Under this category, I grouped mentions of formality/informality in style and descriptions of specific styles, such as *academic*, *magazine*, and *journalistic*. I also included references that were less specific but still suggestive of style as multiple, including phases such as *that style*. **Style as genre** refers to recognizable types, forms, purposes, or modes of writing, such as *research paper style*, *narrative style*, *essay style*, and *memo-style*.[3] Whereas I considered "business style" and "academic style" to refer to *register*, because many genres fall within these registers, I considered references to "cover letter style," "memo style," and "essay-type style" to refer to *genre*. Finally, **style as usage conventions** covers all references to specific citation conventions (e.g., APA, MLA), and to style as usage rules.

Table 6.3 shows how these four references were distributed across the transcripts. The distributions are presented as raw instances (*n*) and percentages among participants who used the term. For example, the top row shows that 13 of the writing minors referred to *style as individual language use* in their entry interviews, which was 32.5 percent of all references to *style* in this group. Table 6.3 also shows differences between the writing minors and nonminors. Most importantly, it shows that a higher percentage of minors referenced *style as register*—both in entry and exit interviews. Furthermore, whereas references to *individual style* increased among the nonminors, they decreased among the minors. Relatedly, the minors' references to *style as register* and *style as genre* both increased from entry to exit interviews. The latter two trends suggest that the minors' underlying views of *style* became more congruent with current theoretical conceptualizations—that is, more focused on the social and less on the individual.

To be clear, the differences shown in table 6.3 are not huge. But they do point to a consistent pattern. More of the minors used the term *style* when discussing the various types of writing they experienced, as seen in example 1 below, or when explaining how they approached a piece of writing in light of their audience, as seen in 2.

1. You don't do one style of writing the entire time. It's all sorts of things.
2. If you're writing towards a younger audience, you have to use a style that they're gonna understand.

Table 6.2. References for "Style"

Reference	Examples
Style as individual language use	• My writing style is mainly descriptive. (Dan, Exit) • You have to think about your own individual style. (Grace, Exit)
Style as register	• . . . when you're writing journalistic style . . . (Brian, Exit) • . . . like a more concise, concrete, direct style of writing. (Lisa, Exit)
Style as genre	• Memo-style was huge [in the business school]. Then cover letter like I said. (Madeleine, Exit) • Almost like a research report. Almost like a—not interview style, but like a column on a certain topic. (Teresa, Exit)
Style as usage conventions	• He has a lot of grammar-style things. (Dan, Exit) • When you do social science you do APA. When you do this, you do *Chicago*-style. (Lisa, Exit)

Table 6.3. Distributions of Style References

	Style as Individual		Style as Register		Style as Genre		Style as Usage Conventions	
	n	%	*n*	%	*n*	%	*n*	%
Minors (Entry)	13	32.5	17	42.5	3	7.5	7	17.5
Nonminors (Entry)	19	41.3	13	28.3	2	4.3	12	26.0
Minors (Exit)	11	26.1	18	42.9	5	11.9	8	19.0
Nonminors (Exit)	15	50.0	9	30.0	1	3.3	5	16.7
TOTALS	58	36.7	57	36.1	11	7.0	32	20.2

In contrast, more of the nonminors used the term *style* as a substitute for *individual voice*, as seen in 3 and 4.

3. I don't know how to describe [voice], I guess, outside of being able to recognize and identify a certain person's style.
4. I think if I continued to do more [blogging] . . . it would help find my own voice as a writer and the style and personality that my writing would show through. Because I think on a blog you can feel like you can just really be yourself.

Students' Uses of *Voice*

My analysis of *voice* revealed fewer gradations in meaning. The three categories that emerged are *social*, *individualist*, and *unclear*. As discussed above, *social* views include references to voices as multiple and rooted in contexts, as seen in 5 and 6.

5. Besides that it was a very different voice because it was so research based.
6. A quick text message kind of voice.

In contrast, *individualist conceptions* are reflected in references to personal voices, as seen in 7 and 8. These capture the notion of autobiographical self, or "who you really are."

7. I think you need to have a voice for yourself that expresses who you are.
8. Also, just being persuasive and having your own writing voice.

Table 6.4 shows the distributions of these references across the interviews. Starting with the top row, we see that 61.9 percent of writing minors who referenced *voice* in their entry interviews expressed individualist views; in contrast, just 23.8 percent expressed social views. Overall, the table shows that just 29.9 percent of students who referenced *voice* expressed social views, which suggests that participants used *style* more than *voice* in a social-constructionist sense. Importantly, for both minors and nonminors, individualist conceptions of voice decreased from entry to exit while social conceptions increased. However, for the minors, the ratio of individual to social views is nearly even in the exit interviews (47.8 percent to 43.5 percent), while this ratio for the nonminors still tilts heavily toward individualist conceptions (57.1 percent to 28.6 percent). Again, the differences are not large. Whereas five mi-

Table 6.4. Distributions of Voice References

	Individualist Views		Social Views		Other/Unclear	
	n	%	*n*	%	*n*	%
Minors (Entry)	13	61.9	5	23.8	3	14.3
Nonminors (Entry)	7	77.8	1	11.1	1	11.1
Minors (Exit)	11	47.8	10	43.5	2	8.7
Nonminors (Exit)	8	57.1	4	28.6	2	14.3
TOTALS	39	58.2	20	29.9	8	11.9

nors articulated social views of *voice* in their entry interview, ten did so in their exit interviews. For the nonminors, the increase was from one to four students.

In sum, the quantitative analysis revealed three apparent shifts in participants' conceptions of *style* and *voice*, especially among the writing minors. First, the minors' references to *individual style* decreased while their references to *style as register* and *style as genre* both increased—suggesting that they developed a more social conception of this construct. Second, more minors than nonminors referred to *voice* in both rounds of interviews, suggesting that this construct entered more into their "discursive consciousness," or capacity to articulate explicitly.[4] And third, more minors than nonminors expressed social views of *voice*, and these references increased from entry to exit interviews. It is important to reiterate, though, that this metalinguistic development was by no means even or linear. My analysis of individual participants' talk about style and voice revealed a great deal of messiness, including apparent contradictions in conceptions. What I aim to show in the next section is that examining this messiness can help to illuminate the kinds of writing and reflective tasks that may push students toward individual or social conceptions of style and voice.

Complexity in Students' Views

The primary kind of complexity that emerged in participants' interviews was a slipping back and forth between individualist and social conceptions of writing, and this often followed a distinct pattern. Individualist conceptions tended to surface as participants spoke in general terms about writing principles and goals, while social conceptions surfaced as they turned to specific assignments or specific strategies they used in a piece of writing.

Consider, for example, Kaitlin, who majored in English and communication studies and minored in writing. In her entry interview, Kaitlin lumps *style* and *voice* together (along with "tone") when referring in general to the positive value that journaling had on her writing development. In her entry interview she explained that journaling "really forced me to hone [my writing] and work on my own personal style and tone and voice." She elaborated by equating *style* explicitly with personality: "Maybe it's more like a shift in my personality, than in my style, but I think the style reflects your personality." Kaitlin also used *voice* to articulate a similar point about personality, as seen here when referring to the impact of the Gateway course on her writing development.

> I think maybe it's [. . .] helped me see it's okay to have a personality when you write. A lot of times when you're writing a lit analysis or you're writing a research paper, it's easy to forget that you're allowed to have a voice, whereas in the minor, [my instructor] really encouraged that.

In this articulation, "voice," like "style" and "personality," is a quality that a piece of writing does or does not "have." Some writing has it; other writing doesn't.

Later in the same interview, however, Kaitlin referred to specific research papers she wrote in her communications major as a "style of writing," one where "you present your findings and tables and charts and then your results, which is kind of *a fun style of writing*." This reference to *style as genre* departs sharply from her view of style as personality. Kaitlin also complicated the concept of individual *voice* when discussing her remediation assignment in her minor Gateway course. As she explained,

> By the end [of the assignment] I'd taken a lit analysis that I'd written on this book about cultural diaspora, and then turned it into a conversation about sexual hegemony. It was something that I really cared about and [my instructor] helped me find *Bitch Magazine* and so that helped me write it in *that voice* where it was just . . .

Here, Kaitlin's pronoun shifts from "my voice" to "that voice," suggesting that there are multiple voices from which to choose. Kaitlin did not continue to describe "that voice" or how she learned to construct it. Rather, she switched gears in midsentence to return to a more individualist take-away about writing; the quote continues:

> I think that the Gateway course really helped me realize that, "Oh, I am allowed to write from my perspective and have my tone and my flavor and help put the 'me' in my writing."

Kaitlin, then, expressed individualist views of style and voice when speaking about writing in general and social views when reflecting on specific writing projects.

Like Kaitlin, Mariana appeared to hold an individualist perspective of both *style* and *voice* when speaking generally about writing. Commenting in her entry interview on decisions she made for her eportfolio, she explained that she "wanted to make sure that it fit me and *my style of writing* the best." And on her future goals as a writer, she explained that, "I still wanna continue to find *my own voice* and to be able to put it into writing." However, commenting on specific papers she wrote, Mariana noted that "I've had a lot of different projects here, and that's the thing that I like about the writing classes here, is that it's—*you don't do one style of writing* the entire time." In this latter reference, style is not personal but situational.

As just shown, developing writers such as Kaitlin and Mariana slip back and forth between individual and social conceptions of writing. They do so, furthermore, depending on the level of writing they are speaking about. Very few students articulated overtly social conceptions of voice or style when discussing general writing principles or goals. Overt talk, that is, about "adapting," "constructing," or "varying" voices was highly unusual. Far more frequent was overt talk about "finding," "owning," or "expressing" one's own voice. This is probably because these individualist conceptions circulate more widely in public discourses about writing—as a quick Google search of "writing and voice" confirms. But the more social conceptions did leak through as participants began to explain the specific assignments and texts they had written.

Another illustration of this general-specific split can be seen in Jon's interview comments. An English major and writing minor, Jon invoked a clearly individualist notion of selfhood and writing in his exit interview when responding to an abstract question about what it means to "write well" at the university level. As he explained, "If you're writing well, you're accurately representing what you actually think about whatever you're writing on [. . .] like you are accurately representing you on the page." Note that this idea of "you on the page" is akin to Ivanič's autobiographical self; it is the representation of one's lived experiences, beliefs, and stances. Jon articulated the same perspective in his entry interview two years earlier in response to a question about what is "most important in learning how to write." As he explained,

> Having a good understanding of yourself is really strong [*sic*] because voice is one of those things that I think can make or break a paper. You can have the strongest argument or whatever. All the evidence, all the analysis, but if you don't have—if you're not in it, I'm not going to care.

Jon articulated a different view of voice, however, in his exit interview when asked to discuss his uses of reflective writing. As a part of his response, he explained that "voice" became a useful concept for him:

> There were some words [about writing] that came up all the time [in my reflections], and there were just writing terms like "voice" and I have a much clearer understanding of what I typically want my voice to be like, depending on audience or how to approach something, and what level of detail based on scope or—again, audience. I don't know, "scope," "voice" and "audience" come up a lot.

Here, Jon refers to voice as a kind of discursive performance ("what I typically want my voice to be like"), which can or should vary "depending on audience" and strategy, or "how to approach something." To be clear, then, Jon articulated a view of voice as both autobiographical self and discursive self, and these two views surfaced at different levels of talk about writing—whether he was talking generally or more specifically about his writing strategies.

There were exceptions to this trend. Some students did talk about voice in overtly social-constructionist terms, even when discussing writing in the abstract. Consider, for example, Angela's explanation in her exit interview of social voice and context.

> I definitely use a different writing voice when I'm writing for online than [when] I'm writing an academic paper. I mean, online I've been things [*sic*] from witty to sometimes a little snarky, I admit it, to more fun and upbeat. I mean, I recently completed an internship at—I don't know if you've heard of this magazine, *Tiger Beat*? It's for thirteen-year-old teen girls about celebrities. Obviously, I wasn't snarky there. I was peppy and energetic. I don't know. *You have to adapt your voice to the situation.*

Angela is explaining here, in overtly social terms, how she adapted her voice for online situations—making it sometimes "snarky" and sometimes "peppy and energetic"—concluding that, "You have to adapt your voice to the situation." This comment suggests that Angela values her ability to craft different voices for different contexts, to write with dexterity across a range of genres, as Ryan McCarty's analysis in chapter 4 reveals with regard to other students in this study. However, it is also important to point out that Angela is responding to a very specific interview question ("How would you describe your voice?"), and that this question is a follow-up to Angela's earlier remark that, to write well in college, "you have to have your own specific voice." That is, with one pointed follow-up question, Angela's use of the term "voice" shifted from an individualist to a social-constructionist perspective. This shows how developing writers—certainly alongside many experts as well (cf. Olinger)—may hold apparently contradictory conceptions about writing simultaneously, and when gently pressed, can shift between them. For Angela, and many other participants, social conceptions of voice and style do not lie far below the surface of more individualist ones that may be more on the tip of their tongues.

Angela was not a writing minor, and therefore she probably did not participate as consistently as did the minors in the kinds of explicit personal reflections on writing that many of the tasks in the writing minor required. The interview itself encouraged her to reflect explicitly on her writing, however, and in the process Angela drew on *voice* as a metalinguistic construct. Therefore, the fact that the writing minors did undergo this deep reflection consistently may help to explain why so many more of them articulated social concepts of language in writing, both as *voice* and *style*.

In general, the WDS participants' talk about *style* and *voice* points to complex and shifting views about selfhood and writing. Participants referred to individual voices/styles and social voices/styles simultaneously, even within the same interview. On this basis, it seems clear that students' beliefs about writing are neither settled nor simple, but shifting and flexible, even in spite of what appear to be strongly held convictions, such as Jon's statement that "if you're not in it, I'm not going to care." Writing instructors and researchers would therefore be wise to listen carefully to students' talk about writing and create opportunities for them to reflect explicitly on *specific* writing experiences and projects.

Note that the WDS interviews were not primarily text-based, or designed to probe participants' tacit knowledge about writing by querying them about their own rhetorical and linguistic choices. However, we can pause to consider what a detailed linguistic analysis of students' written texts might further contribute to our understanding of their views of *voice* or *style*. What, in other words, might an investigation of their performances of writing reveal about their underlying conceptions of these constructs?

Investigating Students' Performances of *Voice* in Writing

This question about the relationship between students' writing performances and explicit beliefs—including their metalinguistic awareness—is a complex one, as McCarty explores in his chapter. On the one hand, many researchers agree that successful production of written texts does not require full metalinguistic awareness (see, e.g., Devitt; Nowacek; Olinger), as writers frequently develop tacit knowledge of the genres they use (Giltrow and Valiquette). As McCarty's chapter shows, a writer like Jonah may be adept at deploying linguistic features of disciplinary genres without having explicit language-level terms for those features. On the other hand, we do have research that reveals that students who command a robust metalanguage about writing may be better able to adopt a critical distance from their writing and thus monitor and evaluate their strategies with a heightened awareness of their rhetorical choices (see, e.g., Cheng and Steffensen; Concha and Paratore). As McCarty shows with regard to another student, Kris, developing writers who are able to speak in detail and with rhetorical understanding of specific genre features (such as why dense noun phrases are used in scientific prose) may also learn to make more strategic choices with regard to whether, and how, they deploy or modify those features. Based on findings like this, it is reasonable to ask whether students who express social-constructionist understandings of language use in writing may be better positioned to notice, create, and adapt written voices in their own writing. This question, of course, is not fully answerable here, yet it will be helpful to show some potential areas where linguistic analysis of students' texts could be useful for probing their writing development.

As one case in point, consider again Angela, who was just quoted above as saying, "I definitely use a different writing voice when I'm writing for online than [when] I'm writing an academic paper." Because such a comment betrays a conscious metalinguistic awareness of *voice* in writing, it is reasonable to expect that Angela is especially adept at creating contextually appropriate voices in the texts she produces.

One of the pieces Angela submitted for the study is a political science research paper entitled "The Transition of One-Party States into Multi-Party States: A Case Study of Mexico and the Demise of PRI." This paper is a formal research study that examines the history of Mexico's contemporary political landscape. Here is a part of her introductory paragraph. Wordings that I comment on are *italicized* and <u>underlined</u>.

> . . . *But* in the 2000 presidential election when PAN's candidate Vicente Fox beat out PRI's Francisco Labistida, *it became clear that* Mexico had transitioned into a multi-party state. This transition did not occur over night, however. *But what events* had led to <u>the demise of PRI's dominance in Mexico</u>? *And more broadly, what factors* make one-party states transition into becoming multi-party states?
>
> *This is the exact question that I addressed in this study*. Understanding <u>the shift from one-party dominance to multi-party competition</u> will allow *us* to have a more complete view of a country's current political circumstances.

In this excerpt I have marked several categories of language that Ken Hyland and others have connected to issues of voice in academic prose. While Angela did not contribute pieces of online writing that we could compare to this one, points can still be made. We might start by asking, first, what kind of voice is created in this stretch of text, and second, how is this voice created through specific linguistic choices.

I would venture to characterize the voice created here, and in the paper as a whole, as at once commanding and engaging. How is this voice created? For starters, there is a clear authorial presence constructed through an overt self-mention (*I addressed*) and referential metadiscourse (*in this study*). Furthermore, the epistemic meanings are confident and assertive (*This is the exact question*; *it became clear that*). In addition to establishing this presence and certainty, Angela chose to direct and involve her reader in several ways. She posed two questions (*what events . . . ? what factors . . . ?*), while also using metadiscourse to characterize the second question in relation to the first (*more broadly*). She used an inclusive pronoun (*will allow us*) to mark the reader and writer as working jointly in the same enterprise. Further, the inclusive pronoun was selected within the larger move of making a promise to the reader that the analysis will indeed have a payoff (*a more complete view of a country's current political circumstances*). In addition to these reader engagement devices, Angela created a conversational voice by beginning sentences with *But* and *And*, which perhaps she knows might offend a hypothetical hardline prescriptivist reader, but she then elevates the voice with long and dense noun phrases characteristic of academic prose (*the demise of PRI's dominance in Mexico*; *the shift from one-party dominance to multi-party competition*). Taken together, these various choices in language work together to mark the writer as a competent and engaging empirical guide, which is very likely an identity and voice that Angela would know to adjust when writing online pieces for "thirteen-year-old teen girls about celebrities," as she puts it.

More generally, we can see these bits of language as traces of a writer making rhetorical choices to create both a writerly self-image (as confident and affable) and a role for the reader (as inquisitive and collaborative). It is the confident and affable presence that enables her to take a stance, and it is the reader-engaged uses of language that enable her to create a credible, persuasive voice.

For Ken Hyland, the voice constructed in any text is "reader-oriented." A recognizable "voice" in formal academic prose, that is, is established by interacting with readers in expected ways and guiding them through the ongoing argument. These include wordings used to identify readers and writer as taking part in a collaborative effort ("As we know, . . ."), to direct readers ("Consider the following"), and to raise questions ("But what would happen if . . . ?"), among many other moves. What additional choices in language might Angela—in an office hour appointment, say—

identify as those she selected to create a certain kind of voice? To what extent would she agree that the textual voice she created is a discursive performance and separate from her sense of her autobiographical self? These are all questions that could assist Angela to further build her metalanguage for reflecting on the details of language in discourse.

Presumably, a student like Angela might engage with these queries differently from a student who embraces a view of voice as individualized self-expression. Let's consider now the case of Jon, who, as explained above, invoked the individualist notion of voice as authentic self-expression: "If you're writing well, you're accurately representing what you actually think about whatever you're writing on [. . .] you are accurately representing you on the page." What's important about this statement is that it does not account for the ways that Jon used language in his literature analysis essays to achieve an authoritative *disciplinary voice*. In particular, one of the papers he submitted as a part of his Capstone eportfolio was an argumentative essay that he wrote for an upper-level course in medieval and Renaissance literature on John Gower's poem *Vox Clamantis*. In this essay, Jon takes what I understand to be a contrarian stance, which is that the rebels depicted in the poem "paint a positive portrait of the very group [Gowers] aims to deface." To make this argument, he deploys a number of rhetorical strategies for building a reader-in-the text with whom he can negotiate claims and position his argument authoritatively.

Hyland examines two of these dialogic strategies as reader-oriented pronouns and directives. While reader pronouns are used to "signal community understandings with the reader" (6), directives are used to call the reader to some action or understanding and thus establish a peer-to-peer writer/reader relationship. Consider how reader pronouns, directives, and other positioning devices enable Jon to create an authoritative voice:

- By examining Gower's text and depiction of the rebels alongside what is arguably one of the most important events in the Bible, **we** can understand better what Gower was trying to do, but also just how greatly he misunderstood both his source material and the events he meant to relay. **Make no mistake**, the rebels were violent and sometimes ruthless, **but never** without good purpose—they were **not** evil in an absolute sense, **but rather** committed acts of destruction as a reaction to the wrongs perpetrated against them.

Such rhetorical devices direct and involve the reader in the unfolding argument, creating a readerly role as insider and keen collaborator. In student papers, these devices contribute toward the voice of an advanced, engaged student.

Jon also used more discipline-specific voicing strategies in this same essay. In particular, he used a rhetorical strategy that Laura Wilder identified in successful student essays in English literature, which she dubs, following Jeanne Fahnestock and Marie Secor, the "appearance/reality" topos. This topos works first by invoking the "apparent" meaning of a text before arguing for the "real" meaning, thus signaling critical engagement with community-based ideas. Wilder found that high-rated student essays used this topos more frequently and effectively than lower-rated ones. This strategy is apparent in a number of key moments in Jon's essay, as seen here.

- This comparison **may seem, at first glance** perfectly valid, and perhaps even convincing; after all, both Satan and those involved with the rising of 1381 were rebels acting out against the pugnant estate and God, respectively [APPEARANCE]. **However**, this reading of the events of 1381 and of Satan's role in Christian theology **fails to present** a complete portrait of either, which manages to not only discredit Gower's claims in Vox Clamantis but also creates an interpretative reversal that contradicts Gower's attempt to vilify the rebels through his usage of demonic imagery [REALITY].

These highlighted uses of language are not unique to Jon's *individual* voice. Rather, as identified by Wilder, they are recurring rhetorical devices closely associated with the field and genre Jon is participating in, an interpretative argument about English literature. To be sure, a more comprehensive analysis of Jon's writing might reveal idiosyncratic patterns of language choices that point to a unique linguistic signature. However, even if this were the case, the point is that what we recognize as the "voice" constructed in Jon's writing is the "amalgamative effect" of functional devices for interacting with the imagined reader.

When we consider these sophisticated positioning strategies in Jon's *performance* of disciplinary writing, it becomes clear that his definition of voice stated earlier as "representing what you actually think" is just one side of the coin. In terms of his development as a writer, it seems plain just from this limited examination that he has also learned how to craft a community-based voice that is valued in interpretative-analytical essays in English. Further examination may reveal that, when writing in other genres and fields, he is equally adept at constructing appropriate and effective social voices. But since this capacity is probably one that Jon is not consciously aware of, does not have the metalanguage to articulate, or does not value as a developing writer (nowhere in his interview does he discuss "good" writing about literature), a linguistic examination of his writing can help fill in gaps left in his self-reports.

Conclusion

This chapter has argued that attending closely to students' talk about writing—including the specific terms they use—can help to illuminate their beliefs about writing, ones that often run below their fully conscious awareness. My analysis has revealed both complex and shifting views of *style* and *voice* among the WDS participants, most prominently the writing minors. The first time I read the interview transcripts, I was initially struck by the overtly individualist, expressive views students articulated. Statements such as "good writing is when you are accurately representing you on the page" and "style reflects your personality" colored my impression of students' views of writing in general, which I initially read as arhetorical and even romantic. Such comments stand in sharp contrast to the social and dialogic conceptions of voice and style that are made explicit in the scholarly literature. However, on more systematic analysis, it became clear that many of the participants held both social and individualist views simultaneously. Further, based on linguistic analysis of select papers, it became clear that even students like Jon, who articulated quintessentially individualist views of voice, are quite adept at *performing* through the texts they produce the kinds of social voices that are valued in student course-work writing. Put simply, students' metalanguage about stance and voice reveals interesting and fruitful contradictions, both within their talk about writing and between their talk and rhetorical performances. Such contradictions only become evident through attentiveness to language-level features in student writing.

Ongoing theorization of voice and style should take these apparent contradictions seriously, considering how they may reveal students' developing views of writing. For instance, when a student like Tim speaks in one breath about learning to "adopt many voices" in writing and then in the next about "his own voice," he is expressing two different conceptions of voice. But this does not necessarily mean he is confused or that the two conceptions are incompatible. His views are not incommensurate with Ken Hyland's view that, to write successfully in the disciplines (or any social context), writers must learn to express *stance* in an authoritative "social voice" that is valued. Tim, that is, can learn to project the voice of a scholar in the field of communication, while still expressing through his writing an individualized discursive identity. Likewise, drawing attention to the fact that students like Jon may project an engaging and authoritative disciplinary voice in their coursework writing does not need to challenge their beliefs that good writing expresses an "authentic" personal voice. The "me" Jon wants to "represent on the page," to use his phrase, can be projected through a commanding disciplinary voice, one that is recognizable to other literature scholars who are reading his paper.

Finally, if we do wish for students to come to think of *style* and *voice* as social and dialogic, it makes good sense to create assignments that encourage them to reflect deeply on the kinds of authorial self-representations that are effective when writing to particular audiences in particular genres. Without those opportunities to reflect, students might be slower to grasp the multiplicity of voices they are already learning to control and weave together in their own writing. Accelerating this capacity, and drawing students' explicit attention to it, could be a more liberating idea for many students than the more static one of "finding their voice."

NOTES

1. Of course, other conceptions of style are relevant to college-level writing—for example, "the plain style" tradition still popular in handbooks such as Strunk and White's *The Elements of Style*.

2. This number does not include unrelated uses of the terms. I excluded, for instance, references to "voice-over" work, teachers' classroom voices, styles of music, film, and teaching. I also excluded the many references to *passive/active voice* when these were used in a clearly grammatical sense.

3 It is beyond the scope of this paper to tease apart *register* from *genre* as theoretical constructs, because these have been used in different ways even among linguists and writing scholars (see Biber and Conrad).

4. Janet Giltrow and Michele Valiquette use these terms (after Anthony Giddens) to distinguish between what we know how to do through experience tacitly, that is, our practical consciousness, and what we are able to articulate explicitly about our knowledge, that is, our discursive consciousness.

WORKS CITED

Adler-Kassner, Linda, and Elizabeth Wardle, editors. *Naming What We Know: Threshold Concepts of Writing Studies*. Colorado UP, 2015.

Anthony, Laurence. AntConc (version 3.4.3) (computer software). Waseda University, 2014.

Bakhtin, Mikhail M. *The Dialogic Imagination: Four Essays by M. M. Bakhtin*, edited by Michael Holquist, translated by Caryl Emerson and Michael Holquist. U of Texas P, 1981.

Bazerman, Charles. "The Life of Genre, the Life in the Classroom." *Genre and Writing: Issues, Arguments, Alternatives*, edited by Wendy Bishop and Hans Ostrom, Boynton/Cook-Heinemann, 1997, pp. 19–26.

Biber, Douglas, and Susan Conrad. *Register, Genre, and Style*. Cambridge University Press, 2009.

Cheng, Xiaoguang, and Margaret S. Steffensen. "Metadiscourse: A Technique for Improving Student Writing." *Research in the Teaching of English*, vol. 30, no. 2, 1996, pp. 149–81.

Coffin, Caroline. "The Voices of History: Theorizing the Interpersonal Semantics of Historical Discourses." *Text*, vol. 22, no. 4, 2002, pp. 503–28.

Concha, Soledad, and Jeanne R. Paratore. "Local Coherence in Persuasive Writing: An Exploration of Chilean Students' Metalinguistic Knowledge, Writing Process, and Writing Products." *Written Communication*, vol. 28, no. 1, 2011, 34–69.

Devitt, Amy J. "Genre Performances: John Swales' Genre Analysis and Rhetorical-Linguistic Genre Studies." *Journal of English for Academic Purposes*, vol. 19, 2015, pp. 44–51.

Elbow, Peter. "Voice in Writing Again: Embracing Contraries." *College English*, vol. 70, no. 2, 2007, pp. 168–88.

Elbow, Peter. "What Do We Mean When We Talk about Voice in Texts?" *Voices on Voice: Perspectives,*

Definitions, Inquiry, edited by Kathleen Blake Yancey, National Council of Teachers of English, 1994, pp. 1–35.

Fahnestock, Jeanne, and Marie Secor. "The Rhetoric of Literary Criticism." *Textual Dynamics of the Profession: Historical and Contextual Studies of Writing in Professional Communities*, edited by Charles Bazerman and James Paradis, University of Wisconsin, 1991, pp. 76–96.

Giltrow, Janet, and Michele Valiquette. "Genres and Knowledge: Students Writing in the Disciplines." *Learning and Teaching Genre*, edited by Aviva Freedman and Peter Medway, Heinemann, 1994, pp. 47–62.

Hiatt, Mary P. "The Feminine Style: Theory and Fact." *College Composition and Communication*, vol. 29, no. 3, 1978, pp. 222–26.

Hood, Susan. "Voice and Stance as Appraisal: Persuading and Positioning in Research Writing Across Intellectual Fields." *Stance and Voice in Written Academic Genres*, edited by Ken Hyland and Carmen Sancho Guinda, Palgrave Macmillan, 2012, pp. 51–68.

Hyland, Ken. "Stance and Engagement: A Model of Interaction in Academic Discourse." *Discourse Studies*, vol. 7, no. 2, 2005, pp. 173–92.

Hyland, Ken. "Undergraduate Understandings: Stance and Voice in Final Year Reports." *Stance and Voice in Written Academic Genres*, edited by Ken Hyland and Carmen Sancho, Palgrave Macmillan, 2012, pp. 134–50.

Hyland, Ken, and Carmen Sancho Guinda, editors. *Stance and Voice in Written Academic Genres*, Palgrave Macmillan, 2012.

Ivanič, Roz. *Writing and Identity*. John Benjamins Publishing Company, 1998.

Jeffery, Jill V. *Voice, Genre, and Intentionality: An Integrated Methods Study of Voice Criteria in the Evaluation of Secondary Students' Writing*. PhD dissertation, New York University, 2010.

Johnson, T. R., and Thomas Pace, editors. *Refiguring Prose Style: Possibilities for Writing Pedagogy*. Utah State UP, 2005.

Matsuda, Paul Kei. "Voice in Japanese Written Discourse: Implications for Second Language Writing." *Journal of Second Language Writing*, vol. 10, no. 1, 2001, pp. 35–53.

Matsuda, Paul Kei, and Christine M. Tardy. "Voice in Academic Writing: The Rhetorical Construction of Author Identity in Blind Manuscript Reviews." *English for Specific Purposes*, vol. 26, no. 2, 2007, pp. 235–49.

Nowacek, Rebecca S. *Agents of Integration: Understanding Transfer as a Rhetorical Act*. SIU Press, 2011.

Olinger, Andrea R. "On the Instability of Disciplinary Style: Common and Conflicting Metaphors and Practices in Text, Talk, and Gesture." *Research in the Teaching of English*, vol. 48, no. 4, 2014, pp. 453–78.

Ramanathan, Vai, and Robert B. Kaplan. "Audience and Voice in Current L1 Composition Texts: Some Implications for ESL Student Writers." *Journal of Second Language Writing*, vol. 5, no. 1, 1996, pp. 21–34.

Shen, Fan. "The Classroom and the Wider Culture: Identity as a Key to Learning English Composition." *College Composition and Communication*, vol. 40, no. 4, 1989, pp. 459–66.

Soliday, Mary. *Everyday Genres: Writing Assignments Across the Disciplines*. Southern Illinois UP, 2011.

Sperling, Melanie, and Deborah Appleman. "Voice in the Context of Literacy Studies." *Reading Research Quarterly*, vol. 46, no. 1, 2011, pp. 70–84.

Tardy, Christine M. "Current Conceptions of Voice." *Stance and Voice in Written Academic Genres*, edited by Ken Hyland and Carmen Sancho Guinda, Palgrave Macmillan, 2012, pp. 34–48.

Wilder, Laura. *Rhetorical Strategies and Genre Conventions in Literary Studies: Teaching and Writing in the Disciplines*. Southern Illinois UP, 2012.

SECTION FOUR

All Writers Have More to Learn

With every new audience, every new genre, every new context, writers have more to learn; past success does not guarantee an immediate ability to write well in a new context. The talented fifth-grader may feel unable to write the descriptive essay required in middle school; the high school senior with top grades and AP scores may feel daunted by the demands of a first-year college writing course; the accomplished graduate student may feel incapable of writing a prospectus, much less a dissertation; the highly successful poet may feel challenged if asked to write a grant proposal. Even with a solid record of effective writing, every writer faces challenging situations that call for further learning, because writing, unlike, say, learning to follow a routine procedure, can never be entirely mastered. Despite some educators' efforts to present writing instruction in sequences of defined levels—learning, for instance, to write sentences before proceeding to paragraphs or paragraphs before essays—there is no series of steps by which instructors can lead students to learn everything they will need to know about writing.

To be sure, more accomplished writers often have a repertoire of rituals, strategies, and other resources to call on as they move from one rhetorical context to another. These approaches can become habitual practices. For example, a writer who knows she works best in the morning in a coffee shop, who ends in the middle of a section so it's easier to continue the next time, and who switches comfortably to another project if she gets stuck on the first will find it much easier to write in a variety of circumstances. The writer who knows how to consider the needs of a given audience, to identify features of various genres, to strategically use the various conventions of written English, and to call on and use advice from other writers for revising will be better able to write effectively in new contexts. It is also true that writers—and instructors—can learn a lot from failure. As Collin Brooke and Allison Carr say, "One of the most important thing students can learn is that failure is an opportunity for growth" (62). Brooke and Carr also call for "pedagogies of failure, or ways of teaching that seek to illuminate the myriad ways writing gets done by examining all the ways it doesn't" (62), which suggests that all students and their writing teachers have more to learn, especially from failure. Anna Knutson's chapter in this section explores how Grace saw herself as failing according to her own criteria, and also how she learned to move past that failure and adopt a novice status that gave her space to develop as a writer. While they did not categorize themselves as failing, students such as Ayanna, Celeste, and Samantha in Naomi Silver's chapter fail to see the value in the eportfolios they created, thereby missing an opportunity to further their writerly development.

The designation of failure presumes some form of assessment, and assessment is, as Peggy O'Neill observes, an essential part of every writer's learning. Assessment in the form of feedback, whether from peers or an instructor, provides writers with guidance throughout the processes of writing. Getting another person's view on an approach to an assignment, receiving responses to a draft, sharing a nearly finished piece with a colleague who has copyediting skills, receiving suggestions for revision from an instructor or a journal editor, and of course, getting a grade are all forms of assessment from which writers can learn. Part of dealing with assessment includes evaluating the assessment. Not every suggestion is worthwhile; peers, instructors, and editors can be wrong. Part of the continued learning of writers involves becoming able to discern which feedback or assessment is most valuable. One of the capacities that marked the development of a number of students in our study was a willingness to disagree with an instructor, to decide that a given bit of feedback or advice was not useful.

With time and practice writers can become better at assessing their own work, determining which will be the most effective approach, identifying the sections that need further development, or developing a revision plan. Still, however, some form of assessment from others enables the continued learning of writers.

Assessment can also provide an indication of writerly development, and the assessment embedded in our study attempted to discern the patterns of learning traced by student participants. Statistical analysis of student responses to entry and exit survey questions provided one way to assess student learning and development in areas including rhetorical ability/dexterity, genre awareness, and the integration of multiple sources. To probe rhetorical ability/dexterity we used this two-part question: "When you need to do a kind of writing task you've never done before, how prepared do you feel to decide: (a) What the writing task is asking you to do; (b) What kind of examples or evidence you should use." All students showed statistically significant growth in this area (p-value of 0.0001), but minors showed greater growth in both numbers and statistical significance. This difference can be attributed, in part, to a curriculum that exposed students to a wide range of genres and devoted explicit attention to the requirements of various types of writing experienced by writing minors.

Another difference in rhetorical dexterity emerged when we looked at disciplinary subgroups. For example, we found that students in science, technology, engineering, and math (STEM) were at the same level of response as their non-STEM peers in the entry survey, but while non-STEM students showed a positive change on this question in the exit survey, the mean of STEM students was actually lower than it had been two years earlier. Although we cannot be certain of the cause, it is clear that the learning of STEM student writers did not include much growth in the area of rhetorical ability/dexterity.

A survey question closely related to rhetorical ability/dexterity asked students to look back at their college career and indicate how frequently they had (a) made an argument and supported it with evidence, (b) expressed a personal opinion on an issue, and (c) written a personal narrative. Results showed no appreciable differences between non-STEM and STEM students in writing argument or personal opinion. Neither group indicated that they wrote a great deal of either, and the non-STEM students indicated slightly more personal opinion writing than their STEM peers. The only statistically significant difference appeared in response to the question about personal narrative, where non-STEM students showed a much more positive response than STEM students. The relatively low response on use of argument is surprising given the campus-wide claims by professors that evidence-based argument is the most important genre for college writers. It is even more surprising given that in response to a survey question about how much they learned about specific genres, all students indicated that they learned to "produce well-supported academic arguments." In the entry survey STEM students showed a lower level than non-STEM for this question, but in the exit survey that difference disappeared. Even though they apparently felt they were not called on to write arguments frequently, all students seemed confident that they had learned how to write in that genre, or it may be that students develop self-awareness but may not be accurate in assessing their own performance.

An area of significant learning for all students was integration of multiple sources, as measured by this question: "In your experience at your institution during the current year, about how often have you worked on a paper or project that required integrating ideas or information from various sources?" Student responses showed statistically significant growth for all students here, but while the minor and non-minor responses were essentially the same in the first year, minors claimed a statistically significant greater ability to do this sort of integration. Yet in response to a question about critical evaluation of arguments, only nonminors showed significant gains. The question "During the current school year, how much has your coursework emphasized making judgments about the value of information, arguments, or methods, such as examining how others gathered and interpreted data and assessing the soundness of their conclusions?" points directly at evidence-based argument, a genre highly valued in disciplines across the entire university. These data suggest that minors may not have been as adept at discriminating among sources, even though they felt comfortable with the process of integrating them. This raises a question about the overall effect of requiring minors to produce eportfolios, a genre that is, as Naomi Silver notes, "comprised of multiple artifacts" (p. 232). As Silver makes clear, eportfolios require more than simply collecting a set of materials and putting them next to one another; the relationships between and among artifacts need to be made visible, the eportfolio itself needs to be composed. Students' ability to do this sort of composing varies, as is visible in digital projects where "some are largely 'digitizations of print-based material' with hyperlinks, images, and possibly video or audio included here and there . . . . and show little evidence of the three dimensions of multimodal writing development" while others are truly web-sensible (pp. 233–34). From our perspective, the ability to create a web-sensible eportfolio offers another marker of writerly development, but students who merely lined up artifacts may well have thought of themselves as adept at integrating multiple sources when they were merely putting materials next to one another. Even if students did not achieve the goal of creating web-sensible eportfolios, minors indicated that they had learned to write in a range of media, and their survey response in this area showed a strong statistical difference from the nonminors.

Taken together these statistical data show student writers' irregular patterns of learning and development, patterns shaped partly by curricular offerings and students' choices, partly by differences between knowing about and actually producing specified forms of writing, and partly by technologies of writing. Yet some groups of students learned in spite of rather than necessarily as a result of their curricular offerings, as statistically similar responses of STEM and non-STEM students regarding evidence-based arguments suggest. Furthermore, the statistically significant differences between nonminors and minors on the question about critical evaluation of arguments suggest that a curriculum that emphasizes rhetorical analysis like that experienced by minors may not result in the desired student learning. While it is clear that participants in this study could identify areas where they developed as writers, it is equally clear that all of these student writers have, as the threshold concept claims, more to learn.

Similarly, irregular patterns become visible in the closer examination offered by Naomi Silver's and Anna Knutson's chapters. Each shows how students excel in some areas while making less progress in others. Initially Grace, the subject of Knutson's chapter, experiences failure as she struggles with a fixed mindset about writing and her abilities as a writer, both of which impede her learning and development. Relying on writing practices developed in high school, she falls into unproductive routines and finds it difficult to move beyond them to take up the genres and practices expected by her college instructors. The turning point for Grace comes with a shift away from the environmental science major to German. In this new language, Grace is finally able to move away from her fixed mindset and deepen her learning. The very unfamiliarity of the German language made it possible for Grace to transform herself into a learner. In her words, "I think I just know English so much better, that I also notice the flaws when I write. . . . Whereas [in] German, it's just, 'Well, I'll fix all the grammar stuff later' . . . it frees me to think about what I want to talk about instead of how I'm saying it" (p. 210). With this turn, Grace learns from her earlier failures and becomes able to learn more about various genres, even though she continues to resist some forms of academic writing.

Assessment loomed large in Grace's learning and her writerly development. Evaluative comments from her high school AP English teacher rang in her ears well into her college career, leading her to struggle for the creativity that teachers valued while also addressing the expectation of her college instructors. Seemingly, the high school English teacher's views led Grace to devalue her ability to produce writing that was well organized and logically sequenced because she felt it was more important to produce creative writing valued by that teacher. Although its source remains unclear, Grace internalized an equation of good thinking with good writing, and this too shaped her assessment of her own writing: "You need to be organized. You need to have good ideas. You have to be a good thinker. . . . If you're a good thinker, then you're a good writer" (p. 203). This evaluative equation hobbled Grace's writerly development, especially because she coupled it with the self-direction to "Just think creatively" (p. 203). Grace's move to major in German was also shaped by assessment. She described instructors in this department, saying all they "want you to do is use the language and not worry about how perfect you're being." With this instructor-authorized freedom, Grace moved past her fixed mindset, past the negative assessment tapes running in her head, and embraced the assessment of her German instructor, who said "It was good" (p. 212).

The criteria for terms like "good," "stupid," or "creative" that shaped Grace's self- assessment and that of her instructors remain undefined. Even though they wielded great power over Grace's learning and writerly development, the meanings attached to these evaluative terms remain obscure. For Silver, the central project is to define and describe the writing development associated with composing in digital, multimodal rhetorical situations. Drawing on the more professional criteria of *Kairos*'s Style Guide along with rhetorical design principles, and web-sensible composition, Silver shows how variously student writers develop. There are, first, the developmental differences between what students say and do. In her examination of Susanne, Ariana, and Abby, Silver shows how their assessment of their own eportfolios remains anchored in alphabetic writing, making it impossible for them to see any relationship between their writing development and the digital dimension of their eportfolios, even when such relationships may be visible. As Silver explains, their evaluation of their eportfolios separates design from argument because these students do not see themselves as multimodal writers.

A related developmental difference lies in the variability of student achievement in alphabetic writing as opposed to the digital aspects of the eportfolio. As Silver explains, "Eportfolios can offer insight into the differential development of student composers who may exhibit highly developed rhetorical awareness and flexibility in one mode, while demonstrating fairly early stages of rhetorical command and metacognitive awareness and regulation in another" (p. 233). Ayanna, for instance, organizes her eportfolio in linear fashion and incorporates "very few hyperlinks or images" (p. 234). This limited repertoire in the digital features of her eportfolio contrasts sharply with the sophistication and rich variety of genre and style evident in her writing, a pattern that is repeated in the eportfolios of a number of other students. Such contrasts make visible the uneven progress students make during their undergraduate years and show how much more even relatively accomplished writers still have to learn.

One of the most important insights in Silver's chapter emerges from her analysis of Kaitlin's eportfolio. Kaitlin's Gateway and Capstone eportfolios show development from a collection she herself describes as a "paperless, online equivalent of a printed portfolio that gives you samples of my writing from my different academic concentrations" (p. 236) to a web-sensible project "that was created online and lives online. The content was made for that form" (p. 240). Silver identifies three criteria that can be used to define students' development as multimodal composers: "(1) the extent to which they see themselves as composing truly 'born digital' texts, (2) the extent to which their integration of these affordances explicitly supports their rhetorical exigency, and (3) the degree to which they are able to demonstrate metacognitive awareness and regulation of their multimodal compositional choices" (p. 240). By meeting all of these criteria, Kaitlin can be described as a multimodal composer, but of greater import is her awareness of the importance of the rhetorical context when composing in any media. As Silver notes, "It is *rhetorical* instruction, not technical instruction, that enabled her to grow as a multimodal composer, and it is worth asking if a more thoroughgoing attention to digital rhetorical instruction might help shift the value judgments of study participants like Ariana, Susanne, and Abby, who seemed to view design rhetoric as little more than fiddling with technology" (p. 242).

Silver's insight about the value of rhetorical instruction speaks directly to the *kind* of learning that developing writers may need to become effective multimodal composers. Just as Grace's learning about writing was enhanced by taking up a different language, one that freed her into a more process-focused writing, so aspiring multimodal writers can benefit from a deeper learning of rhetorical principles. Like many of their peers, these students have more to learn, and thoughtfully planned curricula may guide them toward that learning.

WORKS CITED

Brooke, Collin, and Allison Carr. "Failure Can Be an Important Part of Writing Development." *Naming What We Know: Threshold Concepts of Writing Studies*, edited by Linda Adler-Kassner and Elizabeth Wardle, Utah State UP, 2015, pp. 62–64.

O'Neill, Peggy. "Assessment Is an Essential Component of Learning to Write." *Naming What We Know*, pp. 67–68.

CHAPTER SEVEN

GRACE

A CASE STUDY OF RESOURCEFULNESS AND RESILIENCE

Anna V. Knutson

Grace, an honors student who will go on to graduate with a 3.97 GPA and a Fulbright grant to teach English in Germany, is an exemplary student and an avid reader. Grace's reading practices are significant to her theorization of her own writing development: she believes that "reading helps writing . . . so if you read more, you write better." Based on her academic success, her passion for reading, and her belief that habitual reading transfers to excellence in writing, one would assume, at first glance, that she would be an agile, capable, and confident writer.

However, almost immediately in her first interview for this study, Grace states that she "hate[s] writing," because when she reads her own academic writing, it doesn't "match up" to the novels that she spends so much time reading:

> One of the reasons why I hate writing is because I'll read [my writing], and I'm like, "This isn't just like these masterpieces from all these books that I read." Then I get really upset about it, because . . . it's just a stylistic problem. It just doesn't flow the way I want it to. It's not perfect, and I think part of what makes me so frustrated about it is because I read these great books that I'm never gonna match up to when I write. I just get really disheartened.

In this instance, Grace is engaging in activities that instructors value highly: she is reading for pleasure, reading with the hope of improving her writing, and engaging in what could be construed as metacognitive reflection, or at least self-assessment, by reviewing her academic writing to evaluate her progress. However, these activities don't seem to yield overwhelmingly positive results. As Sarah Swofford suggests (chapter 9), to obtain a full portrait of students' writing development, we must look at data beyond their projects and grades. The apparent (and curious) disconnect between Grace's beliefs about herself as a writer and her success (in terms of grades, test scores, the quality of her upper-division writing, and her overall academic achievements) led me to explore her case in more depth. In doing so, I draw on Grace's experiences in order to illuminate the relationship between self-efficacy, students' beliefs about writing, and writing development.

Why Grace?

Before delving into Grace's case study, I briefly describe how I selected her case and conducted my analysis. As I discuss shortly, Grace is an honors student who, at the start of this study, had declared an environmental science major, which she ultimately dropped due to the amount of argumentative writing the major required. By the time she graduated, Grace had changed her major to German with a minor in environmental science. Her choice to leave her first major due to writing anxiety reveals how central Grace's beliefs and concerns about writing are to her development as a student and a writer.

Like many writing knowledge transfer researchers, I am interested in the relationship between self-efficacy, learning transfer, and writing development, especially in terms of how attempts at transfer that an instructor deems unsuccessful may affect students' self-efficacy and development over time. Since I participated in data collection, first-round interview coding, and data management for this study, I knew upon starting this chapter that there were study participants whose experiences with self-efficacy and transfer might shed light on the relationship between the two phenomena and their role in writing development. When I began analyzing interview data, I had at first planned to conduct a cross-case analysis, exploring questions about the relationship between self-efficacy, transfer, and development as they played out in the experiences of multiple participants in the study. To locate these cases, I compiled all of the interview excerpts that had been coded simultaneously with the two following codes during our first round of coding: "learning transfer" and "writerly self-conception."[1] I chose to explore excerpts coded with both codes because I knew this would help me narrow the data set and locate the cases that could illuminate some aspects of the relationship between self-efficacy, transfer, and development. In doing so, I engaged in what Michael Patton terms "operational construct sampling," a process that involves selecting "case manifestations of a theoretical construct of interest so as to examine and elaborate the construct and its variations and implications" (269). Operational construct sampling entails the purposeful selection of participants to illustrate a specific theoretical construct (or, in this case, the relationship between three constructs: self-efficacy, writing knowledge transfer, and writing development). After extracting excerpts coded with both "learning transfer" and "writerly self-conception" from our qualitative coding program, I was left with 104 excerpts from interviews with 46 study participants.

While conducting focused coding of this slice of data, I found an excerpt from Grace's entry interview, the first quote discussed in the next section, that I found so provocative (and, quite frankly, troubling) that I was compelled to look more closely at Grace's data. I combed through both of her interviews and her writing samples; after doing so, I knew that Grace's data was rich enough to support a single-participant case study, and that only a case study would do her story justice. Joseph Maxwell suggests that case studies differ from sample studies insofar as sample studies explore general questions through data from a larger population, narrowing the sample according to a particular question. In contrast, a case study often starts with a particular case and then states the questions in specific terms, thus "justif[ying] the selection of a particular case in terms of the goals of the study and existing theory and research" (78). My analysis straddled the line between these two approaches, as I began with a set of general questions about the relationship between self-efficacy, transfer, and development before beginning to narrow my sample; ultimately, due to the richness of Grace's data, I ended up narrowing the sample as far as possible: to just one participant.

After I had determined that Grace's data was strong enough to stand alone, I conducted focused coding of her two interviews before triangulating my analysis with her writing samples. In keeping with grounded theory coding, I let the data guide my analysis, allowing codes to emerge from the data before engaging in focused and theoretical coding to highlight salient aspects of the data and theorize relationships between mechanisms operating in the data (Charmaz). Through this process, the story that I will tell shortly began to emerge. At that stage, I realized that Grace could provide not only insight into one possible manifestation of the relationship between self-efficacy, transfer, and development, but also a compelling example of one student's responses to a particular set of writing challenges. As I moved forward with the case study, I discovered that while I cannot claim that Grace's experiences are representative of all college students, or even of the student participants in this particular study, she does provide a focused case study of a phenomenon well documented in writing studies research: the student who comes to college feeling overly prepared, only to learn that her prior writing knowledge no longer serves her, and who ultimately becomes disheartened with the whole enterprise of college writing. As I will discuss in more detail shortly, similar students have been discussed elsewhere in the literature, by Mary Jo Reiff and Anis Bawarshi; Liane Robertson, Kara Taczak, and Kathleen Blake Yancey; and Nancy Sommers and Laura Saltz. While Grace provides a rich, detailed example of how these particular phenomena might interact to create roadblocks for developing student writers, her longitudinal data also reveals how students may overcome their struggles to adapt to writing: ultimately, Grace reveals a great deal of resourcefulness and resilience, which ultimately enable her to cobble together a writing curriculum that works for her. While the choice of "Grace" as a pseudonym was more or less random, and at first glance perhaps seems counterintuitive given her initial struggles to adapt to college writing, I ultimately discovered that the name I chose was consonant with the grace she displayed by overcoming her challenges and persevering through college writing.

Grace's Approaches to Writing

In her entry interview, Grace is asked whether she would attribute her growth as a writer to anything besides reading. Grace's response is saturated with fixed categorizations of types of writing that seem to have presented challenges as she moved from one domain of writing to the next:

> With math you're just like, "Well, I have to put this variable on this side of the equation first," and then there's a system. When you're writing there is no system. As a writer, my writing had always been really formulaic. . . . On ACTs they always test this stupid five-paragraph form—which I don't think is good writing. I mean, it's organized, but it's just like every person's essay is gonna end up just being . . . just all the same.
>
> Writing is a kind of art and shouldn't be so formulaic. . . . It has to be organized, and then I'm always trying to figure out how to match the creativity with the organization. It takes me forever to write. My [AP] teacher . . . he got me away from the whole formulaic thing, because he was just like—he was really just an innovative sort of teacher. . . . If you wrote a perfectly fine paper but it wasn't interesting, he would be like, "Eh." And then I come to university. . . . they prefer you to be more conventional, and I found that really confusing, too. I guess maybe when you're not conventional then you have trouble finding good research. . . . I've gone through some changes in my writing because of that.

Packed into this narrative are three main categorizations of writing:

1. Grace's formulaic approach, learned in math, which she (at first) *unsuccessfully* applied in AP English.
2. The same formulaic thinking, learned in math, which she *successfully* applied in the ACT writing section (she scored in the 98th percentile), although she dismisses the type of writing encouraged and rewarded by this context as not being "good."[2]
3. Grace's creativity in writing, learned in AP English, which she *unsuccessfully* applied in college writing.

In light of Grace's perspective on her experiences with writing, her negative attitude toward writing becomes more understandable: she keeps expending time and energy learning what she seems to view as fixed, unchangeable approaches to writing, only to be met with resistance when she attempts to apply these approaches in new contexts. When describing the only instance where she successfully transfers a type of writing—the formulaic approach that she learned in math, which helped her succeed on the ACT essay exam—she neglects to mention the high score she received on this exam, instead critiquing the assignment itself, which she describes as a "stupid five-paragraph form," which is not "good writing." She ultimately attributes her success to the (flawed) type of writing promoted by the context, rather than to her own ability. In contrast, when she discusses the instances where she applied approaches to writing *un*successfully in new contexts, when she adapts her "formulaic" approach to AP English, and when she struggles to adapt her creative approach to college writing assignments, she attributes her performance to her own individual failures, rather than to the context. Describing high school English, she mentions her "frustration" about her inability to "be right" consistently while writing. Similarly, in the context of college writing, she expresses her "confusion" about the preferences of college instructors for "conventional" writing. Grace's views of her writing ability can be explored through what Dana Driscoll and Jennifer Wells term *attribution*, also known in psychology as "locus of control": when Grace succeeds on the ACT, she attributes her success to the writing task; however, when she struggles to adapt prior knowledge to the new contexts of AP English and college writing, she attributes the failure to herself. This suggests low levels of self-efficacy: even when she does succeed, she doesn't take credit for it, instead attributing her success to the context of writing, which she ultimately critiques.

The two instances where she unsuccessfully applies writing knowledge to new contexts—her application of formulaic thinking in AP English, and her application of creative approaches to writing in college—could be viewed as what Kathleen

Blake Yancey, Liane Robertson, and Kara Taczak term "critical incidents," conflicts between prior knowledge and the demands of a new context, which typically prompt learning. These instances vary dramatically: her description of attempting to adapt her "formulaic approach" from math to AP English is comparatively positive—although she experienced frustration, she was ultimately able to learn from her initial failed attempts to adapt her prior knowledge to this context. In contrast, her failed attempt to adapt her "creative" approach to college has less of a resolution; as I discuss in detail shortly, Grace's views of writing seem to hinge on notions of "creativity," as do those of many of the students discussed by Lizzie Hutton and Gail Gibson in this collection (chapter 3). Grace posits one possible explanation for the writing expectations that obstructed her attempts at "creativity": more creative approaches to writing might prevent her from "finding good research." However, it isn't clear how creativity might realistically impose barriers to locating and integrating "good" research into one's writing. Overall, Grace seems confused about what college writing is, what features it should emphasize, and how it relates to prior research. She does suggest that she has changed as a writer due to these experiences, but the lack of agency in her description of her writing is striking: she has "gone through some changes in [her] writing because of this." This suggests development, of course, but it seems to be completely out of her hands, forced by the expectations (or "preferences") of her instructors, who are framed, interestingly, as "they"; there is no single instructor identified in this excerpt, suggesting that she has a somewhat monolithic view of academic writing.

Grace ultimately does report signs of development in both instances marked by failure, in high school by learning to "match the creativity with the organization," and in college by "go[ing] through some changes in [her] writing," but these experiences seem unnecessarily difficult. Furthermore, they seem to lower her self-efficacy, which might make learning to write in future college classes even more challenging. Grace is not alone: for an example of another student who experienced initial discomfort transferring high school learning into college, see Sarah Swofford's discussion of Natalie in chapter 9. Why, though, was it such a struggle for Grace to adapt her prior writing knowledge to new contexts, and what can her experiences show us about learning transfer and writing development?

The purpose of this chapter is not to diagnose or disparage Grace, or her instructors for that matter; furthermore, I do not mean to suggest that Grace's experiences are universal: elsewhere in this collection, Ryan McCarty provides examples of students who, unlike Grace, integrated writing knowledge from different domains with more ease and success (chapter 4). Instead, I wish to shed light on Grace's struggles with college writing and her responses to these challenges, with the hope that we might learn more about students' transitions into college writing and their subsequent development. As I suggest shortly, students like Grace aren't new to writing studies research: students who struggle to adapt their prior knowledge to college writing have been documented elsewhere in the literature. Although we are familiar with these students, called "boundary guarders" by Mary Jo Reiff and Anis Bawarshi, we know less about whether and how they ultimately overcome their challenges and adapt to college writing. By presenting Grace's longitudinal data as a case study, I provide a glimpse into one student's strategies for overcoming these challenges. In the pages that follow, I explore Grace's perceptions of and experiences with college writing before describing how she overcame her challenges, first by seeking extracurricular writing support, and eventually by pursuing a major in a context so different from her past writing experiences that she was forced to adopt a novice status and rethink her prior approaches to and beliefs about writing.

Grace's Perceptions of Writing Instruction and Theorization of Writing

Grace believes that she has not received explicit writing instruction in college. When asked in her entry interview if her classroom experiences had affected her writing process, Grace states,

> No, I don't really think so—other than the research stuff. That's part of the process. It doesn't tell me how to do it, but it would give me resources . . . or an idea . . . a thesis to make, but it's not actually about writing or how you should be writing. That's where I'm getting my ideas, but . . . not helping with writing at all. It's just that professors just expect you to be able to write. Except I can't.

This response suggests that Grace has yet to become aware of the relationship between form and content: she seems to believe that the only writing support she might obtain from conducting research is "getting . . . ideas"; she seems less aware—at this point, anyway—that she could potentially use sources that she finds through research as a more appropriate model for academic writing than the novels she aspires to emulate.

Furthermore, her stated belief that she "can't" write suggests that Grace seems to be enacting what Carol Dweck terms a "fixed mindset" when it comes to writing development. In contrast to a "growth mindset," or "the belief that your basic qualities are things you can cultivate through your efforts," Dweck defines the fixed mindset as the belief "that your qualities are carved in stone" (7). Upon entering the study, Grace seems quite certain that she just "can't" write, which may explain not only some of her struggles, but also her perception that she has not received explicit writing support or instruction. Dweck notes that "it's startling to see the degree to which people with the fixed mindset do not believe in putting in effort or getting help" (10). If you believe you "can't" write and that nothing can change this, it follows that you would be resistant to seeking and engaging with help. Drawing on Emily Wilson and Justine Post's framework (chapter 1), it seems as though Grace may espouse some views about writing and learning that have ultimately impeded her ability to "critically engage" not only with instructor feedback, but with writing instruction more generally.

Upon graduating, Grace still reports that she believes she hasn't received explicit writing instruction in her undergraduate career: when asked the same question in her exit interview, whether her writing process has changed due to formal writing instruction, Grace states, "The classes don't really teach you how to write." She then adds,

> A lot of the professors . . . don't teach you how to write . . . they just expect you to already know how to do it. . . . I don't know if it's just a personal problem that I just suck at writing. . . . I think it might just be that other things come more naturally than writing does. Then, I think I automatically suck at it, even though it might just be I'm better at other things. . . . They just assume that you know how to write already. . . . Just tell me how you can even—I don't even know how to start writing. I don't know how people can even teach you how to write anyway.

Grace's initial statement places the blame on faculty ("professors . . . don't teach you how to write"); however, she quickly defaults to explanations that make visible some of the beliefs about writing and learning that may be at the root of her problems, including her fixed-mindset views of herself as an incompetent writer: that her struggles are "a personal problem," that she "*automatically* suck[s] at [writing]," that writing doesn't come "*naturally*" to her, and her puzzlement about the idea that writing can even be taught. Grace quickly retreats to a position of inherent inability, and her belief that writing can't be taught—thus suggesting that you either "naturally" or "automatically" can, or you can't. If she believes that writing can't be taught, it is understandable that she perceives that she has not received explicit writing instruction: how can you engage with something that you don't believe exists?

Perhaps unsurprisingly in light of her beliefs about writing, Grace reports experiencing a dearth of individualized writing feedback within her classes:

> Sometimes I go to my professors, and I just tell them how much I hate writing. . . . I did tell my professor that it was probably the reason why I dropped her class. It was really embarrassing, too, because I wish I weren't so bad at it. . . . Why does it have to be so hard? . . . [My professors] never give me . . . there's nothing you can fix if you hate writing. You just hate it. . . . Well, they're always telling me to go to [the] Sweetland [Center for Writing] actually. They're like, "They'll get you all sorts of help," . . . I've just never gone there. . . . I don't know if it will help.

It seems that Grace's perception is that in lieu of individualized writing feedback from an instructor she knows, she is shunted to an unfamiliar place that she does not trust: she doesn't "know if [the writing center] will help." However, Grace's following statement that "there's nothing you can fix if you hate writing" suggests that she believes her problems are so deep, inherent, and in Dweck's terms, *fixed*, that she believes that nothing can help her change or develop, which may explain why she has yet to seek out support through the writing center.

In contrast, as she described earlier in this chapter, it seems as though Grace *does* believe that she received explicit writing instruction in high school. Her "really good," "innovative" high school English teacher made quite an impact on her. She was in his class for two years, which seems to have been a positive experience. Two years of AP English with the same instructor prepared her to succeed in at least two domains of writing: timed essay exams, such as the AP exam and the ACT exam, and his class, which seems to have had quite rigorous—and specific—standards for writing. Grace valued this learning, perhaps so much that it became entrenched, as Chris Anson describes:

> When writers' contexts are constrained and they are subjected to repeated practice of the same genres, using the same processes for the same rhetorical purposes and addressing the same audiences, their conceptual framework for writing may become entrenched, "solidified," or "sedimented." (77)

Anson suggests that the "misapplication of habituated practice" is typical among high school students who have become accustomed to particular types of writing; Grace may be one of these students.

Minor differences between her high school English classes and her college classes seem to genuinely rattle her, and even impede her attempts at invention. For example, describing an English-language paper she wrote in a German class on Faust, she states

> There's just such a difference between my high school teacher and my college professors. Whereas if we discussed something in class in our high school and then you wrote about it—that was just a no-no, because you should be thinking something new. . . . Then here [in college], it's just like, "Oh, whatever." . . . I was afraid to [write] about the stuff that we talked about in class. . . . When I asked [the instructor], "Is it okay if I do like what we were talking about?" He's like, . . . "No, it's totally fine."

Grace's understanding about writing in a range of academic contexts seems to be guided by the preferences and expectations of her high school teacher: indeed, she is concerned, even after two years of college, with the "difference" between him and the multiple college professors that she has since met. Her high school teacher's (seemingly rigorously enforced) expectation that students not write about ideas discussed in class initially presents a roadblock to Grace's attempts to write this paper. It is fitting that this "critical incident" that helped her reframe some of her entrenched knowledge pertained to invention (Yancey et al.); it seems as though many of the struggles she faced in college writing had to do with invention, particularly in terms of coming up with a "creative" idea and "organizing" her thoughts so that she can translate them into writing. As I will discuss shortly, Grace's stance toward writing changes dramatically after she begins coursework for her German major. She seems better equipped to engage with instructor feedback in this German class: when her instructor, who she reports feeling comfortable approaching, corrects her overgeneralized perception that content discussed in class was off-limits for papers, she understands, accepts, and responds to this feedback, which allowed her to write about a topic that she found motivating.

As I have suggested, in addition to entrenched procedural writing knowledge (e.g., rules about writing such as the one described above—that one should never write about ideas from class discussion), Grace seems to have brought some beliefs about writing into college that had played a role in her struggles with writing. An exploration of Grace's constructs of writing, or her sets of assumptions about the nature of writing, is critical to understanding her story of development. The construct of writing emphasized by a given curriculum, Dylan Dryer suggests, may inform "the construct of 'legitimate' or 'standard' writing that students will carry into their future classes, their workplaces, and their private and civic lives" (5). A concern about balancing creativity and organization seems to be central to Grace's own personal theorization of writing, and this concern seems to be connected to her sense that writing ability is inherent, fixed, and reflective of one's thinking, rather than one's ability to communicate effectively in a given social context. When asked what it means "to write well," Grace states:

> You need to be organized. You need to have good ideas. You have to be a good thinker. . . . I feel like writing . . . really demonstrates how you think. If you're a good thinker, then you're a good writer. . . . Just think creatively. It's what makes a good writer.

In this statement, Grace seems to posit writing as a window to the mind. Her fixation on balancing organization with creativity, which persists throughout her interviews, seems to be explained in part in this excerpt: she suggests that good writing relies on good thinking, and that organization and creativity in writing stem from an ability to be organized and creative in one's thoughts. The sense that writing merely reflects good thinking suggests a lack of awareness of writing process, which helps explain her difficulty engaging with writing instruction: if you believe in fixed, inherent ability, it would be extremely difficult to seek help or to approach the situation from a new angle, which are two essential components of adopting a process-based view of writing.

In an excerpt discussed previously, Grace's fixation on balancing creativity and organization is apparent: "Writing is a kind of art and shouldn't be so formulaic. . . . It has to be organized, and then I'm always trying to figure out how to match the creativity with the organization. It takes me forever to write." Her concern with organization seems to be tied to her perception that she has "disorganized" thoughts: in her exit interview, she states that when writing in the English language, "Trying to organize all my thoughts . . . is difficult, for some reason." Given her beliefs about the relationship between "good thinking" and "good writing," her disparaging remarks about her own disorganized thinking come more sharply into focus as a possible obstacle to her development as a writer.

When reflecting on reading her peers' writing, Grace seems similarly concerned with how her "erratic" thinking and her "complex brain" might prevent her from writing well:

> I've spent more time . . . than [my peers] did, but their writing still sounds so much more beautiful. . . . It just is automatically organized. It just came out of their head like that. They just thought, organized, and they could just write it out. For me, it's just like, I'm just thinking, and then I try to think—thoughts are so hard to organize. They're just . . . muddled in my head. . . . They probably just think in a more organized fashion than I do. I'm so erratic when I'm thinking.

Grace's sense that her thinking is inherently more disorganized, or "erratic," than that of her peers, which then leads to her inability to write efficiently and well, points again to a belief in inherent ability, as well as an under-conceptualized sense of writing process. Her peers' thoughts are "automatically organized"; they "just came out of their head like that." In contrast, in Grace's view, some people—like herself—just aren't organized thinkers, and therefore can't write quickly, or "beautiful[ly]." Instead of viewing her peers' writing as the result of hard work and process, or as an opportunity to locate an appropriate genre model for writing in a specific academic context, Grace defaults to a view of inherent ability. However, as Lizzie Hutton and Gail Gibson note in chapter 3, the fact that she has spent a great deal of time (more time than her peers, as she suggests) on writing does suggest her investment in her own writing development.

Grace's fixation on creativity and organization seems to suggest a very specific construct of writing—one that is perhaps unattainable, especially if she believes that writing ability is inherent and can't be taught or learned. As a result of aspiring to these high standards, Grace's writing process is hindered: due to her struggle to balance creativity with organization, she states, "It takes me forever to write." In the exit interview, she discusses her efforts to write creatively as a hindrance to her process:

> Because I want to be creative, . . . I don't want this professor or this teacher to have to read the same kind of stuff over and over again. They probably get billions of papers that sound the same. . . . Trying to be creative also stumps me, makes me slow to start, 'cause I want it to be better than everyone's.

This statement hints at Grace's developing rhetorical awareness: she is concerned about her audience, the professor, "hav[ing] to read the same kind of stuff over and over again"; however, the benchmark to which she aspires, which in this excerpt seems extremely competitive, seems to prevent her from writing, and also serves as a barrier to invention.

However, due to her comfort with more formulaic approaches to writing, Grace's sense that writing just "comes to" the writer seems to be reinforced by her ease with science writing: she states, "If it's a science paper, the evidence will speak for itself. You just add it in as you go." Elsewhere, Grace says,

> [With] science writing you have less research; you just write it. It's more straightforward, and the research will somehow . . . I feel like when I'm researching I'll just feel the thesis coming to me . . . All the support will be coming to you, and then from there you can just find an easy way to just incorporate what they say. Also, 'cause each article was writing in itself, and you could see how they organized it . . . [with] headings. If you're writing a book it's like the same kind of—or an essay. You're just writing a normal

> school essay; to break it down to headings would be a bit weird. If it was like a literature essay, it'd be weird, but in science it's just like, "Yeah, it doesn't matter. You don't need a transition between this and that." . . . If you label it you know what they're gonna talk about. . . . Science is more direct . . . Not gonna be all flowery. I'm gonna be technical. I'm gonna be accurate, but I'm not gonna be flowery.

Again, Grace restates her belief that writing just happens: in this context, "you just write it," and she'll "just feel the thesis coming to [her]," suggesting once again that writing is inherent, rather than a product of learning and process. Interestingly enough, however, this example does hint—for the first and only time in her interview data—at Grace's awareness that academic research might serve as a genre model for undergraduate student writing: "'cause each article was writing in itself, and you could see how they organized it . . . [with] headings." However, she quickly reverts to a less sophisticated view of genre: while she acknowledges that it would be "weird" to use headings in a "normal school essay," she slips seamlessly between discussing "writing a book" and "an essay," almost as though she sees these two types of writing as the same genre. This hints at the same genre confusion that I discussed at the outset: she seems to view novels as being an appropriate genre model for academic writing, which may be one source of her frustration.

It is perplexing that Grace seems to be experiencing such genre confusion in terms of her expectations of her own academic writing, particularly when she expresses a desire to write like the novels she reads. In Grace's case, the decontextualized construct of writing against which she appears to measure herself seems to have not only impeded her attempts to adapt her prior knowledge to new contexts, but the unrealistic standards she has set for herself also seem to have diminished her levels of self-efficacy, resulting in what Dana Lynn Driscoll and Jennifer Wells term a "disruptive disposition." This is particularly troubling given Grace's belief that that good writing is synonymous with good thinking: it seems as though she believes that if one is not a good writer (as she perceives herself), then they are not a good thinker. Grace's previously quoted statements that her "thoughts are so hard to organize," that they are "muddled in her head," and that she is "so erratic when [she's] thinking" suggest that she believes that she is not a good thinker, which implies that she has low levels of self-efficacy when it comes to her cognitive ability more generally in addition to her writing ability specifically.

As I have suggested, throughout her interviews, Grace reveals that she does not believe she is cognitively equipped to be creative and organized at the same time, and that she believes that writing ability is natural and inherent rather than the result of process, effort, and rhetorical efficacy in a given social context. She seems to believe that writing just happens: when she is writing in science, the paper essentially just flows from her, and for her peers who excel in writing in humanities and social sciences, a similar process happens in those contexts; the writing just appears. This theorization of writing, which emphasizes inherent ability at the expense of process, seems to suggest that good thinking leads to good writing, and that if one is a creative and organized thinker, good writing just happens. Grace seems to view her struggles with creativity and organization as stemming from inherent disorganization in her own thinking, suggesting a fixed mindset about her own cognitive and writing abilities. Given that she seems to have entered college with entrenched writing knowledge that has not served her well, coupled with her belief that writing can't be taught or learned, it is unsurprising that Grace struggled so much when adapting to college writing.

Forging Ahead: Resourcefulness and Resilience

Grace is not dissimilar from a group of students discussed elsewhere in the literature: students who come to college believing that they have mastered writing in high school only to face challenges adapting that prior knowledge to meet the demands of their new context. Mary Jo Reiff and Anis Bawarshi call these students "boundary guarders," suggesting that they tend to transfer (perhaps entrenched) genre knowledge wholesale into new contexts, resulting in the misapplication of prior genre knowledge. Upon realizing that their writing knowledge no longer serves them in the new context, these students may, according to Liane Robertson, Kara Taczak, and Kathleen Blake Yancey, "look upon such a setback as a personal failure (and understandably so), which view can prompt not a re-thinking, but rather resistance." Nancy Sommers and Laura Saltz agree that these writers may become resistant:

> . . . freshmen who cling to their old habits and formulas and who resent the uncertainty and humility of being a novice have a more difficult time adjusting to the demands of college writing. . . . These students often select courses to "get their requirements out of the way," blame their teachers for their low grades, and demonstrate an antagonistic attitude toward feedback. They feel as if there is a "secret code" to academic writing or that college itself is a kind of game whose rules—"what the teacher wants"—are kept secret to them, only glimpsed through the cryptic comments they receive on their papers. (134)

Through this lens, Grace's bewildering beliefs about writing generally and her abilities as a writer more specifically begin to make more sense: it seems as though she has come into college feeling prepared as a writer, only to find out that the strategies for writing she spent so much time developing in high school no longer work. In response to her perceived failure, she adopts a resistant stance toward writing generally, believing that writing is, as she states, "just this mysterious process" that she is not equipped to tackle. Although Sommers and Saltz voice concerns about how these students develop over time, Grace reveals one student's unique curricular (and extracurricular) response to these challenges, and eventually, some development.

In response to her struggles with invention, Grace turns to an extracurricular strategy that helps her approach new writing tasks:

> I actually had [my roommate] look at my prompt, 'cause I'm just so stuck . . . I think a lot of it has to do with I have trouble just starting. I find the middle paragraphs are easier to write than intros, and then the intro's the first thing. I can't just leave it missing, but I really feel like I should just start with just the bulk and go back to it. It's weird because with the AP exam . . . you just have to write. It's timed, it's written. You have to do the intro first thing. You can't just go back to it the same way you can on a computer. . . . I'll spend time writing an intro that isn't relevant. . . . then I'll go back and switch it.

In this excerpt, Grace seems painfully aware of how her prior knowledge—writing strategies for a timed essay exam—is impeding her writing process in college. She recognizes that the conditions of the AP exam, which is timed and handwritten, are dramatically different from writing a paper for college. The extended timeline of college writing assignments and the composing power of word processors should allow Grace to engage in a less linear, more recursive process. However, her linear approach to writing, forged through her understanding of AP English exams, seems to prevent her from writing the sections of her papers out of order. This impedes her process of invention, and as a result, she seeks another perspective on the assignment: that of her roommate.

In her exit interview, Grace describes two similar instances where she asked her roommate to read her prompt as a means of seeing the assignment from another perspective. In the first example, she says,

> When it's a writing assignment, there's preplanning that I have to do, research, and just even thinking about how I wanna go about with my argument. — I've tried to ask people, "What is your process?" . . . I think it helps. . . . Sometimes, I ask my roommate

> to look at my prompt again, because I think I just overthink the prompt sometimes. I think too much.

Grace describes two types of extracurricular writing feedback in this excerpt: asking other people about their process, and asking her roommate to read her prompt to prevent her from "overthinking." By seeking the perspective of another student—another thinker, another writer, another construct of writing—she is able to redirect her process, thus helping her generate writing that perhaps aligns more closely with the assignment. By seeking feedback from another student, Grace shows not only movement toward a more growth-oriented mindset, but also a developing awareness of the rhetorically situated nature of writing: she locates an audience beyond her instructor.

In addition to her extracurricular strategies, Grace enacts a curricular strategy (albeit an avoidant one) by dropping her declared major in environmental sciences and opting instead for a minor. Of the major, she states, "I hate that this major is full of writing and persuading people and arguments. I can't write well enough, and so I just—I dropped the class, and then I dropped my major." She goes on to say,

> I just feel like I can't take another two, three classes that will have to have me write, because I have better strengths in science things. I find it easier to write science papers for some reason than it is for an argument paper. . . . I'm not even persuasive in person. How am I supposed to sound persuasive in writing?

Her views of writing in this major still suggest a fixed view of writing development: she is just not persuasive, in person or in writing, thus suggesting that she believes her problems with writing stem from her problems as a person.

However, the shroud of insecurity, low self-efficacy, and fixed-mindset beliefs about writing that had previously enveloped Grace's writing experiences seems to be at least partially lifted when she finds a major that is so different that it forces her to adopt (and embrace) a novice status as a learner: German. Her success in adapting to writing in German can be seen not only through self-reports of her experiences in interviews, but also through the two English-language writing samples that she offered from her German courses, which are much more sophisticated than her writing samples from courses outside of the German department.

Grace's struggles with writing in English-language courses were closely tied to issues with "overthinking" as an impediment to invention; this seems to be somewhat alleviated when she is writing in German:

> In English you're thinking about all the nuances and trying to choose a word, and I just get so indecisive. It's like, "Should I use this word or this word?" There are so many options. Then with the German, it's just like, "Oh, I only know this word for that idea, so I'm gonna go with that word." You're just done with it. You're not overthinking anything.

In her German classes, Grace's self-described "erratic" and "disorganized" thinking seems to be less of a hindrance to her writing process. Writing in a foreign language seems to have forced Grace to adopt a novice status: because she has fewer linguistic resources to choose from, she has to accept her novice status, thus allowing her to move into the assignment without the burden of "overthinking" that impeded her process of invention in her classes outside of German.

In addition to the freedom to fail built into this writing environment, her German classes also allowed for the creativity that she values in writing:

> The German department . . . they like to be really fun about it. . . . They're trying to convert people into becoming majors and minors, which they do very well. . . . They always stress creativity. Just have fun with the language . . . and if you're having fun, and you have everything grammatically correct, and you're learning at the same time, that's totally great. My first essay—I'm really proud of it, but I think [the assignment was] just find a German website and write about it—whatever. I mean, any way that you want. There was something probably more creative to it. I would write it . . . from the perspective of a Gummy Bear. I think our prompt was, "What do you think about the website? Would you recommend it? What else about it?" I was like, "Well, I'm a Gummy Bear, and I like this website 'cause it talks all about me. I'm kinda sad though that it's not long enough 'cause there should really be more written about me, 'cause I'm a Gummy Bear, and I'm awesome, and I'm cute and whatever." Stuff like that—it's just really creative, and then you're excited about writing it. You're just like, "I'm just gonna write this. It's gonna be so hilarious. Everyone's gonna laugh. I'm laughing. I'm having fun."

The novice status imposed by writing in a foreign language seems to free Grace from her anxieties about word choice, style, and subjective judgments of her writing, and the writing curriculum in this context still allows for creativity. By encouraging creativity in terms of content, this environment supports the creativity that Grace values so much while simultaneously obviating her concerns about organization and precision in terms of language.

In stark contrast to her previous statements that suggested a product-oriented version of writing, her description of her writing in German suggests more engagement with process. In German, she is more comfortable taking a longer, process-based approach:

> I think I just know English so much better, that I also notice the flaws when I write. Then I can't continue writing until it sounds just right. . . . Then I get discouraged and I don't want to write anymore. Whereas [in] German, it's just, "Well, I'll fix all the grammar stuff later. Right now, it's just important . . . to just even convey the idea that I want to convey." . . . It's easier to get my ideas when I think about it that way. . . . I go in with this mindset that there will be errors, because I know there will be. It's not my native tongue . . . it frees me to think about what I want to talk about instead of how I'm saying it, or how I'm structuring it, or whether it makes any sense.

Grace finds it easier to "get" her ideas when she isn't concerned about grammar. Although her use of this verb still implies a theorization of writing as a direct communication of one's thinking (she is "getting" or accessing her ideas so that they can then be made visible through writing), she does ultimately enact a mindset that is more comfortable with errors in initial drafts, suggesting a more recursive, nonlinear writing process: she knows that she can circle back and edit later, after she writes through her ideas and revises her draft by attending to "structure." Her knowledge that she is writing in a second language provides her with some freedom to fail when it comes to grammatical perfection, which enables her to focus more on *ideas* than on mechanics and structure, thus helping her forge a writing process, especially when her instructors support her in doing so. In her exit interview, Grace says,

> All [the instructors] want you to do is use the language and not worry about how perfect you're being. Because . . . language isn't even perfect, in general, when you talk and stuff. They don't expect that of you. They just want you to use it, to feel comfortable with it, and to like it. . . . It's not really about how perfect you are. Just use your language. I enjoy doing that. I'll write in German randomly, or I seek out German videos, or whatever, because I like to.

In Grace's view, the instruction in her German major prioritizes scaffolded learning over perfection, which helps her overcome the internalized beliefs about writing and learning that had seemed to hinder her writing in other environments. Here, Grace provides a view of language that emphasizes learning, rather than perfection or a view of language or writing as a direct, transparent communication of one's thoughts. This environment and its effects on her theorization of writing result in increased levels of self-efficacy, as well as her engagement with the subject matter: the fact that Grace seeks out experiences to use her German "randomly" suggests that she is truly motivated to learn this subject, even beyond the curricular environment.

Overall, her acceptance of and subsequent critical engagement with instructor feedback seem to play a major role in Grace's ability to develop as a writer in her German major. When describing her feedback in her German classes, Grace imitates her instructors, perhaps signaling a more personal identification with them as compared to her remarks lumping all university instructors into the unspecified pronoun, "they," as she did when describing her English-language college instructors in an earlier excerpt. She repeats her German instructors' feedback as follows: "'Wow, you're such an amazing—you just did all the grammar right, and you didn't spell anything wrong, and you looked up this vocab, and you used it right.'" In her exit interview, when she states, "I get a lot of encouragement from the professors . . . they're just like, 'Yeah, it was almost . . . perfect grammar-wise.' I've gotten notes saying that, 'This is the best draft that I've ever gotten in this course before,' or whatever." At this point, Grace does not seem to engage, borrowing Wilson and Post's term, "critically," with instructor feedback (chapter 1); however, she is at least more receptive to it: she recognizes that it exists, and she repeats the comments that she remembers, which are all encouraging and supportive.

Grace states in both interviews that she has not engaged with reflection, which is troubling: reflection supported by curriculum may increase self-efficacy. As Kathleen Blake Yancey suggests, "such reflecting contributes to self-efficacy precisely because it helps us understand that we have learned (even if not always successfully); how we have learned; and how we might continue to learn" ("Introduction" 8). Furthermore, curricular reflection may offer writers guided, structured opportunities to theorize their own writing alongside principles espoused by writing research (Taczak; Taczak and Robertson; Yancey, *Reflection*; Yancey et al.), which might have been particularly helpful in terms of prompting Grace to rethink some of her beliefs about writing.

However, despite her statements in both interviews that she has not engaged with reflective writing, it appears that she has: not only does she upload one of her writing samples to our study archive with a note remarking that she had also been required to write a reflective component when submitting it, but her writing samples from her German classes, especially the preface she wrote for her translation of a German's children's story, demonstrate that she ultimately was able to engage in some curricular reflection. The fact that she does not report having engaged in reflection is also indicative of her previous resistance toward writing curriculum:

the reflective assignment that she uploaded seems to have escaped her memory, suggesting that she didn't engage critically with this exercise.

In the translator's preface, Grace adopts an engaging and sophisticated tone while walking her reader through the processes that informed the decisions she made while translating this short story. Despite her statements about reflection, the preface to her translation suggests that she can be a highly reflective writer and thinker when given an opportunity to make her thought processes visible through reflective prose. In reading Grace's description of writing the translator' preface, it becomes clear that instructor feedback was central to this process:

> With my advisor for this translation, this introduction thing, we went through just to see what kind of things I should include. . . . He just let me talk, then he wrote down what I said . . . I think he was [like], . . . "All this stuff that you're telling me can be put into this preface. Just start writing and go from there." I found that to be . . . helpful. . . . I knew that he was gonna look over it afterwards, too. This continued coaching . . . it made me reliable.

This instructor provided Grace individualized writing support consisting of three meetings: brainstorming, a review of a first draft, and a review of a revised draft. Throughout this process, Grace felt supported, and she was receptive to feedback, suggesting that she had become more "accepting" (in Wilson and Post's terms, chapter 1, this collection) of instructor feedback. Furthermore, in this instance, the ongoing feedback that resulted in the translator's preface seemed to have prompted Grace to reflect on her writing and thinking: as I have previously suggested, the preface itself is quite reflective. Since subsequent reflection suggests critical engagement with feedback, this instance seems to reveal that Grace has ultimately critically engaged with instructor feedback in this instance, which Wilson and Post suggest is a sign of development.

Overall, it seems that in their feedback, the German faculty emphasized ideas over perfection. Of another paper, Grace says,

> Once I finished [a draft of a research paper], [my instructor] gave it back and said it was great. . . . He wasn't grading on grammar at that point, because it was just—it's like a checkpoint to make sure you're not going in the wrong direction and being full of errors and whatever. At least you've progressed somewhere. He said it was good, and I'm consistently doing well with that writing. It makes me feel better about writing, like, "Now I wanna write, because I'll do great. If I put the effort in."

Clearly, her motivation and self-efficacy toward writing in this environment are encouraged by this curricular structure: she recognizes that if she "put[s] the effort in," she will be rewarded. Supported by this curricular environment, Grace seems to finally begin to adopt a growth mindset: if she tries, she will learn.

She discusses the role of instructor feedback in more detail when describing her process drafting another English-language paper, which she was "really proud of," in a German class. She notes that

> My professor . . . graded it on ideas. You could always go to him at any time through the whole semester . . . however finished your essay was. . . . He was just, "Whatever." He was just so—ideas—this is what matters obviously.

Feedback is clearly a central part of this story: of the same instructor, Grace says,

> I would be comfortable going up to talk to him, 'cause he was so passionate about [the content of the course]. It's okay to talk to this person, 'cause . . . he'll want to talk . . . to me about this. Some of my other papers, I just feel that I can't talk to anyone about it, and I just kinda go through it.

Grace did take advantage of this instructor's availability for feedback, which helped her change her "five-paragraph mindset" and encouraged her to experiment with novel organizational approaches. Of the paper, she stated,

> It was fun. . . . I went to his office hours. . . . The first thing I said was, "How do I write a ten-page paper? I've never done it before." Then he was like, "Well, you just do it like any other paper. It's just really long." . . . The longest I've ever done was six pages, and it's different if you're into that five-paragraph mindset obviously that's not gonna fill ten pages. . . . It helped me think that there are other organizational styles. Mine ended up being broken into two parts, two arguments.

The feedback in this class emphasized the importance of ideas over perfection, and process over product; this approach seemed to resonate with Grace. It seems as though Grace felt supported, encouraged, and self-efficacious in this environment, which helped her challenge her entrenched writing knowledge: by remarking on her ability to change her "five-paragraph mindset" and experiment with new organizational structures, Grace reveals that she is developing as a writer.

The experience of learning to write in a new language seems to have been destabilizing enough that Grace was forced to dislodge some of her entrenched writing knowledge and approach writing anew, as a novice. Her lack of linguistic resources allowed her to approach writing without "overthinking" it, and the scaffolded nature of assignments and emphasis on growth over perfection allow her to rethink her approaches to learning. Furthermore, the supportive nature of the instructor feedback in this context seems to enable Grace to accept feedback, and eventually to engage critically with instructor feedback and new approaches to writing. The approach to writing that she ultimately adopts seems to be less stilted and linear, emphasizing process over product.

By the time she graduates, Grace ultimately demonstrates more nuanced perspectives about how her self-efficacy shifts when writing for different domains, such as German classes and blogs, which she also points to in her interviews as a freeing form of writing. This is in stark contrast to her earlier decontextualized views of writing as universally "good" or "bad," which suggest that its quality is determined by the quality of the writer's thoughts. Additionally, Grace's self-efficacy seems to improve over time: she says she "hates" writing eight times in her entry interview; in contrast, in her exit interview, she only uses this word once. Perhaps most importantly, it seems as though her counterproductive beliefs about writing and learning shift over time; one of her writing samples from German class, which argues that US perceptions of Freud as a pseudoscientist originate from translation issues, suggests a challenge to her view of writing as an unproblematic container of thought or ideas, and implies instead a more rhetorically informed, socially constructed view of language and writing. Despite the challenges that Grace faced when entering the study, through her extracurricular writing strategies and locating the right major, she ultimately managed to reframe her counterproductive beliefs about writing and learning, unearth her entrenched writing knowledge, and increase her levels of self-efficacy. In the face of adversity, Grace found a way to triumph.

Conclusion

In response to her challenges, Grace demonstrates resourcefulness and resilience: in many ways, she manages to overcome her struggles with college writing by pursuing feedback in extracurricular contexts and seeking refuge in a major where she receives encouragement and individualized writing support from faculty. When she feels unsupported by instructors in her writing process, she, like the participants discussed by Benjamin Keating in chapter 2, seeks feedback in extracurricular contexts, specifically from her roommate. Additionally, she strategically maneuvers within her writing curriculum by dropping a major (environmental science) in which she felt she "[couldn't] write," instead pursuing a major so different from her past writing experiences that she was forced to adopt a novice status: German. Grace's narrative reinforces findings in chapter 2 (Benjamin Keating) and chapter 4 (Ryan McCarty) that suggest that students can be quite strategic and resourceful, and that they are at times capable of forging their own customized curricular pathways—aided by tools such as extracurricular writing supports and strategic choice of major—in order to help them circumvent some of the barriers they encounter in terms of writing development.

Over time, Grace does demonstrate development as a writer, through her self-reports and in the quality of her writing. In her exit interview, she displays increased levels of rhetorical agility and a growing awareness of how her levels of self-efficacy might differ across contexts, which suggests a developmental arc in terms of rhetorical awareness. Indeed, as Lizzie Hutton and Gail Gibson discuss in chapter 3, Grace eventually employs an "academic-creative hybrid" approach to writing, which ultimately signals more confidence, agency, flexibility, and awareness of development. By the time she graduates, instead of framing writing simply as a "necessary" evil, as she does in her entry interview, she recognizes that she has higher levels of self-efficacy for writing in specific domains, such as online writing, as well as academic writing in science and in German classes. This suggests that her view of herself as a writer becomes more rhetorically situated over time: she begins to see the difference between domains of writing, at least in terms of her stance toward them. Although she still claims that she "hates writing," she finds herself better equipped to nuance that claim, specifying that she only hates a *specific kind* of academic writing, and that she actually enjoys and feels more confident when writing online, and when writing for her German and science classes. By providing an example of one student's strategies for adapting to college writing, Grace reveals how procedural writing knowledge and students' personally held beliefs about writing and learning may interact to facilitate or impede transfer and writing development. Furthermore, her experiences suggest that students who fit Reiff and Bawarshi's description of "boundary guarders" may struggle, at first, to adapt to the context of college writing, but in some cases they may enact extracurricular and curricular strategies to overcome their challenges and ultimately develop as writers.

NOTES

1. Although there was a "writing development" code applied during the first round of interview coding, I did not include this code in my search terms. Due to the overlap between the code and the

purpose of the study, most interview excerpts could ostensibly have been coded "writing development." Furthermore, because I, like other researchers in this collection, chose to analyze longitudinal data in order to track development over time, I knew that writing development would be captured in my analysis regardless of whether I used this specific code to locate cases.

2. Grace's discussion of applying her "formulaic approach" from math to her AP English class is discussed in further detail by Lizzie Hutton and Gail Gibson in chapter 3; for an example of another student who discussed transfer between her mathematical learning and her writing development, see Anne Ruggles Gere's discussion of Stephanie in chapter 10.

WORKS CITED

Anson, Chris M. "Habituated Practice Can Lead to Entrenchment." *Naming What We Know: Threshold Concepts of Writing Studies*, edited by Linda Adler-Kassner and Elizabeth Wardle, Utah State UP, 2015, pp. 77–78.

Charmaz, Kathy. *Constructing Grounded Theory*. SAGE Publications, 2014.

Driscoll, Dana Lynn, and Jennifer Wells. "Beyond Knowledge and Skills: Writing Transfer and the Role of Student Dispositions." *Composition Forum*, vol. 26, 2012.

Dryer, Dylan B. "Scaling Writing Ability: A Corpus-Driven Inquiry." *Written Communication*, vol. 30, no. 1, 2013, pp. 3–35.

Dweck, Carol S. *Mindset: The New Psychology of Success*. Random House, 2006.

Maxwell, Joseph A. *Qualitative Research Design: An Interactive Approach*. SAGE Publications, 2013.

Patton, Michael Quinn. *Qualitative Research & Evaluation Methods: Integrating Theory and Practice*. SAGE Publications, 2015.

Reiff, Mary Jo, and Anis Bawarshi. "Tracing Discursive Resources: How Students Use Prior Genre Knowledge to Negotiate New Writing Contexts in First-Year Composition." *Written Communication*, vol. 28, no. 3, 2011, pp. 312–37.

Robertson, Liane, Kara Taczak, and Kathleen Blake Yancey. "Notes toward A Theory of Prior Knowledge and Its Role in College Composers' Transfer of Knowledge and Practice." *Composition Forum*, vol. 26, 2012.

Sommers, Nancy, and Laura Saltz. "The Novice as Expert: Writing the Freshman Year." *College Composition and Communication*, vol. 56, no. 1, 2004, pp. 124–49.

Taczak, Kara. "Reflection Is Critical for Writers' Development." *Naming What We Know: Threshold Concepts of Writing Studies*, edited by Linda Adler-Kassner and Elizabeth Wardle, Utah State UP, 2015, pp. 78–79.

Taczak, Kara, and Liane Robertson. "Reiterative Reflection in the Twenty-First Century Writing Classroom: An Integrated Approach to Teaching for Transfer." *A Rhetoric of Reflection*, edited by Kathleen Blake Yancey, Utah State UP, pp. 42–63.

Yancey, Kathleen Blake. "Introduction: Contextualizing Reflection." *A Rhetoric of Reflection*, edited by Kathleen Blake Yancey, Utah State UP, 2016, pp. 3–20.

Yancey, Kathleen Blake. *Reflection in the Writing Classroom*. Utah State UP, 1998.

Yancey, Kathleen Blake, Liane Robertson, and Kara Taczak. *Writing Across Contexts: Transfer, Composition, and Sites of Writing*. Utah State UP, 2014.

CHAPTER EIGHT

"MY *WRITING* WRITING"

STUDENT CONCEPTIONS OF WRITING AND SELF-PERCEPTIONS OF MULTIMODAL COMPOSITIONAL DEVELOPMENT

Naomi Silver

In their 2006 study of student writing development, *Engaged Writers and Dynamic Disciplines*, Chris Thaiss and Terry Myers Zawacki observe that in regard to still-new forms of composition such as "multimedia writing," there are not yet widely accepted models for thinking about what constitutes exemplary student work, or for understanding the effects of these modes and media on students' writing development. Interestingly, more than a decade later, as a field, we don't yet have robust descriptions of the variety of ways in which students might develop into what we would today call multimodal writers, or writers who can compose in digital contexts. In the past decade, there has been substantial work around developing pedagogical support for students' multimodal composing and flexible, effective models for assessment (e.g., Shipka; Neal; McKee and DeVoss; Whithaus). Attention has been devoted to the need for multimodal assessment to do more than simply apply text-based assessments to these new contexts and rhetorical situations (see, for instance, Sorapure; Penrod; Gallagher). More recently, publications describing a variety of embodied composing processes in digital environments have also begun to appear (see DeVoss et al.; Gonzales), and we are beginning to see useful models for placing multimodal composition within existing frameworks for transfer of learning in writing studies (VanKooten). However, when it comes to analyzing the means by which students become rhetorically savvy multimodal writers, the field seems to remain in much the same place as Thaiss and Zawacki indicated in 2006: we are "not here yet" (93). That is the work of this chapter, then—to begin to define and describe some dimensions of student writing development as students compose within digital, multimodal rhetorical situations.

To this end, we can draw on the conventions and best practices that have emerged for professional multimodal compositions, much as researchers do when looking at student development in disciplinary writing. In chapter 4, Ryan McCarty critiques this reliance on development of disciplinary expertise as a stand-in for student writing development as such, but I turn to the literature on multimodal composition to provide a conceptual framework that is just one indicator of student writing development in this area. So, for instance, we can look at scholarly journals that publish multimodal writing, such as *Kairos*, and consider the degree to which students such as our study participants enact the principles laid out in that journal's style guide as one way to define their development as multimodal composers. The "*Kairos* Style Guide" specifies, among other directives:

- All media and design elements should be non-gratuitous and facilitate or enact the rhetorical and aesthetic argument of the webtext.
- All links should contribute to the possible meanings and readings of the texts. Linking for the sake of linking is discouraged.

These guidelines derive from a "theory of design as an integral element of digital rhetoric practice: design as rhetoric" (Eyman and Ball 68). As *Kairos*'s editors Douglas Eyman and Cheryl Ball argue, "For digital rhetoric, design is equivalent to style; thus, scholars must be concerned with understanding all the available elements of document design, including color, font choice, and layout as well as multimedia design possibilities including motion, interactivity, and appropriate use of media" (68). The authors go on to suggest that the "question is not whether we want style or substance but what kind of style we want to deploy as a component of substance" (68). For our student multimodal composers, then, one question to ask of their writing development is the extent to which they see themselves as composing "texts that are authored to use affordances of screen-based interactions and new media technologies that are neither digitizations of print-based material nor reproducible in print forms" (Eyman and Ball 65), and then, to what extent their integration of these affordances explicitly supports their rhetorical exigency.

Additionally, as much of the assessment literature on multimodal composition suggests, considering how students talk about their processes for achieving a given composition, as well as how they evaluate their success in meeting their own goals for it, can give us additional insights into their metacognitive development in this domain—especially in cases in which students demonstrate more novice facility as multimodal composers. As Colleen Reilly and Anthony Atkins helpfully summarize, for instance:

> Recommendations to use student reflections about digital writing assignments as artifacts that inform or are factored into the assessment of their projects have become commonplace (Hess, 2007; Huot, 2002b; Odell & Katz, 2009; Remley, 2012; Shipka, 2009; Yancey, 2004). [. . .] As Jody Shipka (2009) noted, prompts for student project reflections can encourage substantive and rhetorically sophisticated responses, allowing students to demonstrate their knowledge of course concepts and ability to articulate project goals, discuss rhetorical choices, and constructively evaluate their work. Similarly, Michael Neal (2011) asserted that student reflections about their digital compositions should involve rhetorically oriented rationales of content and design choices. ("Rewarding Risk" n.p.)

Following this lead, then, and using it to build on the rhetorical design principles defined by Eyman and Ball, the degree to which students such as our study participants are able to articulate a "rhetorically oriented rationale" for their multimodal compositional choices can become an additional indicator of their multimodal writing development. This chapter is interested, then, both in what students *do* when facing a multimodal writing task and how they *talk* about what they do; or, to put it in more technical terms,[1] this chapter analyzes participants' metacognitive awareness of the appropriate design principles for a given task and their metacognitive regulation of these principles as they put them into action in their composing processes.[2]

Metacognition and an Expanded View of Writing as Signs of Multimodal Compositional Development

This study captures two domains in which multimodal composition takes place: (1) within single artifacts, composed as a class assignment or an internship project, for instance, and (2) within eportfolios made up of multiple artifacts, composed most often for the minor-in-writing Gateway and Capstone courses, but also in other academic and professional contexts. In the entry and exit interviews conducted for this study, all of our participants were asked directly about their experiences with multimodal and digital media writing, whether in course work or other contexts (see appendix 4 for interview protocols). These questions were aimed at eliciting responses that speak both to rhetorical design principles and to student metacognitive awareness and regulation of these principles. In doing so, the questions assist in making "metacognitive moves for composition [become] observable" (VanKooten), which Crystal VanKooten rightly identifies as a necessary step in our ability to understand student writing development.

Using grounded theory coding to analyze the interviews, the codes "new media" and "portfolio" were developed to capture mentions of these writing experiences in the two domains, and, in 131 interviews, concluded with 475 interview excerpts coded as "new media" and 419 interview excerpts coded as "portfolio." There were 255 instances in which these codes co-occurred. As the number of co-occurrences suggests, these two domains overlap in significant ways in regard to themes that emerged in the student interviews. In regard to the forms of multimodal composition in which they engaged, students in both participant groups had experience blogging, whether for course work, in professional contexts, or for self-sponsored purposes. They also had experience with a variety of social media platforms, and they had created an array of digital media compositions, ranging from PowerPoint and Prezi presentations, to video production, audio podcasting, website design, pamphlet and other print-based multimodal compositions, and more. Additionally, students in both groups had experience creating eportfolios, though due to the eportfolio component of their curriculum, the minors far outnumbered nonminors in this regard.

In interview excerpts connected to both codes, students reflected in a variety of ways on how they understood the design elements of their multimodal compositions in relation to the argumentative elements of their writing. Indeed, the way students frame their sense of this "form-substance" relationship often provides an important indicator of their development as multimodal composers. For many students in the study, composing in modes and media other than "black words on a white page" (Sidney, "Exit"), as one participant put it, was a new experience, and not always a positive one. Several participants explicitly separated design from argument in their discussions of multimodal writing. The following responses, both from the entry interviews of minor-in-writing students, are typical of this impulse: "I think . . . designing the website and uploading the images and making sure everything was in the same format. It just seemed more technical than actually improving our writing" (Susanne); "I think that the technology stuff was not necessary. I don't think that improved my writing at all . . . even the remediation became more of an art project than anything else" (Ariana). In these examples and other similar ones, when students speak of *writing*, it is always in regard to the text-based forms with which they are familiar. These are forms that carry value for students, while design is belittled as merely "an art project," and facility with digital media is merely "technical" know-how. It is of little surprise that these study participants—who have been shown to excel in myriad forms of text-based composition throughout the chapters in this volume—might express initial discomfort with or dislike for compositional forms that do not appear to align with the writing goals they envision for themselves. This perspective is demonstrated by Abby, another minor-in-writing participant, who declares in her exit interview:

> I think that there's just maybe a little bit too much of a focus on online writing just because—just as someone who's coming from a science background who was interested in writing, none of the online stuff is relevant. Learning different writing styles and being able to go to a professional and ask them to help you with this specific type of writing that you're interested in is more important to me than learning how to blog, or to look at an online portfolio, or something like that.

These students' "resistant" stance toward multimodal composition does not necessarily mean they are unable to produce adequate multimodal products, but, as Emily Wilson and Justine Post suggest (chapter 1), their apparent refusal to engage critically with this new composing process, to adopt a metacognitive awareness of its affordances and constraints—even if they do not ultimately enjoy it—suggests limited development in this area.

Other study participants found the challenges of working with digital media and in multiple modes to be interesting and rewarding, though they still tended to approach "substance" and "style" as largely separable. The following exit interview exchange with Katie, a nonminor, demonstrates this approach to design rhetoric:

> Interviewer: You said earlier about your blog too that it made you feel confident because it looked good. . . . Interviewee: Well, it was just a very new, different experience. I've never written like that before and it looked cool. It had the colors and it had the pictures and the video. . . . I was really proud of myself for making something that looked so interesting. . . . I forget what the actual class was about but I remember writing about *Mad Men* and the opening sequence for one of them. . . . I think I played the video and I had other pictures of advertisements from *Mad Men* in there so it looked cool.

Katie is clearly engaged in the content of her argument about *Mad Men*, and is considering her design choices in regard to its presentation; however, her key concern is not how these design elements (images, video) contribute to deepening or extending her argument, but rather their visual effect on the reader ("it looked cool"). It may be inferred that the argument about these opening credits preceded the choice of visual materials, which then become add-ons that do create effect, but remain non-essential to the overall purpose of her composition. In this way, Katie demonstrates an appreciation for the affordances of multimodal composition, but a lack of metacognition about their potential effects on argument, which suggests that her conception of writing itself may not be deeply changed by her engagement with these modes and media.

Julia, a minor-in-writing student, offers a perspective in her exit interview that begins to come closer to the aim of creating her composition's multimodal elements to "facilitate or enact [her] rhetorical and aesthetic argument" ("*Kairos* Style Guide"), and that also addresses the potential technical difficulty of carrying this process forward. She states:

> For me, what I remember most is trying—I chose a visual theme. It was hard because what I wanted to do was do pictures to represent each of the different essays or each of a pair of essays that was like a representation of the different essays. . . . What ended up happening was to get the pictures all to be perfect squares and to get it in the way that—you know, you imagine something and then you really want it to be that way. Eventually, I got it to look how I wanted it to look—[*laughter*]—but, for me, I remember really nit-pickingly trying to get these pictures perfect.

Here, Julia seems to articulate a rhetorical rationale for her multimodal choices (she wants her chosen images to "represent" each category of artifacts she has uploaded to her Capstone eportfolio) that is similar to the relationship between words and images that Karen Shriver calls "stage-setting," namely, when there is "different content in words and pictures, in which one mode (often the visual) forecasts the content, underlying theme, or ideas presented in the other mode" (413).

In Julia's Capstone eportfolio, clicking on an image on her home page will take the reader/viewer to a new page that presents an essay or project thematically related to the image. For instance, the center image in figure 8.1 of two people in apparent wedding apparel kissing each other leads to Julia's Capstone project, titled "For Better or Worse," which explores gender roles in relation to marriage case law. Every other image in the grid similarly "forecasts the content, underlying theme, or ideas" of the artifact to which it links. In regard to design, the perfect symmetry of each image enables the grid format that Julia labored over and provides a visually dynamic first view of the eportfolio. Julia claims earlier in the exit interview that she is "not the most . . . technologically savvy. I'm just not really great with—[*laughter*]—computers." Nonetheless, despite this apparent lack of confidence in

Fig. 8.1. Home page image of Julia's Capstone eportfolio

her technological design abilities, and her relative unfamiliarity with this mode of composition, Julia demonstrates a commitment to her design that allows her to overcome the frustration of the medium's constraints and to realize her rhetorical vision for the "picture-essay" relationship on her eportfolio. In doing so, she evinces both metacognitive awareness and regulation, taking her rhetorical design from "imagination" ("You imagine something and then you really want it to be that way") to realization ("Eventually, I got it to look how I wanted it to look").

Sophie, a nonminor, describes an example of a different rhetorical relationship between visual and textual modes in her entry interview, one of *supplementarity*:

> Prezi sort of allows you to almost communicate your thought process through the presentation, because you can zoom. We had this one map that we're showing and then we want to show another map next to it and, rather than clicking on the next slide, we just zoom out, and you can see both maps next to each other. Which, when you're watching something, it's just much more visually appealing.

Shriver describes a supplementary verbal-visual relationship as "characterized by different content in words and pictures, in which one mode dominates the other, providing the main ideas, while the other reinforces, elaborates, or instantiates the points made in the dominant mode" (413). Sophie, who apparently describes a connection between what appears on two different maps, reinforces this argument for her audience by presenting the connection visually as well as verbally using the Prezi platform's unique "zooming" affordances, and she articulates that relationship in her depiction of the "presentation" itself as "almost communicat[ing] [her] thought process." Although Sophie falls back on the language of "visual appeal" (similarly to Katie) to explain why she prefers the spatial relationship enabled by the Prezi platform to a more linear, slide-based presentation platform, it seems clear that she has an intentional rhetorical design in mind (metacognitive awareness) and is able to choose the appropriate medium within which to facilitate it (metacognitive regulation).

In their interviews, these three study participants, Katie, Julia, and Sophie, each convey a sense of how incorporating multiple modes in their compositions (e.g., visual, spatial) may enhance the meaning of their intended argument. At the same time—while developmental differences among these participants are certainly apparent, from Katie's primarily additive, not-particularly-rhetorical understanding of the relation of argument and media, to Julia's and Sophie's more deliberate and self-aware rhetorically design-based approaches—in all three instances, the incorporation of nonalphabetic modes appears secondary to the dominant text-based argument. It is, of course, often the case in multimodal composition that one mode may be predominant, but students' awareness of when and how they might select these modes can offer additional insights into their writing development. The extent to which writers begin to conceive of "substance" and "style" as necessarily co-occurring, such that their argument could not be enacted without their design, marks a conceptual shift in their understanding of what it means to write, of what might "count" as writing, that may also signal developmental growth.

This shift begins to be visible conceptually in Jenna's exit interview when she is asked about what she learned from the projects of other minor-in-writing students:

> I saw that there were a lot of different ways to say something, if that makes sense. It depends who you're saying it to and why you're saying it. I realize you have to think—there are a lot more decisions that go into how you want to convey something. . . . Like how do you want to—do you want it to be in an essay? Like literally words on a page or do you want to turn it into something with pictures or do you want to put it on a website? All of the things that play into that. If it's just an essay anyone can read it but then if you put pictures with it you're influencing people to see a certain thing or if you put it on a website then how do people navigate your website and where is the emphasis? There's so many decisions that go into that.

Parsing the sequence of steps Jenna makes in her response, at least three important dimensions of multimodal writing development become apparent. First, Jenna's conception of writing appears to have expanded through her collaborations with her Capstone course peers: "There were a lot of different ways to say something"; "There are a lot more decisions that go into how you want to convey something." Second, she views this new compositional terrain as linked to rhetorical situation, to audience, purpose, medium, and context: "It depends who you're saying it to and why you're saying it." And finally, Jenna understands that the choice of medium and mode is inextricable from the effect of the argument: "If it's just an essay anyone can read it but then if you put pictures with it you're influencing people to see a certain thing or if you put it on a website then how do people navigate your website and where is the emphasis?" "Put[ting] pictures with it," then, can not only enhance an argument, making it stronger, but can influence a reader/viewer's interpretation of it. In regard to fully digital media such as websites, design choices such as navigational structure can determine a reader/viewer's experience of the argument as well as create argumentative emphases.

Jenna articulates the ideas that design enacts argument and that writing takes multiple forms with a high degree of metacognitive awareness, but this excerpt does not present evidence of how she herself follows through on her understanding. Examples from two other study participants offer a sense of what it can look like for this compositional development to become visible. In her entry interview, Dana, a writing minor, discusses her experience with remediating an alphabetic essay into an audio essay, and her realization that the argument she wanted to convey could not successfully be enacted using text alone:

> For the remediation, I chose a piece that I wrote for [English] 125 on the Kanye West song. It was an essay that I wrote on an actual song. I thought that I wasted a lot of time

> in the essay explaining how the music sounded or what the lyrics said. I made an audio essay of it, with me reading it and then it cut into the actual music. That was something that couldn't have been done without new media.

Dana's opportunity in the minor-in-writing Gateway course to transform the medium in which she conveyed her message about the Kanye West song enabled her to enact aspects of her argument that were previously not available, and in this way the new medium does more than merely enhance a previously existing argument. Dana's example may be viewed as something of a transitional developmental moment, in that the remediated audio essay draws heavily on the text-based argument that preceded it, but nonetheless accomplishes new rhetorical work made possible by an aural medium.

Lauren, a nonminor majoring in screen arts and culture (film studies), offers a fuller example of compositional development in her entry interview in regard to film-making, in which she begins to understand multimodal and multimedia composition itself as writing. Here, shot selection and continuity editing perform functions that might be taken up, for instance, by selection of evidence and paragraph organization in alphabetic writing. In this way, Lauren, too, shows that her conception of writing has begun to develop as she considers the design elements of composing in a non-text-based medium:

> It's cool because I can express myself in a medium other than words, but I can still express the same ideas that I'm writing about. I mean, I'm like—for my SAC [Screen Arts and Culture] 290 class, we are doing black and white 16mm silent film, so it's really cool cause we had like somebody playing chess—two guys playing chess—and it looked really, really gorgeous. It was like, "I could write about this, but it's so much cooler to see it in this medium," and the way I choose to cut the angles, and where I'm cutting for continuity, and stuff like that, that is kind of like writing in itself.

Though Lauren relies in some ways on the language of visual effect ("it's so much cooler"), her deeper point seems to be that the rhetorical design work that goes into film composition is central to the aesthetic meaning conveyed. Like Dana, she realizes that "writing about" it is possible, but the resulting composition would be entirely different—and ostensibly less successful. Here, then, Dana and Lauren seem to be discovering and exemplifying Jenna's point that "how you want to convey something," the media and modes a writer selects, determines the meanings that may be enacted and communicated.

The participants represented in these several examples of interview excerpts in which there is co-occurrence of the "new media" code and the "portfolio" code offer compelling snapshots of how student writers begin to negotiate and articulate multimodal writing development, helping to make visible the kinds of decisions students make as they transition among modes. The interviews reveal how students can begin to broaden their understanding of composition as they think through what it means to compose in nonalphabetic modes and media, and to communicate their envisioned arguments and designs beyond simply adding in media as nonessential ornamentation or emphasis. None of these participants claims prior expertise with these multimodal and multimedia forms, yet each finds her way to a self-aware demonstration of some of the principles laid out in professional guidelines, such as the "*Kairos* Style Guide," and in multimodal assessment best practices—principles that may be paraphrased in terms of the three dimensions of multimodal writing development Jenna articulated: an awareness of an expanded conception of writing, a deliberate attention to the rhetorical situation, and an intentional enactment of substance via style.

Portfolio Development and ePortfolio Development as Incommensurate Processes

Because the creation of eportfolios plays such a central role in the "new media" experiences of study participants who were enrolled in the minor-in-writing program, the second part of this chapter will turn its focus specifically to an analysis of the effect eportfolios may have on students' writing development. *ePortfolio*, of course, is a contraction of the phrase "electronic portfolio," that is, a portfolio created using a digital platform; consequently, one of the challenges of analyzing the effects of eportfolios on student writing development is the difficulty of distinguishing the effects of portfolio creation in itself from its specifically digital or electronic forms. In other words, it is important to consider both the "portfolio-ness" and the "e-ness" of participant eportfolio compositions in connection to their writing development, and also participant talk in interviews and reflective writing about both of these elements and their interactions. This part of the chapter, then, will aim to disaggregate the "new media" and "portfolio" codes to better understand their related influences on student writing development. In brief, in this analysis, writerly self-identity is found to comprise a new factor in how multimodal writing development becomes observable, such that the most robust development is characterized not only by a composer's expanded conception *of writing*, but also their expanded self-perception *as a writer*. In this broader frame, writers view substance and style as integrally linked, and also view themselves as composers in any mode or medium that enables them best to enact an argument within a given rhetorical situation. However, an additional finding is that development via reflection during eportfolio construction does not necessarily lead to development in multimodal composition—the two seem to proceed independently.

Since portfolio learning and portfolio assessment took off in the mid-1980s (see, e.g., Hamp-Lyons and Condon), a rich literature has been produced on the benefits of portfolio creation for student writing development, particularly in regard to how portfolio composition fosters student self-reflection and metacognition. In a 2009 American Association of Colleges and Universities article, Ross Miller and Wende Morgaine summarize some of these benefits as follows, noting that the reflective work students engage in as they construct a portfolio can:

- build learners' personal and academic identities as they complete complex projects and reflect on their capabilities and progress,
- facilitate the integration of learning as students connect learning across courses and time,
- be focused on developing self-assessment abilities in which students judge the quality of work using the same criteria experts use,
- help students plan their own academic pathways as they come to understand what they know and are able to do and what they still need to learn.

Examples of each of these areas are represented in participants' interview responses. For instance, when asked in his exit interview, "Do you think creating the eportfolio has had an effect on your writing?" Zach replies: "Yeah, definitely—just being able to organize all of this and categorize what I did as an undergraduate and then put a thread through it all. It really helped define me, I guess as a writer—at least in the past—told me what I wanted to try to do with it in the future." In this excerpt, Zach touches on three out of four of Miller and Morgaine's bullet points—building a sense of identity connected to his undergraduate writing ("It really helped define me, I guess as a writer"), facilitating his integration of learning by making visible the implicit linkages among his writing experiences ("put a thread through it all"), and helping him plan an academic pathway ("at least in the past—told me what I wanted to try to do with it in the future").

Ayanna echoes some of these same themes in her response to a similar question in her entry interview:

> I don't think . . . it's affected my *writing* writing, but I think it's affected about how I feel when I write though. I think it definitely makes me feel like more of a writer, more of

> someone who can take risks, and do stuff . . . in general just with any reflective writing I think it gives you a good chance to think about how you've grown as a writer. I think it, especially specifically the ones I have in this portfolio, I think solidified my identity as a writer.

Ayanna touches on the effect eportfolio creation has had on her "confidence" as a writer (a term she uses elsewhere in the interview), and her sense of her capabilities as "someone who can take risks" in writing by inhabiting and effectively responding to a range of rhetorical situations. She also implicitly invokes what Liz Hamp-Lyons and William Condon name as the "three main" characteristics of portfolios, "*collection*, *reflection*, and *selection*" (118, emphasis original), in her discussion of the ways her reflection on the artifacts she selected ("specifically the ones I have in this portfolio") operated to help her consolidate a sense of writerly identity that characterizes her as an integrative learner.

Some participants, such as Ayanna, have already come to this sense of a "solidified" writerly identity through the construction of the Gateway eportfolio earlier in their college course. Other participants, however, demonstrate a marked development in their self-perception as writers from the entry interview's discussion of the Gateway eportfolio to the exit interview's discussion of the Capstone eportfolio at least a year later. For instance, when asked in her entry interview about the possible effect of the eportfolio on her writing, Madeleine replies: "Not any effect other than enhancing the reflective writing that I already was getting the base for in the [G]ateway. . . . I don't think it changed anything." In her exit interview, however, when asked a somewhat broader question regarding "the process of creating the eportfolio, both the selection process, the design process, what effect that kind of combined effort may have had on you as a writer," it seems clear that Madeleine has gained a fuller sense of her own writing experiences and the ways she has grown as a writer, and at this point is able to articulate the effects of "collection, selection, and reflection" on her sense of writerly development over her time in college:

> I think it was really—it was kind of cool to go back and see my writing from the very beginning. . . . I've had five years of writing artifacts. . . . I think it made me realize how much I've changed as a writer. . . . I began to realize that I really had been writing about personal experiences and reflecting on them and articulating them through a bunch of coursework, whether I had intended to or not. In that sense reflecting on it kind of solidified how I view myself as a writer maybe and how I've written while at Michigan.

For this participant, then, when prompted by the Capstone course writer's evolution essay and the composition of her Capstone eportfolio to take a long view of her cumulative writing, a through-line emerges that allows her, too, to "solidify" and integrate a sense of writerly identity bound up with a sense of herself both as a student ("coursework") and as an individual learner who places "personal experiences" within a broader context.

Samantha demonstrates an even more profound shift in perspective from the entry to the exit interview. In her entry interview, she discusses her earnest attempts to meet the demands of the Gateway eportfolio assignment, despite her sense that "I didn't have a concept of what the portfolio was supposed to be for a very long time. I still don't know if I fully do or not. . . . I guess, it forced me to think about how I wanted to showcase myself as a writer. Yeah, I don't know if it's had an impact on my writing though." At this early point in her college writing experience, Samantha evinces a not-uncommon frustration with the eportfolio form. For many students, the apparent artificiality of the genre can be hard to overcome, as is the often-ambiguous sense of audience. As Chris Gallagher and Laurie Poklop report, students often have trouble identifying their audience, as they find themselves writing for multiple readers consisting of instructors, program evaluators, and external audiences such as potential employers, among others (7). This difficulty can be further compounded by the sometimes-conflicting range of purposes eportfolios may serve—from opportunity for self-reflection, to course or program assessment tool, to external presentation of one's best work, and more. For some students, the result can be that no genuine exigency is defined for the eportfolio. Samantha presents this frustration in strong terms in her entry interview:

> I still don't feel like I have a totally, 100% grasp on the functional portfolio. . . . I guess the other thing I had a hard time with the portfolio was the writing is so different. There's the new media writing class and there's my science writing classes and then there's just random assignments. English classes and psych classes. . . . I kept hearing to include blog reports and all these other manner of things. I couldn't—there's nothing cohesive I felt about it. I know you can tag and organize that stuff but I don't know, it still feels pretty disjointed to me.

Samantha gives voice to the idea that, while there may be technical ways to overcome the sense of disjunction among the range of artifacts the Gateway eportfolio prompt asked her to include ("I know you can tag and organize that stuff"), she had trouble seeing this range of her writing become a coherent composition—it remains a mere "collection." The large-scale multiplicity of eportfolio composition, then, can flummox a student like Samantha who—as discussed by McCarty in chapter 4—recognizes generic and disciplinary differences among her various alphabetic and "new media" compositions ("There's the new media writing class and there's my science writing classes and then there's just random assignments. English classes and psych classes."), and does not see them belonging together in a representation of her writing.

In her exit interview, Samantha describes writing the Capstone's reflective essay, which will introduce her eportfolio and ideally explain to a reader how the artifacts it holds represent a genuine and meaningful act of selection that conveys something about her commitments or identity as a writer. At first, the process did not seem to be going well, and it looked as if she might end up facing a feeling of disjointedness and incoherence similar to what she experienced previously: "I'm writing it along and I'm like, 'This is kind of superficial,' which is what they told us purposely to avoid. I was like, 'I'm really not saying anything constructive right now.'" But then she voices a textbook moment of reflective discovery:

> It just eventually came around to me as I was writing. I was like, "I write because I learn." Then it—through that, I want to write so other people can learn. I was like that's why—that's what drives and motivates me to write. That kind of—it's kind of cool because that came out of me just writing this essay here, and it kind of forced me to . . . assess my college career through writing, . . . which is something I wouldn't have done. . . . It was interesting too because it's really my learning style. . . . It's a very integral part of how I learn. I mean, that's—this is the part I love about writing is finding this viewpoint that I didn't set out to find, but then it kind of just happened because I was writing.

In reflecting on the variety of forms of writing she has composed over her college years, Samantha finds a common thread in the idea of writing to learn, and of learning in order to share one's knowledge with others. Drawing on a quotation from Maya Angelou ("When you learn, teach; when you get, give"), she writes in her eportfolio reflection, "I have never been comfortable with the inherent amount of introspection and selfishness that seems to come with 'being a writer' and my personal workaround is that writing is a way to teach." Samantha's experience, like those narrated by Madeleine, Zach, and Ayanna, illustrates the best outcomes of portfolio learning as constructed in the research literature, and it seems clear that in creating their eportfolios these study participants have developed their sense of writerly identity and an understanding of their own learning by engaging in sustained reflection on the writing they have selected to include in them. The story told by this study's "portfolio" code, then, seems to be one of success.

At the same time, however, as certain remarks from some of these same participants suggest, a successful "portfolio" experience is not always tantamount for these students to a sense that composing the eportfolio itself has benefited their expertise as writers in any particular way. That is, while these participants feel they have solidified their identities as writers—as demonstrated by their successful metacognitive regulation and evaluation of their collected writing experiences—they do not seem to have expanded these identities to alter their conceptions of writing itself. In this way, their compositional development may be said to remain bounded as well. Indeed, when asked if they thought "creating the eportfolio has had an effect on [their] writing," it might be recalled that three of these four participants (Ayanna, Madeleine, and Samantha) respond in the negative in their entry interviews. In their exit interviews, while Madeleine does not respond directly to the question, Ayanna says, "I don't know if it's directly changed anything. I think if anything it's just helped me reconcile my thoughts about writing. I don't know if it's directly impacted how to write." Samantha notes, "I don't think it affected my writing. I think it had an effect on how I value writing, or how I think about writing, or why I write, I guess." In all of these instances, from both entry and exit interviews, these participants identify their clear sense of the developmental benefits of the acts of "collecting, selecting, and reflecting" over the span of their writing during college and see these benefits as accruing to their metacognitive sense of themselves as writers, but do not see them as also having an effect on "how to write," on their true "*writing* writing" (Ayanna). The not-so-implicit suggestion here, then, is that eportfolio composition in itself is not writing for these participants—an observation that in turn suggests the research implication that *portfolio* development and *eportfolio* development are not commensurate.

A closer look at the eportfolio as a compositional genre might help to explain a basis for this apparent bifurcation. Comprised of multiple artifacts ideally framed within a coherent webtext, eportfolios can be complex digital compositions. The prompts for the two minor-in-writing eportfolios describe the projects as comprising "a self-curated online collection of your work tied together by self-reflective writing and purposeful design" (see appendix 2a online for the Gateway eportfolio prompt); further, "your portfolio isn't simply a collection: it is a composition itself" (see appendix 2a online for the Capstone eportfolio prompt). The aims of "collection, selection, and reflection" are certainly represented in these descriptions, but simply placing a set of curated artifacts next to one another, accompanied by a reflective document explaining the internal connections the author perceives, does not appear to be sufficient to the eportfolio genre—it must also be "composed" and "purposefully designed." Eportfolios meeting these criteria belong to a category that researchers such as Kathleen Blake Yancey label as "web sensible." Yancey coined this phrase in a 2004 article in which she distinguished it from "what we might call 'print uploaded,' . . . a version of portfolio that is identical in form to the print but that is distributed electronically" (745). Whereas the "print uploaded" eportfolio typically incorporates "digitizations of print-based material" (Eyman and Ball 65) linked in linear fashion, one to the next, the "web sensible" eportfolio is "one that through text boxes, hyperlinking, visuals, audio texts, and design elements not only inhabits the digital space and is distributed electronically but also exploits the medium" (Yancey 745–46). The eportfolio, then, is "a composition . . . operating inside multiple networks" (Yancey et al.), and as such, it asks its composer to operate at least adequately, if not always comfortably, within a networked digital environment.

Returning to Ayanna, Madeleine, and Samantha, their reluctance to attribute their development as writers to the act of composing their eportfolios might be understood as a version of the antipathy voiced by study participants such as Susanne, Ariana, and Abby, who explicitly separated design from argument in their discussions of multimodal writing. For these three successful portfolio learners, too, "*writing* writing" remains alphabetic writing—"black words on a white page," as Sidney states in her exit interview—and unless they make the broader leap of coming to see themselves as *multimodal writers*, like study participants Jenna, Dana, and Lauren, they often do not view their writing itself as having changed, despite the very positive effects of this particular act of digital and multimodal composition on their sense of writerly self-efficacy. For this very reason, eportfolios can offer insight into the differential development of student composers who may exhibit highly developed rhetorical awareness and flexibility in one mode, while demonstrating fairly early stages of rhetorical command and metacognitive awareness and regulation in another.

Students in the minor-in-writing program have complete freedom to choose their eportfolio platform and design their eportfolio as they wish. The eportfolio prompts encourage them explicitly to consider the extent to which, as the "*Kairos* Style Guide" puts it, "media and design elements [are] non-gratuitous and facilitate or enact the rhetorical and aesthetic argument" of their eportfolios. The Gateway eportfolio prompt, for instance, asks students to consider the "reading experience" they wish to create, the kinds of "interactivity" that will further these aims, and the "media" that will support it (see appendix 2a online for the complete prompts). Consequently, all of the eportfolios created for the minor-in-writing program are web sensible to at least some extent; none of them is a simple "print uploaded" portfolio as Yancey defines it.

That said, the eportfolios vary tremendously in the extent and effectiveness of their rhetorical design, and some are largely "digitizations of print-based material" with hyperlinks, images, and possibly video or audio included here and there. Ayanna's and Madeleine's Capstone eportfolios both belong to the latter grouping. The writing they each include is varied in style, genre, and sophistication, and each writer reveals unique interests and commitments in her selection of essays. In terms of design, Ayanna's is organized linearly, and incorporates very few hyperlinks or images, while Madeleine's is topically organized and does include supplementary images related to several artifacts, as well as some internal hyperlinks that connect writing samples organized along a graphical timeline (see figure 8.2). However, both eportfolios consist entirely of digitized and/or embedded print-based artifacts. Samantha's Capstone eportfolio is much more visually dynamic, incorporating colorful, apparently stock photographs (they are not attributed), but it shares Ayanna's linear organization and collection of digitized and embedded print-based artifacts. Because they all contain extensive reflective writing, these eportfolios do tell a coherent narrative about their composers, and do demonstrate the portfolio learning each participant speaks of in her exit interview.

However, the eportfolios are minimally web sensible, and show little evidence of the three dimensions of multimodal writing development Jenna articulated in the first half of the chapter, which can provide a framework for analysis of eportfolio-based multimodal and multimedia composition here: that is, awareness of an expanded conception of writing, a deliberate attention to rhetorical situation, and the intentional enactment of substance via style. Consequently, while these three participants clearly develop as "portfolio" composers from the Gateway to the Capstone experience, as articulated in their interviews and also in their eportfolio reflections, the design of their Capstone eportfolios and the modes and media of the artifacts the students include suggest that they have attained a less robust development as multimodal and multimedia composers by the end of their college educations. The story the data tell about "new media" writing development thus appears to be a more circuitous, and also more troubled, one.

ePortfolio Development as Entailing Both Expanded Writing and an Expanded Writer

Nonetheless, this study does present evidence of "portfolio" and "new media" writing development progressing together, and it is to one such example that I turn in the final section of this chapter. Kaitlin's Gateway eportfolio reveals that she is already a disciplinarily adept writer by her second year of college. She presents artifacts from her Gateway minor-in-writing course as well as from courses taken

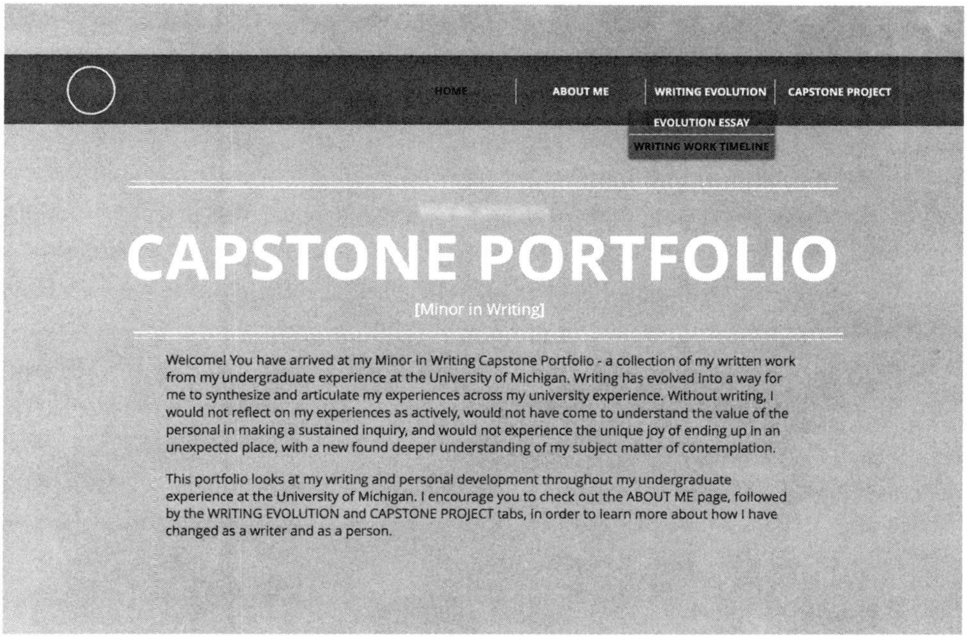

Fig. 8.2. Home page of Madeleine's Capstone eportfolio

for her double major in English literature and communication studies. The essays themselves, in all three areas, display markers of a confident, rhetorically savvy and flexible writer (see McCarty, chapter 4, for an analysis of advanced disciplinary rhetorical moves in writing), and the brief, reflective introductions to each essay further show that Kaitlin possesses a robust level of metacognitive awareness and regulation of her writing in its varied genres and disciplines.

To give one example, Kaitlin's English essay entitled "Evidence of Psychological Realism in Nella Larsen's *Passing*" begins: "Psychological realism may be described as that genre of prose fiction that derives its singularity from a tight focus on the world inside the mind. Rather than leading readers through a plot by way of neutral narration, pieces of this genre tend to place. . . ." This paragraph first states a premise in solid academic form (and with canny use of hedging: "may be described," "tend to"), opens up a contrast in the next sentence, and then continues to develop the definition and turn to the specific features of the novel that align with it. In the next paragraph, the essay begins a close reading of a specific scene in the novel that provides the initial evidence for the claim offered in the essay's title. Kaitlin establishes her idea quickly and clearly, and goes on deftly to support it.

Her reflection on this essay, while written in a more informal register, interestingly comments on these very aspects of her writing, and further extrapolates from them to make a broader claim about how the essay represents her capabilities as a writer of evidence-based arguments:

> I've chosen this bit of writing as an example because I find that the vast majority of academic writing and even a lot of group work correspondence stems from the same basic format: make a statement and back it up. Regardless of whether or not you've read the book I'm talking about, you should be able to see here that there is a clear presentation of an argument and solid evidence to substantiate it.

Kaitlin's other reflective introductions in the Gateway eportfolio do similar work, focusing less on the content of the essay presented and more on a thoughtful (and sometimes witty) analysis of what the essay demonstrates about a particular aspect of her writing abilities. Indeed, in her entry interview, she speaks about the role that reflective writing has played in allowing her to "take a step back from all of the details and the specifics and see [her writing] as a bigger picture . . . It helps me remove myself from the details and say, 'Has this accomplished the task' . . . I guess, from a broader outline perspective, than the individual assignment specifications itself." As a portfolio, and approached holistically, Kaitlin's Gateway eportfolio displays all four of the qualities that Miller and Morgaine identify as significant: it defines a provisional writing identity, reveals integration of learning, showcases self-assessment, and outlines an initial academic path. On her home page, by way of introduction to the eportfolio, she writes: "The texts that I have chosen to include here are ones I hope will give you the best picture of my writing style, and since my goal is to convey my adaptive skills as a writer, I've included pieces I think demonstrate the range of topics and styles I've tackled so far. What you'll find here is an organized collection of writing from my collegiate career at the University of Michigan." And she delivers on this promise.

At the same time, as an *e*portfolio, it is rather surprising. In appearance, Kaitlin's Gateway eportfolio is very similar to Madeleine's Capstone eportfolio—text-only on an unobtrusive background. In a short paragraph on the home page, preceding the description of the artifacts I quoted above, she explains this look, writing, "Welcome to my electronic writing portfolio! Despite its format, this is not a blog. Rather, it is the paperless, online equivalent of a printed portfolio that gives you samples of my writing from my different academic concentrations" (see figure 8.3). Here Kaitlin seems to be offering a precise definition—and celebration—of Yancey's "print uploaded" digital portfolio, "a version of portfolio that is identical in form to the print but that is distributed electronically" (745). And indeed, like Ayanna's,

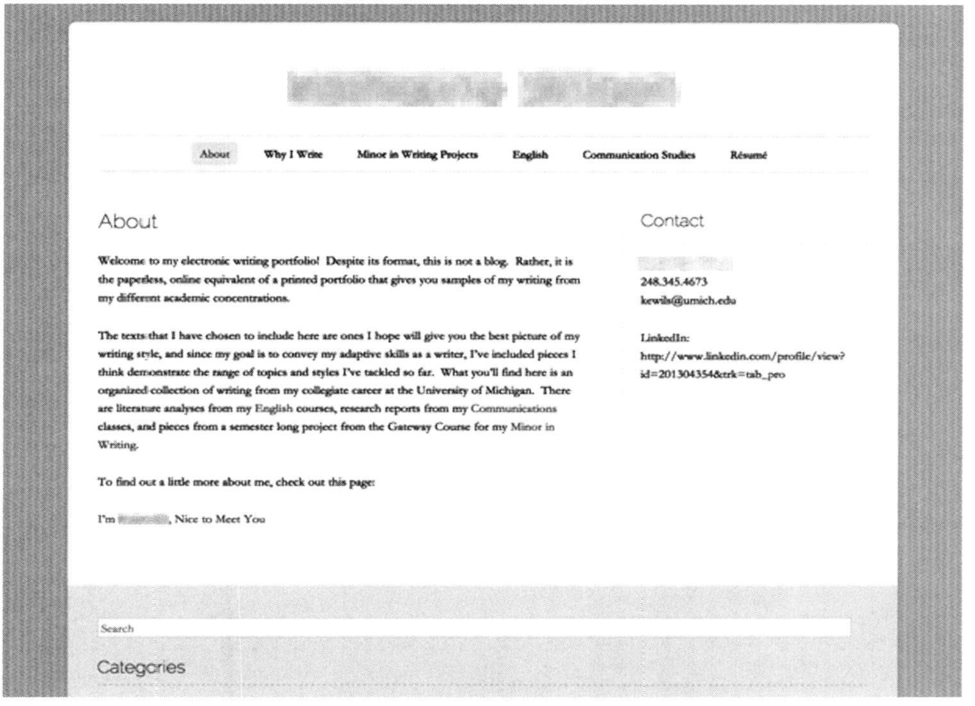

Fig. 8.3. Home page of Kaitlin's Gateway eportfolio

Madeleine's, and Samantha's eportfolios, Kaitlin's offers only "digitizations of print-based material" (Eyman and Ball 65). In her entry interview, also like them, she downplays the effects of creating the eportfolio on her writing as such, and instead focuses on how the process helped her obtain a new perspective on her writing: "maybe not so much in the fact of my writing as maybe my perception of my writing where I guess I didn't really have a picture of myself as a writer before. . . . it just kind of gave me more confidence that I have done this, so I shouldn't be doubting that I can do it again." Based on these design features of her Gateway eportfolio, then, it appears to be far less robust an example of composition in its genre—the web sensible eportfolio—than the print-based artifacts she includes in it. And her unenthusiastic interview statements about her eportfolio as a mode of writing do not seem to display the same metacognitive awareness present in virtually every other statement she makes in the interview about her writing goals, commitments, and development. Kaitlin's Gateway eportfolio thus seems to provide a clear example of uneven writing development among modes and media.

Yet on a closer look, the picture turns out to be a bit more complicated. Like

Madeleine, Kaitlin incorporates internal hyperlinks that connect to splash pages and artifact pages, weaving them together and creating additional pathways among them. She includes external hyperlinks that point to evidence and examples for arguments, as well as a high number that provide connections to cited material. Her remediation project, intended for an online magazine, is the only multimodal artifact in the eportfolio, and incorporates a wide variety of images—those that are worked into the writing itself, as, for example, in a sentence prior to a pair of images, which uses ellipses to indicate that the reader should now turn to the images to complete the thought, as well as those that act as simple illustrations of a point made.

Additionally, one of the essays included in Kaitlin's eportfolio, "Why I Write Revisited," explicitly addresses the topic of "new media" writing in a way that demonstrates a higher degree of metacognitive awareness than was apparent in the entry interview, as well as thoughtful analysis of the significance of this mode for deepening argumentation and revision:

> Comparing traditional writing and new media writing is to me the difference between a printed set of papers and a piece that lives on the web. What made me start to accept new media was its gift of using hyperlinks to forever banish the bibliography to the seventh circle of literary hell. Even better, hyperlinks give you the power to seamlessly provide research and evidence for a point with nothing more than the click of a mouse. With new media you also suddenly have the ability to illustrate writing with pictures and graphics that there previously was never room for. And with new media, pieces truly do *live*. On the web, you don't just publish something; rather you have the capability to keep going back and editing what you've already put out there.

Here, Kaitlin narrates a change of mind regarding "new media," which is amplified in her entry interview in her comments on how reading Andrew Sullivan's article "Why I Blog" in her Gateway class influenced her perspective on the value of blogging (from an apparent "waste of time" to something that "can be completely professional"). She demonstrates that she is open to reconceptualizing what might count as "writing," and expresses that she writes rhetorically, with her audience's needs in mind—a point she makes several times in her entry interview (e.g., "for the love of God, don't be mean to your audience"). In these ways, though the rhetorical design of Kaitlin's Gateway eportfolio is very similar to the less web sensible Capstone eportfolios of Ayanna, Samantha, and Madeleine, and her multimodal writing development has not progressed in tandem with her writing in text-based modes and genres, similar to Jenna, it is already possible to see elements of meta-

Fig. 8.4. Home page of Kaitlin's Capstone eportfolio

cognitive awareness and regulation regarding multimodal and multimedia composition that preview the genuine development found in her Capstone eportfolio.

From the first glance, the differences in appearance between Kaitlin's Gateway and Capstone eportfolios (see figure 8.4) are striking—from the bold use of color and images that dominate the very brief "Welcome" text, to the playful icons indicating different elements to be found throughout the site, to the unifying visual theme of travel and mapping.[3] Indeed, this eportfolio reads more like a website created to reach an audience of fellow travelers than a collection of work compiled for a school-based purpose—an impression borne out by the subordination of the section titled "Portfolio" to the bottom of the page, as just one element among others. In her exit interview, Kaitlin herself comments on the differences between the two eportfolios, clearly indicating her preference for the later one:

> I hated my Gateway portfolio. . . . It was just bland and boring. I was very nervous to put anything personal on it. It was not visual. It was just a bunch of text that really wasn't broken up by anything. It wasn't really multimedia. I mean, there were links, but just in the text, like here's a blue word here and there. . . . I had this idea that it really needs to look like a resume, but just like a normal paper thing but online so you don't actually

> have to have paper. . . . Whereas, with the Capstone portfolio, I was challenging myself not to take paper and put it online, but something that was created online and lives online. The content was made for that form. I think that was the biggest difference in my mind.

Kaitlin's commentary here about the differences she perceives between the two eportfolios, and her intent in composing the Capstone eportfolio to be something "that was created online and lives online," marks a striking conceptual leap in regard to multimodal and multimedia composition. Further, her statement that "the content was made for that [online] form" suggests that she considers design, or "style," to be the means by which her content, or "substance," is conveyed. In this way, by the time she reaches the end of her Capstone course and has created this Capstone eportfolio, she has developed from a champion of "print uploaded" digital writing to a committed creator of "web sensible" digital texts. Another way to put this would be to suggest that Kaitlin seems fully to meet the criteria laid out in the first half of this chapter, that an important way to define the study participants' development as multimodal composers would be to consider:

1. the extent to which they see themselves as composing truly "born digital" texts (their intentional enactment of substance via style);
2. the extent to which their integration of these affordances explicitly supports their rhetorical exigency (a deliberate attention to the rhetorical situation);
3. the degree to which they are able to demonstrate metacognitive awareness and regulation of their multimodal compositional choices (an awareness of an expanded conception of writing).

Looking further into Kaitlin's eportfolio and the process she describes in her exit interview for creating it, these criteria seem to hold up, and to extend into an expanded sense of writerly identity as well. In this interview, when asked, "Do you think that creating this e-portfolio has had an effect on your actual writing?" Kaitlin responds, "Definitely." She expands this answer with information that also develops the ideas about "online" composition quoted above:

> Mostly because when I start writing, I usually want to write for pages and pages and pages. The challenge was how can I achieve the same effect but in a visual format or in a format that is something besides a printed 8 x 11 piece of paper? . . . I would start

> writing for paragraphs, like for each bullet point. I said, "Okay, how can I figure out how to make it academic but at the same time not go on for pages?"

Here, Kaitlin can be seen thinking about how to demonstrate an ethos as a multimodal composer and connect with the community of readers she has in mind for her website. In particular, she's focused on how to convey an "academic" argument in a form more suitable to web-based writing. She is explicitly engaged at these moments in thinking through the transition from print-based to digital rhetoric in regard to the composer, audience, and textual elements of the rhetorical situation.

Looking at the Capstone eportfolio itself, it becomes apparent how she develops a solution to her dilemma, one that makes full use of the affordances of the digital medium in an intentional and rhetorically savvy way. She goes on to say in her interview, "I would pick out quotes where it was making the point that I wanted, but over an image, so you're not just immediately assaulted with a ton of text. You have to scroll over it to see it." Kaitlin introduces the key texts and characters in her composition visually (see figure 8.5), but when you mouse over each image, it offers you a brief quotation that serves as one response to her guiding question on this page about what adventurers have to teach others who want to follow in their footsteps—or, as she frames the question on the project splash page, "Why do people adventure, and what do they know that I don't?"

Finally, when you click on the image, it takes you to a slide show where you again see the image in full, along with the full quotation, and clicking through the slide show reveals this view for each of the images on the original page. It might be disputed how "academic" this particular solution is—it appears more directed at a general audience of "adventurers," and "academic" in Kaitlin's words might mean something in this context more like "research-based"—but in terms of its design rhetoric and its exploitation of the affordances of the web template, it constitutes highly successful web writing and a sophisticated response to the composer's original rhetorical challenge.

Like Jenna, Dana, and Lauren, who each found their own way to understanding themselves as multimodal composers, despite having no prior expertise with multimodal and multimedia forms, Kaitlin, too, describes the hurdles involved in learning to compose and design for a digital rhetorical situation:

> I had never done that before. Nobody had challenged me to do that before, so doing this portfolio definitely taught me how to do that. . . . It was a lot of learning to write in a way that made the content work for the form, the form work for the content, which we

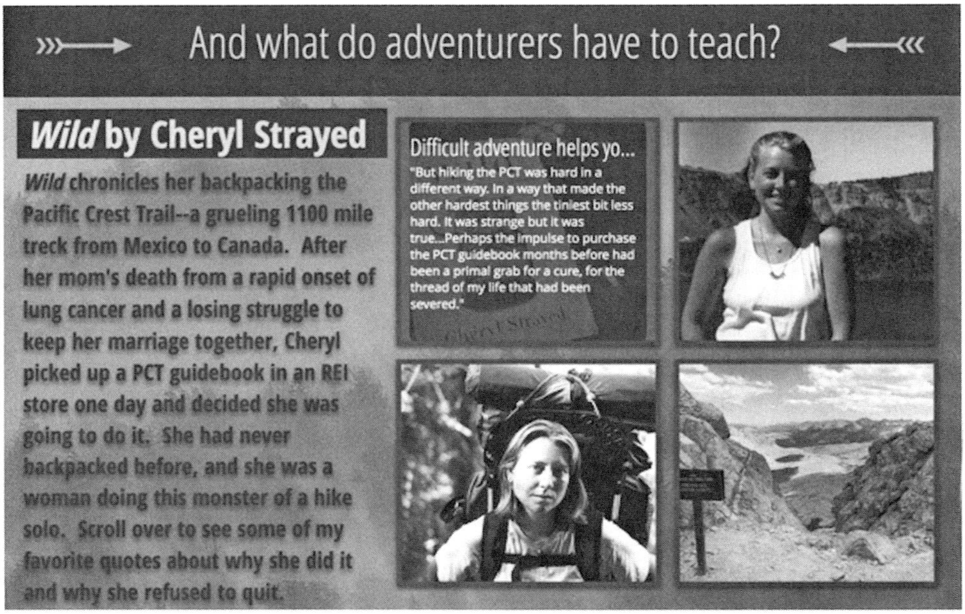

Fig. 8.5. Scroll-over effect in Kaitlin's Capstone eportfolio

> talk about that with essay classes but never in something like this. That was definitely a unique challenge and I think a good growing challenge.

In these comments, it becomes clear that, since her entry interview, Kaitlin has deeply rethought what it means to write and to be a writer. Becoming a multimodal composer entails a new kind of "learning to write," one that "uniquely" enabled her growth and development. However, as she also astutely notes, multimodal writing is ultimately quite similar to print-based writing in its imperative to attend to the rhetorical situation of the composition—here, as in "essay classes," an effective writer must be intentional about presenting content so that the form meets the needs and expectations of the audience. Reflecting in her interview on how she understands her writing development as a result of this project, Kaitlin makes a direct link to the rhetorical instruction she has received in more traditional writing classes, and her need to transfer this learning into the new digital context. In other words, it is *rhetorical* instruction, not technical instruction, that enabled her to grow as a multimodal composer, and it is worth asking if a more thoroughgoing attention to digital rhetorical instruction might help shift the value judgments and critical engagement of study participants such as Ariana, Susanne, and Abby, who seemed to view design rhetoric as little more than fiddling with technology.

Conclusion

This chapter raises two central questions, then, about "new media" and "portfolios" in their connection to student writing development. One has to do with what is learned from analyzing student multimodal and multimedia writing development in all of its forms—in singular artifacts and in large, multifaceted compositions such as eportfolios. The other has to do specifically with how to understand the value added by the "e-ness" of eportfolios, that is, what other aspects of student writing development might surface when "portfolio-ness" and "e-ness" are working together?

Taking the second question first, this chapter's analyses have demonstrated a robust "portfolio effect" across the study participants' eportfolios, as represented in their interviews and their reflective writing. In regard to their digital dimension, it has been noted that even the more "print uploaded" versions of the minor-in-writing eportfolios are web sensible to some degree, such that their "e-ness" adds a not-negligible dimension to their "portfolio-ness," whether or not this addition is realized or acknowledged by the writer. In the broadest sense, the need to build the eportfolio in an online platform requires design decisions for even the more print-based versions. Kaitlin, for instance, in responding to a question in her entry interview about what the most memorable aspect of creating the eportfolio was for her, said, "I think probably doing all of the reflective writing and also the horrible experience that it was to pick a background. You wouldn't think that that'd be so hard, but I think I went through about 100 different ones before I ended up with the one that I had." Although she did not embrace design rhetoric at this point in her writing development, Kaitlin nonetheless took her design choices seriously enough to search for just the right neutral blue background for her "paperless, online equivalent of a printed portfolio." Further, as Jenna noted ("If you put it on a website then how do people navigate your website and where is the emphasis?"), the very fact of creating a navigation for the eportfolio requires decisions about organization and presentation that would not be needed in a purely print-based portfolio. Creating the navigation also creates connections among artifacts, and "draws a thread" that might not otherwise become visible in the same way, and these connections are further emphasized by the use of hyperlinks and graphical elements, as in Madeleine's Capstone eportfolio. Consequently, even study participants who do not embrace the potentials of multimodal composition as readily as Kaitlin ends up doing, nonetheless engage in rhetorical design work by the very fact of creating their portfolio as an *e*portfolio. The "e-ness" becomes a value added to the important developmental work created by the "portfolio effect," and it is worth asking if this effect would be as robust without it—a potential topic for a future paper.

Returning to the first question, one of the key insights shared by study participants who demonstrate robust multimodal writing development is the emergence of a flexible and capacious conception of how writing is defined, of what "counts" as writing—not only black text on a white page, not only traditionally conceived academic genres, but images, film, sound, websites, and more. Study participants who embrace the affordances of multimodal and digital media production, and who learn to address their constraints as rhetorical problems to be solved or worked around, evince a highly metacognitive relationship to the rhetorical situations they compose within. This characteristic is not unique to these multimodal composers, of course. Several chapters in this book demonstrate students' abilities to navigate among a range of text-based genres and disciplinary conventions. In chapter 3, Lizzie Hutton and Gail Gibson profile study participants who find ways to integrate "academic" and "creative" domains of writing, coming to understand "writing and their writerly growth as entailing both generative activity and adherence to communicative norms, instead of viewing these approaches as requiring an either-or choice" (p. 105). Ryan McCarty also examines how students turn formal, discipline-based writing instruction and self-sponsored writing experiences to their own ends, navigating among them and drawing elements from different genres and domains to meet their personal needs "as educated communicators across a range of contexts" (chapter 4, p. 130). A multimodal composer such as Kaitlin makes similar moves in her exploration of how to communicate her research and original ideas about travel and adventure (what she calls the "academic" dimension of the project) through web-based design that speaks to a broad audience. Like some of the participants in Hutton and Gibson's chapter, she might be said to integrate "academic" and "creative" domains of writing for her own communicative ends. In bringing modality and media into the rhetorical mix in a highly reflective capacity, alongside discipline, genre, or style, writers such as Kaitlin and Jenna perhaps make even more literally visible the innovative negotiations and play in which all of the highly developed participant composers represented in this volume engage.

Returning to the value added of the "e" in eportfolio, however, this chapter has also shown that eportfolio development does not only demonstrate the expanded conception of writing articulated by Jenna, but that this work of expansion and extension is, as Kaitlin puts it, "a good growing challenge." That is to say, it produces a developmental effect both for the writing and in the writer. Kaitlin herself articulates this connection in her exit interview, stating, "It's hard for me to separate writing development from personal development because I think that the two really are tied together." Kaitlin's reference to "personal development" here corresponds to the discoveries of a writing "identity" voiced by Zach, Ayanna, Madeleine, and

Samantha via their acts of portfolio reflection. Yet in Kaitlin's case, the discovery points to the transformational effect becoming a multimodal composer has had on her personal writerly growth. Once such metacognitive awareness and regulation of the expanded possibilities for enacting substance via style within a digital rhetorical situation become visible, there appears to be no going back. When students find their way to deep multimodal writing development, then, their expanded senses of writing and of themselves as writers function as threshold concepts about whose effects there is still much more to learn.

NOTES

1. Gregory Schraw's overview of these widely used terms is a useful point of reference here. He defines metacognitive knowledge or awareness and its subcategories of declarative, procedural, and conditional knowledge, and metacognitive regulation and its subcategories of activities for planning, monitoring, and evaluating one's knowledge. See, for example, Schraw, "Promoting General Metacognitive Awareness."

2. It should be noted that students who display both robust metacognitive awareness and robust regulation may still create fairly novice compositions if they are new to the modes and conventions such genres demand. Nonetheless, I would argue that these students demonstrate genuine development as multimodal composers.

3. To be sure, these features are made available as part of the "Nomad on the Road" theme from Wix. The point here is not that Kaitlin created them all from scratch (though she has incorporated several original photographs and other elements), but that throughout the website, she makes creative and intentional use of them to enact a specific rhetorical purpose.

WORKS CITED

DeVoss, Dànielle Nicole, Sara P. Alvarez, Michael Baumann, Michelle Day, Khirsten L. Echols, Layne M. P. Gordon, Ashanka Kumari, Laura Sceniak Matravers, Jessica Newman, Amy McCleese Nichols, Caitlin E. Ray, Jon Udelson, and Rick Wysocki. "On Multimodal Composing." *Kairos*, vol. 21, no. 2, 2017, kairos.technorhetoric.net/21.2/praxis/devoss-et-al/index.html. Accessed 23 October 2017.

Eyman, Douglas, and Cheryl Ball. "Digital Humanities Scholarship and Electronic Publication." *Rhetoric and the Digital Humanities*, edited by Jim Ridolfo and William Hart-Davidson, U of Chicago P, 2015, pp. 65–79.

Gallagher, Chris W. "Staging Encounters: Assessing the Performance of Context in Students' Multimodal Writing." *Computers and Composition*, vol. 31, March 2014. pp. 1–12.

Gallagher, Chris W., and Laurie L. Poklop. "ePortfolios and Audience: Teaching a Critical Twenty-First Century Skill." *International Journal of ePortfolio*, vol. 4, no. 1, 2014, pp. 7–20.

Gonzales, Laura. "Multimodality, Translingualism, and Rhetorical Genre Studies." *Composition Forum*, vol. 31, Spring 2015, compositionforum.com/issue/31/multimodality.php. Accessed 23 October 2017.

Hamp-Lyons, Liz, and William Condon. *Assessing the Portfolio: Principles for Practice, Theory, and Research*. Hampton P, 2000.

"*Kairos* Style Guide." *Kairos: A Journal of Rhetoric, Technology, and Pedagogy*, kairos.technorhetoric.net/styleguide.html. Accessed 12 September 2017.

McKee, Heidi A., and Dànielle Nicole DeVoss, editors. *Digital Writing Assessment and Evaluation.* Computers and Composition Digital Press/Utah State UP, 2013, ccdigitalpress.org/dwae/. Accessed 23 October 2017.

Miller, Ross, and Wende Morgaine. "The Benefits of E-portfolios for Students and Faculty in Their Own Words." *Peer Review*, vol. 11, no. 1, Winter 2009, www.aacu.org/publications-research/periodicals/benefits-e-portfolios-students-and-faculty-their-own-words. Accessed 24 October 2017.

Neal, Michael. *Writing Assessment and the Revolution in Digital Texts and Technologies.* Teachers College P, 2011.

Penrod, Diane. *Composition in Convergence: The Impact of New Media on Writing Assessment.* Lawrence Erlbaum Associates, 2005.

Reilly, Colleen A., and Anthony Atkins. "Rewarding Risk: Designing Aspirational Assessment Processes for Digital Writing Projects." *Digital Writing Assessment & Evaluation*, edited by Heidi A. McKee and Dànielle Nicole DeVoss, Computers and Composition Digital Press/Utah State UP, 2013, ccdigitalpress.org/dwae/04_reilly.html. Accessed 24 October 2017.

Schraw, Gregory. "Promoting General Metacognitive Awareness." *Instructional Science*, vol. 26, 1998, pp. 113–25.

Shipka, Jody. "Negotiating Rhetorical, Material, Methodological, and Technological Difference: Evaluating Multimodal Designs." *College Composition and Communication*, vol. 61, no. 1, September 2009, pp. 343–66.

Shriver, Karen A. *Dynamics in Document Design: Creating Texts for Readers.* John Wiley and Sons, 1997.

Sorapure, Madeleine. "Between Modes: Assessing Student New Media Compositions." *Kairos*, vol. 10, no. 2, Winter 2006, kairos.technorhetoric.net/10.2/binder2.html?coverweb/sorapure/index.html. Accessed 24 October 2017.

Thaiss, Chris, and Terry Myers Zawacki. *Engaged Writers and Dynamic Disciplines: Research on the Academic Writing Life.* Boynton/Cook, 2006.

VanKooten, Crystal. "Identifying Components of Meta-Awareness about Composition: Toward a Theory and Methodology for Writing Studies." *Composition Forum*, vol. 33, Spring 2016, compositionforum.com/issue/33/meta-awareness.php. Accessed 24 October 2017.

Whithaus, Karl, editor. "Special Issue on Multimodal Assessment." *Computers and Composition*, vol. 31, March 2014, http://www.sciencedirect.com/science/journal/87554615/31?sdc=1. Accessed 24 October 2017.

Yancey, Kathleen Blake. "Postmodernism, Palimpsest, and Portfolios: Theoretical Issues in the Representation of Student Work." *College Composition and Communication*, vol. 55, no. 4, June 2004, pp. 738–61.

Yancey, Kathleen Blake, Stephen J. McElroy, and Elizabeth Powers. "Composing, Networks, and Electronic Portfolios: Notes toward a Theory of Assessing ePortfolios." *Digital Writing Assessment & Evaluation*, edited by Heidi A. McKee and Dànielle Nicole DeVoss, Computers and Composition Digital Press/Utah State UP, 2013, ccdigitalpress.org/dwae/08_yancey.html. Accessed 24 October 2017.

SECTION FIVE

Writing Development Precedes and Extends Beyond College

One consequence of the relatively segmented nature of the US educational system is that we in writing studies tend to think about writing development in terms of what happens during the undergraduate years, as the research reviewed in the Introduction shows. Our questions and methods have varied across the years, but we have not, as a field, given much sustained attention to the practices and beliefs students bring with them from their high school experiences with writing. Yet, as many participants in this study make clear in their interviews, the influence of high school writing instruction extends far into college writing. Grace, the student discussed in several chapters, presents one such case, where the admonitions of a high school AP instructor continue to shape her thinking about writing and herself as a writer well past her sophomore year in college. But Grace is not alone. Many students describe their writerly selves in terms of their high school experiences. Some left high school feeling that they were not *writers* because they had concentrated on other areas, had received negative feedback on their writing, or somehow lacked the appropriate skill, background, or preparation. Others left high school convinced that they could be successful college writers because they had been in an AP course, had received affirmation from writing instructors, or had done comparatively better writing than their peers.

Frequently students' high school–based assumptions about their own writing abilities proved to be wrong. First-year students in our study who claimed they weren't writers found that they actually had an undiscovered talent for writing or actually really enjoyed the processes of writing. In contrast, students who felt very well prepared for college discovered that the kind of writing expected for the AP exam didn't align well with the kind of writing expected by college writing instructors. Student participants who had enjoyed deep personal connections with their high school writing instructors were unable to find similar support in college, and as a result, felt diminished as writers. This absence had consequences for their writerly development because, as Emily Wilson and Justine Post show in chapter 1, the instructor-student relationship influences how students respond to feedback. Study participants who had been accustomed to producing highly successful one-draft writing, usually the night before a high school assignment was due, struggled with college expectations for extended development of ideas or had little understanding of how to undertake substantial revision of their writing. Talking with such students made us aware of the profound and often long-lasting effects of students' high school writing experiences.

It was particularly painful because many students reported that their college writing instructors had admonished them to forget everything they had learned in high school, as if it were possible to erase all the relationships, understandings, and experiences they had developed during the previous four years. Students who had been successful high school writers resented having what they knew about writing dismissed so completely, and they felt betrayed when the advice of high school teachers proved to be significantly different from the instruction they encountered in their college writing classes. Students who had been less successful in high school writing often expressed confusion about what expectations they should address, and expressed hope that their college writing instructors would share with them the "secrets" for being a good writer.

While we could not, in the context of this volume, give full attention to all the ways that high school writing experiences shape how students perform in college writing, we did not feel that we could end this collection without gesturing toward the importance of directing writing research toward deeper understandings of what student writers bring to the college classroom and the complex effects of this baggage upon their writerly development in college.

Our field has done a somewhat better job of attending to the experiences of college student writers after graduation. There is a body of literature on the nature of professional writing (e.g., Anderson; Anson; Bernhardt and Farmer; Couture; Odell, Goswami, and Quick) that considers the nature of writing in the workplace and, in some cases, makes recommendations for improving the alignment of college writing with what is expected in professional life. The lived experiences of college student writers entering the world of work have received much less attention, but Anne Beaufort has provided leadership in this area. Her *Writing in the Real World* looks at the experience of four students as they make the transition from academic to professional writing, focusing on the overlapping knowledge domains, opportunities for transfer of learning, and traits and conditions that foster further writing development. Beaufort's *College Writing and Beyond* provides additional information about the experience of moving from being a student to working by following one student as he negotiates this transition.

One of the chapters in this section explores how two students negotiated the transition from high school to college writing, and the other describes how four student writers moved beyond college. Looking a few years in each direction from college writing does not address all of the issues raised by recent discussions of the lifelong journey of writing development, but these two perspectives can inform the larger conversation, and our thinking has been influenced by the principles articulated by Bazerman et al. regarding the long view on writing development. These principles are:

- Writing can develop across the lifespan as part of changing contexts.
- Writing development is complex because writing is complex.
- Writing development is variable; there is no single path and no single endpoint.
- Writers develop in relation to the changing social needs, opportunities, resources, and technologies of their time and place.
- The development of writing depends on the development, redirection, and specialized reconfiguring of general functions, processes, and tools.
- Writing and other forms of development have reciprocal and mutually supporting relationships.
- To understand how writing develops across the lifespan, educators need to recognize the different ways language resources can be used to present meaning in written texts.
- Curriculum plays a significant formative role in writing development. (7)

All the chapters in this collection show how these principles take on life in the writing experiences and perceptions of the students in our study. Nearly every chapter speaks to the complexity of writing and the variability of writerly development as shaped by shifting contexts and resources. Naomi Silver in chapter 8 and Lizzie Hutton and Gail Gibson in chapter 3, among others, give particular attention to the relationship between personal and writerly development. The chapters in this section focus on expanding the span of life considered in writing development. Sarah Swofford's chapter looks at the context shifts experienced by two students as they move from high school to college, reconfiguring the resources they brought from high school to meet the expectations of college writing. But before she narrates their experiences, she argues that the concept of the "typical" student at any college or university contributes to a homogenization of the very different writing experiences and perceptions that students bring from their high schools. Sometimes "typical" is constructed from local lore, and in other cases from institutional data, but in either case it can obscure features integral to understanding and fostering student writing development. She claims, "Using both broad demographic data and rich individual qualitative studies offers a fuller perspective on the writing experiences, resources and development that students bring into college" (p. 255). To put this claim into action Swofford demonstrates how Descriptor Plus, a College Board product that profiles communities and high schools across the country, can be used to understand where students come from, based on geodemographic data. A tool such as Descriptor Plus can provide at least a general overview of the kinds of resources students would have had access to in high school, and thereby complicate conceptions of the "typical" student.

Swofford goes on to show how qualitative research on individual students can augment the broad-stroke portraits offered by the "big data" of Descriptor Plus by narrating the stories of Natalie and Marie. Both came from communities different from those of more "typical" students at UM, which meant that they had access to fewer local resources—such as college-educated mentors, cultural experiences, and educational opportunities. Although there were similarities between their home communities, and each felt she was well prepared, these two students brought very different resources to college writing.

In her community Natalie had enjoyed a good deal of positive attention for her writing, both in and outside school. She was encouraged and supported by her teachers and, in Swofford's words, experienced writing development in "relational" terms. At the university Natalie faced the challenge of finding a network of support to emulate the one that sustained her writing development in high school. Natalie's confidence was "knocked a little bit" as she realized that her high school and the adults who supported her had not actually prepared her as well as she thought. But as she faced the challenge of responding to new writing expectations, Natalie called on others, including her roommate, instructors, and peers, for support. Marie, on the other hand, felt that her high school had given her good preparation in grammar and formatting, so she remained confident as a writer. From the beginning to the end of her undergraduate career, Marie maintained the view that skills that might be described as dealing with surface features of writing marked her as a good writer. In her engineering program, where collaborative writing projects are the norm, she frequently used these skills by taking the role of editor. Sharing writing projects with peers and making substantive contributions to the success of the group, Marie's feeling of being well-prepared remained largely intact. Ultimately, as Sarah reports, both students became successful writers, but their high school experiences clearly shaped the strategies they employed and their views of writing.

Anne Gere's chapter looks at the other end of student experience, probing the concepts and capacities students take with them as they graduate and move on. Looking first at coded excerpts from exit interviews, Gere begins by noting how commonly students indicated that writing would be important in their futures. Many expressed very specific goals for the writing abilities they wanted to develop or pointed to skills they had developed in college writing that would be useful in their future lives. Other students talked about what they could do with writing, describing the repertoires they had developed or the greater confidence they felt. A number of students talked about the value of learning to reflect about their own writing and about other aspects of their lives. On a bittersweet note, a number of students, both minors and nonminors, spoke of the impending loss of opportunities to write regularly. Often in the context of explaining the strong personal connection they felt with writing, these students worried about "losing" writing as they moved beyond the university. This aggregation of student comments offers multiple perspectives on students' writing development.

Moving from this broad overview of students' comments about their college writing experiences, Gere looks closely at four recent graduates to learn about their transitions into new contexts with new writing challenges by conducting interviews to learn about their writing experiences two or more years after graduation. Stephanie, the first of these, graduated with a double major in math and English and is currently working for an insurance underwriting firm. In explaining her choice to major in English as well as math, Stephanie looked back to her strong high school preparation—writing fifteen- to twenty-page papers, for example—and credited her high school writing experiences as being instrumental in leading her to write an honors thesis in English. She also made special note of the importance of feedback, from both instructors and peers, in fostering her writerly development. Significantly, even though her position in the insurance firm did not provide feedback on her writing per se, Stephanie carefully saved a special folder of writing on which she has received positive comments and referred back to it when she faced a new writing task.

Linda, an Asian studies major and writing minor, reported a very different work experience and had actually resigned from her position with an auto parts supplier shortly before her follow-up interview. A prolific writer from childhood, Linda aspired to be a professional writer and took her first job with the hope that it would enable her to continue writing. Unfortunately, that didn't work out, and Linda decided to leave her position to devote more time to writing. Linda's commitment to writing was especially striking since, by her account, her writing received very little attention in high school. It was not until she reached the university that she had instructors who really helped her. Prior to that she had to rely on extensive reading and her own imagination. Like Stephanie, Linda assigned great value to getting feedback on her writing, and was discouraged by the difficulty of finding feedback since she had graduated.

Enrolled in a highly competitive PhD program in biology, Kris reported the greatest disjunction between her high school writing experiences and what she encountered in her undergraduate studies. She attended a "technical" high school where writing was given little attention, and she felt so lacking in writerly confidence that she enrolled in a developmental writing course during her first semester of college. In assessing her college writing experiences, Kris made it clear that writing courses did not play a role in the development of her capacities and confidence as a writer. She credited her omnivorous reading and her course work in philosophy with giving her new perspectives on writing, particularly writing in science. Like Stephanie, she found the experience of writing an honors thesis pivotal in her writerly development. As was true for both Linda and Stephanie, Kris highlighted peer review as one of the most important contributors to her development as a writer, and she took pleasure in the fact that the norms of science writing required her to collaborate regularly with colleagues and receive feedback from them.

Unlike Stephanie, Linda, and Kris, Dan, a communications major and writing minor, had very little use for peer feedback during his college years. In this, Dan, a writing minor, resembles the nonminors whom Benjamin Keating discusses in chapter 2. In both cases, peer review is held in low regard. For Dan, though, the issue seemed to be the control he wanted to exert over his prose and his desire to receive comments from his instructors. He described his decision to focus on writing as a process of elimination—in high school he wasn't good at math, didn't like reading, and found science intimidating. Dan currently holds a position as social media coordinator for a baseball team, where he is required to write constantly. He arrived at his position by way of writing for the *Michigan Daily*, a role he took up because of his confidence in himself as a writer. On reading a sports story Dan said to himself, "I can write a better story than this"(p. 305), and this insight led Dan to a successful undergraduate career of sports writing. Ironically, the feedback Dan eschewed as an undergraduate plays a central role in his daily work. "I wish I had bought in more to the classmate feedback" (p. 307), he lamented. Dan's boss does provide feedback, in some ways replacing the instructor feedback that Dan valued as an undergraduate. And as was true during his college years, Dan still wants to control the story. Speaking of social media, he claimed, "I like to think of it as talking from a position of power . . . you can say, 'Why don't you look at—'" (p. 309).

In concluding, Gere points to the continuities that extend from high school through college and on into the postgraduation years for each of these students. Although each developed in several ways during college, many of the patterns they build on and the assumptions they held remained solidly present. Gere also describes the adjustments each has had to make in response to the need to integrate the visual and textual—charts and graphs for Stephanie, painted images for Linda, scientific figures for Kris, and captions for Instagram images for Dan. For each of the four the repertoires and rhetorical flexibility they developed as undergraduates provide resources to meet the challenges they encounter in their new roles.

Together these two chapters show the considerable similarities between the transitions from high school to college and from college to postgraduation positions while simultaneously illuminating some of the variations in patterns of development. These longer views of writing development affirm the principles that writing development is complex, follows many different paths, responds to shifting contexts, and is shaped by curriculum. Most of all, these chapters call for further research on writing development across longer stretches of time.

WORKS CITED

Anderson, Paul. "What Survey Research Tells Us About Writing at Work." *Writing in Nonacademic Settings*, edited by Lee Odell and Dixie Goswami, Guilford, 1985, pp. 3–83.

Anson, Chris, and L. Lee Forsberg. "Moving Beyond the Academic Community: Transitional Stages in Professional Writing." *Written Communication*, vol. 7, no. 2, 1990, pp. 200–31.

Bazerman, Charles, Arthur N. Applebee, Virginia W. Berninger, Deborah Brandt, Steve Graham, Paul Kei Matsuda, Sandra Murphy, Deborah Wells Rowe, and Mary Schleppegrell. "Taking the Long View on Writing Development." *Research in the Teaching of English*, vol. 51, no. 3, 2017, pp. 351–60.

Beaufort, Anne. *Writing in the Real World: Making the Transition from School to Work*. Teachers College Press, 1999.

Beaufort, Anne. *College Writing and Beyond: A New Framework for University Writing Instruction*. Utah State UP, 2007.

Bernhardt, Stephen, and Barbara W. Farmer. "Work in Transition: Trends and Implications." *Expanding Literacies: English Teaching and the New Workplace*, edited by Mary Sue Garay and Stephen Bernhardt, SUNY Press, 1998, pp. 55–80.

Couture, Barbara. *Functional Approaches to Writing: Research Perspectives*. Frances Pinter, 1986.

Odell, Lee, Dixie Goswami, and David Quick. "Writing Outside the English Composition Class." *Literacy for Life*, edited by Richard W. Bailey, The Modern Language Association, 1983, pp. 175–94.

CHAPTER NINE

REACHING BACK TO MOVE BEYOND THE "TYPICAL" STUDENT PROFILE

THE INFLUENCE OF HIGH SCHOOL IN UNDERGRADUATE WRITING DEVELOPMENT

Sarah Swofford

The transition from high school to college is a critical period for undergraduates. For students, this transition is both exciting and scary, as it represents an accomplishment, but also the movement from one educational context to an entirely new one, where expectations and norms are often unclear. For the general public (and many educators), discussions often center around the degree to which students' transitions are "smooth," "easy," or "successful." Though describing students' transitions in these ways is tempting, we must reject these overly simplistic portrayals. The complex range of students' experiences before they come to college have the power and the potential to shape their experiences once they arrive, and in this way, to influence their development as undergraduate writers (Swofford). In this chapter, I argue that using both broad demographic data and rich individual qualitative studies offers a fuller perspective on the writing experiences, resources, and development that students bring into college. We must consider this prior background to fully conceptualize writing development at the undergraduate level. As an example of such a method, I use geo-demographic data and individual case studies of two undergraduates at the University of Michigan (UM), Natalie and Marie.

To make sense of these students' college experiences and undergraduate writing development more broadly, it is crucial to look not just at the students' projects and grades. We must also examine where they have come from, how they position themselves, and how they have been positioned with regard to their communities and their academic lives. At UM, there is a sense that entering classes of first-year students are generally fairly homogeneous. “Typical” students enrolling as first-years at UM come from affluent backgrounds, and most matriculate at well-resourced high schools. Both Natalie and Marie, in contrast, graduated from high schools considered “good schools,” but had less access to resources than many of their UM peers. Understanding the “typical student” who enrolls at a given institution is important, as this knowledge offers context for the kinds of instruction students have typically encountered before they arrive in first-year writing. It is tempting, though, for instructors and writing programs to focus on the “typical student,” without recognizing the variations that may occur even among relatively homogenous populations. When researchers and instructors gloss student populations to provide a profile of a “typical” student, we often actually describe aspects of social class, which encode norms of shared writing and academic know-how and discourses. In creating these profiles, we mark the ways that students already understand what is valued in academic writing classrooms. These profiles can be useful, particularly as writing programs understand the “wide view” of the student population or help new instructors know something of their classes before the semester begins.

They can also be dangerously seductive in that they offer a way to statistically erase populations of students whose experiences do not match the profiles we create. Students’ actual experiences reveal complexities in the transition that we often would prefer to overlook or simplify. For example, Natalie and Marie are similar to the “typical” profile of a UM student in that they come from communities that highly value education and provide a high school curriculum that, at minimum, explicitly states it is designed to “prepare” students for college. However, their experiences also reveal important distinctions, which suggest that examining student writing development should reach back to the communities and schools students engage with before coming to college.

At some institutions, the profile of the “typical” student is based on campus legend. At others, it’s based on institutional data. At UM, it seems to be a combination of these two factors. In 2008, UM purchased access to data called Descriptor Plus, which is a College Board product intended for use in admissions. Descriptor Plus offers two primary data sets—Neighborhood Clusters and High School Clusters. Neighborhood Clusters (NC), the data used in this study, are profiles of communities across the country based on geodemographic data. UM purchased access to this data as a means of combating the growing homogeneity of entering first-year classes after the state passed Proposal 2, which banned affirmative action. When the university started using the data, it found that more than 75 percent of students came from the five highest-income NCs (G. Nelson). NC data offer a detailed snapshot of the students' communities before they come to college, providing an interesting perspective on the types of high schools students come from and how their home communities might shape their expectations of college. NC data can also help researchers and instructors understand the kinds of guidance students have probably received about going to college, the kinds of secondary institutions they most often enrolled in (which could, potentially, reveal something about how they are prepared for postsecondary education), and the kinds of financial aid that students from their neighborhoods most often seek.

While this information is undoubtedly important, it cannot possibly capture the complexity of individual students' experiences and backgrounds. NC data, as demonstrated below, are necessarily broad and lack nuanced details. The data offer information about neighborhoods and communities, but cannot suggest how individual students' experiences line up with those profiles. For an institution like UM, these kinds of community profiles can be particularly interesting because there are fewer local connections between the institution and the places students come from, given that most students do not come from the area surrounding the university. At smaller, regional institutions, collecting information similar to that found in the NC can be useful to inform research on student populations, because more nuanced (but still broadly sweeping) profiles of the student population can reveal the smaller percentages of students whose experiences may not be the "norm" at a given institution. This information can also inform the broad generalizations that writing programs and individual instructors often make about their students, and the ways that we characterize "typical" students at a given institution.

Understanding where students come from, even in the broadest strokes, should also inform the theories of writing development that we build. NC data offer us a way to see patterns in our students' precollege communities, but it must acknowledge the complexity of individual student experiences, a complexity we can only layer onto NC data by asking students to explain their development both before *and* during college. In this way, we can see the various communities that shape students' understandings of writing before they transition into first-year writing. Before students arrive at college, the adults around them offer opportunities for literate practice and often shape the exposure to the various literacies these students encounter. The adults and communities around students sponsor these literacies (Brandt), which in turn shape the kinds of writing and discourses students expect to see and create when they enter college. As Shirley Brice Heath argues in her seminal work *Ways with Words*, different communities develop shared norms for language and literacy practices, and these literate practices shape students' understandings about how they will communicate (both verbally and in writing) in postsecondary academic writing contexts.

Bringing together the NC data and case studies of illustrative students demonstrates how both researchers and writing instructors might use similar data to reveal students' complex, individual backgrounds and to better inform our sense of the students we serve and how we can shape pedagogy and policy to support them. The important role of secondary education in students' writing experiences has long been a focus of research conducted on the transition from high school to college. Much of this research has taken the form of calls for collaboration between high school and college instructors (Addison and McGee; Appleman and Green; Creech and Clouse; M. Nelson). These calls reflect the sense that student experiences in high school somehow influences their experiences in college, and the emphasis of this work is on how collaboration can better "prepare" students for college writing. While these calls for collaboration are both important and valuable, they have not been addressed in sustained, far-reaching ways. However, there seems to be a growing conversation about how students' specific experiences in secondary contexts can shape their experiences with college (Hannah and Saidy).

First-year writing is an important site for facilitating transfer (Beaufort; Rounsaville, Goldberg, and Bawarshi), but reaching back across the border of first-year writing to secondary writing contexts is also necessary to truly understand development. Recent scholarship on transitions both hints at and calls for more attention to what comes before students enter our classrooms. This research points to the ways that students' experiences are complex, arguing that "any social context proves affordances and constraints that impact use of prior knowledge, skills, strategies, and dispositions, and writing transfer successes and challenges cannot be understood outside of learners' socio-cultural spaces" (Adler-Kassner et al. 8). Nevertheless, writing research has not fully examined how the "prior" shapes the "now" when it comes to student writing development.

Attention to individual students' experiences and how those experiences shape student development can be logistically difficult, particularly when we try to gather a more complete range of student experiences. So, on the one hand, we have literature with calls for collaboration, which have gone systematically unheeded (though answered both locally at various institutions and through initiatives such as the National Writing Project), and on the other hand, a burgeoning field of work that dives deep into small groups and/or individual students' responses to transition, allowing theories of identity to inform our understandings of student learning and development (Wardle and Clement 161).

A method that surveys a broad population of students, identifies interesting subgroups, posits how their prior knowledge might shape their development, and then *asks* them about their experience could help develop a better theory of the wide range of precollege experiences and the complexities of students' writing lives. We need to reach not only ahead of students' collegiate experiences, as Anne Gere suggests (chapter 10), but *behind* them, beginning with a fuller understanding of high school and then, the context surrounding their precollege development, and someday, even further back. Therefore, the demographic data represented in this study offers a method for guiding inquiry into student experiences, pointing writing researchers to which populations of students may have experiences that can offer insight into the trajectories they explore. The experiences students have before college with writing can heavily influence the kinds of resources they engage with at the undergraduate level and how they navigate the differences between what they bring with them and the development they experience in college, and, therefore, our very assumptions about how to characterize successful growth and student writing development.

The connections between the "big data" information in the Descriptor Plus data set and individual case studies complicate the current research on writing development and the transition to college. The College Board NC information offers a very broad, sweeping understanding of the kinds of resources students have access to in their communities. It gives a more detailed profile than the monolithic understandings of the "typical student" that proliferate on many campuses. However, this data does not allow us to see the effects of how students' communities shape their writing development, nor does it offer perspective on the complexity of students' individual experiences. So, in addition to the NC data and the neighborhood profiles it offers, it is essential to examine the experiences of individual students, so that we add rich detail to these broad profiles and see to what extent they describe students at a given institution. In this chapter, I argue that students' precollege writing experiences are shaped by the resources available in their neighborhoods and neighborhood schools, how students' relationships with "expert" adults in their home communities influence their attitudes and expectations of writing in college, and how their familiarity with the tasks and discourses in academic writing allow and constrain students' sense of their own expertise and capacity for growth as writers.

Neighborhood Clusters

NC data, as pictured below, offer a map of the various communities that represent the College Board's description. Some of these NCs are more dense in one or two regions, while others are more broadly distributed across the nation. The majority of the students in this study are from neighborhoods described as "affluent." As an example of the kinds of information that NC data can provide, figure 9.1 represents NC 78, one of the common clusters for students in this study. The image in figure 9.1 contains a description of this cluster:

> This neighborhood is at the top of the economic heap with top salaries and home values. There is little diversity among the highly educated, professional residents, and both students and parents value education. Some students choose private and religious schools but all attend schools with good academic programs. They take advantage of AP and honors coursework and perform near the top on admissions tests. They submit a prolific number of applications to a variety of colleges, often private, across the country. Although some will apply, financial aid is not a priority.

The information portrayed in figure 9.1 offers several key insights, including the average educational attainment in the neighborhood, home values, and rates of homeownership (which in some states can offer a sense of how well-resourced the local public schools may be). This information can describe communities and local schools, and how those places have contributed to the writing experiences that students have before they arrive in college.

The NC information in figure 9.1 suggests that a student coming into first-year writing from this NC is likely to have encountered many community members who have gone to college and who offer institutional knowledge and support. It is also likely that schools in communities as well-resourced as this one have more experienced teachers, who are given more resources and who have had more time to develop pedagogies that support writing development. As Sarah McCarthey describes, teachers in low-income schools face overwhelming pressure to raise test scores, and many experienced teachers choose to work in higher-income schools where there is more "insulation" from these pressures (47).

While we certainly cannot make assumptions about what individuals experience in any given NC, we can see that a high school in NC 78 would "prepare" students for the writing experiences they were likely to encounter at UM, in the sense that the adults around them had experienced similar writing tasks and situations. The students who enroll at UM from Cluster 78 communities would probably have been surrounded by many adults with college and postgraduate degrees, and, therefore, a large number of adults with extensive experience in academic discourses. Students in these communities have probably had more experience with

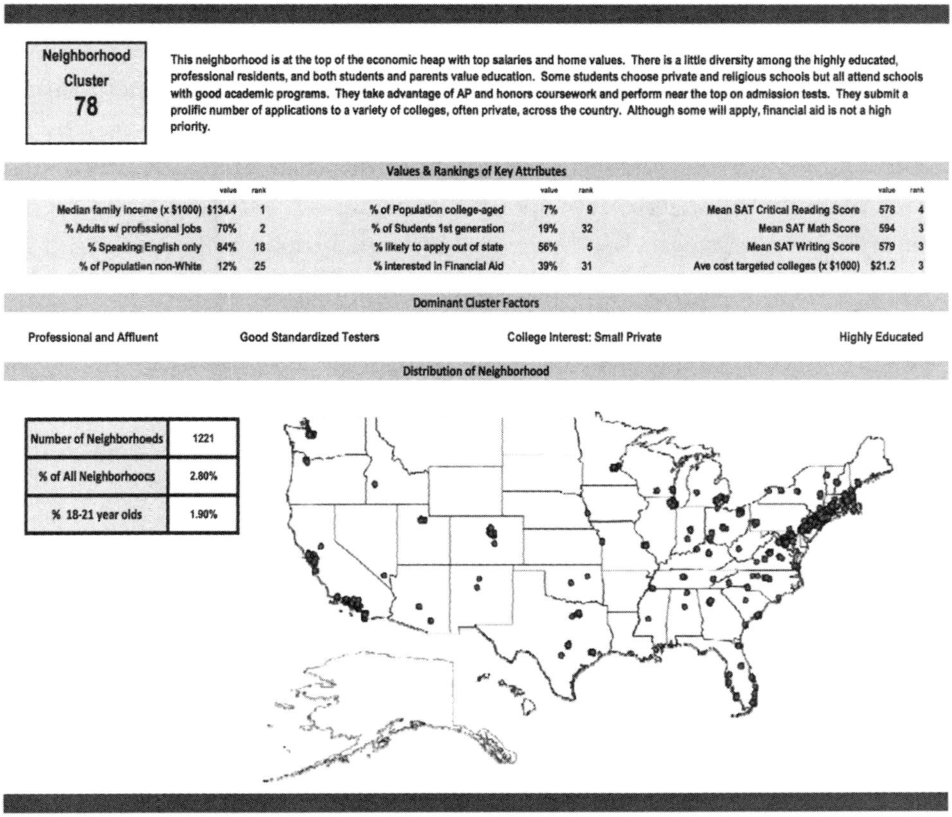

Fig. 9.1. Cluster 78, one of the most common clusters for participants in this study

these academic discourses, because the adults around them have personal experience with the value of academic writing.

To examine how NC data might offer new insights into the development of students in this study, I divided up the thirty clusters defined by the College Board into five "Megaclusters" based on the College Board's description of income in each cluster description: lower income, lower-middle income, middle income, upper-middle income, and upper income. As evidenced by table 9.1, the UM students in this study ($N = 178$) reflect the university's fairly affluent population. Nearly 60 percent of the participants in this study came from neighborhoods within the highest income Megacluster, while fewer than 10 percent of the participants came from the lowest income Megacluster.

Guided by geodemographic data found in the NCs, I now explore the experiences of two students in this study, Natalie and Marie, whose backgrounds do not match those of the "typical Michigan student" (and, for that matter, the most common background of students who participated in this study). For both of these students, experiences in high school shaped expectations of what writing in college would be like. These participants' experiences demonstrate the complexity and diversity of individual writing development. While we certainly cannot say that socioeconomic status, social class, or the type of neighborhood a student comes from determines their growth or development as an undergraduate writer, this kind of information offers a helpful starting point for better understanding what students bring to college writing classes. Writing development, as Natalie's and Marie's experiences suggest, does not begin in first-year writing. College instructors should understand that "high school writing" is by no means a monolithic experience. What we can see in this data of Natalie and Marie's development suggests that their precollege writing experiences played a key role in their collegiate writing development.

A Tale of Two Students

Natalie and Marie represent students who are at once typical and atypical. Natalie, a sports management major, was also a writing minor who used the minor curriculum to explore and develop her own identity as a writer. In her interviews, she expresses a sense of engagement and interest in writing, and frequently discusses not only the writing she completed in her courses, but the writing she does outside of academic contexts. As I will describe in more detail below, Natalie's college writing development is marked by a sense of disorientation—her expectations of what would be valued in college writing were subverted early in her first semester of college. However, Natalie moved through these early disorienting experiences with a sense

Table 9.1. Neighborhood Clusters for Study Participants

Group #	Group Description	Total #	# of Minors	# of Nonminors
1	Low income	16	6	9
2	Lower-middle income	23	3	20
3	Middle income	28	13	15
4	Upper-middle income	6	3	3
5	Upper income	105	45	60

Note: All the cluster data, including counts and how the clusters were grouped together can be found on our Fulcrum platform at https://doi.org/10.3998/mpub.10079890

that being flexible would allow her to gain new writing skills and strategies, though her experiences in her first semester of writing at the college level would cause her to question the ways she felt she was prepared in high school for writing in college.

Marie, on the other hand, began her time at UM as an undeclared major in the College of Literature, Science, and the Arts, but quickly changed majors and entered the College of Engineering, where she earned a BSE in chemical engineering. Marie feels a close connection to her discipline, regularly identifying herself as "an engineer" and describing her writerly identity in terms of herself as an engineer. She professes having an easier time with "technical writing," pointing out that this is true for most engineers. Despite her relatively high level of confidence, though, Marie struggles to adapt her writing to new contexts and clings instead to the expertise in grammar that she developed as a high school student.

If a "successful transition" to college is defined as a student beginning college and continuing on to graduation, then both of these students are successful. Natalie graduated magna cum laude and Marie finished with a GPA just a hair under 3.5. These students certainly had success at UM, and in that respect they are not necessarily "atypical." They describe working hard in their courses and being very engaged in their academic work. That attitude toward academic work is common in descriptions of "typical" Michigan students around campus.[1] Both Natalie and Marie detail going to high schools where they took advantage of honors and AP course offerings, and they describe these courses as helping them feel prepared for college writing. Natalie and Marie make interesting cases for considering how students' precollege experiences influence their writing development, because they are students for whom those experiences were salient enough that they choose to mention them several times throughout their two interviews in the study. Neither the entry nor the exit interview protocol explicitly asked students to refer back to high school, and though Natalie and Marie are not the only students who chose to do so, they are especially interesting because their communities are not similar to those of the majority of the other students in this study.

Natalie and Marie's experiences offer a window into how both the NC data and rich qualitative case studies might inform our understandings of the complexity of undergraduate writing development. Natalie's community falls into Megacluster 1, and Marie's into Megacluster 2, which means they are part of the just under 22 percent of students in this study from communities with incomes in the low to lower-middle range. Nearly 60 percent of the students in this study came from communities in Megacluster 5, the most affluent cluster. These populations are consistent with the demographics of the university as a whole (or, at least with the most recent data available at the time of this writing). To better understand how Natalie and Marie's backgrounds shaped their writing development, I briefly describe their NC information before using that information to contextualize the perspectives that both women offer of their own experiences through their interviews.

Natalie's experiences as a writer at UM are especially interesting, because how she navigated her transition from high school to college writing appears to be deeply connected to her background. As table 9.1 shows, just 10 percent of the students in this study come from a background similar to Natalie's, but as her case study will demonstrate, their experiences suggest that this population of students merits keen attention. Specifically, Natalie comes from what the College Board calls "Cluster 79," which is described in the Descriptor Plus document as follows:

> This is a unique, urban, blue collar neighborhood of low income families with very high educational aspirations. It is modestly diverse with parents who generally have had at least some college. Students attend schools with solid curricula where they take advantage of the AP and honors offerings. They get good grades; have solidly above average test scores and extremely high aspirations. They look at a modest number of selective privates and public flagships across the country. Financial aid is sought by most and will play a big role in their attendance.

This cluster description sits in contrast to Cluster 78, pictured in figure 9.1. The majority of students in this study (and in the minor alongside Natalie) came to UM from neighborhoods like the one described in Cluster 78, neighborhoods where most families are affluent. Natalie's neighborhood is very different. Though the cluster description suggests that students at high schools in neighborhoods like Natalie's are encouraged to apply to selective universities and colleges, students in Natalie's neighborhood are less likely to have the financial resources required for college than her peers at UM from more affluent neighborhoods. They are also surrounded by fewer adults with college degrees than students who come from the more affluent clusters.

Like Natalie, Marie comes from a neighborhood that the College Board characterizes as having fewer economic resources than that of the "typical Michigan student."[2] Marie's neighborhood falls into the second Megacluster, described as "lower-middle income" in the College Board's profile. Specifically, she graduated from a school in NC 59, which the College Board characterizes in the following way:

> Residents of this neighborhood have lower middle incomes and own homes which are of moderate value. A traditional blue-collar community, most parents have some expe-

rience with college but less than half have a baccalaureate. A large majority of students attend public high schools where they engage and excel in solid curricula which include a solid number of AP/honors courses. They have very high educational aspirations and score well above average on admissions tests. Most are mobile, interested in financial aid, and likely to apply to nationally selective privates and public flagships.

Like Natalie's NC information, Marie's NC description offers key information about how students in neighborhoods like hers are positioned for college. Students in these neighborhoods are not surrounded by adults who have baccalaureate or postgraduate degrees, which means they may not have access to the same kind of support that students in Cluster 78 are likely to have. However, the cluster information also makes it clear that these students are not in "failing" schools. Rather, these are schools that work hard to prepare students for success in college. Schools in Cluster 59, like the schools in Natalie's cluster, offer students a curriculum that is, at least in its stated intention, meant to prepare students for college. It is tempting to place students on a binary of preparedness—they are either prepared or they are not, and public perceptions of high schools suggest that "good" high schools prepare students for college, and "failing" high schools do not. Fully investigating the nature of "preparedness" is beyond the scope of this chapter, but such work can and should examine what "prepared" means in the context of how developing writers perceive their transitions into college.

Natalie and Marie's interviews, for example, reveal that even though their high schools offered them a curriculum intended to prepare them for college, and even though they succeeded with that curriculum, they had a range of complex experiences, including at times feeling very unprepared compared to their classmates at UM. These two case studies offer a perspective on the scope of experiences that students may have as they bring their precollege experiences into collegiate writing contexts. While the information about Natalie's and Marie's neighborhoods of origin in contrast to those of their peers is certainly illuminating, this information does not reveal the scope or process of their development as writers at the university. To better understand how those precollege experiences shaped their development, I looked to the interviews, where both students were asked to reflect on their experiences with writing and to consider how they were developing as writers. In this way, both data sets (the NC and the interview transcripts) revealed how these students navigated their divergent undergraduate writing trajectories. This in turn allows for an analysis that suggests that both "writing development" and "successful transition" might be more capacious terms than we currently recognize.

Writing in Community

Both Natalie and Marie identify their precollege experiences as a site of writing development, and they both situate at least part of their development as writers in how they participate in communities with other writers. Though they share a sense that the writers around them contribute to their development, they experience the importance of writing in community in very different ways. Understanding Natalie's precollege background offers insight into her development in college; she identifies the adults around her as key to her writing growth and success.

Perhaps because she comes from a small school and a small community, Natalie views her continued writing development as relational, at least in part. In her entry interview, Natalie identifies the source of her confidence in her writing (which later she describes as "over-confidence") as coming from her high school experiences. As a high school student, Natalie was given opportunities to write for the town newspaper, and to write for what she called a "sports journalism thing" in her local community. As she engaged as a writer, trusted adults encouraged her efforts. Natalie describes this encouragement: "I was also told, 'Natalie, you're a good writer. Keep pursuing writing,' or 'keep working hard,'" and she returns to these comments as a source of her precollege confidence again and again throughout both of her interviews, and ostensibly, throughout her undergraduate writing experiences. For Natalie, writing before college (particularly writing she did outside of the classroom) was something she enjoyed and felt confident in—a skill that brought her recognition in her hometown and her high school.

She describes these experiences with writing in warm terms, and notes her small community offered few "cultural opportunities," a lack of experience that she hoped coming to college would address. The complexity of Natalie's characterization of her community must not be overlooked here. In this moment, she both validates the trusted adults all around her who supported her extracurricular writing, yet worries that perhaps these adults, despite their best efforts, might not have the cultural capital that would be more highly valued in her postsecondary writing contexts. However, at no point does Natalie wholly denigrate her community of origin. She clearly values the opportunities she was given there as a writer, but she is reaching outside of that community for new opportunities at college.

In this way, Natalie roots her development as a writer in her relationships with trusted, encouraging adults, but also in her relationship with herself. Though she experienced a sense of dislocation when she transitioned into college writing, and is jarred by the new expectations for her work, she does not take up the narrative that she is not good at writing as we witnessed with Grace, who was profiled in

Anna Knutson's chapter (7), nor does she adopt a narrative of failure. Instead, she uses a process of reflection and evaluation to consider her writing experiences. The feedback she receives from her instructors in college similarly provokes growth; as she described in her entry interview, "initially I don't think that I appreciated what he [first-year writing instructor] was telling me, appreciated the things he was trying to get me to do. . . . [but] I think that it got me to be more open, I guess, to revision and suggestion." As Emily Wilson and Justine Post suggest (chapter 1, this volume), there is great potential for growth when students find that the feedback they receive is different than the feedback they expect, particularly when, as is the case with Natalie, that feedback provokes greater reflection on her own writing. This process seems to allow her to collect herself and to create a framework for the expectations of writing at college. In part, her success at this reframing might lie in her focus on herself as a writer and on her own development, as demonstrated in her keen attention to growth: "I guess as a writer I would say I at first was very hesitant, hard to get things done, hard to express what I'm trying to say, I guess now, stepping back and being able to see where I come from and the experiences I had, like that very much frees me as a writer." Here, Natalie acknowledges that the transition into college writing has resulted in a sense of dislocation, but that the dislocation that has been so uncomfortable actually produces an opportunity to look at her own development. Natalie also relates her sense of growth to a sense of freedom. At no point in the interview does she directly say that she felt bound or restrained in her previous encounters with writing, but the repetition of feeling "freed" as a writer suggests that she may have felt restricted by the kinds of writing she was exposed to in high school.

As she moved into college, armed with the confidence of high school success and the encouragement of adults in her community, Natalie felt she knew what to expect. As she describes her early expectations, "I came into Michigan thinking, 'Oh I got this. I just need to do what I've been doing and be able to grow with whatever help I can get.' But I had no idea what I was doing." In this description of her transition to college, Natalie notes the good reasons she expected to continue being successful with her writing: her previous work had been well regarded, and she had no reason to believe that the writing strategies she had developed as a high schooler would be unsuccessful in her new writing context. However, what she discovers as she begins to write in her college classes is not the seamless transition she recalls expecting. Rather, she describes her transition to college as one marked by disruption. The expectations that had been established by her experience in high school and by the adults around her were not fulfilled, and she suggests that her earlier confidence was erroneous, or at least naïve.

Natalie's assumption that she could continue to do what she had been doing in high school is tempered by her acknowledgement that she needs to rely on the relationships she builds in college to receive the help she needs to grow and develop as a writer. As Ben Keating describes in chapter 2, some students build writing communities of their own to support their writing development. Natalie engages in this kind of self-sponsored search for peer support in her writing. The acknowledgment that she would need to rely on someone to give her help so she could grow is aligned with the relational strategies she developed in her home community. In this moment, though, she also notes that even this strategy did not completely address the new challenges she faced. However, her reflection on the difficulties of transitioning into college writing reveals a willingness to repurpose her previous knowledge for new tasks and contexts. She mentions in her entry interview how small her school is, and nearly in the same breath describes how she's learned to work through her feelings of disruption and dislocation by relying on the relationships she forms with other writers:

> I think the faculty and the courses I've taken. . . . I think they push you to be more definitive in what you're writing. I think that was the big thing. I also think that just listening to people smarter than you is a big thing. I think I learned to take a step back and listen to what other people are writing and read what they are writing and realize that was good writing in its own way. I could learn from that.

Here, Natalie reflects on how she navigated the feeling of disruption that her transition to college produced. She recalls listening to people she perceived as "smarter," and of reading their work as part of that listening process. Earlier in the interview, she seems to be casting about for a way to incorporate what she is noticing about what is "good" writing in college contexts into what she knew to be "good" when she arrived, and as a means of building a framework that connects what she already knows to the new knowledge she is developing. She recognizes that what is valued in academia is not what was valued in her small town, so she reaches back to what she knows—the relationships she referenced as being critical to her earlier writing development. As Wilson and Post (chapter 1) note, student/instructor relationships play an important role in helping students learn to critically engage with feedback. Here, Natalie offers an example of how relationships with instructors have shaped her development as a writer.

She looks to faculty for advice, and cites "listening" to people in what seems to be both spoken and written language. Here, Natalie takes her prior knowledge (the sense that her relationships with people help her develop her writing) and combines that knowledge with a growing sense that paying keen attention to her audience supports "good writing." Natalie seems to be looking for the writing advice she had received in high school, when her teachers and community members encouraged her to write and to keep writing. Natalie views this move to college as a chance to experience culture and knowledge beyond that of her home community, and she similarly looks to other writers as a resource to pull from as she seeks to develop her own work. The initial sense of disruption she describes seems to make her reel a bit, but she recovers and uses her relational strategies to find a way to move forward with her writing.

Like Natalie's, Marie's sense of her writing community and the community she came from also shapes her developmental trajectory as a writer. Marie's writing confidence is fairly rigid. Her confidence in her abilities is real, but it's possible that her confidence comes at the expense of greater growth and development. Her reliance on what she calls her grammar skills and formatting appear in her entry interview and thread through her undergraduate years, as she continues to insist that her grammar skills, what we might call conventions, bring her success. As Ben Keating notes (chapter 2), Marie's focus on grammar is not uncommon for nonminors in this study, and like her fellow nonminors, her focus on grammar probably contributed to her resistance to peer review. She finds collaborative writing projects very useful, but she dislikes the fact that her peer reviewers did not have the same kind of stake in her writing as in projects where all members wrote together.

In this way, Marie's common refrain is her deep investment in writing with others. The writing that Marie describes in her engineering courses asked her to build relationships with other writers, a process that demonstrates much of her development throughout her undergraduate years. She notes that considering her group members as one audience helps her shape her writing, but also that she takes on the role of "editor," relying once again on her skills with grammar to complete her share of the work rather than engaging more in the invention of the text her group produces:

> [The grammar] definitely helped there [in group projects], 'cause in high school, you were writing it for the teacher. You just write it and it's done in high school. Definitely when I got here, it was more of a group course where everyone works together, and everyone had groups, where we analyzed each other's papers, and we helped each other. It helped me. It definitely helped me to be able to write things that people actually want to read, which I think is good.

Marie uses her skills with grammar as a way to navigate both the relationships with other writers and the writing they produce. Later, in her exit interview, Marie notes that her competency with grammar is the strength she brings to each group project. Her group writing became so important to her, in fact, that when she was asked to select a piece of writing to upload to the archive for each semester she was in the study, she consistently selected a group project to submit, even in the semesters when she describes taking courses that asked her to write independently. Because of her strong commitment to collaborative writing, though, it's difficult to determine to what extent Marie's writing developed, because it's impossible to determine what portion of those texts she composed.

From the interviews, though, it is clear that she does stretch her prior knowledge about writing in the matter of audience, noting that a sense of audience helps writers produce successful texts:

> To write well, someone has to want to read what you have written. I think if you're writing and nobody wants to read it, then I feel like, what's the point? . . . Definitely a big part of writing well is making sure other people want to read what you've written and a lot of that comes with talking about things maybe in a different light, a way that people have never thought of something before, or bringing up things, maybe ideas people have never thought of, things like that.

In this moment, Marie has a keen sense of audience, and she maintains that appealing to audience is one key factor in producing "good" writing. Like Natalie, Marie has a clear sense of relationships, but for Marie, the relationship at the center of her single-author writing is between herself, as the writer, and her audience. Marie notes that considering audience is important regardless of what kind of writing she is producing, which facilitates growth in her writing as she progresses through her degree. Marie's sense of audience seems particularly keen, and it is certainly possible that her orientation to her discipline contributes to her sense of herself as a writer. Again and again, she describes herself in both the entry and the exit interviews as "an engineer," and in both interviews she describes the "technical" audience who might encounter her writing. She is remarkably attentive to what this audience might value in reports and other kinds of technical documents and genres. Even her focus on the conventions of Standard English reflects this attentiveness to audience, as she notes that "correctness" in reports and other professional documents is important for engineers. In this way, Marie chooses to enter a community of writers that, according to her description, highly values the set of skills that she brings from her high school writing.

Though Natalie describes using relationships with other writers to develop the skills where she felt she needed practice, Marie uses the skills she feels she already has to leverage her relationships with other writers at her new institution. The kind of development she experiences, in this way, may not offer her as much room for writing growth, but her strategy certainly seems to give her a kind of capital to offer her classmates in their group conversations. Discounting her decisions as largely unsupportive of her development would negate the ways she leverages the resources she brings to college. Marie uses her skills with grammar as a way to navigate her relationship with both the other writers and the writing they produce. Marie is content to transfer her skills from high school to college, and does not seem to wish to push the boundaries of her previous understanding as Natalie does. This, of course, does not mean that Marie fails to transfer knowledge from her previous context, nor does it suggest she does not grow as a writer; rather, she simply limited her discussion of her writing development to a specific set of writing skills (grammar, conventions, and formatting). Both students' focus on the role of community indicates the central role it plays in their writing development, and it is further evidence that students employ resources from their precollege writing environments as they grow as writers. These two students, bolstered by the social connections to writing in their home communities, find ways to construct and engage in writing communities in college, which allows both of them to succeed as writers (though in very different ways). As Gere (chapter 10) indicates, writing communities also facilitate student development after college, so the fact that Natalie and Marie bring this resource with them offers them support that extends from high school through college and beyond.

Confidence and Being Humbled

As previously mentioned, Natalie began her time at UM with confidence in herself as a writer. This confidence was fed by the writing she created for her community and the encouragement she received there. Moving from high school to first-year writing, however, seemed to be a particularly jarring moment for her. Natalie returns to her transition into college again and again, and each time her description of that moment in her experiences as a developing writer evokes a sense of the difficulty she felt in this new context. In her exit interview, she states,

> I was definitely confident coming in [to college]. I also think maybe over-confident, maybe I wasn't sure—I had done really well in the things that were put in front of me

> in high school and those kinds of tasks. I hadn't done deeper stuff. I hadn't been challenged I guess in other ways with writing. . . . I think I was confident, and maybe over confident. I think I was humbled my first—maybe my first writing class and realized that there were people and professors and students out there that were really stretching to write.

Natalie is an adept student, but her description of entering college does not evoke the positive, "easy" transition many people believe is common (or, for that matter, desired) of successful students. As she describes it, she began college as a confident student and writer. As a high school student, Natalie did "really well" with the assignments and writing tasks she was asked to undertake, and in this comment, it is clear that she brought with her a confidence born of previous success. Natalie considered herself a writer before she came to UM, and found occasion to write both in and out of the classroom, and as previously mentioned, her community sponsored and supported her as a writer. She reflects on her prior experiences, and rather than finding them wholly positive, some of those reflections lead her to wonder about the value of her high school experiences, as in this moment in her entry interview, when she questions the quality of her writing before college:

> I was told in high school that this is good, but it wasn't good. I don't think it was good. Looking back, I don't think it was good at all. I think that first year, there was lots of road bumps, and I didn't—my confidence was knocked a little bit, but in a good way. I needed to go back to the core of what writing was going to be for me.

Here, Natalie again frames her transition to college as one marked by disruption, as her previously held assurance is "knocked a little bit" in postsecondary writing. This disruption, though, is framed as a necessary one. She references a sense that the writing she expected to be rewarded was not, that the writing she perceived in high school as "good" is not considered "good" in college. The movement from what she felt confident was good in high school to her growing sense of what might be good in college is one she describes again and again in her interviews as rising and falling. In this way, Natalie demonstrates how student writing development does not need to be linear—picking up new skills at each step along the way—to be "real" development. Instead, she describes a developmental trajectory marked by fits and starts, and one where her sense of self-efficacy is as key to her progression as the skills she gathers along the way.

The disruption that Natalie experiences in her transition to college is one that might pose barriers to "success" for some students. However, Natalie sees it as contributing to her growth as a writer and a student. She frames being "knocked a little bit" as a catalyst, as pushing her past the initial discomfort and forcing her to stretch herself as a writer. Natalie's willingness to adapt her strategies and to reconsider what made her writing "good" contributed to her writing development, as it gave her space to grow and to risk small failures. This kind of rhetorical flexibility, as Gere notes (chapter 10), is an important feature of students' continued writing development, because it enables them to connect the writing they learned in college with their understandings of how they will continue to grow as writers. She did well in her classes, so the sense she describes of "being knocked a little bit" isn't one that describes literal failure—either of her individual classes or in her degree program. Rather, this is the description of a student who experiences what might be called a "snag." Her first-year writing class, in particular, seems to create a place of tension, or as Natalie describes it, "struggle." Natalie notes in her entry interview that she found the class to be a difficult experience:

> I think if you were to ask me what I first got out of it [first-year writing], I would have been very disgruntled because it was a class that, I think I struggled through it. I did well academically, but I struggled through concepts and all of that. I think I was stuck in, well, in what I was doing prior. . . . It's a small class, but initially I don't think I always appreciated what he was telling me, appreciated all the things he was trying to get me to do.

Natalie's struggle with first-year writing is certainly sympathetic. Many other students would remark on their experiences in similar ways. She readily acknowledges, though, with good-natured grace, that the course was difficult for her, not just in an academic sense or that her grades weren't what she expected. More than grades, it seems that the root of Natalie's frustration is in the difficulty she had in seeing how this experience connected to her previous experiences with writing before she came to college. She notes that while she was "struggling" to understand the concepts underlying her first-year writing class, she relied on "what [she] was doing prior," which seems to be a reference to her experiences in high school.

Though Natalie remarks on her growth as springing from the sense that what she had learned in high school was not going to be accepted as well as she had expected, Marie's sense of confidence in her precollege writing skills was, on the surface, much more surefooted, as she articulates in her entry interview:

> I know in high school I did the standard English classes, and I took AP English classes, and a lot of that was writing a lot. I did very well in them. I did really well on the AP test.

> Actually, I started off in LSA [the College of Literature, Science, and the Arts] when I got here. I took the first-year writing courses, and I did well in those. I think when I got into engineering, it was no longer required of us. Actually, in the College of Engineering, it's kind of a joke. Engineers don't write . . . it's kind of a joke there. I'm good at grammar. I had a grammar Nazi [*sic*] in high school, so I'm good at that. I think it's almost a level of expectation that's not necessarily there in the College of Engineering. You're expected to be able to write well and show your ideas efficiently and condensed. I think that takes away a lot of the creativity of writing. You're supposed to condense everything and say it as quickly and . . . as concisely as possible. (entry interview)

As Grace's profile in Knutson's chapter (7) similarly suggests, students use their experiences in high school English classes that explicitly purport to be preparation for college (like AP courses) to set their expectations for what writing in college will be like. They attempt to transfer these skills, with varying degrees of success and struggle. When Marie reflects back on her movement from high school into first-year writing, she focuses on how she was able to utilize what she did well—grammar—in her college writing courses as well. She sees a connection between what she did before and what is expected of her in her new writing context, and she capitalizes on that connection. She demurs at calling herself a writer ("Engineers don't write"), and instead turns to focus on what she already knows ("I'm good at grammar"), citing her precollege writing experiences as giving her skills she uses to write in college. While Natalie takes up a "writerly identity," Marie resists that description, instead taking up the identity of "engineer," which she seems to believe precludes being (or seeing herself as) a writer.

Though Marie's chosen identification with her discipline offers space for her professionally, it seems to constrain the kinds of writing she engages with and the kinds of growth she makes available to herself. It is certainly helpful for students to take up professional identities, and such identification gives Marie a writing community where she can engage with other engineers and their writing. She has a clear sense of the writing that engineers do, but in her exit interview she also expresses a desire to write so that she can consider "a different perspective." In that moment, there is a glimpse of the kind of flexibility and adaptation that Natalie develops, and given more opportunities to do such thinking, Marie may have found other kinds of writing and other audiences with whom to communicate. It may be that the boundaries of her discipline did not invite her to participate in the kind of reflection and writerly revision that Natalie was able to do through her wider range of writing experiences.

Marie does not describe her transition from high school to college writing in terms of her struggles with it or in terms of the way it negatively affected her confidence with writing. Rather, she creates a narrative that focuses on the skills that bring her a sense of confidence, again relying on her training in high school focusing on "local" concerns such as grammar: "In terms of within engineering, I think I'm pretty confident in the way I write, and I think a lot of that is because in high school I had all that grammar training, and all that. It's not necessarily technical, but things every writer should at least know, like grammar." From her precollege experiences, Marie has gained a firm confidence in her abilities with grammar and formatting documents. This sense of expertise allows her to feel she experiences success in college similar to her success in high school. Like Natalie, Marie situates her level of confidence with writing in the experiences she had with it before coming to UM. As I will discuss in greater detail below, Marie does not look for opportunities for growth, though, and instead seeks places to utilize the skills she feels she has already mastered relying on her grammar to excel in "technical writing" and in her chosen discipline.

Flexibility and Writing Taxonomies

While Natalie seems to experience a sense of disruption in her transition to college writing, with a corresponding blow to her writing confidence, Marie seems to find a writing trajectory where she believes she already has the skills to be successful. Natalie describes the experiences that shaped her college writing practices in her entry interview, noting that though she had been introduced to the writing process before she arrived at UM, that process was not like the processes she was expected to adopt in college writing:

> [T]hey tell you over and over again you have to—I mean, growing up, they tell you you have to—these are the steps. You brainstorm, then you prewrite and then you draft. Then you draft again. They have those posters on the front of elementary school classrooms. I always hated that, like I didn't like that.

Natalie's precollege understanding of writing process, informed by her teachers' explanation of the "steps" and the classroom posters in her elementary school, is in no way unique to her experience. Posters outlining a very straightforward, linear writing process litter the landscape of classrooms across the country, and the first time that most students are introduced to the idea of a process for writing is typically in K–12 classrooms. The concept of writing as a process is a foundational concept of writing instruction at the primary and secondary levels, and as Natalie noticed, it is similarly important in first-year writing. It is not surprising, then, that

Natalie points to these posters as an example of what was so frustrating about her transition to writing in college. As a young writer, she had a sense that this linear process didn't work for her, but it was the only process she was offered. Moreover, when she entered college, she found that the processes emphasized in first-year writing were markedly different than those she had been exposed to in elementary and secondary education. Here again, there is a sense that transitioning to college was disorienting for Natalie. Though she didn't care much for the process she was offered, that process was one she had developed familiarity with and one where she knows what is expected of her.

As the Council for Writing Program Administrators' "Outcomes for First-Year Writing" indicates, "Composing processes are seldom linear: a writer may research a topic before drafting, then conduct additional research while revising or after consulting a colleague" (*WPA Outcomes*). These recursive writing processes valued in postsecondary writing instruction felt at least somewhat at odds with the kinds of processes Natalie had been exposed to in the past, perhaps because she feels that the relationship between her writing process in secondary school and her writing process in college are not connected. Though she expresses discomfort with the linear processes of her previous education, it was what she was most familiar with, and Natalie describes a sense of dislocation in this moment of her transition. In her first writing class at the university, she seeks to understand the concepts underlying the new kinds of writing (and the new expectations for that writing) that she knows exist. As Natalie describes feeling "stuck" in what she had learned before, it seems that she felt she had to create a new conceptual framework for the writing concepts she was being introduced to in her first-year writing class. At first, these concepts seem disconnected from what she had learned about writing previously. As far as Natalie can tell, she does not have her previous frameworks about what is "good" in writing to rely on, which caused her to feel "disgruntled."

While Natalie seems to bring a strong recollection of her *process* from secondary education, Marie identifies the grammar instruction she received in high school as a source of power in her transition to college writing and in her continued development as an undergraduate writer. She takes her understanding of grammar, or conventions, and her sense of their significance in the kinds of writing she encounters, and uses that sense, alongside her understanding of her prior experiences with writing, to develop a taxonomy of the writing she experiences in college, dividing "writing" into two distinct categories—"creative" and "technical," a move similar to those described by Lizzie Hutton and Gail Gibson in chapter 3. She describes her sense of these categories in her entry interview:

> I think they [past experiences] did [teach me], because I got such a good education in the grammar and everything. I never really was that creative. I could fake it when I needed to write an essay in high school or something, but when it comes to editing something, I've always been really good at that. That definitely helps in the technical writing also, 'cause you still need to be grammatically correct. You still need to have the formats down correctly and all that stuff, otherwise it's distracting from what you're actually trying to say in the paper. I think [high school] definitely helped.

In this moment, Marie describes how she understands "writing" to work. For her, there are simply two kinds of writing: creative and technical. This taxonomy is limited, and Marie's assessment of her expertise in these two categories is grounded in how she can use what she already feels she has mastered (grammar) in writing each one. She notes that her grammatical expertise in "technical writing" (which she never fully defines) "helps," and there is a clear sense that she does not feel as comfortable with "creative" writing. As Marie describes her trajectory through her undergraduate degree and the various forms of writing she encountered along the way, she maintains that her background in grammar from high school is one major key to her success. As Gere notes in chapter 10, the kind of genre taxonomies that Marie describes persist in students' understanding of their future as writers.

The limitations of Marie's writing taxonomy become clear when she attempts to describe how her first-year writing experience shaped her as a writer. For example, Marie's taxonomy of technical and creative writing does not leave much room for the genres of writing that are most common in academic writing in the humanities. Marie seems unsure in her entry interview how to classify the writing she encountered in her first-year writing course, especially in relation to the writing she had previously encountered in high school:

> My first-year writing class, it was a different kind of writing than what I had done before. In high school it was much more analytical. . . . When I got here, I took English 125, and it was definitely more creative. There was analyzing portions, but each essay we did, there was an argumentative essay, an analytical essay, different creative writing essays, and different exercises we did. I definitely think they helped. I got better as I progressed in that class. I think, as I said, it's definitely helped me, even in engineering, just being able to think of different ways to think about things and different ways to look at things. I think it's helped.

Here, Marie notes that there is a kind of writing she is less certain of how to classify, and for a moment, she applies what seems to be a third category—analytical writing—to her taxonomy. However, later in the interview, she classifies her writing in high school as "creative," and for the remainder of both the entry and the exit interview, she places the writing she encounters in college as either "technical" or "creative." Though Marie seems to define "creative" writing here as having "different ways to think about things and different ways to look at things," much of the writing she describes doing in first-year writing could certainly be described as analytical. It is unclear why Marie felt she needs to operate within such a limited taxonomy as a writer, but here, she bumps up against something new, and rather than revising her understanding, she doubles down on her previous concepts of what it means to write. In doing so, she also constrains her understanding of herself as a writer. She explains that she knows herself to be competent at "technical writing," in large part because of her abilities with "grammar," but that she does not feel as comfortable in "creative" forms or kinds of writing. Because most of the writing outside of the reports she creates in her engineering courses is writing that Marie classifies as "creative," she is left with limited options for developing new skills or writing expertise. As she creates this taxonomy that values the skills she already has, she unknowingly limits her options for becoming more expert as a writer.

Characterizing Development in Transitioning Writers

Natalie's comments about her movement from high school to college writing, on the surface at least, focus on the difficulties she experienced and the unease she felt about the confidence she arrived with. Her apparent difficulty, though, reveals a growing expertise—she notices that being "challenged as a writer" offers her opportunities to develop her abilities. Marie, on the other hand, articulates a confidence in her abilities that does not seem to facilitate a trajectory of growth. Marie's apparent expertise reveals chinks in the narrative of how "smooth transitions" into college offer more success to students. In these two comments, Marie and Natalie's reflections on their precollege writing experiences appear parallel but point to their divergent development. This divergence is a place where the profile of the "typical student" falls short of the reality of students' complex and diverse experiences and growth as writers.

In Natalie's case, the description for her NC, Cluster 79, aligns fairly well with the experiences she describes in both of her interviews. The high school she went to appears to have offered her opportunities to practice writing extensively both inside and outside of the classroom. Her experiences writing for the town paper and in local sports journalism are especially noteworthy. She also describes supportive teachers and a curriculum that, while limited, offered her ways to feel confident as a writer. In her comments about her teachers' encouragement, Natalie displays a sense of her teachers as trusted professionals and mentors. When they told her she was good at writing, she believed them, and that belief shaped her experiences with writing after she left high school. Her teachers cared deeply about her success and told her that she should keep writing, and so she did.

Similarly, Marie's cluster information offers a perspective on her development that is supported and expanded on by the data from her interviews in the study. Her high school offered course work intended to prepare students for college, and Marie took advantage of those courses. As a result, she feels well prepared for college and relies heavily on the skills she was told would lead her to success as an undergraduate writer. In high school, Marie had found an area of expertise and holds fast to that expertise as she moves through college, especially since she occupies a discipline where the kinds of writing skills she feels most confident with are highly valued.

Marie and Natalie illustrate the ways that students' experiences as developing writers do not begin when they enter first-year writing. Rather, this development reaches back to its beginnings in their communities and local primary and secondary schools. Understanding how those complex and varied experiences shape individual students' growth is tricky, though, and requires that instructors have at their disposal information that is often difficult to obtain and time-consuming to sift through for each and every student. "Big data," such as the information provided by the College Board in their NCs, does not and cannot tell us what individual students have experienced before they come to college. But as this chapter demonstrates, this kind of data can suggest patterns of development among student populations. This research is important because, as the analysis of Marie and Natalie's experiences suggests, it illustrates the fine-grained complex differences between students who, on the surface, may appear to have very similar backgrounds.

When we, as instructors and researchers, erase those fine-grained complexities, we risk alienating the students who are experiencing their transition into and through college in different ways than those expressed in the dominant narratives on our campuses. This kind of analysis can and should work to inform both our "big picture" sense of the students we teach and to destabilize the questions we ask about our students' growth and development as undergraduate writers.

The cluster and group counts used in this study are available on our Fulcrum platform at https://doi.org/10.3998/mpub.10079890

NOTES

1. This sense I base on my own experiences as a teacher of first-year writing at UM, and on conversations I had with students in those classes, where they shared their understanding that the "Michigan difference" (a campus-wide slogan) meant that most students were good students. This sense led many of my students to feel inadequate in the sense that they were "behind" their peers.

2. By which I mean, "typical" in the sense that they represent the majority of students both in this study and at the university in general.

WORKS CITED

Addison, Joanne, and Sharon James McGee. "Writing in High School/Writing in College: Research Trends and Future Directions." *College Composition and Communication*, vol. 62, no. 1, 2010, pp. 147–79.

Adler-Kassner, Linda, Irene Clark, Liane Robertson, Kara Taczak, and Kathleen Blake Yancey. "Assembling Knowledge: The Role of Threshold Concepts in Facilitating Transfer." *Critical Transitions: Writing and the Question of Transfer*, WAC Clearinghouse/UP of Colorado, 2017, pp. 17–47.

Appleman, Deborah, and Douglas E. Green. "Mapping the Elusive Boundary between High School and College Writing." *College Composition and Communication*, vol. 44, no. 2, 1993, pp. 191–99.

Beaufort, Anne. *College Writing and Beyond: A New Framework for University Writing Instruction.* Utah State UP, 2007.

Brandt, Deborah. "Sponsors of Literacy." *College Composition and Communication*, vol. 49, no. 2, 1998, pp. 165–85.

Creech, Kimberly Kaye, and Pamela Jane Clouse. "Outcomes of a Partnership for College and Career Readiness and a Senior English Transition Course." *National Association of Secondary School Principals. NASSP Bulletin*, vol. 97, no. 4, 2013, pp. 314–34.

Hannah, Mark A., and Christina Saidy. "Locating the Terms of Engagement: Shared Language Development in Secondary to Postsecondary Writing Transitions." *College Composition and Communication*, vol. 66, no. 1, 2014, pp. 120–44.

Heath, Shirley Brice. *Ways with Words: Language, Life, and Work in Communities and Classrooms.* Cambridge UP, 1983.

McCarthey, Sarah J. "The Impact of No Child Left Behind on Teachers' Writing Instruction." *Written Communication*, vol. 25, no. 4, 2008, pp. 462–505.

Nelson, Gabe. "'U' Gauges Geographic Diversity." *The Michigan Daily*, 28 Mar. 2007, https://www.michigandaily.com/content/u-gauges-geographic-diversity

Nelson, Matthew C. *"What Would You Advise Us to Do?" Status, Knowledge, and Asymmetry in Cross-Level Interactions among Teachers of Writing.* Dissertation. University of Michigan, 2008.

Rounsaville, Angela, Rachel Goldberg, and Anis Bawarshi. "From Incomes to Outcomes: FYW Students' Prior Genre Knowledge, Meta-Cognition, and the Question of Transfer." *WPA: Writing Program Administration*, vol. 32, no. 1, 2008, pp. 97–112.

Swofford, Sarah. *Linguistic and Rhetorical Ideologies in the Transition to College Writing: A Case Study of Southern Students.* Dissertation. University of Michigan, 2015.

Wardle, Elizabeth, and Nicolette Mercer Clement. "Double Binds and Consequential Transitions: Considering Matters of Identity during Moments of Rhetorical Challenge." *Critical Transitions: Writing and the Question of Transfer*, edited by Chris M. Anson and Jessie L. Moore, WAC Clearinghouse/UP of Colorado, 2017, pp. 161–79.

WPA Outcomes. Council of Writing Program Administrators, 2014, http://wpacouncil.org/positions/outcomes.html. Accessed 7 July 2017.

CHAPTER TEN

WRITING BEYOND THE UNIVERSITY

Anne Ruggles Gere

Even in their sophomore year, students in our study were thinking about their goals for life after college, and writing figured prominently in their projections. Responses to survey questions about the importance of writing for success in undergraduate academics, in graduate school admission, in achieving long-term academic goals, and in being able to change careers were so highly positive in the sophomore year that there was no statistical difference between students' sophomore and senior year responses. The only statistically significant difference appeared in the question that asked students about the importance of writing for "achieving career goals," which showed a more positive response in the exit survey, but with a p-value of .083 it was not a strong difference. Students included in this study—both minors and nonminors and both early and late in their undergraduate years—clearly saw writing as essential to their lives after leaving the university. To be sure, this group elected to participate in a study of writing, so they may be somewhat atypical, but their other similarities to so many of their nonstudy peers suggest that many undergraduates think writing will be important in their futures. Furthermore, their view of writing and future work echoes Deborah Brandt's findings in *The Rise of Writing: Redefining Mass Literacy* regarding the information economy's transformational effect on the importance of writing in the workplace.

Interview questions about the role students expected writing to play in their futures elicited similarly positive responses, although explanations varied. Not surprisingly, one of the most common responses focused on writing's importance to students' future professional lives, with more than forty students, including both minors and nonminors, explaining how they expected writing to contribute to their careers. These students, despite sharing this view, construed the details of writing's importance in many different ways. The variations included the importance of various genres of writing that students imagined themselves writing in the future, such as personal statements, sales reports, or legal briefs; the value of writing for a range of academic or employment contexts, such as explaining scientific data, making a presentation to a client, or translating statistical data; and digital modes, such as blogs, tweets, and other social media. Another group of approximately eighteen students enumerated specific writing strategies or repertoires that they expected to use in the future, strategies such as seeking advice about drafts, shifting style or register for different audiences, and editing for clarity and correctness. A handful of students looked toward continuing to write for personal pleasure, and three talked about wanting to become published authors. These imagined futures, in all their variety, demonstrated students' capacity to reflect on writing's meaning and purposes in their lives, another mark of development.

Unpacking the aspirations and goals students attached to their future writing offers another perspective on writing development, because it provides insight into what they think writing is and what it can do. A number of students stated that they wanted to develop specific features in their writing, with "concise" and "clear" being the most prominent. This explanation offered by Jake was typical: "Being concise, being clear, just getting the point across in a way that people can understand. Pretty mundane." Students also indicated that correctness was another important feature: "You can't make a mistake and have grammatical errors in your sentences," Abby said, reflecting a view of writing similar to Marie's in chapter 9 by Sarah Swofford. Students like these appeared to see writing in instrumental terms, portraying it as relatively transparent, a means of conveying ideas and information that have already taken shape. This does not mean these students didn't see writing in other ways simultaneously. As Lizzie Hutton and Gail Gibson show in chapter 3, a number of students saw writing in bifurcated terms, divided into two domains. One, which they termed "academic," represented already formed ideas, and the other, which they called "creative," generated new ideas. Students showed similar inclinations toward binary thinking as they looked toward their own futures as writers.

A number of students hoped to pursue graduate work and alluded to the relationship between genres and disciplines as they talked about fields they wanted to enter via graduate school—including law, medicine, veterinary science, philosophy, and nursing. To be sure, some students simply talked about writing as key to the admissions process: "I need to write to get into school," said Mary. But more students made connections like this one, from Annie: "Well, I'm applying to law school . . . so I think that the writing that I do for political science . . . it's the usual profession to go from political science to law school. I think writing those types of papers will probably be most helpful." Annie could see how writing in one genre could be helpful in another, and she valued the opportunity to make the connection as part of her preparation for graduate school.

Students also connected disciplines and genres in discussing more immediate goals. Samuel, a student in the business school, had a very specific goal: "If I can write a case that presents the company's history, goes into their challenges, and then that case can be used in the business club that I'm part of, that would be something I'd be really proud of, so that's one of my main goals, too." Chassi said, "I'm going to have to emphasize science writing as something that I have to get good at, or I should get good at. Gathering information as a writer is going to be very important, and also synthesizing it in a meaningful way." Dariella, a biology major, explained, "I could go more science-y and learn how to write really good scientific papers, which I think would be more useful for the career path that I'm headed towards." She went on to articulate a more expansive view of the ways she might use writing in her future career: "I would like to apply science to real-life situations, so I think I'd want to try to make that connection. Maybe I could take scientific findings and apply those through writing to a real-world situation. I don't know what kind of job that is." Although she cannot tie it to a specific career path, Dariella expresses a goal that appears much more frequently among graduating seniors, as I will show below. But it is worth pausing to note this goal of translating, of seeking to convey disciplinary language in terms that people outside the field can understand, because it was articulated by a number of students, both minors and nonminors.

Connections between writing and their goals for employment in fields such as business, education, sports management, nonprofits, journalism, music, and public policy punctuated many student interviews. Some were quite specific about the ways they expected to use writing in their work. As Maggie put it, "I don't want to go on and write books. I just want to be able to redo people's promotional materials for their fitness centers or something like that." Kelly explained: "As a vet you can make newsletters and stuff for your clinic, so I guess there's a little bit of writing there that I think I'd like." Charlotte, a journalism student, explained her goals as "Learning to write objectively and cite two sides of a story . . . a lot of the research aspect, just because journalism requires a lot of research." Margaret, a violinist, talked about writing program notes and press releases for her recitals and concerts. Erica, a pre-med student, confessed that she had originally thought writing was not part of her future, but her work in a lab changed her mind: "I kind of realized that my very narrow-minded thought process of not needing to be a strong writer in the medical field was just not accurate." With comments like these, sophomores demonstrated awareness that writing can take many forms, and that these various manifestations of writing become part of the activity systems of specific work environments. At the same time, these students expressed a sense of agency, that they could adapt writing to their own purposes.

A related theme focused on the many things students felt they could do with writing. Some sophomores expressed this as confidence in their entry interviews. Looking back at her writing in the first two years, Kaitlin, who appears in several chapters in this volume, commented, "It just kind of gave me more confidence that I have done this, so I shouldn't be doubting that I can do it again." Another, Natalie, who also appears in Sarah Swofford's chapter (9), said about her experience in writing courses, "It's given me tools to be able to speak better, to show myself better, and, going back to the reflective thing, to tell people why I'm doing what I'm doing." Reflection permeated writing instruction, and as this quote indicates, enabled students to enumerate the repertoires they could call on: "The writing process, argumentative writing versus research writing versus creative writing. They're all really different. I think it's really cool that it shows my diversity as a writer," said Megan. Tim, a pre-law student, noted, "Most everything settles out of court, and a lot of that is memos and writing, and finding sources that back up your point and all that stuff so it's basically like the writing process in real life, and that's why I kinda think I'll be good at it." Woven through these comments are indications of rhetorical flexibility based on a repertoire of approaches to writing. This, along with the students' writerly confidence, constitutes another dimension of writing development.

No doubt, the reflection encouraged by writing instructors contributed to students' ability to identify some of their own strengths, and it surely helped them to see how they could transfer their repertoires of strategies from one context to another. For example, in talking about a writing course, Joy commented on learning "about the ethics in writing and how to be a more credible writer. Those are skills that I can carry over to magazine journalism. . . . I would definitely take what I've learned in this class and apply it to making videos for *Her Campus*," a nationally circulated online magazine. Sophia talked about using reflection outside of the academy: "I had to apply, over the summer, for that job. It was a lot about reflecting on past experiences in terms of leadership, and working in teams and stuff like that. That kind of forced me to think about all the experience I'd had up until that point and flesh them out into a way that made me seem desirable as a candidate." Because she had learned how to reflect on her writing, Sophie was able to transfer that capacity to writing a job application. In addition to transferring learning from one context to another, the repertoires students claimed gave them rhetorical flexibility: "My style changes based off of what type of paper it is," said Jack. Jonah claimed, "I think that [reflection] eventually will translate into, will help me in a job in the future, just being able to adapt and learn different ways of writing. . . . I'm probably not going to be writing research papers or essays about stuff, but I think it does translate into other ways of working." This capacity for using reflection to identify one's own writerly abilities and to figure out how to use them in new situations points to another dimension of writing development.

Seeing writing as a flexible set of capacities that can be used for a variety of purposes in multiple contexts both indicates and fosters writing development. Few first-year students can enumerate a repertoire of writing strategies and imagine ways to use them in the future, so the fact that students begin to show this capacity by the sophomore year is evidence of change that can be described as a form of development. At the same time, the ability to approach writing in more than one way, to feel comfortable with more than one genre, to recognize more than one way to present ideas fosters writing development because those who see writing in flexible terms are better able to add to their repertoires. At the sophomore level a majority of both writing minors and nonminors expressed this type of comfort.

One area where minors and nonminors differed was in expressions of strong personal connections to writing. Angela, a nonminor, talked about journaling regularly and claimed "writing is in my life," but many more minors claimed that writing was very important in their lives. In exit interviews they said they wanted to continue writing forever, they saw themselves as writers, and several said that they would like to publish an article or a book. Sentences such as Susanne's "I would like to be involved with writing throughout my life," Willa's "My hope is that writing is always in some regular part of my life because I know I'm happier when I am, you know, journaling or getting to write papers and stuff like that," and Mariana's "I definitely don't want to ever stop writing" punctuated their interviews. To some extent, these differences can be attributed to the fact that minors had made a commitment to writing, but these variations also remind us that writerly development takes multiple directions. The fact that fewer nonminors expressed a desire to continue writing does not suggest that they did not develop as writers; they simply developed differently.

Although nonminors made fewer statements about a personal connection to writing, several of them spoke poignantly about a sense of impending loss. Sara explained, "I don't want to stop writing because it is something that I feel like I've done for so long . . . it's very similar to a language. At the end of my sophomore year, I was entirely fluent in French, but I haven't had an opportunity to speak French . . . so I've lost it a lot. I feel like the same thing will happen with my writing." Dariella echoes Sara's analogy between writing and learning a language by saying she is fluent in three languages—English, Spanish, and writing. Louisa described a personal writing club she and friends had created, where "we come in with our stories, and we brainstorm together, and we bounce back and forth. I'm hoping that continues . . . ," but she didn't sound confident that it would. Amy lamented, "I realized how little writing I did over the whole semester. It kind of made me think maybe I should do more writing on my own just so I can keep up with it and not forget it." "I'm afraid I'll lose writing," said Stephanie. Implicit in these concerns about loss is an assumption that writing—and writing development—needs continual practice, that it cannot be taken for granted.

I was interested in learning more about the contours of students' writerly development—its relative importance and role, its relationship to field-specific genres, students' rhetorical repertoires, and the associated gains and losses after graduation. This interest led me to look closely at the complete data—surveys, interviews, and archives of writing or eportfolios—for four students, two minors and two nonminors, and to conduct follow-up interviews with each to learn more about their writing development after graduation. I selected the four from a group of approximately thirty minors and thirty nonminors for whom we had the most complete collections of data. I chose students who represented variety in gender, major, and postgraduation occupation. My final selections were based on alumni's willingness and ability to participate in an interview either in person or via Skype.

Stephanie: The Math Side and the English Side

Stephanie graduated in 2014 with majors in both English and actuarial math and wrote an honors thesis on Edmund Spencer's *The Faerie Queen*. The writing she archived as a nonminor included a first-year essay titled "Identity through Commonality: The Effectiveness of Comedy and Tragedy." This paper, an analysis of the ways Aristophanes's *Lysistrata* and Aeschylus's *Persians* portray the consequences of Athenian aggression, was written for a Great Books course open to honors students only. In reflecting on her high school preparation, Stephanie claimed that she arrived at the university especially well prepared, noting that she had been asked to write lengthy analytical papers in high school. Unlike Natalie in Sarah Swofford's chapter, Stephanie's assessment of her preparation proved to be highly accurate. Another of the papers she archived focuses on issues of agency and free will in Chaucer's "Troilus and Criseyde," and Stephanie makes a complex argument about the various forms of agency and free will assigned to characters in the poem. In another paper, titled "Two Wrongs Make a Right: An Analysis of Necessary Rape in 'Sir Degaré,'" Stephanie draws on textual evidence to show how rape enables a princess to free herself from her father. In all three cases the writing is sophisticated, and the arguments are well documented and convincing.

The same is true for her honors thesis, titled "Refashioning the Epic: An Analysis of Spenser's Breaks within *The Faerie Queene*." Here, as in her other archived selections, Stephanie does complex literary analysis, arguing that Spencer draws on both epic and lyric traditions to create a unique form that wrestles with chronological and allegorical time and moves into the realm of the unwritten word. In every case, Stephanie's writing draws on considerable research, demonstrates an ability for original thinking, and conveys complex ideas in lucid prose. She demonstrates all the capacities of an accomplished writer, and she values writing as part of her academic experience. For example, at the beginning of her exit interview, Stephanie described the role of writing in her life as "Huge . . . it has huge importance in my life. I'm an English major—and math as well—and I'm always writing essays. I'm always researching. I'm always thinking about how to interact with the writers I'm reading about." But in the second semester of her first year, having matriculated as a math major, she came to a realization: "I realized I'm missing something, so I took Shakespeare with Professor T and it made me realize that I was a writer." In reflecting on her response to the college Shakespeare course, she looked back at her high school experience: "It wasn't just taking AP Lit because that's how you're going to get to the good schools; it was, this is a part of you. This definitely brings you joy." For Stephanie, writing is not only a place to demonstrate her considerable academic capacities; it is also a source of deep pleasure. The mixture of affective and intellectual investments in writing explain its "huge" importance in her life, and it also explains why she invested so much time and talent in writerly development.

Since Stephanie was already a very proficient writer when she arrived on campus, it would be easy to claim that she developed very little during her college years, but her own assessment is that she grew a lot as a writer during her time as an undergraduate. In particular, she felt that she gained greater confidence in her writing abilities. In her exit interview, she claimed, "I wasn't nearly as confident as I am now. I think that having just the sheer amount of writing that we've been doing at the university has helped with that, but I wouldn't say that I was a newbie coming in either." In reflecting on her confidence, Stephanie looked back at her high school argumentative essays and "the 15–20-page term papers" she was required to write. "That was normal for us," she claimed. Although she did not write in a wide variety of genres during her college years, Stephanie felt that her writing became better and better as she moved forward. Both the quantity and quality of the writing she produced, especially in her senior year, led Stephanie to see herself as a highly competent writer when she graduated. Looking at the entire collection of writing that she had archived during her undergraduate years, she was impressed by the totality of what she had accomplished, saying "this is pretty good." She also looked at her recently completed thesis and observed: "The fact that I've completed a 57-page scholarly piece of writing and people actually think it's legit and worth honors is a huge huge growth. Coming in freshman year, I don't think I ever would have thought that I would have been able to do anything like that." Stephanie's case shows how writing development interacts with personal growth, and both achievement and confidence are interwoven with and supported by affective dimensions such as the pleasure and joy she finds in writing, whereas Grace, also an honors student, who appears in chapter 7 by Anna Knutson, found the path toward writing development much more complicated and difficult.

Stephanie's high school experiences laid the foundation for her decision to major in English as well as math, but writing took on increased importance as she negotiated the spaces between her two majors. At the same time, however, she expressed concern that she would "lose" writing by working in the insurance business: "I definitely want to keep writing. Going into the insurance business, I'm definitely nervous that I'm going to be losing it." Like many minors, Stephanie's immersion in writing, particularly her honors thesis, made her treasure the "joy" that writing brought her, and the prospect of graduation made her fear that she would not be able to continue it.

Her interview with me two years later confirmed that Stephanie was right to be nervous, because as she moved into her position as a trade credit underwriter she had to abandon the scholarly writing she had enjoyed as an undergraduate. She said, "Unfortunately I kind of lost that type of writing. Now I am doing more analytical, a lot of persuasive writing." Her job requires her to summarize data for more senior colleagues who have to make financial decisions. She explained how she writes: "Here's what I recommend. Here are seven or eight bullet points of financial ratios and positive or negative news and press releases. Here's how the soybean crop is going in Brazil and all that." She also described writing "diplomatic emails to brokers, the people who stand between us and our clients, trying to sugarcoat the no's and make the yes's kind of sound like we're doing them a favor." This variation in genres—the recommendation versus the diplomatic email—demonstrates Stephanie's rhetorical repertoire, and she credits her honors thesis with preparing her for both the persuasive and diplomatic writing. In her undergraduate exit interview she indicated that she did not see any influence of her math writing on her English essays, although she acknowledged the reverse. In talking about her postgraduation writing, however, she described the interaction of her math and English majors as key to her writing: "The math side helps me weave from step one to step two to step three, whereas the English has helped me say why that is step one." This integrated view, which demonstrates Stephanie's development as a writer, served her well, insuring her success in taking up the new genres required by her work: "Usually when I write the persuasive essay I get the answer that I want so I think I'm still a confident writer, definitely more confident now in the persuasive and analytic." Stephanie built on her college writing experiences to broaden her rhetorical repertoire. She benefited from arriving at her firm when two colleagues were out on maternity leave, which enabled her to "skip that pure data entry nine-month period" and start analytical writing immediately. In contrast, others in her entry cohort weren't doing "the persuasive writing the analytical writing easily until a year in," but she was also more prepared than her peers who lacked her experience with writing extensively as an undergraduate.

In addition to building on genres she had practiced in college, Stephanie continued familiar writing processes after graduation. During her exit interview, for example, she noted that peer review was a regular part of class, sometimes in small groups and sometimes with everyone in the class workshopping one student's draft. She also described long meetings with the cohort of students who were all writing honors theses. They would talk together about their projects, share ideas and strategies for their writing, and exchange drafts: "We would pass drafts back and forth and say, 'Hey, can you read these four pages of my chapter and let me know what makes sense.'" In her view, sharing drafts and ideas with the cohort of seventeen honors students had a major effect on her writing: "They've influenced my writing so far that it's not all my writing; they've shaped certain aspects of my thesis." In her interview with me, Stephanie talked about the social nature of her writing as a trade credit underwriter, explaining that she works in a group of nine where each has an area of specialty: "I know the agricultural sector in the US and South America as well as the RV industry, projectors and the tech industry. Someone else knows all about the metal prices around the world." She made it clear that she and her colleagues rely on one another for data about various industries, but they also bounce ideas off one another as they prepare to write about their recommendations: "Hey, I'm looking at company X that's selling to company Y but on these kind of weird payment terms. Has anyone see something like that and how do you price it?" Stephanie may not send her draft for someone in the group to read, but her writing process includes social practices similar to those of her undergraduate years.

Feedback from instructors was also important to Stephanie as an undergraduate. As she explained in her exit interview, she saw her professors as resources and often sought their advice: "If I ever had an essay where I wasn't 100 percent sure of the thesis or just wanted to talk through some of the problems I'd been having, the professors were always willing to meet with me to discuss it and bring other viewpoints." These kinds of encounters, in addition to exchanging drafts with peers, made the social nature of writing clear and important to Stephanie. Her professors, particularly the supervisors of her honors thesis, led her toward more self-critique as well. In the required course for thesis writers, students were required to evaluate their own work and progress: "We had to do evaluations every other week, saying this is what we're supposed to be doing on our thesis in order to get it done by the deadline." This combination of looking to more expert writers and becoming better able to evaluate her own writing appears in Stephanie's description of her work as an underwriter: "When I do persuasive summaries and whatnot, I save all of them just because per legal requirements we have to save them for two years. When my manager says, 'Hey, that was a really good review,' I save a copy of it into a different folder in an email, and I will look back at those and say what do I do here that was so different than the other ones that may not have been flagged for being great." Even in an environment where she is not getting explicit feedback on her writing, Stephanie has found a way to continue her practice of using feedback to reflect on and improve her writing. Significantly, that reflection involves the same sort of critical engagement that Emily Wilson and Justine Post describe in chapter 1 as crucial for writerly development.

Another dimension of writing that mattered to Stephanie in both her undergraduate and work life was its capacity to help her organize her thoughts. In some cases this took the form of outlining or developing a plan for writing, but it also fulfilled larger personal needs. In the interview at the time of her graduation, Stephanie noted that when she began at the university she thought outlining was a waste of time and never did it. However, by the time she graduated she felt that outlining had some value. Significantly, outlining meant organizing ideas in preparation for writing an essay ("I turn to writing as a way to organize my thoughts"), but it also served to relieve stress: "If things are getting really overwhelming, a lot of times I just make lists, or I journal just to get all of the ideas that are floating around in my mind on paper." This use of outlining demonstrates one way that writing fosters personal growth because it provides strategies for students like Stephanie to deal with the inevitable challenges of being college students. In her interview with me, Stephanie claimed, "Outlining is like a new commandment for me . . . it's less formal than what it used to be simply because I don't have to write a five-page paper in seven hours. So it's less structured because I feel like the 'assignment' is less structured. It doesn't matter if I have two bullet points or four or twelve, so long as it's persuasive enough to get the answer I want." As with genres, feedback, and social dimensions of writing, outlining—in the broadest sense—continued to be important to Stephanie as she moved from student to professional. She also clung to the idea of writing as a system for organizing ideas and creating structures to think with.

Since she has nearly completed her training as an underwriter, as she looks ahead in her career, Stephanie has several choices. She could become an actuary and create spreadsheets to guide insurance companies in pricing, she could remain as an underwriter, she could go to law school and become a legal counsel in the insurance industry, or she could go into claims. At this point she is leaning toward claims, largely because it would enable her to do more writing: "You are drafting decision letters regarding the language of the policy, what a certain comma means, and how that is going to determine whether or not the claim is accepted or denied. That's where I'd like to move toward, getting a little more Englishy." The "huge" importance of writing in Stephanie's life seems to be guiding her career choices, and she has found ways to continue many of the writing practices she used in college. For Stephanie, writing development means adapting strategies and understandings of writing to new contexts. Strengthened by growing confidence in her abilities, her visible accomplishments, the deep pleasure she takes in writing, and her ability to look back at her work at the same time she looks ahead, Stephanie is poised to continue developing as a writer.

Linda: I Go to the Place Where Stories Are Born

Stephanie acknowledges that her position in the insurance business does not afford opportunities to write in depth as she did in college, but she seems comfortable with the compromise. In contrast, Linda, a 2015 graduate and a writing minor, appears unwilling to move away from the writing that matters to her. In her follow-up interview with me, Linda said, "I've always loved writing. I've been writing since I was a kid. . . . Since I was a kid I had a dream that I was going to be a professional writer. . . . I knew from a young age that was what I wanted to do. I can't exist without writing." This was not an exaggeration because, as she went on to explain, Linda had just left her sales position with an automotive supply company after working there for about a year and a half. "I ended up leaving the company to pursue writing because that job was not very writer-friendly. It was a great first job, but that's not really where my career is. I'm hoping to find another job more focused on writing. . . . Writing is one of the things I'm meant to do." Unlike Stephanie as well as Kris and Dan, the other two students considered here, Linda arrived at the university with a firmly established writerly identity, forged out of youthful experiences.

The landing page of Linda's Capstone eportfolio is filled with colorful petroglyphs of animals and a greeting, "Welcome to Wild Wood." In the introduction she explains that she has constructed the eportfolio as a showcase of her best writing in college. One of her essays, "Becoming Catskin," shows why she selected "Wild Wood" as the title for her eportfolio and shows how writing became so important to her. This essay begins: "I lie on the ground feeling like a tightknit ball of bones slung over with a pink jacket. I feel, rather than see, the three elementary schoolgirls behind me Dory, Yolanda, and Tamia. Their skin is as black as mine. One of them kicks my back. I don't move. I don't cry, not anymore." The narrative continues, showing how these three girls regularly attacked her and how she often fled to the forest near the elementary school playground to escape the bullying girls. In the forest, which became a tropical rainforest for her, she created a safe space to interact with animals and meet her imaginary friend Arden, a six-foot gryphon who took the place of her absent father and helped her through her parents' divorce.

As the narrative goes on, Linda eventually fights back against the bullying girls and returns their punches, kicks, and insults. Teachers, who had either ignored or been unaware of the bullying Linda regularly received, punish her for fighting, and the punishment included forbidding her return to her beloved forest. In her desolation, she discovers the power of writing:

> At first, I only feel the ache of losing my forest. Then I search deeper, and discover a new part of my mind. There, in that new space, I create words, and then write them on the empty page. Now, I know what I will do. I will write tales about my rainforest. Maybe then, I can go back to that wonderful place, even if it's just for the length of a story. I plow through line after line of my notebook, until I have filled a full page with makebelieve adventures. I cannot stop writing. My hand is bound to the paper by a new power. There is no restraint to this power. There are only words.

Her eight-year-old self's experience with trauma makes writing an integral part of Linda's identity, and she continues to ground her creative writing in nature-based fantasy stories through all her schooling and into her young adult life. Beginning with her elementary school notebook, Linda filled pages with her writing. She wrote short stories in middle school and her first novel in high school. She is currently completing a second novel. The major project included in her eportfolio was a novella that she is currently revising into a novel she hopes to publish.

Linda's identity as a writer is remarkable given how little support she received before entering the university. As she explained in our interview, it was not until college that she had "teachers who really helped show me, people who were professional writers themselves and knew about the craft." Prior to that she had to rely on reading and her own imagination. Fortunately, she had a parent who fostered reading. One of the personal essays included in her eportfolio includes a description of the difficult summer after her parents separated, leaving her mother with two young daughters and very little money. Linda writes:

> Then a miracle happened; the local library moved into a strip mall that was only one mile from our house. . . . Almost every day that summer, Mother would dress us in sunhats and walk hand-in-hand with us to the library. I remember few things from my childhood as vividly as that library. Every time we went there my sister and I left carrying as many books as we could carry in our tote bags. We would spend our nights poring over our treasure trove in the family room.

Immersion in reading played a significant role in Linda's development, enabling her to turn to writing when faced with personal and social challenges. Yet there is little evidence that Linda's literacies received school support; hers was self-sponsored writing. In reflecting on her writerly experiences during high school, she noted that before college she received very little feedback on her writing. In college in both the writing minor and her other courses she found "a professional writing environment to really grow in," and received useful responses to her writing from both peers and instructors. Before that, "I didn't really have a feedback loop," she explained. For Linda, as for the great majority of students in our study, feedback contributed substantially to writerly development.

An Asian studies major as well as a minor in writing, Linda took advantage of many opportunities for writing in college, as was evident in the wide variety of material she included in her eportfolio: nine essays for courses in Asian studies, some written in Japanese or Chinese; several poems; photographs; three personal essays; an audiobook; and a video essay. Animals and nature are dominant throughout the entire collection. For Linda, "the place where stories are born" is always in the natural world, peopled by animals. Her poetry features geese, bucks, a swan, a blue heron, and a seascape; her photobook contains images of animals, plants, and birds; her video essay offers instructions for sewing stuffed animals. The one piece that doesn't fit the pattern is "Roots to Grow and Wings to Fly," the personal narrative about her experience of her parents' divorce and her life with a single mom. In the introduction, she acknowledges that it really doesn't fit with the rest of the material in the eportfolio but explains that she included it because she thought it was one of her best pieces. I would add that this narrative adds another dimension to Linda's writerly identity because it elaborates on the pain that made writing so important to her. She deliberately undercut the conceptual unity of her eportfolio, but she did it to exercise her own critical judgment. Like other students whose writerly development generated a willingness to disagree with academic requirements, Linda challenged the instructor's emphasis on coherence by asserting her writerly authority.

The essays written for Linda's courses in Asian studies focus on animals in nature, just as her fiction does. Her paper "When God Was a Fox" argues that Inari, the god of agriculture, was a deity who took animal form; her "Tales of Tirvagvoni" examines the ways animals are portrayed in four different stories; and a paper on Potania Theron, goddess of animals and wilderness, redefines the nature of this goddess. Although Linda credits the writing minor for much of her development as a writer, she makes clear that her Asian studies classes were "very big on essay writing" and provided both peer and instructor feedback. Furthermore, the material she studied gave her "some new material to write about," and she felt that what she wrote for Asian studies contributed to her fiction writing: "I think if I hadn't taken those courses, I wouldn't have written some of my creative writing pieces." From an electronic perspective Linda's eportfolio might be seen as not particularly well integrated because it does not include links across selections. However, the pervasive emphasis on wilderness and animals makes clear the conceptual connections that hold the entire eportfolio together.

Another unifying factor in Linda's eportfolio is visual. In addition to the images of petroglyphs on the landing page, she includes a photobook titled "The Invisible World," which includes over forty pictures of things that usually escape notice. Linda describes the images this way: "Wildflowers growing at the side of the road, or the odd-shaped rock in someone's front yard—these are things that seem small and insignificant but actually hold a world of photogenic magic." The photogenic magic connects directly with Linda's writerly identity, as she explains in the photobook introduction: "Writing to me is about escaping the ordinary for the fantastical, for when I write I may choose to replace my reality with my innermost desires and fascinations. For me, the wilderness has always been the refuge of my dreams, because nature in just about any form inspires me as a writer." The importance Linda assigns to nature in her writing is remarkable in that she, a child of the city, had few opportunities to connect with the natural world, but in her view that circumstance made nature even more valuable to her. In her "Why I Write" essay she explains: "The sheer scarcity of wilderness in my life caused my childhood fascination with all things animals and nature. That fascination is what ultimately led me to discover myself as a writer." Although Linda developed the range and complexity of her writing across four years, her motivations and goals remained relatively unchanged.

When Linda took a position in sales with an auto supply company after graduation, she thought that it would provide opportunities to continue her development as a writer. Although she estimated that she wrote about one-third of the time, most of the writing consisted of emails about orders, queries about problems with materials received, and presentations about sales data for her department. She also spent a lot of time producing and rearranging spreadsheets designed to track and improve efficiency in plant production. Initial training for her position included a few online videos about writing conventions such as formatting emails and using professional language, "things I already knew," Linda commented. She soon realized that writing as she understood it was not valued in her workplace. There were no opportunities for creativity, nor was feedback provided. "It was the polar opposite of the writing I did at UM," she sighed. After a year and a half, Linda left this position, determined to spend more time engaged in the writing she values so highly.

Linda has continued to write, but she describes it as a lonely process because she hasn't found a community of writers where she can give and receive feedback. "I briefly joined a writing support group, but they weren't the group I was looking for. They were more a place where you could go to write for a few hours a week. There wasn't any sort of feedback or critique," she said. Linda's search for a community of writers underscores the importance she and many other students attach to writing among other writers. In some cases they, like Stephanie, adapt elements of their new context to address their desire for the company of other writers, and in other cases, like Linda, they continue to search for greater continuity with their college writing practices. Fear of an abrupt loss of their writing community echoed in the exit interviews of many students, just as the value students ascribe to communities of writers appears in many chapters in this collection. Linda's experience demonstrates the pain of losing such a community.

She is thinking of applying to MFA programs as a way of finding a community of writers, and she continues to write regularly: "I think the most important thing is to take time off and just write as much as possible. The only way to do it at this point is just do it. That's why I write every day." Meanwhile, ever resourceful, Linda turned to images, this time images she creates herself: "I took up acrylic painting, and it's very beneficial to my fiction writing." She explains, "I use it to flesh out scenes or explore character and settings . . . I'm not a person that outlines novels; I think art kind of takes that place and acts as the outlining aspect of writing a novel. I draw before, during and after writing. . . . After a session, I might do a quick painting of a scene that I liked in the novel, maybe to brainstorm ideas for revising." She is even considering creating illustrations for her novel. In the absence of the feedback she finds necessary to developing her writing, Linda produces art that enables her to both plan and revise her fiction. This integration of art and writing fits into the larger pattern of Linda's writerly development, a pattern of close connections between the visual (largely of the natural world) and the narratives she creates.

Linda's identity as a writer was firmly established long before she entered the university, and her development during her undergraduate years can be described as solidifying that identity more than broadening her rhetorical repertoire. To be sure, she was a very successful student who produced a number of academic essays that required identification and integration of scholarly resources, and she wrote in both Japanese and Mandarin as well as English. But in her academic essays she focused on topics and themes closely related to her interest in writing fantasies centered in the natural world. As she noted, she saw her work in Asian studies as providing resources for her fiction. Feedback on her writing constituted the most powerful influence on Linda's development as a writer, and she came to value and even depend on it as part of her process of writing. Since graduating, Linda has become even more convinced about her writing goals, and she seems unwilling to settle for less than full-time attention to her novel. Linda the writer is a maker, of images and of imaginary worlds.

Kris: I Am Confident in My Inabilities

Like the students Sarah Swofford describes in chapter 9, Kris, a nonminor, brought from high school a set of assumptions that shaped her view of college writing. Because her high school emphasized a technical program she did not feel confident as a writer or prepared for the first-year writing requirement, so she enrolled in the developmental course that provides support to students prior to the first-year writing course. After that she took a first-year writing course, and as she put it, "That pretty much ended the writing courses that I took except for I transitioned to more philosophy-based courses, and I really enjoyed the writing aspect of those classes. It kind of contrasts with scientific writing which was a lot of fun. Then for my upper level writing requirement I did a thesis, an honors thesis." Unlike Stephanie or Linda, Kris did not arrive at the university feeling well prepared for writing or convinced that she had any special talent as a writer. Her enrollment in the developmental course, probably based on her experience with the university's directed self-placement essay, marked her as someone who felt the need for extra support as a writer. Yet, by the time she graduated, Kris had become a confident and effective writer who wrote an honors thesis as well as a successful application for a highly competitive graduate school fellowship.

Kris's development as a writer owed little to writing courses, however. Her study in philosophy and the natural sciences, extensive reading, high-stakes writing for career advancement, and the honors thesis provided the grounding for her growth as a writer. After completing the developmental course and the required first-year course, Kris took several philosophy courses because she liked the way it led her to think and because she enjoyed reading philosophy. Reflecting on this choice in her exit interview, Kris explained that writing in philosophy pushed her in new directions, which helped her to "reflect on the way we write in science." But her love of science took priority, even in philosophy, leading her to write about scientific concepts and issues in philosophical terms. For instance, she wrote a philosophy paper arguing that all children should be vaccinated. Although scientific evidence about the faulty basis of the antivaccination movement provided the exigency for her paper, her argument was based on philosophical principles. In her exit interview, she explained, "One of my goals is to be able to communicate with people who aren't in academia but need access to scientific information. . . . We need to be able to communicate our research to these people. I'm from a rural community myself, and I want to make science accessible to people there." In her view, effective communication meant explaining a concept to people who don't understand it: "That is the biggest thing I learned from working in the lab, not from the writing classes I had. I wish I would have had this more in my writing classes." Kris's interviews do not include more detailed explanations of how writing courses could have served her better, but she made it clear that her science professors did an excellent job of showing her how to make her writing more effective.

At the same time, Kris's exit interview suggested considerable personal agency in her writerly development. She described herself as a voracious reader. "We read a lot in science, and I read a lot for fun. I've always loved, loved, loved reading, and I began to realize reading and writing were intimately tied together." During her first two years as an undergraduate Kris "got fed up with the competitive grading and standardized testing" in higher education and was ready to leave the university. Her parents persuaded her to stay, but she remained more on her own terms: "I started reading. I just read everything I could get my hands on in science. Then it came to my junior year. I started taking microbiology classes. It was crazy to me because people were taking these exams, and they had studied out of the book a lot. I just knew the answers because they came out of the primary research and all the books that I had read." Self-sponsored reading not only enabled Kris to thrive in her microbiology courses, it fostered her development as a writer because even though many of the authors she read intimidated her with their knowledge and style, they also inspired her because of her passionate interest in science. As she put it, "Ultimately nothing is going to be more interesting, more important to me than my research." Powered by extensive reading and a deep commitment to science, Kris took on challenges that furthered her writerly development.

In her exit interview Kris said, "The three most important things I've written so far, in terms of advancement of my career and where I'm going, is that I've had to write abstracts for conferences, I've had to write for grad school, and then I had to write for a grant as well. Those experiences were very necessary, but they also taught me a lot about writing and its importance." None of these things—participating in conferences, applying to graduate school, and seeking a National Science Foundation fellowship—is required of an undergraduate student, and each of them represents a significant challenge. In reflecting on her conference participation, Kris acknowledged a lot of anxiety: "What's really nerve wracking about this is that I don't even like standing in front of my peers in class. At a conference I'm standing in front of grad students, post docs, and professors." Even though making conference presentations was "nerve wracking," it increased Kris's confidence, making her feel that she successfully brought her reading and writing together. Graduate school applications require students to create written representations of themselves that will be convincing to admissions committees, and Kris willingly undertook this challenging project. The most successful STEM students arrive in graduate school with a fellowship to support their research, and Kris applied for and received one, another instance of her choosing to engage in high-stakes writing that she chose. Kris's claim that these three pieces of writing were necessary rings true because together they helped to position her as a successful graduate student in microbiology. They simultaneously tested her commitment and capacity for writing and enhanced her confidence as a writer.

Although Kris did not include her honors thesis as one of the three most important pieces of writing, she asserted that the process of writing it was "transformative," and her description of the process suggested that the thesis made a significant contribution to her development as a writer. Part of the thesis's powerful effect derived from the fact that it was based in the lab. Kris's struggle with the competitive grading in undergraduate courses diminished when she joined a lab group: "I was all against academia until my junior year when I joined a lab. This was the second semester of junior year. I didn't really decide to jump on the thesis boat until senior year when I had only six months of research under my belt." Kris's was an unusually tight schedule since she had to complete graduate school and fellowship applications during the same semester when she was writing her thesis, but it gave her "a fantastic experience." She said her process involved "reading a ton of primary literature, beating my head against the wall, doing several drafts, and then sending it to my advisor." Kris's description of the benefits of writing the thesis included this: "It's really great to think about your research in that way and have to do a literature review." But she saved the greatest praise for her advisor, characterizing him as "very very helpful. He is a fantastic guy, and I couldn't speak more highly of him." She described his response to her writing this way: "'Well look at this section. You might want to try this.' He let me make my own mistakes and then correct my own mistakes by saying, 'This is what you did well. In science we do it this way, so go back and redo it.'" This combination of guidance and freedom, particularly freedom to make mistakes, moved Kris into the company of more confident and effective writers.

When asked in her exit interview what contributed most to her writerly development, Kris said, "Peer review, I think, is the most important lesson I've learned in the classroom because we were forced to do that in first-year writing. Then I actually picked up on that and I was like, wow, that's helpful." She also, however, associated peer review with her lab and the study groups associated with her science courses. "It's very nice to sit down, especially with somebody who's kind of your age, or just a little bit older, and say 'Will you read this' because what we find, even when we discuss science. . . . your ideas, while they can be really great, are kind of consistent with your own logic. Then somebody will come in, and they'll be like 'That doesn't make any sense,' 'That makes a lot of sense,' 'I don't know what you're talking about.'" Because she had come to value peer response so highly, Kris actively sought it: "With my thesis, I got a group of my friends together. I bought them dinner and I was like 'Will you read this?' They were like 'I guess,' and I got some really great feedback." Like the students Ben Keating describes in chapter 2, Kris transformed a practice that had been "forced" on her into an essential part of her writing by translating it into scientific terms.

Other dimensions of Kris's development as a writer came directly from her experience as a student of science. Concision, for instance, emerged from page limits imposed by scientific genres such as abstracts and grant proposals. When she first entered the university, Kris "always associated writing well with writing long, kind of just filling the page," but in her science classes she found that "the most important documents I've written had an extremely short and strict page limit. It is so hard to communicate your ideas in a short amount of space." Reflecting on her difficulty in adjusting to such limits, Kris suggested that instructors could modify their approach: "Instead of always saying okay, you need to write this much, saying you can only write this much to communicate your ideas." Another thing Kris learned from studying science centered on the role of writing itself. As she put it, "A lot of what we learn as undergrads is not really a reflection of the actual profession and what the professors do, especially the dichotomy between writing and science." She went on to explain that she began from the assumption that writing wasn't very important in science, but by her senior year she saw writing as central. Along with this developmental shift came another. In her exit interview Kris explained that initially the process of creating an archive of her writing for this study had been a grade-conscious and essentially mechanical process: "My first couple of semesters I was like, it's a writing assignment. There you go. There's another writing assignment. There you go. I think you can definitely see at the beginning they're just some pieces that I wrote and received good marks on." She went on to say, "Whereas at the end I wasn't concerned about the marks. I was like, this is something that I feel passionately about, and you can see that reflected in my writing." For Kris the passion for writing, the appreciation of concision, and the increased valuing of writing itself grew out of her development as a student of science and her growing understanding of what the life of a professional scientist entails.

Unlike nearly all the students in this study, Kris did not leave the university when she graduated; she continued as a graduate student. With her prestigious NSF fellowship and excellent academic record, she had many graduate school options, but she chose to remain at UM because it seemed to offer the best program in her area. When I interviewed her, she had just finished her second year of graduate school and was continuing the same line of research on bacteria that she had begun in her undergraduate honors thesis. As we talked, a number of continuities with Kris's undergraduate experience emerged. She affirmed the importance of reading for her development as a writer: "I guess what was most significant in my progression as a writer in any particular area was what I was reading along with it. If I read something . . . I get excited about writing more." As Ryan McCarty notes in his chapter 4 discussion of Kris's developing scientific writing, reading journal articles was a way for her to learn the genre as an undergraduate. As a graduate student, however, her reading serves more as a form of invention or a means of getting ideas for both her writing and her research. This shift indicates her further development as a writer because she has moved beyond simply following models to actively contribute to conversations in her field.

Kris remained deeply committed to her research, particularly the study of bacteria begun in her honors thesis, and she was edging closer toward her goal of publishing it, "just adding more information, additional experiments, to clear things up, solidify." Communicating science to a nonacademic audience likewise remained an important writing goal for Kris, and she talked enthusiastically about making a presentation on her research to students in her former high school in northern Michigan. She continued, "One of the biggest questions I still struggle with is how do I . . . justify spending your taxpayer dollars on what I do? I feel like every academic should be compelled to do that."

Even though she remained in the same university in the same department with the same advisor, Kris experienced many discontinuities in her development as a writer when she became a graduate student. Her long-term ambivalence about writing took new form as she met different challenges, came to wider understandings, and took up new writing practices. The biggest change, as Kris saw it, was the increased amount of writing required. "In my first two years of graduate school I've probably spent at least 50 percent of my time writing, balancing that with experiments." She continued, "If you would've told me that at the beginning, I would not have signed on. It's truly a love-hate relationship because you learn so much when you're forced to sit down and take all of the ideas that are in your head. . . . Then you write them down and then you realize there are pitfalls. Then, as academic communication goes, you get back those pitfalls." Part of Kris's love-hate relationship with writing results, no doubt, from the inevitable critiques (making pitfalls visible) that are part of peer review, whether for undergraduates or scientists submitting papers for publication. Although the demands on her as a writer increased, Kris came to terms with them:

> At the outset I was just very uncomfortable with my abilities to write and I was able to distance myself from my lack of skill by saying "Well I don't need that, it's not what I do." . . . Once I was able to swallow the pill that writing and science are linked I could respect writing and what it does and how it communicates. That changed my perspective. . . . I'm more open to the idea that I can be a writer and a scientist.

Kris's deep commitment to communicating science to audiences outside academia helped her move past her negative feelings about writing and embrace the opportunities it provided.

Using new strategies also changed Kris's perspective on writing. In preparing manuscripts for publication she had to develop figures, a standard feature of scientific articles. She described the figures as the narrative spine of an article; readers should be able to scroll through figures and tell the story of the article. In her view, figures help writers because each one addresses a question, "You have the 'what is my question that this figure is going to answer?' and then each figure takes you step by step through and then you're just doing the writing to supplement that." At another point in the interview Kris said she found outlines helpful, and it appears that figures serve a similar function by creating a structure into which she can write. Another strategy she described can be seen as a version of writing to learn. She explained that in preparing for her preliminary exam presentation she followed a process where "you write all the questions that you can come up with that could possibly be asked on any given slide and then you go back through and you write answers to all those questions." Although she did not use writing-to-learn terminology, Kris's explanation echoed its central premise: "You need to feel fundamentally sound in your ability to write about your project . . . writing forces you to put all your ideas on paper in a way that you can communicate them." Writing enabled Kris to make a much more effective presentation, and thereby helped her see another way that it fostered her career in science.

Another instance of this new role for writing in Kris's life had both personal and professional dimensions. During her exit interview as an undergraduate she claimed that she had never done any reflective writing. However, in her follow-up interview with me she explained that she has taken up a new practice: "I write independently for catharsis—it has nothing to do with science. . . . I can put all my ideas in one place, and the process of writing opens up my mind and frees up some space." Sometimes the writing deals with interpersonal issues, and she writes as "an outsider looking in and explaining the situation." While this writing is not directed toward professional goals, it carries benefits for these goals because it enables her to focus on her work: "I could get an experiment done with extreme focus, whereas before I was splitting the time between 'I need to add this much, but that person said . . .'" Writing about personal issues enables Kris to simultaneously deal with them and to become more focused on her work in the lab. It also nurtures her personal and social development to, as she puts it, "be a better human being."

In her exit interview, Kris made very clear statements about not using social media. When asked if she used any form of new media writing, she responded that she did not, but she did acknowledge that she read her sister's blog about business school, and speculated that new media might provide a means of communicating her views on science to a wider audience: "I would love to be able to share—people don't understand why I get excited, and I'd love to be able to share why I get excited, you know? I think maybe a blog or something like that, is the way to do that." Two years later, Kris was not writing a blog to share her excitement about science with others, but she had required students to tweet what they had learned from a workshop she offered, and she said, "I have a Twitter feed, and I follow almost exclusively scientists. I scroll through and I pick up papers. . . . There is a lot of writing and exchanging going on out there." Social media now shape both her reading and writing, and it has contributed to her development as a writer by creating yet another link between reading and writing while simultaneously providing another way to exchange ideas with other writers.

The most substantial contribution to Kris's writerly development centered on how her view of herself as a writer and of the nature of writing shifted during her first two years of graduate school. As a high-achieving student who saw herself as a scientist rather than a writer, she struggled to incorporate the writer role. She noted that it was really in elementary school that she first began to think, "I'm not a particularly good writer, but I'm a science person, and because I'm a science person I'm not a good writer," much like Marie in Swofford's chapter 9. This dichotomy shaped her thinking throughout most of her undergraduate education. In part, as noted above, her perspective shifted because she recognized that writing would enable her to accomplish her goal of making science more accessible to wider audiences. However, a more profound change took shape when her principal investigator, with whom she was writing proposals and papers, admitted "that writing wasn't easy for him." She explained, "As a like-minded science person this idea that okay we've doing something and I still don't think I'm good at it, and I've been a very successful scientist for X number of years . . . has been extremely helpful." Along with understanding that an admired mentor also found writing difficult, Kris came to understand more about writing. Specifically, she learned that "it didn't have to be perfect . . . it's never going to be perfect and it's not that I am a writer or I'm not a writer." With this recognition she was able to see that she did not have to think of writing in bimodal terms; she could be a person who writes to communicate. She also acknowledged a range of audiences and purposes: "It's me communicating with myself through writing about an experience that I'm trying to go through or writing a letter to my mom or writing a scientific article for the community." She was able to free herself from a need for perfection and value what writing enabled her to do.

Along with this recognition came another. One of the questions I asked in our interview referred back to her exit interview statement that she was developing confidence as a writer. "Is that still happening?" I asked. Kris responded:

> I would amend that statement. I'm confident in my inabilities. I'm confident that I can write a first draft, and that it will be terrible, but I will have a first draft with all of my ideas in one place. Then I'm confident that I can find, whether it be professors or other resources, to give me feedback and comments, incorporate those comments, and edit. I'm confident in the writing process, and I'm not sure that I'll ever be confident in my writing abilities, but I don't want—in some ways that's good because I don't want it to breed complacency. I'm never going to sit down and think, well, I'm a great writer. I'm just going to sit down and power this out because that's not the way it works for me. It takes several iterations and so I'm confident in being able to utilize resources and get things done, but not in my raw writing abilities.

With this statement Kris identifies herself as a writer who understands and depends on processes that she has developed. Because she sees writing in social terms, she is comfortable asking for help rather than relying entirely on her own abilities. Although she doesn't mention her extensive reading here, that background surely contributes to her confidence in being able to effectively use the help she receives; she has honed an ability to identify when and how to use the resources available. In a deep and hard-won way she understands writing as never entirely finalized and never quite perfect, and within these terms she is confident in her ability to perform successfully as a writer.

Dan: I Need to Control the Story

Like Kris's, Dan's postgraduation journey led him to a much deeper appreciation for the social and collaborative dimension of writing, but he arrived at this place via a very different route. A communications major who graduated in 2015, he now serves as social media coordinator for a professional baseball team. Dan's application to the minor in writing explained that he wanted to enter the program because he was a new staff member for the *Michigan Daily* and felt that the minor would add "an academic context" to his journalistic writing experience. One theme that emerged in Dan's entry interview and in the writer's evolution essay he wrote before graduating is an ambivalent view of collaboration in writing, one interwoven with varying statements about confidence. In the entry interview, he claimed that he was nervous about his writing abilities when he entered the university, unsure that he would measure up to its standards, and anxious to have others read his work so he "would feel better about it." This uncertainty echoed in his evolution essay when he explained that he kept writing even though he didn't really enjoy it; writing was his fallback because, as he states, "I struggled with math and science, was bored by history and politics and didn't pick up Spanish quickly enough, so I stuck to writing." Unlike the other three students profiled here, Dan was not a reader. "I didn't read books for fun. . . . I couldn't even finish the Harry Potter series because I was more content seeing the movies," he claimed. Lacking a solid grounding as a reader, and making comments about seeking reassurance from other readers and turning to writing as a last academic resort suggest a writer who lacked confidence and depended on collaboration with others to assure the quality of his writing.

Yet it was confidence in his own writing abilities that led Dan to write for the *Daily*. The backstory, which he repeated in his application to the writing minor and his "Why I Write" paper, is that he was reading a *Daily* article about a hockey game and thought "I can write a better story than this." He began writing sports stories for the *Daily*, attracted positive attention from editors, and went on to become an editor himself. Dan's story can be read as the narrative of a very successful student journalist who found a niche for himself early in his college career, and in his evolution essay Dan explains how his perspective on writing shifted. He explains, "Writing wasn't fun in the beginning because the assignments weren't interesting." What he did find interesting was a first-year writing assignment that required him to go out and conduct interviews. His writing in response to this assignment was, to Dan's ear, "one of the first examples in which I didn't sound like I disliked writing." Journalistic writing, which meant writing about others, suited Dan because, as he said during his entry interview, "I need to control the story." He claimed to enjoy the control: "I control what is included and excluded. No one gets to determine my writing process but myself. . . . The power that I can wield in a single phrase is incredible." Here there is no indication of the nervous writer who seeks support and reassurance from others. Instead Dan expressed enough confidence in his own abilities to be rather dismissive of peer review. "I have a good sense of what is my best writing," he said. He also asserted that he could write a paper and "it wasn't going to be the end of the world if I didn't talk to someone about it." When he did receive feedback from peers he felt free to reject it, claiming that he knew better what he was trying to accomplish and preferred the "best" feedback that would come from instructors. Dan's confidence in his own writing and his ability to discern its best parts led him reject, at least while he was an undergraduate, the collaboration made possible by peer feedback. At this point in his writerly development he seemed to see collaboration as undercutting the control he sought in writing.

In his senior year writer's evolution essay Dan offered a more complicated explanation of the control inherent in writing stories about others. He acknowledged that writing about others rather than himself could be seen as avoiding the vulnerability that comes with self-disclosure. He wrote:

> I don't write about others because I'm afraid of being vulnerable—really, there's some vulnerability to doing that itself—but it's a strange concept to open up to others about things that would otherwise be kept inside, especially because it doesn't serve as much of a purpose as sharing information does. In a way, it was easier and more informative to write about someone else's vulnerabilities than my own.

These two sentences both deny and affirm Dan's reluctance to make himself vulnerable through self-disclosure in writing. He says he is not afraid to reveal himself but describes it as strange and lacking the purpose and ease of "sharing information."

The equation between information and purpose offers another angle on the issue of control. Purposeful writing about information can be controlled whereas self-disclosure could lead to loss of control or vulnerability.

Nearly all of the work included in Dan's eportfolio demonstrates his desire and ability to exert control in writing. For Dan, control is a comprehensive term that includes everything from his topics—a focus on others rather than himself—to sentence-level decisions about syntax and punctuation that shape meanings. The majority of selections come from his work as a *Daily* sports reporter and feature accounts of sporting events, profiles of key players, and interviews with coaches, all organized like a sports blog with the newest at the top. These, along with a rich collection of sports-oriented photographs, display Dan's considerable ability as a sports journalist and introduce him to prospective employers. Both in several of the sports clips and other selections included in the eportfolio, Dan adopts a humorous style that can be read as a form of control. A revised version of the "Why I Write" essay from his Gateway portfolio takes the form of a series of statements with a number of humorous asides, such as attributing his interest in telling the stories of others (rather than his own) to his "inner 'Gossip Girl'" and suggesting that "everyone has read the *Daily* and thought they could do better." In his evolution essay Dan acknowledges that he prefers to deflect attention away from himself and cites a piece titled "Karma," a humorous first-person account of tempting fate by being dishonest and lazy to see if he will be punished. He explains, "I found ways in my [creative nonfiction] course to write a personal essay (as instructed) without writing about myself. . . . I developed the ability to put myself into the story without being the focus which has long been important to my work at the *Daily* and beyond." "Feature," a genre-bending use of sports-event narrative style to describe a young man's attempts to hook up with a woman at a bar offers another example of the humorous deflection. Similarly, Dan's Capstone project, "Journey to Adulthood," recounts his attempts to accomplish feats such as administering the Heimlich maneuver, cooking a meal, building a fire, sewing a button, and jump-starting a car to prove his maturity. The one exception is "Remembering," a serious account of Dan's body image issues. Otherwise, he demonstrates considerable ability to "control the story" and deflect attention away from himself with humor, information, or the language of sports.

Although he was not particularly interested in the social dimension of peer response to his writing in the context of a course, Dan was keenly aware of and attuned to responses from audiences for his journalism. When asked, during his entry interview, what constitutes good writing, he said, "Originally I would say it meant getting an A. Now I would revise that to saying it's writing to your audience . . . when the person who read it thought, okay, I think this piece was well written and was understood." He goes on to explain, "A great piece of writing transcends a good piece of writing when other people continue to talk about it." Audience awareness loomed large for Dan, and writing for the *Daily* gave him immediate feedback from his audience: "The scary thing and the great thing about the *Daily* is that it tracks the number of reads you get online so when a piece does really well or a piece doesn't do well, maybe, you can go back and make yourself more paranoid about that." Dan's humorous comment about becoming paranoid tempered but did not obviate the seriousness with which he thought about the effects of his writing on his audience. Furthermore, he made it clear that he drew on audience response to develop as a writer: "I'll go back and check out a piece that I might have worked on longer or that got more reads, and I'll reflect on that and I'll think, okay. Yeah. I did well here. Or, like, I'll hit myself, 'Damn it, Dan,' or something like that."

Two years later, when I interviewed him, Dan had a very different view of feedback from his peers: "I'm realizing now that I wish I had bought in more to the classmate feedback." He explained, "That was tough for me to accept really early on and probably into the senior year just because . . . I thought back then, 'I know what I'm doing. I don't need another student to tell me this.'" In his position as social media coordinator for a professional baseball team, Dan finds collaboration central to his work: "When you jump into a thing like social media . . . you have to be willing to collaborate with anyone and everyone. . . . I'm taking anyone's voice who can offer it to me." Dan's social media—Twitter, Facebook, and Instagram—plunged him into a cacophony of other voices. In addition to responding to and drawing on readers who commented on his tweets and posts, Dan enjoys a collaborative relationship with his boss: "I can shoot my boss . . . an idea like 'Hey what do you think about this?' Sometimes it might be like, 'Wait, just too far,' 'Probably not the voice we want,' or something, and he'll say 'I wouldn't do that.' It's fair. I'm appreciative of that." On other occasions, Dan's boss is encouraging: "I like what you're doing. What if you tried . . . working with these keywords you've used?" As he became more comfortable in his role, Dan sometimes questioned his boss's suggestions, saying "I don't know if I necessarily think that works . . . it was tough for me to say it to him at first." From one perspective, the boss takes on the role of an instructor, offering praise, guidance, and correction, but Dan's ability to question his boss's judgment illuminates another dimension of the relationship, especially when the boss says, "Yeah, you're right. It doesn't really sound that great now that I think about it. Love what you had." In this version of collaboration Dan felt comfortable evaluating and ultimately rejecting his boss's advice—much as students described in Emily Wilson and Justine Post's chapter 1 critically engaged with instructor feedback—and, thereby, retained control of the story.

When I asked Dan about the ways he had changed and developed as a writer since graduation, he had a ready answer: "You have to be able to take criticism and feedback in real time. The stakes are higher, and I've had to grow into that. I've had to be like, 'Okay, I'm putting something out there on the internet, and it's going to be seen by millions of people. I have to be ready to live with that. I was not accustomed to that type of writing." Because his audience is so large and so immediate, Dan is keenly aware of the social nature of writing: "Collaboration is something I really, really enjoy. The more and more you collaborate the more ideas you get." Here collaboration includes responses from both his boss and his readers, and Dan was reminded of the multiple perspectives of peers who responded to his writing in college: "The minor took in a lot of different voices. I had friends from chemistry, sciences, and those who were in political science." The rich collection of his readers' voices mirrors what Dan experienced as an undergraduate, but the stakes are much higher in his social media position, and he has learned to collaborate with a wide and diverse audience.

Social media not only offers Dan a large audience, it shapes or controls the development of his writing. When I asked him to reflect on his development as a writer, he first took a global perspective, saying, "I imagine in two more years I might have some different answers. I think that writing is one of those great things that as you get older you don't necessarily get worse at it." But then he quickly shifted, stating,

> I want to stress just how big and important social media counts as a form of writing. . . . This Twitter profile isn't just a chance for me to talk with friends. It's really a chance for me to continue writing and to think about saying something in fewer characters. . . . The new media focus is critical to how I think about writing. . . . I'm intrigued by how writing changes through these mediums.

Dan's development as a writer is evident in the way he continues to think about the nature of writing itself and the shaping effect of the various forms of social media he uses. In addition to using the tools of social media effectively on a daily basis, he reflects on the significance of this form of writing. He has to think about concision in a new way, finding ways to convey his ideas in fewer characters. He also has to write in "real time," with little opportunity for revision, but, as interchanges with his boss show, collaboration remains part of his writing process. "It's like editing on the fly," he explains. Of course, social media also create the audiences that shape Dan's writing by responding to what he posts or tweets, and it fosters additional forms of collaboration. One audience positions Dan in relation to other developing writers: "I am seeing a lot of upcoming writers or a lot of upcoming students, because they're interacting with me on Twitter on an everyday basis or on Facebook." Dan can be seen as a mentor figure to the upcoming writers and students he interacts with, helping prepare them for the ever-larger role social media will play in writing. Another shaping or controlling force on Dan's writing is the baseball team itself and the way it performs. As he puts it, "There's nine guys on the field, and if they do well, I can be funnier and I can be more sarcastic." Still, however, Dan sees social media as giving him another way to control the story: "Social media—I like to think of it as talking from a position of power. . . . You can say, 'Why don't you look at. . . .'"

Part of Dan's development as a writer led him to adopt a more inclusive view of collaboration. In his professional role he came to see a value in peer response that had been invisible to him during his undergraduate years. While he still looks to authority—his boss took the place of instructors—he also recognizes the value of the multiple voices who respond to his writing on social media, for both their contributions to his thinking and the ways he can support their growth as writers. Dan's desire to control the story remained constant, however. From his undergraduate years to the present he focuses on the stories of others rather than his own; he uses humor, information, and sports narratives to deflect attention away from himself; and he believes that social media, along with other technologies of writing, give him a position of power so that he can control the story.

Conclusion

Despite significant differences in their levels of writerly confidence and their writing experiences as undergraduates, these four students followed a number of similar paths in writing development after college. There were no clear variations between minors and nonminors in the ways they conceptualized writing or their capacities as writers. All saw writing as essential to the work they were doing, and they felt prepared to take up the writing challenges of their new positions, even as they recognized the need to adapt their writing processes to new contexts. All of them became even more aware of the audiences for whom they were writing, whether colleagues in the insurance business, other scientists, the hoped-for agent or publisher, or baseball fans, and they adjusted their writing accordingly. All, with the possible exception of Linda, adapted their processes of writing to unfamiliar genres, including recommendations on insurance pricing; articles for scientific journals; and tweets, posts, and captions. And Linda's shift toward integrating painting and writing may lead her toward a multimodal genre that includes both text and image. The entire group saw writing in positive terms and expressed pleasure about what they were able to accomplish with it. They had repertoires that enabled them to approach writing in more than one way and to work comfortably with new genres.

The social dimension of writing was clearly visible to all four. They actively sought some form of feedback and reflected on what they learned. Stephanie's practice of saving and rereading praise-winning reports; Dan's exchanges with his boss and constant attention to fans' responses to his tweets, posts, and captions; Kris's lab-based collaborations; and Linda's attempt to find a writing community all show how these writers translated their college experiences with feedback into their work environments. None of the four mentioned having experience with peer review in high school, but all reported being introduced to it in their university courses, and they each found ways to replicate peer review as they stepped into their new roles. In many ways, then, these four young adults successfully enacted the writerly behaviors that student responses in the exit survey anticipated. Writing enabled them to achieve professional aspirations, they proceeded reflectively as they faced writing challenges, and they felt capable as they faced new and field-specific rhetorical situations.

One of the challenges faced by all four concerned new ways of integrating the visual and textual. To be sure, Dan and Linda had experience with creating the eportfolio required of writing minors and so knew something about multimedia writing, but Dan's undergraduate writing did not include creating captions for Instagram images, and Linda had no prior experience connecting painting with her fiction writing. Stephanie's English-major writing did not include incorporating charts, and Kris had never before had to create figures for science publications. Each of the four met these challenges, but the fact that incorporating the visual was required in these very different lines of work is worth noting as we think about what writing is in the twenty-first century.

Despite their similarities, these four young adults established writing patterns as undergraduates that continued and took firmer form as they assumed new positions. Linda continued to focus on creating fantasies based in the natural world. Stephanie kept doing research, analyzing it, and writing about what she concluded, even though she shifted from literary texts to commodities. Dan went on controlling the story by using humor and sports narratives. Kris carried on with her process of collaborating to write about science. Implicit in these patterns were assumptions about the nature of writing. For Linda it continues to be a safe place constructed by the imagination, for Stephanie it is a means of persuading others, for Dan it is a vehicle for sharing information and offering humor, and for Kris it is a way to provide useful information to people outside the academy.

All of these students are only two or three years out of college, and each faces many challenges ahead. Stephanie will need to decide which area of insurance she wants to pursue and whether she will seek another degree. Kris faces a long road of graduate school, dissertation, postdoc, and the uncertainty of academic employment. Linda has to make both short-term and long-term decisions about how she will maintain herself as a novelist. Dan is already thinking about where he might go next in the world of sports journalism. As they move forward writing will continue to play an important role in their professional lives, and based on the patterns of development they have already shown, it seems likely that they will continue to draw and build on the ways of writing they developed as undergraduates.

WORK CITED

Brandt, Deborah. *The Rise of Writing: Redefining Mass Literacy*. Cambridge UP, 2015.

CONCLUSION

After six years, thousands of hours collecting and analyzing various forms of evidence, and hundreds of conversations about approaches, interpretations, and drafts, we have learned a great deal about how college student writers develop, and we are happy to share our work with others interested in more deeply understanding how undergraduate writers develop. We come away from this work with a new awareness of the complexity of writing development, its many forms and variations, and the multiple methods that can illuminate various aspects of it. Creating this collection posed the challenge of limiting and selecting, since it was not possible to include discussions of all the data we collected.

Our project benefited from and built on previous longitudinal studies, and we hope other scholars and researchers will in turn build on this study, perhaps drawing on some of the data we offer online. We looked carefully at other studies of writing development and expected our own work to follow similar lines, and to some extent our study affirmed previous investigations. We found, for instance, that the writerly development of many students was marked by developing expertise in the discourse communities of the disciplines in which they concentrated. At the same time, though, we encountered many students who complicated the equation between disciplinary expertise and writing development by coupling it with other, more self-directed goals. We found that students developed facility with various genres, but they also created their own categories for *kinds of writing*. We found that patterns of students' writerly development were multiple and irregular, but we could also discern some commonalities among specific subgroups. We expected that existing concepts would guide much of our work, and they did. Threshold concepts played a role in the questions around which chapters in this collection developed, as did rhetorical theory. These helped us develop ways to show what the learning and development of student writers looks like. However, a number of our questions—about language-level analysis, extended views of development, and multimodal writing, for instance—reached beyond them.

It would be very satisfying to conclude this collection by offering a list of declarative statements about student writing development, the sorts of statements that could provide unambiguous support for specific curricular or policy moves. This desire for certainty takes on urgency given the growing importance of writing in this country. One assumption shared by nearly all our study participants centered on the major role writing would play in their lives beyond the university. These students probably had not read Deborah Brandt's *The Rise of Writing*, which asserts that we are witnessing "the turn to writing as a mass daily experience" (3). This turn means that people, both at work and leisure, are spending a major portion of the day with fingers on keyboards, it means that we are living and writing among others who write, and it disrupts the long-standing dominance of reading-based literacy in favor of one in which reading frequently occurs as part of writing rather than as an end in itself. Our participants may not have read Brandt, but they enacted her claim that young adults pursue writing-based literacy, "teaching themselves to 'write over reading,' commandeering, redefining, and in some cases, refusing reading to advance their writing development" (14). In light of such claims, to say nothing of the current anti-intellectual climate that questions the value of higher education, we would like to offer clear and certain statements, but reading across the chapters included here reveals that nearly every possible declaration has to be qualified. The pages that follow offer several observations that emerge from this study, and each is accompanied by the "but" that demonstrates the complexity of writing development.

College Writing Has Transformative Effects on Students

Evidence collected by this study makes it clear that student participants developed new capacities across their undergraduate years, and many articulated their growth in definitive terms. Some described their writing experience as transformative, commenting on the ways it changed both their writing and how they see themselves. Others talked about their newfound passion for writing, claiming that writing would always be part of their lives. And still others pointed to the specific skills they had learned, such as developing an argument and tailoring it to a specific audience's interests. Looking across surveys, interviews, and the written artifacts of participants, we found compelling evidence that a great majority of participants felt they had become different writers in college. Their claims took varying forms, sometimes analytical, sometimes emotion-filled, and sometimes surprised at what had been accomplished, but nearly always positive.

We found, for instance, evidence of students' growing awareness of audience in interviews as well as selections of student writing, and in entry interviews many indicated that audience awareness was a new concept, not something they had learned about in high school. When asked in interviews what constituted good writing, a very frequent and unprompted student response was "audience awareness." As recounted in section one, the number of coded responses about the importance of audience increased significantly between sophomore and senior year across the entire group of participants. For some students, the teacher/instructor remained the primary audience, while others imagined multiple audiences as well as the possible effects their writing could have on them. Students also talked about the kinds of effects they wanted to have on audiences—to be not boring, to have a particular impact, or to reach wide groups of readers online. In chapter 2, Benjamin Keating explains how many students who participated in peer review saw their classmates as authentic audiences, from whom they learned ways to address multiple audiences. Lizzie Hutton and Gail Gibson found, as they recount in chapter 3, that increased audience awareness accompanied deepening understandings of genre, enhancing students' confidence about addressing various audiences, as Shannon exemplified: "[I can] mold my style to any different venue or audience or purpose for what I'm writing" (p. 104). The rhetorical flexibility demonstrated by students such as these is one marker of writing development.

In addition to student claims, our study showed clear evidence of audience awareness in student writing. Ryan McCarty demonstrates in chapter 4 how students such as Kris and Jonah address audiences within their disciplinary homes by tracing the patterns of nominalization, dense noun clusters, and specialized lexical items they both use in writing for STEM readers. At the same time both Kris and Jonah extend their audience awareness by taking up other strategies. For Kris it means adopting what McCarty calls "argumentative methods from outside her usual STEM contexts" (p. 122) to reach non-STEM readers. Jonah takes a more all-encompassing approach, drawing on resources from his several writing experiences to "write with dexterity across a range of situations" (p. 128) and to address a variety of audiences.

The patterns that Laura Aull traces in chapter 5 show similar transformations in student writing at the level of word and phrase choices that signal generality and certainty. Aull's automated text analysis of lower- and upper-division student writers shows how students move from a majority of boosters and minority of hedges in writing to the reverse as they transition from lower-division to upper-division courses so that they write in fewer generalities and begin to more closely approximate academic writing. Large-scale changes like this speak directly to the transformative shifts that signal writing development.

But Transformative Effects Are Not Uniform and Not Always Visible to Students

Despite such evidence of transformations, we have to acknowledge that they did not occur for all students. Some continued to see audience only in terms of the professor or instructor and spent considerable energy trying to figure out what the professor wanted. These students expressed frustration when they could not determine and produce what the instructor would reward with the coveted A, but they did not turn to more expansive considerations of audience. Only some students moved toward what Hutton and Gibson (chapter 3) describe as an academic-creative hybrid, where students negotiate successfully between "views of writing and their writerly growth as entailing both generative activity and adherence to communicative norms, instead of viewing these approaches as requiring an either-or choice" (p. 105).

Individual students in our study reinforce the claim of researchers such as Richard Haswell, Lucille McCarthy, Marilyn Sternglass, Anne Beaufort, Nancy Sommers and Laura Saltz, and Lee Ann Carroll, that student writing development is always uneven and irregular. Naomi Silver's investigation of students' experiences with multimodal composition in chapter 8 displays this irregularity in very clear terms, demonstrating that the same student can "exhibit highly developed rhetorical awareness and flexibility in one mode, while demonstrating fairly early stages of rhetorical command and metacognitive awareness and regulation in another" (p. 233). This pattern of uneven development also emerges in a student such as Grace, in chapters 3 and 7, who feels capable with formulaic writing but considers herself unable to produce writing inflected by creativity.

Another feature of writing development highlighted by researchers such as Nancy Sommers and Laura Saltz is the distance between what students say and what they do. In some instances, students talk about aspects of writing they do not enact in their own composing. A variation on this difference is students who accomplish things in writing that they do not acknowledge in talking about it. In chapter 6, Zak Lancaster illustrates this phenomenon in his analysis of Jon, who in his exit interview describes good writing as "you are accurately representing you on the page" (p. 175), which suggests an arhetorical view of writing. Yet Lancaster's analysis of selections of Jon's writing shows that this student uses rhetorical strategies very effectively. As Lancaster observes, interviews "reveal interesting and fruitful contradictions, both within [students'] talk about writing and between their talk and rhetorical performances" (p. 182).

Curriculum Shapes Writing Development

At every level the curriculum influences how students develop as writers. In our study, for instance, the fact that peer review is a significant part of all first-year writing courses, and virtually no one is exempted from first-year writing, means that our student participants had the common experience of peer review. This helps explain why peer review looms so large in students' discussions of their writing and why a number worried about how they would replace these opportunities to share writing when they graduated. On another campus where peer review does not necessarily figure so prominently in the curriculum, students might pay it less attention. Likewise, the existence of an upper-level writing requirement, ostensibly to develop facility in disciplinary writing, had a shaping effect on the writing experiences of all study participants. As noted in the introduction to section two, and especially in Ryan McCarty's chapter 4, the linkage between disciplinary expertise and writing development occupies a prominent position in scholarship on writing development, as exemplified by Anne Beaufort, Mary Soliday, Nancy Sommers and Laura Saltz, and Chris Thaiss and Terry Zawacki. In this view, the curricula of student majors play a key role in their development as writers.

Students in our study confirmed that learning to emulate the discourses of their fields of study shaped their writerly development. Zach, who appears in McCarty's chapter, describes himself in the exit interview, saying: "I am now a perfectly well adapted scientific writer, streamlined to convey concepts and findings in a concise and objective manner. . . . It has historically been a necessity to write this way in science in an effort to convince skeptical readers that your findings are based on truth rather than opinion" (p. 115). Zach's prose suggests his ability to enact scientific writing effectively, and he sees it as a mark of his growth as a writer.

An especially powerful curricular force for the students in our study was the minor in writing, and comparisons of students in the two groups of writing minors and nonminors demonstrate a number of ways the curriculum of the minor shaped writing development. As Benjamin Keating documents in chapter 2, students in the minor had, overall, more positive feelings about their experiences with peer review than the nonminors. He writes: "For minors, peer review took place in a classroom setting where students were able to choose their own writing projects and claim authority over them. Overwhelmingly, they perceived peer review as a highly useful and enjoyable experience" (p. 74). It shaped the way minors understood the revision process and fostered a dialogic view of writing. Keating observes that nonminors did not experience the same curriculum and "reported more negative experiences with school-sponsored modes of peer review" (p. 74). Further, in some cases nonminors equated skill in grammar with writing competence, thereby, claims Keating, slowing their writerly development.

Lizzie Hutton and Gail Gibson add a further insight into the curricular influence of the minor in chapter 3 as they distinguish between students "who saw writing and writing development as entailing mainly learned competence in the genre-specific communication of thought" and those "who saw writing development as entailing competence in the generation of thought, and who emphasized the development of a highly personal writerly identity" (p. 93). Nonminors largely populated the first category while minors tended to fall into the second. Hutton and Gibson explain this difference in curricular terms, noting that course work in the minor remained "detached from a specific disciplinary affiliation beyond writing studies itself" (p. 93). These authors go on to explain that students who integrated the two domains of "creative" and "academic" writing also tended to be minors, who "often praised the space that the minor courses provided for their processing of these different constructs" (p. 93).

An important feature of the minor curriculum was, of course, the eportfolio, and Naomi Silver demonstrates how this requirement shaped the writerly development of minors in chapter 8. By dividing the "portfolio effect" from the "eportfolio effect," Silver makes clear the varying paths of development followed by minors. Some students, such as Ayanna, integrated learning through processes characteristic of portfolios—collection, reflection, and selection—but failed to see writing in the eportfolio as "real" writing and ultimately created a Capstone eportfolio that cannot be described as web-sensible. A few of the minors profiled by Silver, such as Kaitlin, do come to see their work in eportfolios as "real" writing and create web-sensible projects that draw on the full resources of their platforms. The writers in the latter category develop a more capacious concept of writing and "evince a highly metacognitive relationship to the rhetorical situations they compose within" (p. 244). In contrast, students who did not become multimodal writers had a more limited concept of writing, demonstrating that even within the same curriculum marked differences in writerly development may appear.

But Students Subvert or Supplement Curriculum

Silver's account of the varying paths of development among minors suggests one way students subverted the curriculum. A stated learning goal of the minor, "to compose in a variety of modes, including a range of new media such as blogs, interactive maps, online magazines, etc.," was subverted by students who did not think of eportfolios or other multimodal projects as "real" writing and thus did not become the multimodal composers the minor was designed to produce. Keating describes a different type of subversion in chapter 2 when he narrates how nonminors looked beyond classroom-based peer review. As Keating reports, many nonminors described peer review in negative terms, recounting how their peers lacked sufficient knowledge and simply went through the motions. Accordingly, these nonminors themselves failed to take school-sponsored peer review seriously. Yet they valued peer review enough to seek it out on their own, like Charlotte, who explained, "I do use peer editing as a huge thing. . . . I like using people who I know I can trust as far as peer editing, which usually happens to be my mom a lot, or my friends that work at the *Daily*, or past teachers" (p. 64). From one perspective it can seem that peer review did not work for students such as Charlotte, but she subverted the classroom version of peer review by supplementing it with a self-sponsored version.

Supplementing the curriculum appears in another form as Ryan McCarty describes how students such as Zach, who proclaims himself a "perfectly adapted scientific writer," then took up another approach to writing: "I believe that even more societal value can be drawn from scientific truths by conveying them in a way that draws on the passion of the audience, not just the rationality . . . such an endeavor must be undertaken carefully and subtly so as not to distract from the empirical evidence" (p. 115). Zach retains the scientist's respect for empirical evidence but insists that his writerly development should include more than scientific writing. McCarty goes on to recount the several ways that students see discipline-focused writing as something to be supplemented with other approaches to develop as writers. Leo sees "every class" as contributing to his writerly development (p. 116); Katie values "the different assignments and the different audiences" she writes for (p. 117); Kris notes the importance of writing to audiences beyond the scientific community "in communicating your research" (p. 122); and Jonah aims to "learn more ways in which to perfect various forms of writing" (p. 128). As McCarty puts it, many students who attained the goal of emulating the discourses of their disciplinary communities reached beyond that to a writerly development that was "multifaceted, drawing on a range of personal interests, general education courses, courses in their majors, work experiences, and extracurricular activities" (p. 129).

In talking with students who had already graduated and moved on to the next chapter of their lives, Anne Gere in chapter 10 found more examples of students supplementing the curriculum of their disciplinary homes. Stephanie, who entered the university determined to major in actuarial math, supplemented this curriculum with a major in English and found that the combination served her very well when she took a position in the insurance industry. Kris, who also appears in McCarty's chapter, supplemented her biology major with courses in philosophy and claimed that writing philosophy papers gave her insights into the ways scientists write, and at the same time helped equip her to write for audiences outside the scientific community. Both of these lessons proved to be important as she pursued an academic career in biology. Linda, specializing in Asian studies, supplemented her major with a minor in writing and claimed that the combination served her need to develop as a fiction writer. Dan, a journalist and communications major, also supplemented his major with a minor in writing, and it was there that he encountered, and initially dismissed, the peer review that became central in his job as a social media coordinator.

Students' Personal and Social Development Is Linked to Writing

The Anderson et al. study referenced in the Introduction (p. 7) found that three characteristics of good writing assignments—clear writing expectations, meaning-making writing tasks, and interactive writing processes—can "affect students' perceived development socially and personally" (227). The authors suggest that this finding centering on social and personal development "opens a new category of the benefits of writing in college" (227), and findings from our study offer a look at this category. Interview transcripts from this study are filled with students' expressions of pleasure, frustration, resistance, pride, inadequacy, delight, ambivalence, and a variety of other feelings. Frequently these feelings appear to have a shaping effect on students' ways of writing and their perceptions of their writerly selves. In turn, we found claims that writing led students to various forms of personal and social development. Abby, for instance, said that positive responses to her writing "made me more confident with not only my writing abilities but what I have to say in general, people want to hear." Madeleine, a minor, voiced this view in her exit interview: "College is such a transformative time that writing can become the mode through which you kind of make sense of what you've been through. I think this is what my writing experience has been like. It's not just in the academic sense. Not that that's not valid, because it totally is. It can also play a role in personal development and reflecting on your experiences."

As noted in the introduction to section one, students frequently took pleasure in their ability to achieve a desired effect on or elicit a positive response from an audience. They talked about the delights of sharing writing with peers and being a writer among writers. These positive feelings associated with writing led students to feel more capable, more socially adept, more in charge of their own learning. Of course, students' feelings did not always take positive form. Study participants expressed resentment about peer review that was not effective and did not, therefore, confer its full benefits for their writing or themselves. In this and many other contexts students' emotional responses contributed to or limited their writerly development and their writing development played a role in their personal and social development.

"Critical engagement," the term Emily Wilson and Justine Post use in chapter 1 to describe the most effective student responses to instructor feedback, represents a mixture of affect and action. This engagement, which includes seeing broad purposes for writing, imagining audiences beyond the instructor, reflecting on one's own writing, and evaluating feedback rather than accepting it without question, steps beyond the more obvious feelings of acceptance or resistance to show how writers' personal and social development is bound up with their writerly development. Capacities such as taking a broader view, being reflective, and assessing critiques lead to personal and social growth as much as to the development of writers.

Take, for instance, Adrienne, whom Wilson and Post discuss. In her entry interview Adrienne expresses resentment because "I didn't get the grade I wanted," on a paper written for an English class, gives no attention to the feedback, and "quit thinking about English as a major" (p. 38). Her lack of critical engagement with the feedback is accompanied by a relatively impulsive response. Wilson and Post cite high school expectations for feedback as an obstacle to critical engagement with feedback, and Adrienne expresses frustration that her "professors aren't filling out a checklist" (p. 46) as her high school teachers did.

Grace, a student featured in Anna Knutson's chapter 7, also expresses strong feelings about writing in her entry interview, claiming that she "hates" writing and believes she "can't write" (p. 193). The struggle for Grace centers on the need to reconcile formulaic and more creative writing: "It has to be organized, and then I'm always trying to figure out how to match the creativity with the organization" (p. 196). As Knutson puts it, "[Grace] does not believe that she is cognitively equipped to be creative and organized at the same time" (p. 205), and "that writing ability is natural and inherent rather than the result of process and effort" (p. 205). Like Adrienne, Grace abandons her intended major, shifting from environmental sciences to German, explaining: "I hate that this major is full of writing and persuading people and arguments. I can't write well enough and so I just—I dropped the class, and then I dropped my major" (p. 208). Grace's underdeveloped concept of writing took her on a circuitous route to writerly development that included eventually finding a "reset" button in her new major and simultaneously drawing on new personal and social capacities.

Natalie, who appears in Sarah Swofford's chapter 9, describes herself as "definitely confident coming [to college]; I also think maybe over-confident" (p. 272), but she quickly learned that the standards for writing in her high school were very different from those at the university: "I was told in high school that this is good, but it wasn't good. Looking back, I don't think it was good at all. I think that first year, there were lots of road bumps, and I didn't—my confidence was knocked a little bit, but in a good way" (p. 272). Unlike Grace and Adrienne, Natalie does not proclaim herself a bad writer or take up a narrative of failure, thereby demonstrating a level of personal and social maturity. Instead she, in the terms Wilson and Post use, engages critically with the feedback she receives and describes herself as feeling "freed" as a writer.

But Students Help Shape the Terms of That Personal/Social-Writing Development Link

Although students such as Adrienne and Grace express significant doubts about their writing abilities early in their undergraduate careers, each shifts the terms of the linkage between writerly and personal/social development. In her exit interview, however, Adrienne praises feedback from an instructor who looked "at the overarching thing. She was really great at keeping in mind form," and explains how she responded: "It was killing my darlings, but it was learning form and purpose" (p. 39). Here Adrienne engages critically with feedback that helped her improve her writing, and her response also shows that she has grown enough personally and socially to look past high school expectations.

In becoming a German major, Grace found herself in a writing environment that "emphasized the importance of ideas over perfection, and process over product" (p. 213). Knutson speculates that learning to write in a new language may "have been destabilizing enough that Grace was forced to dislodge some of her entrenched writing knowledge and approach writing anew, as a novice" (pp. 213–14), and in the process she became more receptive to instructor feedback. As Knutson notes, Grace did not describe herself as engaging in reflection, but it is difficult to imagine that reflection did not figure in her decision to switch to a major with instructors who provided individualized writing support. In this environment she could combine writerly with personal and social development.

Natalie, in chapter 9, demonstrated a capacity to engage critically with the feedback she received and to acknowledge that it represented very different expectations from those of her high school teachers. She could have become resentful about not being well prepared for college writing, but she showed personal and social maturity by seeking to replicate in college the supportive network she had experienced in her small hometown. Because she saw writing feedback in relational terms, she sought out peers who could help her negotiate the new expectations. In so doing, Natalie connected her social intelligence with her developing understanding of writing. With this move she righted herself after having her confidence "knocked a bit" and continued on a path that combined both writerly and social/personal development.

Language-Level Analysis Reveals Large-Scale Aspects of Development

Large-scale language-level analysis makes visible features of students' writing and their comments about writing that cannot be seen through examination of individual texts or transcripts. The meanings students attach to words such as *voice* or *style* or any number of others, such as *revision* or *argument*, affect how they write, how they think about what writing can do, and what developmental paths they take. Looking across a large collection of student comments, as Lancaster does in chapter 6, can provide insights into how students understand and use metalanguage about writing. Knowing, for instance, that students in a curriculum like the writing minor collectively think of style more in terms of register than do nonminor students, who think of it in more individualistic terms, can help shape the curriculum for both groups of students. Similarly, analysis that shows how students' understanding of style shifts (or doesn't) from a greater emphasis on its individual qualities to seeing its relationship to genre or register casts light on developmental trajectories. The insights drawn from such analysis can provide valuable information about the development of student writers. Lancaster's finding of the often contradictory views expressed by students, as they slip from individualist to social descriptions of style and back again, and the link between these perspectives and students' understanding of their various writing projects, suggests the value of looking closely at the role of assignments in writing development.

Seeing patterns that contribute to features such as generality and unnuanced certainty, both features of relatively inexperienced writers, can, as Aull demonstrates in chapter 5, explain student writing in ways that may lead to effective instruction. Specific words and phrases can be identified as boosters and hedges, and their frequency patterns can be measured to understand the kinds of language choices students make. Aull shows that it is possible to identify *how* students' micro-level choices illuminate "macro-level constructs like audience and purpose, showing how they are realized and discoverable" (p. 158). In showing how students use their linguistic resources, Aull suggests that the assignments to which students write exert a shaping force on their micro-level choices.

In addition to informing curricular planning and understandings of writerly development, large-scale analysis can serve pedagogical purposes. Using, or encouraging students to use, language-level analysis of writing produced in classrooms can reveal the micro-level choices that shape larger effects such as certainty, generality, writer-in-text, voice, and style. Such analysis can help students become more attuned to monitoring and appreciating their own development as writers. For instructors, this analysis can lead to productive discussions about writing and the many choices it entails. Perhaps most important, instructors can learn to create assignments that encourage students to reflect on how they represent themselves in writing for a given audience in a given genre. As both authors in section three noted, the projects or assignments that students undertake contribute significantly to the language choices they make. The importance of devoting serious attention to writing assignments or prompts cannot be overemphasized, because they contribute directly to writerly development. Dan Melzer has shown that the great majority of assignments in US colleges and universities focus on conveying information and ask students to address the teacher as examiner, giving students little opportunity to approach multiple audiences or work with various genres. Language-level examination of student writing can reveal the limitations of poorly conceived assignments and at the same time make clear to students and faculty strategies for developing more effective ways to address specific audiences in a variety of genres.

But Language-Level Analysis Can Also Reveal Useful Information about Individual Students

Large-scale analysis of language-level features of writing can provide useful information about patterns in groups of students, but language-level analysis of student writing can also be productive for understanding the writing of individual students. Ryan McCarty's analysis of the ways Kris and Jonah use nominalization, noun clusters, and scientific terms, for example, illustrates important aspects of their writerly development. Similarly, Lancaster's examination of how Kaitlin and Mariana talk about the terms *style* and *voice* provides insights into their conceptions of social and individual aspects of writing.

As this study has found, some students lack the language to describe their writing or simply don't recognize what they are doing. Other students describe writing in terms quite different from what they actually do as writers. Analyzing student writing at the level of language can clarify the complexity of writing development by showing how students are actually using language. Lancaster illustrates this point with a qualitative language-level examination of texts written by Angela and Jon. In Angela's case, there is continuity between her expressed views about a socially inflected approach to style and her performance as a writer. But Jon projects a social or disciplinary voice in his writing even though he expresses a much more individualistic view in his interviews. This qualitative analysis validates the claim that there can be significant variation between the statements and performances of developing student writers and at the same time shows how those variations align with analysis of the writing collected from larger groups.

Writing Development Is Shaped by Prior Experiences and Perceptions

While it seems obvious to say that writing development at the college level extends back into high school and forward into writing after graduation, most studies of writing development at the college level have concentrated on the undergraduate years without much attention to what came before or after. At the beginning, the design for this study did not include extension in either direction, but as we examined the evidence from college students' reflections on their writing as well as transcripts of their interviews, it became clear that students see their own writing development in an arc that extends back to high school and forward past graduation.

Students such as Adrienne and Linda demonstrated in different ways the shaping influences of high school writing on college student writers. Adrienne, whom Wilson and Post introduce in chapter 1, arrived on campus as a confident writer who had received A's in high school and planned to be an English major. In addition to receiving a lower grade than she expected on an English paper, Adrienne explained, "I didn't feel like [my writing] was appreciated" (p. 38), suggesting that she had experienced appreciation from her high school teachers. In her entry interview she expressed particular resentment about having to write "what the teacher thinks" (p. 38), comparing it unfavorably to the more "objective" checklists her high school teachers had used. The intensity of Adrienne's struggles with the differences between her high school and college writing experiences became visible when Adrienne decided not to major in English. In her entry interview she explained, "I'm just less confident [as a writer]" (p. 38).

Linda, who appears in chapter 10, made few references to her writing instruction in high school, except to note that she had not received much attention or encouragement. She had, however, developed a very clear sense of her identity as a writer in high school. Her self-sponsored writing provided emotional sustenance as well as a vehicle for personal growth because in writing she found a means to deal with and move beyond the traumas and challenges she faced. For Linda, college writing offered a valuable set of opportunities for receiving helpful feedback, learning important strategies, and strengthening her identity as a writer. The apparent deficits in Linda's high school writing experiences made college writing a welcome change.

Just as high school writing experiences shaped the ways students encountered college writing, so college writing contributed to students' views of their futures as writers. As survey data discussed earlier shows, most students in this study felt that writing would be important to their success in life after college. Stephanie, Dan, and Linda were no exception. Although their goals varied considerably, each felt that writing would play a key role in their future lives and made choices to prepare for that future. Stephanie's double major in math and English gave her an ideal mix of analytical and interpretive skills. Dan combined his extracurricular experience as a journalist with a major in communications and a minor in writing to give himself the broadest possible preparation for becoming a writer after graduation. Linda drew on her major in Asian studies for material to incorporate into her fiction, and the minor in writing put her in contact with committed writers who gave her a community in which to practice her craft.

But Students Also Transform Their Approaches to and Thoughts about Writing

Although she abandoned the idea of majoring in English, Adrienne did minor in writing, and between her entry and exit interviews her views of writing and herself as a writer shifted again. Rather than critiquing instructors for seemingly subjective and arbitrary feedback, she actively sought feedback very different from the checklists she had wished for earlier. Describing one instructor's feedback, she explained, "I wanted more. 'How is it working as a whole? What is your feeling as a whole?' . . . I feel like I didn't get enough feedback" (p. 38). Instead of resenting a lack of appreciation for her writing, Adrienne became a confident enough writer to seek and welcome what Wilson and Post call "tough-yet-generative feedback" (p. 39).

For Linda, the transforming effects of college built on the foundation she had established in high school. She embraced opportunities to receive feedback from peers and instructors. As a minor in writing, she became part of a cohort of writers, received helpful feedback from instructors, and had opportunities to work on projects in which she was deeply invested. Her courses in Asian studies provided inspiration and information she could use in her writing, and she also developed a rich sense of the relationship between the verbal and visual.

Kris, who began college writing in a developmental course, found her way to more effective writing by reading extensively and taking a cross-disciplinary approach. As McCarty notes in chapter 4, one move was to consider the difference between writing in biology and in physics, contrasting a more interpretive emphasis with a more quantitative one. Another of Kris's moves was to consider the differences between writing in philosophy and biology. This cross-disciplinary perspective gave her a window on the nature of scientific writing, and at the same time broadened her repertoire so that she could write about science for nonspecialist audiences. Throughout this process of transformation Kris remained convinced that her writing should remain her own: "You don't automatically pick up on somebody else's style and make that your own. You still have to form it in such a way that it's your own style" (p. 121).

Looking Ahead

This collection includes a rich array of insights into college students' writing development. Each chapter considers the study data from a different angle, contributing to a kaleidoscopic view of student writers. Despite their wide-ranging topics, methods, and conclusions, each contributor privileges the student perspective, attending closely to what student writers say and do. Yet even with the variety of insights offered, this collection touches on only a few of the many possible topics associated with writing development and draws on a relatively small percentage of the available data. To encourage other researchers to take up additional issues and questions, we are making the study data available at https://doi.org/10.3998/mpub.10079890 so that others can join us in investigations that can lead all of us to do even better at preparing students for the life-long journey that is writing development.

WORKS CITED

Anderson, Paul, Robert M. Gonyea, Chris M. Anson, and Charles Paine. "The Contributions of Writing to Learning and Development: Results from a Large-Scale Multi-Institutional Study." *Research in the Teaching of English*, vol. 50, no. 2, 2015, pp. 199–237.

Beaufort, Anne. *College Writing and Beyond: A New Framework for University Writing Instruction.* Utah State UP, 2007.

Brandt, Deborah. *The Rise of Writing: Redefining Mass Literacy.* Cambridge UP, 2015.

Carroll, Lee Ann. *Rehearsing New Roles: How College Students Develop as Writers.* SIU Press, 2002.

Haswell, Richard H. *Gaining Ground in College Writing: Tales of Development and Interpretation.* Southern Methodist UP, 1991.

McCarthy, Lucille Parkinson. "A Stranger in Strange Lands: A College Student Writing across the Curriculum." *Research in the Teaching of English*, vol. 21, no. 3, 1987, pp. 233–65.

Melzer, Dan. *Assignments across the Curriculum: A National Study of College Writing.* Utah State UP, 2014.

Soliday, Mary. *Everyday Genres: Writing Assignments across the Disciplines.* SIU Press, 2011.

Sommers, Nancy, and Laura Saltz. "The Novice as Expert: Writing the Freshman Year." *College Composition and Communication*, vol. 56, no. 1, 2004, pp. 124–49.

Sternglass, Marilyn S. *Time to Know Them: A Longitudinal Study of Writing and Learning at the College Level.* Lawrence Erlbaum, 1997.

Thaiss, Chris, and Terry Myers Zawacki. *Engaged Writers and Dynamic Disciplines: Research on the Academic Writing Life.* Boynton/Cook Heinemann, 2006.

APPENDIX 1

DEMOGRAPHIC INFORMATION

Number of students, start of study:	182
Number of students, end of study:	169
Minors:	60
Nonminors:	109

Gender

Male nonminors	15
Male minors	16
Female minors	44
Female nonminors	94

Majors

The participants who completed the study represented forty-seven majors, including the following:

American Culture
Anthropology
Architecture
Art and Design
Asian Studies
Biology
Biomedical Engineering
Biomolecular Science
Biopsychology, Cognition, and Neuroscience
Business Administration
Communication
Computer Science
Creative Writing
Earth and Environmental Science
Ecology and Evolutionary Biology
Economics
Education
English
French
Geological Sciences
German
History
Industrial and Operations Engineering
Informatics
International Studies
Latin American and Caribbean Studies
Linguistics

Mathematics
Microbiology
Movement Science
Museum Studies
Music Performance
Neuroscience
Nursing
Organizational Studies
Philosophy
Physiology
Political Science
Psychology
Public Policy
Screen Arts and Culture
Sociology
Spanish
Sports Management
Statistics
Women's Studies

Other information related to majors and minors.

Minors

1 Triple major, single minor
8 Dropped the minor and were dropped from the study
9 Single major, double minor
16 Double major, single minor
38 Single major, single minor

Nonminors

2 Single major with two minors
2 Triple majors, zero minor
4 Double majors with a single minor
29 Double major, zero minor
36 Single major, zero minor
36 Single major with a single minor

APPENDIX 2

SWEETLAND MINOR IN WRITING PROGRAM DETAILS

An extended version of Appendix 2 can be found on our Fulcrum platform at https://doi.org/10.3998/mpub.10079890

Overview and Learning Goals

The 15-credit Sweetland Minor in Writing Program requires an application. Admitted students take both Gateway and Capstone courses within Sweetland, and must allow at least one "gap" semester between the two courses to enable greater opportunity for their growth as writers. In addition to these two required Sweetland courses, minors take two upper-level writing requirement (ULWR) courses (rather than the one required of all students), and are encouraged to select one in their major area of study and the other outside of it, to broaden their exposure to genres of disciplinary writing. Minor students also select one more course focused on argumentative writing, creative nonfiction writing, professional writing, writing and other arts, or digital media writing. Fulfilling these requirements means taking a writing-focused course nearly every semester and encountering a broad range of genres, modes, and media.

Learning goals for the minor state that students will:

- Produce complex and well-supported arguments that matter in academic and nonacademic contexts.
- Explore different strategies for organizing, revising, and proofreading writing of varying lengths and genres.
- Identify and implement rhetorical choices that meet the demands of specific genres, audiences, and rhetorical situations.
- Compose in a variety of modes, including a range of new media such as blogs, interactive maps, online magazines, etc.

- Identify the expectations that characterize writing in the major, and use this knowledge to write effectively in a range of genres in that discipline.
- Learn the language to describe writing processes, rhetorical choices, genre expectations, and disciplinary discourse to discuss writing-in-progress and writing development over time.
- Collaborate with other writers to improve writing-in-progress.

Electronic Portfolios

The two Sweetland courses required by the minor, the Gateway and Capstone, address these goals explicitly and at the same time give students a good deal of latitude in how to accomplish them. One significant feature of the program is the creation of an electronic portfolio in both the Gateway and Capstone courses, creating a kind of reflective bookending of each student's writing experiences and growth. Though each of the two eportfolios is guided by an assignment prompt, students can select their own platform (often a templated one such as WordPress or Wix, though a small number of students hand-code them), and have complete freedom of design. The major writing projects for the two courses also foreground student interests and commitments. The Gateway course leads students to compose a reflective essay called "Why I Write," and the Capstone course asks them to look back at their college experiences in a "Writer's Evolution" essay, accompanied by an annotated bibliography of their own prior writing. Though both projects require a guiding idea and evidence, there is no required format or genre, allowing students to write poems, narratives, and manifestos as well as more conventional essays.

Gateway Course Projects

The primary work of the Gateway course consists of two paired projects, the **Repurposing an Argument** project and the **Remediating an Argument** project. In the former, students are asked to select "a piece of writing you've already completed on a topic that's dear to your heart and/or mind, a topic you'll want to continue living with this semester" and "repurpose it for a new audience and with a new or extended argument." The latter assignment prompts students "to try to present the *same argument* [as in the Repurposing project] to the *same audience*, but in a *different medium*," so as "to consider the ways that medium and form affect argument, audience, and purpose." Students also complete a project asking them to explore the phrase "**Why and How I Write**," to begin to synthesize more deeply their sense of the work they have done during the semester and to begin to think about goals for their writing in the remainder of the program.

Capstone Course Projects

In the Capstone course, students engage in the culmination of their minor in writing work in the **Capstone project**, a "long-term, research-based project of your design [that] invites you to identify a specific scholarly and/or creative conversation happening in the world to which you'd like to contribute. [. . .] Your project can take any form you deem appropriate for your overall argument and audience—as long as it is governed by a tightly focused guiding idea or argument and demonstrates this idea through meaningful engagement with research." These projects span the full semester, and multiple drafts, including a proposal; production plan; annotated bibliography; rough draft, rough cut, or mockup, depending on the medium; peer review and instructor feedback; and more. Students also complete an **Evidence-Based Essay on Your Development as a Writer (Evolutionary Project)** that asks them to demonstrate and reflect on their evolution as writers, and in particular, what they explored and learned during their college writing career and the minor in writing program.

APPENDIX 3

SAMPLE OF WRITING DEVELOPMENT SURVEYS

The questions below are drawn from across all survey items. Full surveys and results can be found on our Fulcrum platform at https://doi.org/10.3998/mpub.10079890

The first set of questions was designed by researchers at the Sweetland Center for Writing. Students chose responses to the following set of questions on a scale from 1 to 4, with 1 indicating "very much" or "a lot" and 4 indicating "never" or "not at all."

Questions about students' high school writing experiences

1. **How often did you do the following writing tasks in high school? (Exit survey version: How frequently did you do the following over the course of your college career?)**[1]

   Sample response options include: Write a sustained and detailed argument of more than five pages in length; summarize the main ideas from an assigned reading; evaluate and respond critically to an assigned reading; make an argument and support it using evidence; express a personal opinion on an issue; interpret a literary text; write essays or papers in subjects other than English; write a personal narrative.
2. **How often did you use the following writing processes during high school?**

   Sample response options include: Revise an essay multiple times; follow citation guidelines; provide and receive feedback on peer writing; conduct research using online databases or other web-based sources;

1. An asterisk indicates questions that appeared in both entry and exit surveys.

identify credible research sources; compose or revise online; create a portfolio of your writing.

Questions about students' first-year composition writing experiences

1. **How much did you learn about the following in your First-Year Writing Requirement course? (Exit survey version: How much did you learn about the following in your courses at the University?)***

   Producing well-supported academic arguments; reading and using complex texts to create and support your argument; writing in a variety of different genres; shaping writing for different audiences and purposes; revising, editing, and proofreading writing over multiple drafts; giving and receiving feedback on writing-in-progress; knowing how to approach new kinds of writing tasks.
2. **How frequently do you use what you learned in your First-Year Writing Requirement course about the following when writing for other courses?**

   Same response options offered as above.

Questions about students' writing experiences outside of class

3. **Do you write for any of the following extracurricular activities? Mark all that apply.***

   Sample response options include: Paid employment; internship; activist or advocacy work; faith-based activities; recreation or hobbies; fan activities (e.g., fan fiction, sports blogs, etc.); creative writing; personal writing (e.g., journaling); other (please specify); I don't do any extracurricular writing.
4. **How important do you believe writing will be for the following? (Exit survey version: How important do you believe writing has been for the following?)***

   Sample response options include: Your undergraduate academic success; your admission into the graduate or professional program; your ability to achieve your long-term academic and career goals; your ability to enter your chosen career field; your ability to change careers or pursue new opportunities

5. **In the last four years, what kind of writing has been most important to you, and why? (Free response)**
6. **Do you experience difficulties with any of the following in your academic writing? Please check all that apply.***
   Sample response options include: Adapting how you write for different academic disciplines or genres; avoiding abstract, indirect language; coming up with a topic or idea to write about; constructing an argument using appropriate evidence; general English syntax; having a vocabulary for talking about writing; integrating and citing sources effectively; knowing where to get feedback on drafts; punctuation; register (e.g., appropriate degrees of formality, slang, etc.); revising a paper through multiple drafts; stating a clear, confident position; using visuals effectively in writing; writing in a variety of different media; no significant issues; other (please specify).

Questions about student academic and intellectual engagement in their university

The following questions come from the National Survey of Student Engagement (NSSE). Students chose their responses on a scale from 1 to 4, with 1 indicating "very often" and 4 indicating "never."

1. **In your experience at your institution during the current school year, about how often have you done each of the following?*** Asked questions in class or contributed to class discussions; made a class presentation; prepared two or more drafts of a paper or assignment before turning it in; worked on a paper or project that required integrating ideas or information from various sources; included diverse perspectives (different races, religions, genders, political beliefs, etc.) in class discussions or writing assignments; come to class without completing readings or assignments; worked with classmates outside of class to prepare class assignments; tutored or taught other students (paid or voluntary); participated in a community-based project (e.g., service learning) as part of a regular course; talked about career plans with a faculty member or advisor; discussed ideas from your readings or classes with faculty members outside of class; received prompt written or oral feedback from faculty on your academic performance; worked harder than you thought you

could to meet an instructor's standards or expectations; worked with faculty members on activities other than course work (committees, orientation, student life activities, etc.); had serious conversations with students of a different race or ethnicity than your own; had serious conversations with students who are very different from you in terms of their religious beliefs, political opinions, or personal values.

2. **During the current school year, about how much reading and writing have you done?***

   Number of: assigned textbooks, books, or book-length packs of course readings; books read on your own (not assigned) for personal enjoyment or academic enrichment; written papers or reports of twenty pages or more; written papers or reports between five and nineteen pages; written papers or reports of fewer than five pages.

3. **During the current school year, about how often have you done each of the following?***

   Attended an art exhibit, play, dance, music, theater, or other performance; exercised or participated in physical fitness activities; participated in activities to enhance your spirituality (worship, meditation, prayer, etc.); examined the strengths and weaknesses of your own views on a topic or issue; tried to better understand someone else's views by imagining how an issue looks from his or her perspective; learned something that changed the way you understand an issue or concept.

4. **Which of the following have you done or do you plan to do before you graduate from your institution?***

   Sample response options include: Practicum, internship, field experience, co-op experience, or clinical assignment; community service or volunteer work; participate in a learning community; work on a research project with a faculty member outside of course or program requirements; foreign language course work; study abroad; independent study or self-designed major; culminating senior experience (Capstone course, senior project or thesis, comprehensive exam, etc.).

5. **Mark the box that best represents the quality of your relationships with people (other students, faculty members, administrative personnel) at your institution.***

   Relationships with other students
   Relationships with faculty members
   Relationships with administrative personnel and offices

6. **To what extent does your institution emphasize each of the following?***

   Spending significant amounts of time studying and on academic work; providing the support you need to help you succeed academically; encouraging contact among students from different economic, social, and racial or ethnic backgrounds; helping you cope with your nonacademic responsibilities (work, family, etc.); providing the support you need to thrive socially; attending campus events and activities (special speakers, cultural performances, athletic events, etc.); using computers in academic work.
7. **To what extent has your experience at this institution contributed to your knowledge, skills, and personal development in the following areas?***

   Sample response options include: Acquiring a broad general education; acquiring job or work-related knowledge and skills; writing and speaking clearly and effectively; thinking critically and analytically; analyzing quantitative problems; using computing and information technology; working effectively with others; voting in local, state, or national elections; learning effectively on your own; understanding yourself; understanding people of other racial and ethnic backgrounds; solving complex real-world problems; developing a personal code of values and ethics; contributing to the welfare of your community; developing a deepened sense of spirituality.

Questions about student experience with writing at their university

The following questions were adapted from NSSE's "Experiences with Writing" Topical Module, which was developed by the Council of Writing Program Administrators (CWPA) and NSSE.

1. **During the current school year, for how many of your writing assignments have you done each of the following?***

   Sample response options include: Brainstormed (listed ideas, mapped concepts, prepared an outline, etc.) to develop your ideas before you started drafting your assignment; talked with your instructor, classmate, friend, or family member to develop your ideas before you started drafting your assignment; received feedback from your instructor, classmate, friend, or family member about a draft before turning in your final assignment; visited a campus-based writing or tutoring center to get help with your writing assignment before turning it in; used an online tutoring service to get help with your writing assignment before turning it in; proofread your final draft for errors before turning it in.

2. **During the current school year, in how many of your writing assignments did you*:**

   Narrate or describe one of your own experiences; summarize something you read, such as articles, books, or online publications; analyze or evaluate something you read, researched, or observed; describe your methods or findings related to data you collected in lab or field work, a survey project, etc.; argue a position using evidence and reasoning; explain in writing the meaning of numerical or statistical data; write in the style and format of a specific field (engineering, history, psychology, etc.); include drawings, tables, photos, screen shots, or other visual content in your written assignment; create a project with multimedia (web page, poster, slide presentation such as PowerPoint, etc.).

3. **During the current school year, for how many of your writing assignments has your instructor done each of the following?***

   Sample response options include: Provided clear instructions describing what he or she wanted you to do; explained in advance what he or she wanted you to learn and the criteria he or she would use to grade your assignment; provided a sample of a completed assignment written by the instructor or a student; asked you to: do short pieces of writing that he or she did not grade, give feedback to a classmate about a draft or outline the classmate had written, write with classmates to complete a group project, or address a real or imagined audience such as your classmates, a politician, nonexperts, etc.

Questions about students' comfort and confidence in writing

The following questions come from the Daly-Miller Writing Questionnaire. Students chose responses to the following set of questions on a Likert scale from 1 to 5, with 1 indicating "strongly agree" and 5 indicating "strongly disagree."

Please indicate your level of agreement with the following statements*:

Sample response options include: I avoid writing; I look forward to writing down my ideas; I am afraid of writing essays when I know they will be evaluated; handing in a composition makes me feel good; my mind seems to go blank when I start to work on my composition; I would enjoy submitting my writing to magazines for evaluation and publication; I'm nervous about writing; writing is a lot of fun; I have a terrible time organizing my ideas in a composition course; it's easy for me to write good compositions; I don't think I write as well as most other people.

Self-reporting and English-language acquisition questions

The following questions were designed by researchers at the Sweetland Center for Writing.

1. **Thank you for participating in this survey. Before you submit your responses, we have just a few more brief questions. How would you describe yourself as a writer? (Free response)**
2. **Do you speak or write in languages other than English? If so, please indicate which languages you speak and/or write with proficiency.**
3. **What language(s) do you speak at home with your family?**
4. **When you were growing up, did at least one parent or guardian speak English as a first language?**
5. **Where did you attend school for the following years? (Students indicate whether they were in the US, outside the US, or a mixture of both.)**

    Kindergarten or preschool, ages 3–5
    Elementary school (grades 1–4), ages 6–10
    Intermediate school (grades 5–6), ages 11–12
    Middle school or junior high school (grades 7–8), ages 13–14
    Secondary school or high school (grades 9–12), ages 15–18

In this section, students chose responses to the following set of questions, designed in-house, on a scale from 1 to 4, with 1 indicating "very much" or "a lot" and 4 indicating "never" or "not at all."

1. **How frequently did you do the following over the course of your college career?**

   Sample response options include: Create and use video digital media and audio digital media; create web pages; create and work with podcasts or enhanced podcasts, blogs, or microblogs; create electronic presentations using PowerPoint, Prezi, or other presentation software; evaluate websites for credibility, scholarly sources, etc.; create online games; create remixes or mashups; publish or write online; create and use electronic portfolios; create animation; create apps; use digital editing tools such as Photoshop or other software.
2. **In the last four years, what kind of writing has been most important to you, and why? (Free response)**

APPENDIX 4

SAMPLES OF INTERVIEW QUESTIONS

The entire set of interview questions can be found on our Fulcrum platform at https://doi.org/10.3998/mpub.10079890

These questions are drawn from across all sets of interviews: minor entry, nonminor entry, minor exit, and nonminor exit.

Questions for both Minors and Nonminors

General—writerly self-image

1. How would you describe yourself as a writer when you began at UM? How would you describe yourself as a writer now? What language have you developed to talk about yourself as a writer or how you learn to write? How do you describe the role of writing in your life?
2. To what extent would you say you have grown as a writer? To what would you attribute this growth?
3. What are your goals for yourself as a writer? Minors only: Have these changed since entering the minor in writing?

Transfer

4. Thinking across your college writing experiences, what do you think it means to write well?
5. What do you think is most important in learning to write?
6. Which First-Year Writing Requirement course did you take? What did you learn in this class that you have continued to use in your writing? What language did you develop in this course to talk about yourself as a writer or how you learn to write?
7. What is your concentration? Have you had an opportunity to do writing in your concentration? What kinds? What effect have those experiences had on you as a writer? How confident do you feel about writing in your concentration?

Writing Experiences

8. What experiences in and out of the classroom have had an effect on your writing?
9. How has your writing process changed as a result of these experiences?
10. If I use the term "reflective writing," what does that mean to you? Have you used reflective writing in your own writing processes?
11. What experiences have you had working with other writers in your courses (or in other contexts)? Have you done workshopping or peer review? Group or collaborative writing projects?
12. If you were going to give someone advice about writing, what are some of the things they should think about as they begin writing a paper?
13. What is your concentration? Have you had an opportunity to do writing in your concentration? What kinds of writing? What effect have those experiences had on you as a writer? How confident do you feel about writing in your concentration?
14. Have you had any experiences with new media writing (e.g., writing for blogs or websites, using sound or video, PowerPoint presentations, etc.)? If so, what have those experiences looked like? What effect have those experiences had on you as a writer?
15. You've been uploading pieces of writing to the study archive on CTools. How has that process been going for you?
16. What pieces did you choose for the archive? Why did you choose them?

Future

17. What kinds of writing do you think will be most valuable for your career?
18. If you could tell your teachers one thing about writing, or how to teach writing, what would you say?
19. Any other comments?

Questions for Minors Only

Gateway course

1. What impact has the minor Gateway course (Writing 200) had, overall, on your writing?
2. What impact has it had on your sense of yourself as a writer?

3. What have your experiences of working with other writers in the course been?
4. The minor Gateway course emphasized reflective writing in various forms. How would you describe your experience with this kind of reflection?
5. Are you still using reflection in your current writing (whether assigned or voluntary)? Do you find yourself using reflective writing in other contexts besides writing papers?
6. How would you describe your experiences using new media writing (blogs, remediation project, etc.) in Writing 200?
7. The next couple of questions are about your Gateway portfolio. Can you walk me through it a bit?
   a. Separate from the other new media writing you did in Writing 200, how would you describe your experiences creating the portfolio in particular? What were your aims for the portfolio? What kinds of choices did you make in building it?
   b. What impact would you say creating the portfolio has had on your writing? What was the impact of the reflective writing in the portfolio?
   c. How has your writing process changed as a result of these experiences in the Gateway course?

Capstone course

8. What overall impact has the minor Capstone course (Writing 400) had on your writing? Has this course influenced your writing process? How so? Has this course had in impact on your sense of yourself as a writer?
9. What effect has the experience of the Capstone project had on you as a writer? Why did you choose the project that you chose?
10. The next few questions are about your Capstone eportfolio. (Have the student pull his or her eportfolio up on the computer screen.) Can you tell me about the most memorable aspect of your experience with the eportfolio? What were your aims for the eportfolio (what narrative did you hope to tell)? How do you feel your eportfolio addresses those aims? Did you design the eportfolio (navigation, links, media, visual design, etc.) to create a particular reader experience? Can you give some specific examples of your design choices?
11. Did you notice any relationships among your artifacts as you created your eportfolio? What relationships did you want your readers to notice?
12. Do you think creating the eportfolio has had an effect on your writ-

ing? How so? What did you learn from the reflective writing in the eportfolio—both the evidence-based essay you wrote and the contextual reflections?

13. What could people interested in writing development—including program administrators such as those at Sweetland—learn about writing development from your Capstone eportfolio?

Gateway to Capstone

14. Now we'd like you to reflect back on your Gateway course as well. How did your experience in the Capstone course compare to your experience in the Gateway course?
15. What have your experiences been of working with other writers throughout the minor?
16. What differences do you see between the Gateway and Capstone eportfolios?
17. The Gateway and Capstone courses emphasized reflective writing in various forms. How would you describe your experience with this kind of reflection? Are you still using reflection in your current writing (whether assigned or voluntary)?

Questions for Nonminors

Writing Experiences

1. Thinking back over the last two years, what experiences in and out of the classroom have had an effect on your writing? How has your writing process changed as a result of these experiences?
2. If I use the term "reflective writing," what does that mean to you? Have you recently used reflective writing in your own writing processes (whether assigned in courses or voluntary)?
3. What have your recent experiences been of working with other writers in your courses (or in other contexts)? Have you done workshopping or peer review? Group or collaborative writing projects?
4. Now that you are about to graduate, what advice would you give to college students about writing? What are some things they should think about as they begin writing a paper?

5. Have you had any experiences with new media writing, such as writing for blogs or websites, or making an electronic portfolio, Mportfolio, or digital portfolio? What were the specific experiences?
   a. *If yes to electronic portfolio*, probe:
      1. How has this experience affected your writing or sense of yourself as a writer?
      2. How do you think these experiences would have been different if this had been a hard-copy or paper portfolio (the kind people put in three-ring binders), not an electronic portfolio?
      3. Have these experiences pushed your writing in any new directions? How so?
      4. Has your eportfolio helped you understand the writing and learning you have done elsewhere in the university in new and different ways?
      6. You've been uploading pieces of writing to the study archive on CTools. How has that process been going for you?
      7. Why did you choose the pieces you chose to upload for the archive? What was it like looking back over your old writing and uploading some of it for this study? Did this process make you think differently about your writing?
      8. Finally, what do you think instructors should know about teaching writing at the undergraduate level?

APPENDIX 5

INTERVIEW CODEBOOK

The extended codebook, complete with representative quotations of code exemplars, can be found on our Fulcrum platform at https://doi.org/10.3998/mpub.10079890

1. **Archived work**. This code describes any discussion of either the work that nonminor students have uploaded to the study archive or the process of uploading. *This code is specific only to the nonminor interviewees.*
2. **Audience awareness**. This code describes any instance in which the speaker considers a reader or readers, whether real or ideal.
3. **Collaboration or peer feedback**. This code indicates any mention of students' reactions to collaborative writing experiences or peer feedback, whether assigned or not.
4. **Feedback (instructor)**. This code describes any mention of instructor feedback or response to written work *that is not specifically tied to an instructor's grade or formal assessment of that work*. (Note: There is a separate code for specific references to *grades or evaluation*, which may overlap with some of these instances. Also note that there is a separate code for *collaboration and peer review*.)
5. **Good teaching**. This code describes the speaker's evaluation or consideration of pedagogical approaches, whether positive or negative.
6. **Good writing**. This code describes the speaker's conception of effective or successful writing, in whatever discipline. This can include claims about notions of correctness (grammar, spelling, etc.) in writing.
7. **Grades and teacher evaluation**. This code indicates moments where the interviewee refers to a teacher's assessment of written work, whether in the form of a grade or not. (Please note the separate code for *feedback (instructor)*.
8. **Kinds of writing**. This is a fairly broad category, encompassing any instance where the reader refers to differences in genre, disciplinary differences or conventions, differences in approach or subject matter,

or writing flexibility. For some students, descriptions of or distinctions between kinds of writing can become vague; we coded these moments as well, because they seem telling regarding students' abilities to distinguish between genres (see final example).

9. **New media**. This refers to any mention of new media and the technology that supports it. We did not code mentions of the writing minor eportfolio with "new media" unless the technological aspects of the portfolio were explicitly mentioned.
10. **Portfolio**. This primarily refers to any mention of the eportfolio created for the Gateway course, although we also looked for mentions of any kind of portfolio use. See also note about *new media*, with which this code can but does not necessarily overlap.
11. **Process**. This refers to any mention of composing, including explicit discussion of brainstorming, prewriting, organizing, and revising. It sometimes overlaps with the *feedback (instructor)* code. For this code, we did not include references to how a paper ends up looking, in terms of organization, etc.
12. **Professional goals**. This refers to any discussion about the intersection of writing and the student's professional goals, including future graduate or professional school writing.
13. **Purpose**. This refers to the intention behind a particular piece of writing, one's clarity of purpose in the writing itself, or the larger ideas that might motivate one's writing, whether professional, academic, personal, etc. It encompasses any awareness that writing is driven by intention. (Note, however, the separate codes for *writing goals* and *professional goals*, which may but do not necessarily overlap.)
14. **Reflection**. This refers to any *explicit* discussion of writerly self-awareness, reflective writing, or thinking back on specific writing assignments or growth. This also can refer to specific instances of *not* reflecting *when a student is asked about reflective writing but does not or cannot respond*. However, we did not include in this code moments that may indicate a writer's attitude toward their writing without the writer purposefully articulating or engaging in reflection.
15. **Transfer**. This refers to any mention of how ideas or lessons transfer from class to class or apply in other contexts. *When possible*, please try to code as specifically to an individual course as possible: *Transfer 125*, *Transfer 220 (minor Gateway course)*, *Transfer 225*, and/or *Transfer General* for discussion of any other courses where writing assignments

appear to apply in other contexts. This category also can refer to specific instances of nontransfer when a student is asked about his or her first-year writing requirement and specifically comments about the class not having a later benefit.

16. **Voice**. This refers to any mention of issues of style or tone, personality, or authenticity in writing.
17. **Writerly self-conception**. This refers to any description of oneself as a writer—how, what, and why one sees oneself writing, whether past or present. It often coincides with *professional goals* and *writing development*. This category includes any discussion of student's confidence around writing assignments and writing tasks.
18. **Writing development**. This is a broad category that refers to any discussion of how a student sees his or her writing developing or improving over time. It was frequently co-coded with *writerly self-conception*. It also surfaces in some discussions of reflection, or looking back on growth from previous writing.
19. **Writing goals**. This category refers to any comments about specific goals a student has for his or her writing. This category may overlap with *professional goals*, such as when a student indicates an interest in publishing or pursuing other work as a writer.

APPENDIX 6

LIST OF PARTICIPANTS BY NAME AND CHAPTER

(see following page)

Student Pseudonym	chap. 1 (Wilson & Post)	chap. 2 (Keating)	chap. 3 (Hutton & Gibson)	chap. 4 (McCarty)	chap. 5 (Aull)	chap. 6 (Lancaster)	chap. 7 (Knutson)	chap. 8 (Silver)	chap. 9 (Swofford)	chap. 10 (Gere)
Abby					focus			mention		mention
Adrienne	focus									
Amanda					focus					
Amy		mention								
Angela		focus				focus				
Annie										mention
Ariana	mention			mention				mention		
Ashley			focus							
Ayana			focus		focus	mention		focus		
Brian						mention				
Carol										mention
Celeste		mention								
Charlotte		focus								
Chassi			mention							
Courtney			focus			mention				mention
Dan			focus			mention				focus
Dana	mention		mention					focus		
Dariella	focus	focus	mention							mention
Eva		mention	mention							
Gabi										mention
Grace		mention	mention			mention	focus			
Helen										mention
Isabella										mention
Jack		mention								mention
Jake			focus							mention
Janice						mention				
Janie	mention	focus								
Jenna	mention							focus		
Jon						focus				
Jonah		mention	mention	focus						
Joy	focus	mention	focus			mention				mention
Julia								focus		
Justin					focus					
Kaitlin		mention				mention		focus		mention
Katie	mention	focus		mention				focus		

Kelly									mention
Kris				focus					focus
Lauren	focus	focus	mention				focus		mention
Leo			mention	mention					
Linda									focus
Lisa						mention			
Louisa									mention
Madeleine						mention	focus		mention
Maggie									mention
Margaret						mention			
Mariana						mention			
Marie								focus	
Mary									mention
Megan									mention
Mike			mention			mention			
Natalie	mention	mention						focus	mention
Nicole									mention
Olivia			mention						mention
Owen					focus				
Patricia						mention			
Raquel			mention						
Rebecca		mention							
Sadie		mention							mention
Samantha			mention				focus		
Samuel		mention							mention
Sarah									mention
Shannon		mention	mention		focus				
Sidney	focus	focus					mention		
Sophie							focus		mention
Stacey		mention							
Stephanie		mention	mention						focus
Susanne					focus		mention		
Teresa			mention			mention			
Tim	focus		mention			focus			
Willa									mention
Zach		mention		mention			focus		

Additional appendices corresponding to chapters 5 and 9 are available on our Fulcrum platform at https://doi.org/10.3998/mpub.10079890

CONTRIBUTORS

Laura L. Aull is Associate Professor of English and Linguistics at Wake Forest University. Her work can be found in journals addressing composition studies, applied linguistics, and writing assessment, and she is the editor for *Assessing Writing*'s "Tools and Tech" series. Her current research focuses on corpus linguistic analysis of stance and other discourse patterns in academic genres, particularly argumentative essays, across student levels. She is the author of *First-Year University Writing: A Corpus-Based Study with Implications for Pedagogy*.

Anne Ruggles Gere is Arthur F. Thurnau Professor and Gertrude Buck Collegiate Professor at the University of Michigan, where she directs the Sweetland Center for Writing and serves as chair of the Joint PhD Program in English and Education. A former chair of CCC and a former president of NCTE, she is the 2018 president of MLA. She has written a dozen books and over 100 articles. In addition to research on writing development, she is engaged in a large-scale project of integrating writing-to-learn pedagogies into gateway STEM courses.

Gail Gibson is the Director of the Kessler Presidential Scholars, which provides financial, academic, and other supports to low-income and first-generation students at the University of Michigan. She earned her doctorate from the Joint PhD Program in English and Education at Michigan. Her academic research focuses on college access programs and writing instruction for students considered underprepared. She currently oversees a two-year pilot program investigating beliefs about belonging and community service among first-generation college students. A former journalist, Gibson previously served as a national legal correspondent for the *Baltimore Sun*.

Lizzie Hutton is Director of the Howe Writing Center and Assistant Professor of English at Miami University. Her research considers college students' reading-writing knowledge transfer. Her current project involves a historically based retheorization of Louise Rosenblatt's transactional theory. Also the author of a collection of poems, Lizzie has scholarly and creative work published or forthcoming in *College English*, *Journal of English Linguistics*, the *Yale Review*, and *Antioch Review*, among other journals. She received her PhD in English and Education from the University of Michigan, where she was also a longtime research assistant at the Sweetland Center for Writing.

Benjamin Keating is Assistant Teaching Professor of Writing at Wake Forest University. He received his PhD from the University of Michigan's Joint Program in English and Education, where he was a graduate student research assistant at the Sweetland Center for Writing. His research interests include antiracist pedagogy, collaborative learning, qualitative methods in writing research, and professional writing. Before his doctoral studies, he worked as an editor at a nonprofit focused on K–12 education policy. His current project explores disability, whiteness, and language diversity in college writing peer review.

Anna V. Knutson is Assistant Professor of English and Director of Composition at East Tennessee State University. While earning her doctoral degree in the Joint Program in English and Education at the University of Michigan, she served as a graduate student research assistant in the Sweetland Center for Writing. She has collaboratively authored articles published in *College English*, *Computers and Composition*, *Kairos*, and *WPA: Writing Program Administration*. Interested in writing program administration, learning transfer, and digital literacies, Anna is currently exploring writing knowledge transfer between social media and academic contexts among intersectional feminist college students.

Zak Lancaster is Associate Professor of English at Wake Forest University, where he teaches courses in writing and linguistics and coordinates the Writing Associates program, a WAC/WID initiative. His research focuses on the language of stance and evaluation in academic discourse, writing in the disciplines, and second-language writing. His articles have appeared in *Written Communication*, *College Composition and Communication*, and the *Journal of English for Academic Purposes*, among other interdisciplinary journals.

Ryan McCarty is a PhD candidate in the Joint Program in English and Education at the University of Michigan. His research investigates the learning students do when translating across the range of languages they use outside of school, at work, in their chosen majors, and across the curriculum. This research draws on his experience teaching at a multilingual high school, an urban community college, and at the university level, as well as on several projects with undergraduate and graduate writers across the disciplines.

Justine Post is Assistant Professor of Rhetoric and Composition at Ohio Northern University and director of the university's Writing Center. She completed her PhD in the Joint Program in English and Education at the University of Michigan, where she conducted a mixed-methods case study theorizing on the role of feedback in the first-year writing classroom. Her research uses qualitative and quantitative methods to explore the intersections between instructor and student perceptions and actions in the writing classroom, work that directly informs her approaches to teaching and administrating writing at Ohio Northern.

Naomi Silver is Associate Director of the Sweetland Center for Writing at the University of Michigan, where she teaches in the Center's Minor in Writing and Peer Writing Consultant programs. Her research and publications focus on multimodal writing, electronic portfolios, and reflection in digital contexts. She is chair of the CCCC Committee on Computers in Composition and Communication (7Cs), and codirects the Sweetland Digital Rhetoric Collaborative. As co-investigator on the Writing Development of Undergraduates at the University of Michigan study, she participated in Cohort VI of the Inter/National Coalition for Electronic Portfolio Research.

Sarah Swofford is Assistant Professor of Composition and Rhetoric and the Writing Program Administrator in the Department of English, Theater, and Liberal Studies at the University of South Carolina Beaufort. She received her PhD from the Joint Program in English and Education at the University of Michigan, where she studied the influence of language ideologies in rural southern students' transitions to college writing. Her research interests focus on influential factors in students' transitions to college writing, rural education, first-year writing, writing pedagogy, and student writing development in and beyond their undergraduate writing experiences.

Emily Wilson is a PhD candidate in the Joint Program in English and Education at the University of Michigan. She works as a graduate student research assistant at the Sweetland Center for Writing. Her undergraduate degree is in education, and her master's degree is in English. Before starting her doctoral program, she spent eleven years as a high school English teacher. Her dissertation research involves studying how literacy mediates identity for adolescents who grow up in the military.

INDEX